BLOOD & BELONGING

JOURNEYS INTO THE NEW NATIONALISM

MICHAEL IGNATIEFF

VIKING

VIKING
Published by the Penguin Group
Penguin Books Canada Ltd, 10 Alcorn Avenue, Toronto,
Ontario, Canada M4V 3B2
Penguin Books Ltd, 27 Wrights Lane,
London W8 5TZ, England
Viking Penguin, a division of Penguin Books USA Inc.,
375 Hudson Street, New York, New York 10014, U.S.A.
Penguin Books Australia Ltd, Ringwood, Victoria, Australia
Penguin Books (NZ) Ltd, 182–190 Wairau Road,
Auckland 10, New Zealand

Penguin Books Ltd, Registered Offices:
Harmondsworth, Middlesex, England

First published 1993

1 3 5 7 9 10 8 6 4 2

Printed and bound in Canada on acid free paper

Canadian Cataloguing in Publication Data

Ignatieff, Michael
    Blood and belonging

Includes bibliographical references.
ISBN 0–670–85269–4

1. Nationalism.   2. Nationalism—Quebec (Province).
I. Title.

JC311.I45 1993   320.5′4   C93–094634–0

CONTENTS

THE LAST REFUGE

WARLORDS

The UN checkpoint was a sand-bagged portakabin manned by two Canadian infantrymen guarding a road barrier between the Croat- and Serb-held sections of Pakrac in central Croatia. The road to the checkpoint wound its way between pulverized bungalows, upended cars in the ditches, waist-high grass in abandoned gardens. Just visible in the grass, as we approached the checkpoint, were two teenage Croatian spotters, with their binoculars trained on the Serbian side.

The UN had just waved us through into Serb-held territory when fifteen armed Serbian paramilitaries surrounded our van. They had been drinking at a wedding in their village. The drunkest one, with dead eyes and glassy, sweat-beaded skin, forced the van door open and clambered in. 'We watching you,' he said, making binocular gestures with his hands. 'You talk to Ustashe,' and he pointed back at the Croatians hiding in the grass. Then he took the pistol out of his belt. 'You fucking spies,' he said. He ordered the driver out at gunpoint, took the wheel and began revving the engine. 'Why can't I shoot this?' groaned the cameraman in the seat behind. 'Because he'll shoot *you*,' someone in the back of the van muttered.

The Serb put the van into gear and it was moving off when one of the UN soldiers yanked open the door, grabbed the keys and shut off the ignition. 'We'll do this my way,' the UN soldier said, breathing heavily, half pulling, half cajoling the Serb out of the driver's seat. Another young Serb in combat gear pushed his way into the van and shook his head. 'I am police. You are under arrest. Follow me.'

This was the moment, in my journeys in search of the new nationalism, in which I began to understand what the new world order actually looks like: paramilitaries, drunk on plum brandy and ethnic paranoia, trading shots with each other across a wasteland; a checkpoint between them, placed there by something loftily called 'the international community', but actually manned by just two anxious adolescents; and a film crew wondering, for a second or two, whether they were going to get out alive.

The writ of the 'international community' ran no further than 150 metres either side of the UN checkpoint. Beyond that there was gun law. The paramilitaries took us to the police station in the village where the chief spent an hour establishing to his satisfaction that because our translator's grandfather had been born on the Croatian island of Krk, he must be a Croatian spy. But then a telephone call arrived, instructing the chief to release us. No one would say who had given the orders. It appeared to have been the local Serb warlord. This was my first encounter with a warlord's power, but it was not to be my last.

I am a child of the Cold War. I was born in the year of the Berlin Airlift of 1947 and my first political memory of any consequence is of being very afraid, for one day, during the Cuban Missile Crisis of 1962. Looking back now, I can see that I lived through the last imperial age, the last time when the nation states of the world were clearly allocated to two opposing spheres of influence, the last time when terror produced peace. Now terror only seems to produce more terror.

If the twenty-first century has already begun, as some people say it has, then it began in 1989. When the Berlin Wall came down, when Václav Havel stood on the balcony in Prague's Wenceslas Square and crowds cheered the collapse of the Communist regimes across Europe, I thought, like many people, that we were about to witness a new era of liberal democracy. My generation had almost reconciled itself to growing old in the fearful paralysis of the Cold War. Suddenly a new order of free nations had begun to take shape from the Baltic republics to the Black Sea, from Tallinn to Berlin, from Prague to Budapest, Belgrade and Bucharest. In August 1991, when Muscovites defended the Russian Parliament against the tanks, we believed that the civic courage which had brought down the last twentieth-century empire might even be strong enough to sustain Russia's transition to democracy. We even thought, for a while, that the democratic current in the East might sweep through our own exhausted oligarchies in the West.

We soon found out how wrong we were. For what has succeeded the last age of empire is a new age of violence. The key narrative of the new world order is the disintegration of nation states into ethnic civil war; the key architects of that order are warlords; and the key language of our age is ethnic nationalism.

With blithe lightness of mind, we assumed that the world was moving irrevocably beyond nationalism, beyond tribalism, beyond the provincial confines of the identities inscribed in our passports, towards a global market culture which was to be our new home. In retrospect, we were whistling in the dark. The repressed has returned, and its name is nationalism.

CIVIC AND ETHNIC
NATIONALISM

As a political doctrine, nationalism is the belief that the world's peoples are divided into nations, and that each of these nations has the right of self-determination, either as self-governing units within existing nation states or as nation states of their own.

As a cultural ideal, nationalism is the claim that while men and women have many identities, it is the nation which provides them with their primary form of belonging.

As a moral ideal, nationalism is an ethic of heroic sacrifice, justifying the use of violence in the defence of one's nation against enemies, internal or external.

These claims – political, moral and cultural – underwrite each other. The moral claim that nations are entitled to be defended by force or violence depends on the cultural claim that the needs they satisfy for security and belonging are uniquely important. The political idea that all peoples should struggle for nationhood depends on the cultural claim that only nations can satisfy these needs. The cultural idea in turn underwrites the political claim that these needs cannot be satisfied without self-determination.

Each one of these claims is contestable and none is intuitively obvious. Many of the world's tribal peoples and ethnic minorities do not think of themselves as nations; many do not seek or require a state of their own. It is not obvious, furthermore, why national identity should be a more important element of personal identity than any other; nor is it obvious why defence of the nation justifies the use of violence.

But for the moment what matters is that nationalism is centrally concerned to define the conditions under which force or violence is justified in a people's defence, when their right of self-determination is threatened or denied. Self-determination here may mean either democratic self-rule or the exercise of cultural autonomy, depending on whether the national group in question believes it can achieve its goals within the framework of an existing state or seeks a state of its own.

All forms of nationalism vest political sovereignty in 'the people' – indeed the word 'nation' is often a synonym for 'the people' – but not all nationalist movements create democratic regimes, because not all nationalisms include all of the people in their definition of who constitutes the nation.

One type, civic nationalism, maintains that the nation should be composed of all those – regardless of race, colour, creed, gender, language or ethnicity – who subscribe to the nation's political creed. This nationalism is called civic because it envisages the nation as a community of equal, rights-bearing citizens, united in

3

patriotic attachment to a shared set of political practices and values. This nationalism is necessarily democratic since it vests sovereignty in all of the people. Some elements of this ideal were first achieved in Great Britain. By the mid-eighteenth century, Britain was already a nation state composed of four nations – the Irish, the Scots, the Welsh and the English – united by a civic rather than an ethnic definition of belonging, i.e. by shared attachment to certain institutions: the Crown, Parliament and the rule of law. But it was not until the French and American revolutions, and the creation of the French and American republics, that civic nationalism set out to conquer the world.

Such an ideal was made easier to realize in practice because the societies of the Enlightenment were ethnically homogeneous or behaved as if they were. Those who did not belong to the enfranchised political class of white, propertied males – workers, women, black slaves, aboriginal peoples – found themselves excluded from citizenship and thus from the nation. Throughout the nineteenth and early twentieth century, these groups fought for civic inclusion. As a result of their struggle, most Western nation states now define their nationhood in terms of common citizenship and not by common ethnicity. One prominent exception is Germany.

Napoleon's invasion and occupation of the German principalities in 1806 unleashed a wave of German patriotic anger and Romantic polemic against the French ideal of the nation state. The German Romantics argued that it was not the state which created the nation, as the Enlightenment believed, but the nation, its people, which created the state. What gave unity to the nation, what made it a home, a place of passionate attachment, was not the cold contrivance of shared rights, but the people's pre-existing ethnic characteristics: their language, religion, customs and traditions. The nation as Volk had begun its long and troubling career in European thought. All of the peoples of nineteenth-century Europe under imperial subjection – the Poles and Baltic peoples under the Russian yoke, the Serbs under Turkish rule, the Croats under the Habsburgs – looked to the German ideal of ethnic nationalism when articulating their right to self-determination. When Germany achieved unification in 1871 and rose to world-power status, her achievement was a demonstration of the success of ethnic nationalism to all the captive nations of imperial Europe.

Of these two types of nationalism, the civic has a greater claim to sociological realism. Most societies are not mono-ethnic; and even when they are, common ethnicity does not of itself obliterate division, because ethnicity is only one of the many claims on an individual's loyalty. According to the civic nationalist creed, what holds a society together is not common roots but law. By subscribing to a set of democratic procedures and values, individuals can reconcile their right to shape their own lives with their need to belong to a community. This in turn assumes that national belonging can be a form of rational attachment.

Ethnic nationalism claims, by contrast, that an individual's deepest attachments are inherited, not chosen. It is the national community which defines the individual, not the individuals who define the national community. This psychology of belonging may have greater depth than civic nationalism's, but the sociology that accompanies it is a good deal less realistic. The fact, for example, that two Serbs share Serbian ethnic identity may unite them against Croats, but it will do nothing to stop them fighting each other over jobs, spouses, scarce resources and so on. Common ethnicity, by itself, does not create social cohesion or community, and when it fails to do so, as it must, nationalist regimes are necessarily impelled towards maintaining unity by force rather than by consent. This is one reason why ethnic nationalist regimes are more authoritarian than democratic.

They may also prove authoritarian because they are, in essence, a form of democracy conducted in the interests of the ethnic majority. Most of the new post-Cold War nation states give lip-service to the idea of a society of civic equals, and provide safeguards for minority rights. In reality, new nations like Serbia and Croatia, the Baltic states, the new Asian republics, have institutionalized ethnic majority domination. Ethnic nationalism is a particular temptation for those ethnic majorities – like the Baltic peoples and the Ukrainians – formerly ruled by the imperially backed Russian minority.

It is sometimes argued that authoritarian ethnic nationalism only takes root where civic nationalism has never established itself. On this account, ethnic nationalism is flourishing in Eastern Europe because forty years of communist single-party rule effectively destroyed whatever civic or democratic culture there once had been in the region. If so, it ought to be true that ethnic nationalism does not sink deep roots in societies with extensive democratic traditions. Unfortunately this is not the case. European racism is a form of white ethnic nationalism – indeed it is a revolt against civic nationalism itself, against the very idea of a nation based on citizenship rather than ethnicity. This revolt is gaining ground in states like Britain, Italy, France, Germany and Spain with ample, if varying degrees of democratic experience.

There is also a host of examples – Northern Ireland, India and Canada, to name three – where ethnic nationalism flourishes within states formally committed to civic democracy. In Northern Ireland, between 1920 and 1972, the Loyalist Protestant majority used the British parliamentary system to maintain a comprehensive form of majoritarian tyranny against the Catholic minority. Being steeped in the British democratic and legal tradition did nothing to stop Loyalists from bending democracy to nationalist ends. In India, forty-five years of civic democracy have barely contained the ethnic and religious nationalisms which are currently tearing the country's federal system apart. In Canada, the picture is more optimistic, but the analytical point is the same. Full inclusion within a federal democratic system has not abated the force of Quebecois nationalism.

In all of these places, the fundamental appeal of ethnic nationalism is as a rationale for ethnic majority rule, for keeping one's enemies in their place or for overturning some legacy of cultural subordination. In the nations of Eastern Europe, ethnic nationalism offers something more. For when the Soviet empire and its satellite regimes collapsed, the nation state structures of the region also collapsed, leaving hundreds of ethnic groups at the mercy of each other. Since none of these groups had the slightest experience of conciliating their disagreements by democratic discussion, violence or force became their arbiter. Nationalist rhetoric swept through these regions like wildfire because it provided warlords and gunmen with a vocabulary of opportunistic self-justification. In the fear and panic which swept the ruins of the communist states people began to ask: so who will protect me now? Faced with a situation of political and economic chaos, people wanted to know who to trust, and who to call their own. Ethnic nationalism provided an answer that was intuitively obvious: only trust those of your own blood.

BELONGING

But if nationalism legitimizes an appeal to blood loyalty, and in turn blood sacrifice, it can only do so persuasively if it seems to appeal to people's better natures, and not just to their worst instincts. Since killing is not a business to be taken lightly, it must be done for a reason which makes its perpetrator think well of himself. If violence is to be legitimated, it must be in the name of all that is best in a people, and what is better than their love of home?

Nationalists are supremely sentimental. Kitsch is the natural aesthetic of an ethnic 'cleanser'. There is no killer on either side of the checkpoints who will not pause, between firing at his enemies, to sing a nostalgic song or even recite a few lines of some ethnic epic. The latent purpose of such sentimentality is to imply that one is in the grip of a love greater than reason, stronger than the will, a love akin to fate and destiny. Such a love assists the belief that it is fate, however tragic, which obliges you to kill.

Stripped of such sentimentality, what then is this belonging, and the need for it, which nationalism seems to satisfy so successfully? When nationalists claim that national belonging is the overridingly important form of all belonging, they mean that there is no other form of belonging – to your family, work or friends – which is secure if you do not have a nation to protect you. This is what warrants sacrifice on the nation's behalf. Without a nation's protection, everything that an individual values can be rendered worthless. Belonging, on this account, is first and foremost protection from violence. Where you belong is where you are safe; and where you are safe is where you belong. If nationalism is persuasive because it warrants violence, it is also persuasive because it offers protection from violence. The warlord is his people's protector; if he kills he does so in defence of the noblest cause: the protection of the innocent.

But belonging also means being recognized and being understood. As Isaiah Berlin has written in *Two Concepts of Liberty*, when I am among my own people, 'they understand me, as I understand them; and this understanding creates within me a sense of being somebody in the world.' To belong is to understand the tacit codes of the people you live with; it is to know that you will be understood without having to explain yourself. People, in short, 'speak your language'. This is why, incidentally, the protection and defence of a nation's language is such a deeply emotional nationalist cause, for it is language, more than land and history, which provides the essential form of belonging, which is to be understood. One can, of course, be understood in languages and in countries other than one's own; one can find belonging even in exile. But the nationalist claim is that full belonging, the warm sensation that people understand not merely what you say but what you mean, can only come when you are among your own people in your native land.

COSMOPOLITANISM AND PRIVILEGE

Anyone whose father was born in Russia, whose mother was born in England, whose education was in America, and whose working life has been spent in Canada, Great Britain and France, cannot be expected to be much of an ethnic nationalist. If anyone has a claim to being a cosmopolitan, it must be me. I wish I spoke more languages than I do, I wish I had lived in more nations than I have, and wish that more people understood that expatriation is not exile: it is merely the belonging of those who choose their home rather than inherit it.

For many years, I believed that the tide was running in favour of cosmopolitans like me. There seemed so many of us, for one thing. There were at least a dozen world cities – gigantic, multi-ethnic melting pots which provided a home for expatriates, exiles, migrants and transients of all kinds. For the urban professional populations of these major cities, a post-national state of mind was simply taken for granted. People in these places did not bother about the passports of the people they worked or lived with; did not care about the country-of-origin label on the goods they bought; they simply assumed that in constructing their own way of life they would borrow from the customs of every nation they happened to admire. Cosmopolitans made a positive ethic out of cultural borrowing: in culture, exogamy was better than endogamy, and promiscuity was better than provincialism.

There was nothing new in itself about this cosmopolitan ethic. We have lived with a global economy since 1700, and many of the world's major cities have been global entrepôts for centuries. A global market has been limiting the sovereignty and freedom of manoeuvre of nation states at least since Adam Smith first constructed a theory of the phenomenon at the outset of the age of nationalism in

1776. A global market in ideas and cultural forms has existed at least since the Enlightenment republic of letters. Rootless cosmopolitans have existed as a social type in the big imperial cities for centuries.

Two features, however, distinguish the big city cosmopolitanism of our era from what has gone before. First of all is its social and racial diffusion. Twentieth-century democracy and unprecedented post-war prosperity have extended the privileges of cosmopolitanism from a small white moneyed male elite to a substantial minority of the population of the nation states of the developed world. Suddenly, there are a lot of us about, and our sense of sharing a post-nationalist consciousness has been mightily reinforced by cheap air travel and telecommunications.

The second obvious change is that the global market we live in is no longer ordered by a stable imperial system. For two hundred years, the global expansion of capitalism was shaped by the territorial ambitions and policing authority of a succession of imperial powers, the British, French, German, Austro-Hungarian and Russian empires of the nineteenth and early twentieth centuries; and the Soviet and American joint imperium after the Second World War. Since 1989, we have entered the first era of global cosmopolitanism in which there is no framework of imperial order.

There have been three great re-orderings of the nation-state system of Europe in this century: at Versailles in 1918, when the new nations of Eastern Europe were created from the ruins of the Austro-Hungarian, Turkish and Russian empires; at Yalta in 1945, when Roosevelt, Stalin and Churchill allocated the nation states of Western and Eastern Europe to two spheres of influence; and between 1989 and 1991, when the Soviet empire and the communist regimes of Eastern Europe collapsed. What distinguishes the third of these is that it has occurred without any imperial settlement whatever. No treaty exists to regulate the conflict between the territorial integrity of nation states in Eastern Europe and the right to self-determination of the peoples within them. For every resolution of this conflict by civilized divorce, Czech-style, there have been a dozen armed conflicts. The basic reason is obvious enough: the imperial police have departed.

The Americans may be the last remaining superpower, but they are not an imperial power: their authority is exercised in the defence of exclusively national interests, not in the maintenance of an imperial system of global order. As a result, large sections of Africa, Eastern Europe, Soviet Asia, Latin America and the Near East no longer come within any clearly defined sphere of imperial or great power influence. This means that huge sections of the world's population have won the 'right of self-determination' on the cruellest possible terms: they have been simply left to fend for themselves. Not surprisingly, their nation states are collapsing, as in Somalia and in many other nations of Africa. In crucial zones of the world, once heavily policed by empire – notably the Balkans – populations find themselves without an imperial arbiter to appeal to. Small wonder then, that, unrestrained by stronger hands, they have set upon each other for that final settling of scores so long deferred by the presence of empire.

Globalism in a post-imperial age only permits a post-nationalist consciousness for those cosmopolitans who are lucky enough to live in the wealthy West. It has brought chaos and violence for the many small peoples too weak to establish defensible states of their own. The Bosnian Muslims are perhaps the most dramatic example of a people who turned in vain to more powerful neighbours to protect them. The people of Sarajevo were true cosmopolitans, fierce believers in ethnic heterogeneity. But they lacked either a reliable imperial protector or a state of their own to guarantee peace among contending ethnicities.

What has happened in Bosnia must give pause to anyone who believes in the virtues of cosmopolitanism. It is only too apparent that cosmopolitanism is the privilege of those who can take a secure nation state for granted. Though we have passed into a post-imperial age, we are not in a post-nationalist age, and I cannot see how we will ever do so. The cosmopolitan order of the great cities – London, Los Angeles, New York, Paris – depends critically on the rule-enforcing capacities of the nation state. When this order breaks down, as it did during the Los Angeles riots of 1992, it becomes apparent that civilized, cosmopolitan multi-ethnic cities have as great a propensity for ethnic warfare as any Eastern European country.

In this sense, therefore, cosmopolitans like myself are not beyond the nation; and a cosmopolitan, post-nationalist spirit will always depend, in the end, on the capacity of nation states to provide security and civility for their citizens. In that sense alone, I am a civic nationalist, someone who believes in the necessity of nations and in the duty of citizens to defend the capacity of nations to provide the security and the rights we all need in order to live cosmopolitan lives. At the very least, cosmopolitan disdain and astonishment at the ferocity with which people will fight to win a nation state of their own is misplaced. They are, after all, only fighting for a privilege cosmopolitans have long taken for granted.

SIX JOURNEYS

There is only so much that can be said about nationalism in general. It is not one thing in many disguises, but many things in many disguises; nationalist principles can have dreadful consequences in one place, and innocuous or positive ones in another place. Context is all. I wanted to see nationalism in as many of its guises as possible. But where was I to go?

The itinerary I chose was personal, but hopefully not arbitrary. I chose places I had lived in, cared about, and knew enough about to believe that they could illustrate certain central themes.

I began my journey in Yugoslavia, because I had lived there for two years as a child and knew it well enough in Tito's heyday to be astonished that it should have been the place where the infamous phrase 'ethnic cleansing' was coined. The thirty-five years of Tito's rule did not seem to me just an interlude of peace in an interminable history of Balkan inter-ethnic warfare. In the Yugoslavia I had loved, Croats, Serbs and Muslims had lived as neighbours. What then had turned neighbours into enemies? How exactly had nationalist paranoia torn apart the structure of inter-ethnic accommodation and produced the new order of partitioned, ethnically homogeneous states?

My next journey was to Germany, the nation which both invented ethnic nationalism under the Romantics and then disgraced it under Hitler, and which now is struggling to contain ethnic nationalism in its modern Western European form: the white racist youth gang. Post-war Germany thinks of itself as a civic democracy, yet its citizenship laws remain defined by ethnicity. It is the society in Europe most tormented by the choice between succumbing to its ethnic nationalist past and building a civic nationalist future.

Of the fifteen successor states of the Soviet empire, Ukraine is the largest: a nuclear superpower getting its first experience of national independence and discovering how difficult it is to dig itself out of centuries of Russian rule. It was a natural choice of destination for a journey into the ruins of the former Soviet empire. But there was a personal reason for choosing the Ukraine. My grandparents and great-grandparents were Russian landowners who owned an estate in the Ukraine. What better way, I thought, to explore the deep inter-penetration of Ukrainian and Russian identity than to return to that estate and to see how my ancestors were now remembered in a new state.

The same personal agenda led me to choose Quebec, where those same Russian grandparents ended their lives in exile. The nationalism I know best, the one which has torn my country – Canada – apart for thirty years is Quebecois. Here is a nationalism in a modern, developed and democratic society, a demand for cultural and linguistic self-determination which raises a fundamental issue – equally relevant to Scotland and Catalonia – if you already are a nation and enjoy substantial autonomy, why do you need an independent state of your own?

Since nationalism is so often called a form of tribalism, Quebec also offered an opportunity to observe how tribal and national consciousness interact among an aboriginal people of northern Quebec, the Cree, who have adopted the language of national self-determination to confront Quebec's plans for economic development in the north. How, in turn, do Quebec nationalists confront a nationalist challenge within?

As a Crimean Tartar nationalist told me in the Ukraine, only a man who has no mother knows what a mother means. Only a man without a state knows what a nation state means. Of the many stateless peoples in the world – from the Crimean Tartars to the Palestinians – the largest are the Kurds. The creation of the Kurdish enclave in northern Iraq, by the Gulf War armies of the West, allowed me to see for myself how limited autonomy and self-rule have transformed a people who have never had a home of their own. In the Kurdish struggle for a homeland, they have had to fight against four of the most virulent secular and religious nationalisms of the twentieth century: Kemal Atatürk's Turkey, Ayatollah Khomeini's Iran, Saddam Hussein's Iraq and Hafez Assad's Syria. Can their own national struggle finally bring the Kurds together? In other words, can nationalism create a nation?

My final journey took me back to consider the braying national identity of my adopted country, the British Isles. Where better to observe this identity under stress than in the streets of Belfast, where for seventy-five years the Protestant Loyalist community has been defending its right to be British against the most violent nationalist movement in Western Europe, the IRA? What exactly is Loyalism loyal to? Is it a cargo-cult of Britishness, or is it a mirror in which the British can see the distorted image of who they really are? Coming home to the fierce Britishness of Ulster allowed me to confront the central conceit which cosmopolitans everywhere, and the British in particular, have about the tide of ethnic nationalism destroying the fixed landmarks of the Cold War world: everyone else is a fanatic, everyone but us is a nationalist. If patriotism, Samuel Johnson remarked, is the last refuge of a scoundrel, so post-nationalism and its accompanying disdain for the nationalist emotions of others, may be the last refuge of the cosmopolitan.

CROATIA
&
SERBIA

THE ANCIEN
REGIME

Wild strawberries were served in a silver cup at breakfast, I remember, followed by hot rolls with apricot jam. The dining room looked over the lake, and when the window was open you could feel the mountain air sweeping across the water, across the white linen tablecloth and then across your face.

The hotel was called the Toplice, on the shores of Lake Bled in Slovenia. The diplomatic corps spent the summer there, in attendance upon the dictator who took up residence across the lake. My father, like the other diplomats, came to gossip and take the waters. Every morning, he bathed in the heated pools beneath the hotel. I played tennis, ate wild strawberries, rowed on the lake and conceived a passion for an unapproachable Swedish girl of 12. Such are my *ancien régime* memories, and they are from communist Yugoslavia.

I remember an evening listening from the bottom of our dining room as the then foreign minister, Koča Popović, suavely smoked cigarettes in an ivory holder and told how his partisan unit had 'liquidated the Chetniks', the Serbs who had fought on Hitler's side at the end of the war. I had never heard the word 'liquidated' used like that before.

It was obvious, even to me, that the communist elite had won power not merely by defeating a foreign invader, but by winning a vicious civil war. The reality of Tito's police state was just as obvious. We lived in Dedinje, a hillside suburb overlooking Belgrade, only several hundred metres from Tito's residence. Wherever you walked, there were men in plain clothes, strolling about or whispering into walkie-talkies. Tito himself was the hidden god of the whole system. With his sleekly groomed hair, permanent sun-tan, shiny silk suit and black onyx ring on his finger, he resembled nothing so much, my father said, as a prosperous south German refrigerator salesman.

Obviously he was more imaginative and sinister than that. I remember how, on a cruise in the Adriatic, my parents kept hiding a book from the crew, stowing it under their bunk, locking it in their luggage. The book turned out to be Milovan Djilas's *The New Class*. Djilas, Tito's companion in arms was still in Tito's jail for denouncing his dictatorial tendencies.

We travelled everywhere in the Yugoslavia of the late 1950s – through Bosnian hill villages, where children swarmed up to the car, barefoot and in rags; to the great mosque of Sarajevo, where I removed my shoes and knelt and watched old men pressing their foreheads on the carpets and whispering their prayers; to the Dalmatian islands and beaches, then unvisited by Western tourists; to Lake Bled in Slovenia. Parts of southern Serbia, central Bosnia and western Hercegovina were so poor that it was not clear how ordinary people survived at all. Ljubljana and Zagreb, by contrast, were neat, prosperous Austro-Hungarian towns that seemed to have nothing in common with the bony, bare hinterlands of central Yugoslavia.

At the time all expression of economic resentment, together with nationalist

consciousness itself, came under Tito's ban. The society marched forward, willingly or unwillingly, under the banner of 'brotherhood and unity'. To call yourself a Croat or Serb first and a Yugoslav second was to risk arrest as a nationalist and chauvinist.

I had no idea how complicated and ambiguous the division between national and Yugoslav identity actually was. I knew, for example, that Metod, my tennis coach in Bled, always called himself, first and foremost, a Slovenian. I remember him saying bitterly that he hated serving in the Yugoslav National Army, because both he and his brother were ragged by the Serbs for being Slovene.

Was that the only time I saw the cracks that were to become fissures? I think so. For everywhere else, I remember people who told me, happily, that they were Yugoslavs. In retrospect, I was there at the most hopeful moment. Tito was still lionized for having kept the country out of Stalin's empire; there were the first signs of the economic boom of the 1960s; soon to come was the liberalization of travel, which allowed millions of Yugoslavs to work abroad and for a time made Yugoslavia the freest of all the Eastern European communist countries.

I hold on to my *ancien régime* memories. Everyone now says the descent into hell was inevitable. Nothing seemed less likely at the time. My childhood tells me that nothing is inevitable: that is what makes what did happen tragic.

THE NARCISSISM OF MINOR DIFFERENCE

As Balkan nationalists tell it, their history is their fate. Croats will explain, for example, that the root cause of the bloodshed in the Balkans is that they are 'essentially' Catholic, European and Austro-Hungarian in origin, while Serbs are 'essentially' Orthodox, Byzantine and Slav, with an added tinge of Turkish cruelty and indolence. The Sava and Danube rivers, which serve as borders between Croatia and Serbia, once demarcated the boundary between the Austro-Hungarian and Ottoman empires.

If this historical fault-line is emphasized often enough, the conflict between Serbs and Croats can be read off as inevitable. Yet it is not how the past dictates to the present but how the present manipulates the past which is decisive in the Balkans.

Freud once argued that the smaller the real difference between two peoples the larger it was bound to loom in their imagination. He called this effect the narcissism of minor difference. Its corollary must be that enemies need each other to remind themselves of who they really are. A Croat, thus, is someone who is not a Serb. A Serb is someone who is not a Croat. Without hatred of the other, there would be no clearly defined national self to worship and adore.

In Croatia, Franjo Tudjman's ruling HDZ (Croatian Democratic Alliance) party presents itself as a Western-style political movement on the model of the Bavarian Christian Democrats. Actually, the Tudjman state resembles the Serbian regime of Slobodan Milošević much more than either resembles anything on the Western European parliamentary model. They are both post-communist one-party states, democratic only in the sense that their leaders' power derives from their skill as manipulators of popular emotion.

An outsider is struck, not by the differences between Serbs and Croats, but by how similar they seem to be. They both speak the same language, give or take a few hundred words, and have shared the same village way of life for centuries. While one is Catholic, the other Orthodox, urbanization and industrialization have reduced the salience of confessional differences. Nationalist politicians on both sides took the narcissism of minor difference and turned it into a monstrous fable according to which their own side appeared as blameless victims, the other side as genocidal killers. All Croats became Ustashe assassins; all Serbs became Chetnik beasts. Such rhetorical preliminaries, needless to say, were an essential precondition of the slaughter that followed.

Yet what remains truly difficult to understand about the Balkan tragedy is how such nationalist lies ever managed to take root. For ordinary people know that they are lies: all Croats are not Ustashe; all Serbs are not Chetniks. Even as they use these phrases, people know they are not true. It cannot be repeated too often that these people were neighbours, friends and spouses, not inhabitants of different ethnic planets.

A nationalist minority on both sides went to work on their deeply intertwined common past, persuading all and sundry, including outsiders, that Serbs and Croats have been massacring each other since time immemorial. History has no such lesson to teach. In fact, the protagonists were kept apart for much of their past, in separate empires and kingdoms. It was only the assassination of Croat politicians in the parliament in Belgrade in 1928 which set off the slide into ethnic warfare during the Second World War. While the present conflict is certainly a continuation of the civil war of 1941–5, this explains little, for one still has to account for the nearly fifty years of ethnic peace in between. It was not merely a truce. Even sworn enemies on either side still cannot satisfactorily explain why it broke down.

Moreover, it is a fallacy to regard either this war or the civil war of 1941–5 as the product of some uniquely Balkan viciousness. All of the delusions that have turned neighbours into enemies are imports of Western European origin. Modern Serbian nationalism dates back to an impeccably Byronic style of national uprising against the Turks. Likewise, the nineteenth century Croatian nationalist ideologue, Ante Starčević, derived the idea of an ethnically pure Croatian state indirectly from the German Romantics. The misery of the Balkans stems in part from a pathetic longing to be good Europeans – that is, to import the West's murderous ideological fashions. These fashions proved fatal in the Balkans because national unification could be realized only by ripping apart the plural fabric of Balkan village life in the name of the violent dream of ethnic purity.

Likewise, even genocide in the Balkans is not a local speciality, but an importation from the grand Western European tradition. Ante Pavelić's wartime Ustashe regime, which Serbs mistakenly regard as the true face of Croatian nationalism, couldn't have lasted a day in office without the backing of the German Nazi regime, not to mention the tacit approval of that eminently European authority, the Catholic Church.

In sum, therefore, we are making excuses for ourselves when we dismiss the Balkans as a sub-rational zone of intractable fanaticism. And we are ending the search for explanation just when it should begin if we assert that local ethnic hatreds were so rooted in history that they were bound to explode into nationalist violence. On the contrary, these people had to be transformed from neighbours into enemies.

Thomas Hobbes would have understood Yugoslavia. What Hobbes would have said, having lived through religious civil war himself, is that when people are sufficiently afraid, they will do anything. There is one type of fear more devastating in its impact than any other: the systemic fear which arises when a state begins to collapse. Ethnic hatred is the result of the terror which arises when legitimate authority disintegrates.

Tito achieved the national unification of each of the six major peoples of the south Balkans. He understood that a federal state was the only peaceful means to satisfy the national aspirations of each people. For each republic to unify on their own, they would have had to initiate the forcible deportation of populations. As much as a quarter of both the Croat and Serb populations have always lived outside the borders of their republics. Tito created an intricate ethnic balance which, for example, reduced Serbian influence at the heart of the federal system in Belgrade, while promoting Serbs to positions of power in Croatia.

Tito's containment of nationalism, built as it was on a personal dictatorship, could never have survived beyond his death. Even by the early 1970s his socialist rhetoric of 'brotherhood and unity' was falling on deaf ears. In 1974, he compromised with nationalism, allowing the republics greater autonomy in the new constitution. By the end of his reign, the League of Communists, instead of counterbalancing the ethnic clientism among the elites in the republics, was itself fragmenting on ethnic lines.

This fragmentation was inevitable given Tito's failure to allow the emergence of civic, rather than ethnic-based, multi-party competition. Had Tito allowed a citizens' politics in the 1960s or 1970s, a non-ethnic principle of political affiliation might have taken root. Tito always insisted his was a communism with a difference. In the end, his regime was no different from the other communist autocracies of Eastern Europe. By failing to allow a plural political culture to mature, Tito ensured that the fall of his regime turned into the collapse of the entire state structure. In the ruins, his heirs and successors turned to the most atavistic principles of political mobilization in order to survive.

If Yugoslavia no longer protected you, perhaps your fellow Croats, Serbs or Slovenes might. Fear, more than conviction, made unwilling nationalists of ordinary people. But most people did not want it to happen; most people knew, if they drew back for a second, that rushing to the protection of their ethnic group would only hasten the disintegration of their common life.

Ethnic difference *per se* was not responsible for the nationalistic politics that emerged in the Yugoslavia of the 1980s. Consciousness of ethnic difference turned into nationalist hatred only when the surviving communist elites, beginning with Serbia, began manipulating nationalist emotions in order to cling to power.

This is worth emphasizing since most outsiders assume that all Balkan peoples are incorrigibly nationalistic. In fact, many people bitterly lament the passing of Yugoslavia, precisely because it was a state which once gave them room to define themselves in non-nationalist ways. In a poignant and bitter essay, 'Overcome by Nationhood', the Croatian writer Slavenka Drakulić describes how, until the late 1980s, she had always defined herself in terms of her education, profession, gender and personality. It was only the maddened atmosphere of the Croatian-Serbian war of 1991 that finally stripped her of all of these defining marks of identity except simply being a Croatian. What is true of an intellectual cannot be less true of village people. The nationalist language games of the elite only appeared to give a voice to their fear and their pride. In reality, nationalism ended up imprisoning everyone in the Balkans in the fiction of 'pure' ethnic identity. Those with multiple identities, for example, from mixed marriages, were forced to choose, between inherited and adopted families, and thus between two fused elements of their own selves.

Historically, nationalism and democracy have gone hand in hand. National-ism, after all, is the doctrine that a people have a right to rule themselves, and that sovereignty reposes in them alone. The tragedy for the Balkans was that, when democracy at last became possible, the only language that existed to mobilize people into a shared social project was the rhetoric of ethnic difference. Any possibility of a civic, as opposed to ethnic, democracy had been strangled at birth by the communist regime.

Serbia's Slobodan Milošević was the first Yugoslav politician to break the Titoist taboo on popular mobilization of ethnic consciousness. Milošević por-trayed himself both as the defender of Yugoslavia against the secessionist am-bitions of Croatia and Slovenia and as the avenger of the wrongs done to Serbia by that very Yugoslavia.

Milošević's programme, first set out in the Serbian Academy of Arts and Science Memorandum of 1986, and consistently followed ever since, has been to build a Greater Serbia on the ruins of Tito's Yugoslavia. If the other republics would not agree to a new Yugoslavia dominated by the Serbs, Milošević was prepared to incite the Serbian minorities in Kosovo, Croatia and Bosnia-Herce-govina to rise up and demand Serbian protection. These minorities served as Milošević's Sudeten Germans – pretext and justification of his expansionary design.

So much is obvious. More complicated is the relation between the Milošević project and Serbian opinion. It would make matters simpler if we could demonize the Serbs as incorrigibly nationalistic and assume that Milošević was merely responding to their ethnic paranoia. The reality is much more complicated. While there were extreme nationalist elements, like the Chetniks, still seething with resentment at Tito's campaign against their war-time leader, Draža Mihaj-lović, the majority of urban Serbs in the early 1980s displayed little nationalistic paranoia, and even less interest in their distant rural brethren in Knin, Pale, Kosovo or western Slavonia.

What needs to be explained, therefore, is why most ordinary Serbs' general indifference to the Serbian question turned into rabid anxiety that Serbs in the diaspora were about to be annihilated by genocidal Croatians and fundamentalist Muslims. Milošević certainly exploited 'the Serbian question' to serve his dema-gogic ends. But the Serbian question was not of Milošević's making. It arose inevitably out of the collapse of Tito's Yugoslavia. Once the multi-ethnic state disintegrated, every national group outside its republic's borders suddenly found itself an endangered national minority. As the largest such group, the Serbs felt particularly vulnerable to the rise of Croatian nationalism.

While the Croats, like the Slovenes, professed to support the emergence of a loosely confederal Yugoslavia, in reality both republics were set on the course of independence by the late 1980s. The drive towards national self-determination was fuelled by economic resentment. As the bills came in for Yugoslavia's expansion in the 1960s and 1970s, and its foreign indebtedness increased, the two richest republics, Slovenia and Croatia, became resentful that their econ-omic success was creamed off to pay for backward Bosnia and 'Balkan' Serbia. Both Tito's suppression of the Croatian spring of 1970, and Milošević's expan-sionist behaviour – especially Serbia's absorption of the autonomous provinces of Kosovo and Vojvodina – convinced Croatian and Slovenian nationalists that they had no future inside a federal Yugoslavia. Independence strongly appealed to the local intelligentsia and the communist elite: it would make them big fish in a small pond.

Croatians claimed the right of national self-determination, and they soon had influential backing from the newly reunited Germany. But no one in Germany or the European Community scrutinized with sufficient care the implications of Croatian independence for the rights of the 600,000-strong Serbian minority.

Croatia's independence constitution described itself as the state of the Croa-tian nation, with non-Croatians defined as protected minorities. While most Croats sincerely believed that their state offered full rights to the Serbian minority, Serbs did not regard themselves as a minority, but as a constitutionally protected nation, equal to the Croats. When the Croats revived the Šahovnica, the red and white chequered shield, as their new flag, Serbs took one look and believed the Ustashe had returned. The Šahovnica was both an innocently traditional Croat emblem and also the flag of the war-time regime which had exterminated a large, if still undetermined number, of Serbs. When Serbs were dismissed from the Croatian police and from the judiciary in the summer and autumn of 1990, the Serbian minority concluded they were witnessing the return of an ethnic state, with a genocidal past.

Defenders of the Croatian position insist that these fears were manipulated by Milošević. They certainly were, yet in the broader context of the collapse of the inter-ethnic Yugoslav state, Serbs had reason to be afraid. War was the result of an interacting spiral of Serbian expansionism, Croatian independence and Serbian ethnic paranoia in Croatia.

The final explosion was detonated in the summer of 1991 by battles in Serbian areas of Croatia for control of the key seat of local power, the police station. In Serb villages like Borovo Selo in Western Slavonia, when the Croatian state dismissed local Serbian policemen, they proceeded to arm and set themselves up as vigilantes. When the Croats tried to restore their authority in Serbian areas they were fired upon and roadblocks were set up at the entrances to villages. With the Croatians unable to control Serbian areas of their state, the Yugoslav National Army stepped in, at first to restore order and then to smash Croatian independence. Croatia then had no option but to fight for its survival. After six months of tenacious resistance, it found itself, at the ceasefire of February 1992, with a third of its national territory occupied by the rump state of Serbian Krajina and its supply routes to the Dalmatian coast blockaded by the Serbian paramilitaries in Knin. Twenty-five thousand UN troops now keep the two sides apart at checkpoints scattered across all of Croatia's main road networks. The war in Croatia has subsided into an armed truce, but the basic conflict between Serbs and Croats rages on south of the Sava River, as the two fight to divide Bosnia-Hercegovina at the expense of the Muslims.

THE HIGHWAY OF
BROTHERHOOD AND
UNITY

I began my journey where it used to begin every summer of my Yugoslav childhood, on the highway between Belgrade and Zagreb. This was the highway we travelled, in a magnificent black Buick, with lots of fins and chrome, to Lake Bled in Slovenia. It was called the Highway of Brotherhood and Unity and it was built, with a typically Titoist mixture of genuine national enthusiasm and socialist forced labour, to link together the economies of the two central republics, Croatia and Serbia. For 300 kilometres, it runs parallel to the Sava River, through the Slavonian plain, some of the flattest and richest farmland in Europe.

I began by visiting Tito's birthplace in Kumrovec, which is off the Highway of Brotherhood and Unity on the Slovenian border, in a hilly region of north-eastern Croatia known for the sharp tang of its white wine and the disputatiousness of its people.

Kumrovec was preserved as in one of the socialist newsreels I used to see in the Belgrade cinema in the 1950s. The sun was shining. The apple blossom was shimmering in the spring breeze. Peasants rolled through the village on haycarts.

Outside the whitewashed farmhouse, there was a bronze statue of Tito as partisan hero, in his greatcoat, striding ahead, deep in thought. Inside the house where the great leader was born, to a Croatian father and Slovenian mother (the perfect Yugoslav parentage), I inspected the maize-filled mattress where he may have slept; his report card in an Austro-Hungarian school; his photograph as a Comintern agent during the 1930s; his fake Swedish passport used during the partisan war; his field glasses, his splendidly vain white partisan uniform, with red and gold epaulettes; the map of his war-time campaigns, which showed how much of the partisan campaign was fought where the Bosnian war rages now; his post-war 'travels for peace' as head of the non-aligned movement: each capital visited was rewarded with a red star. Some places, like Cairo and New Delhi, had a dozen red stars each; other remote places, like Santiago, Chile or Ottawa, Canada, only one.

I was shown around by the local schoolteacher, a small, disappointed man with the red-rimmed eyes and broken veins of a drinker. When I asked his name, he made a small, nervous bow.

'Ivan Broz.'

'So you are a relative?' Tito was a *nom de guerre*. His family name was Broz.

'A distant cousin,' said Ivan, poker-faced. But later, when he was showing me the marshall's partisan uniform, he whispered, 'Once we took it out of the display case for a dusting, and I tried it on.' He looked about furtively, smiling and showing his stained yellow teeth. 'It fitted perfectly.'

Had he ever met Tito in person? Once, he said, when Tito took President Nixon to see his humble beginnings in Kumrovec. Ivan, then a schoolboy, was chosen to present a bouquet to Pat Nixon, while a girl was chosen to present flowers to the American President. For weeks, they were drilled in their bow and their curtsey, and then when the great moment came, it was over in a flash. 'Afterwards, the girl received a pen set and a signed autograph from the President. I got nothing. Such is life.'

But Tito?

Ivan remembers the dictator's eyes trained upon him. 'He was a politician. You never knew what he thought.'

Did people still come to visit here, I wanted to know. Oh yes, Ivan assured me. But the place was empty. There were no coaches in the parking lot, no families picnicking in the park, no one but me poring over the exhibits.

In one of the cases, there was a photo of Tito at an international conference, sitting behind a little sign reading: Yugoslavia. Someone had violently scratched out the name of the country with a ballpoint pen.

Why, I asked. Ivan shrugged his shoulders. 'It is not a popular name now in Croatia,' was all he would venture.

'Did you always feel more Croatian than Yugoslav?' I asked him. 'Always,' said Tito's sad cousin.

Back on the Highway of Brotherhood and Unity, I soon become aware what an odd highway it is. First of all, all the green destination signs have been painted over. I stop at one of them and take a closer look. The highway sign says I am headed towards Lipovac, but when I peel back the Lipovac decal on top, the word Belgrade appears beneath. The highway still does go all the way to the Serbian capital, but as far as Croatia is concerned, that destination has disappeared. Officially speaking, therefore, I am on a highway to nowhere.

About forty kilometres past Zagreb, the Croatian traffic begins taking the exits, leaving the highway to me. Soon I am the only civilian car on the road, beside the UN jeeps and lorries heading out from Zagreb to the checkpoints along the route. I have a superb four-lane motorway all to myself. I stop, get out, cross both lanes and back again. No one. Then I get into the car, take it up to 115 miles an hour, feeling full of adolescent elation. I roar up to a toll booth, only to discover that its windows are smashed and the booths are empty, though the hazard lights continue to blink on and off. I back up and take the toll booth at full speed.

I have no company except for hawks, who circle above the deserted highway looking for field mice, and feral cats who prowl along the grassy uncut verges. But from time to time, I can just make out the flash of sunlight on the binoculars of Croatian spotter teams dug into the motorway exit ramps. They must be wondering what a civilian car is doing using this deserted stretch of motorway as a drag-strip.

I have Austrian plates on the car. With Croatian or Serbian plates, I couldn't proceed beyond any of the checkpoints ahead. I am also equipped with a UNPROFOR pass, the essential passport for the UN protection zones I am about to enter. In the boot of the car are some canisters of extra petrol, to get me through the Serbian zones, which are under petrol embargo. Besides the canisters, there is a flak jacket. I've put it on once, and took it off immediately. It is ludicrously cumbersome and in practice useless. All you think about when you are wearing one are the parts of your body that remained exposed. Besides, the canisters have already leaked on to the flak jacket, ensuring that if I do get hit while wearing it, I will only burst into flames.

About seventy kilometres east of Zagreb, I spot the first signs of war: the guard rails on the central median strip have been chewed up and strewn about one of the carriageways. Then I begin to feel the track marks left behind in the road surface by the passage of tanks and armoured personnel carriers. Further on, the road is pocked and pitted with mortar blasts. On one of the motorway bridges, I spot my first sign of the cross with four cyrillic C's in each quadrant, standing for the Serbian motto: 'Only Unity can Save the Serbs.' On the next motorway bridge, I see the U for Ustashe, together with the chequered flag, the Šahovnica. On my left a rusted and burnt-out bus, lying on its side by an exit ramp, its roof sheared away by some form of incoming fire. I have reached the edge of the war-zone.

JASENOVAC

At the Jordanian headquarters at Novska, seventy kilometres east of Zagreb, a UN jeep meets me and leads my car down a shell-pocked slip road, over a pontoon bridge, past the Serb and Croat checkpoints and drops me off at a blasted and wrecked shell of a building which used to house the Jasenovac museum and memorial centre.

Between 1941 and 1945, trains drew up at the rail-head ramp on the other side of a vast, low, marshy field that slopes down to the Sava River. Jews and Serbs, gypsies and Croatian communists were herded out of the sealed wagons and pushed down the ramp to the rows of barracks behind the barbed wire. They were put to work in the brick factory, and when they were used up they were burned in the brick ovens or shot in the back of the head and then dumped in the Sava River.

No one knows exactly how many people died in the bare field behind the museum where the barracks and barbed wire once stood. Serbs and Croats cannot even reach agreement about this. Serbs maintain the figure is 700,000. There isn't a Serb village in central Croatia which didn't lose someone in this place. Croats insist that the number is no more than 40,000. Independent researchers have put the total number of people exterminated at Jasenovac in the region of 250,000, but no one can be sure.

It is just as difficult to come to terms with what happened only two years ago, when the war of 1991 reached Jasenovac. For I am walking into a museum that has been systematically destroyed. Every book in the library has been ripped up and tossed on to the floor. Every glass exhibit case has been smashed. Every photograph has been defaced. Every file has been pulled out of every drawer, every table and chair has been up-ended, all the curtains have been cut to ribbons, all the windows have been smashed and all the walls have been daubed with excrement and slogans. Some quite amazing hatred of the past has taken hold of the people who did this. As if by destroying the museum, they hoped to destroy the memory of what was done here.

Several thousand Croat militia were billeted in the museum in October 1991, and it is likely that they vandalized the place, although the walls have also been defaced with graffiti left behind by the Serbs who shelled the centre and retook it from the Croats.

I wade through rooms shin deep in ripped books and torn photographs, and with these I can struggle to piece together what the exhibits might have been like. On the floor, a picture of a crowd of prisoners waiting at the barbed wire lies beside a photograph of a young woman, her hair in plaits, leaning on a fence. Next to that a photo of a prelate shaking hands with an SS officer lies on top of a pile of ripped-up prisoners' files, and beside that, shredded portraits of Tito. The whole history of Yugoslavia seems to lie among the shattered glass and filth at my feet.

I can see how the children struggled to understand what they were told by the museum guides, because their drawings lie scattered all over: barbed wire, barracks and guards in bright water colours, the walking skeletons at the brick-works, as seen through the eyes of a 9-year-old, trying to understand.

Among the shards of glass and masonry I find scraps of film, ripped from the projectors in the museum cinema. Bending down in the filth, I hold the frames up to the light through the shattered windows open to the sky. In one strip of film I see frame after frame of an old man weeping, in another, a starved woman tottering down the road, in another strip of film, eighteen frames of a headless corpse.

Light streams through a gaping shell hole in the roof of the lecture theatre, and a lectern is all that remains standing in the burned-out wreckage of seats and cinema screen and wall panelling. On the front of the lectern there are the words, in Serbo-Croatian, which mean: Lest We Forget.

I walk out into the field behind the museum, now strewn with artillery shell casings, towards the railway cars, their ventilation holes sealed with barbed wire. I ask myself how such a place can ever be drained of its capacity to poison the living.

After 1945, Tito had the camp bulldozed in the hope that Serbs and Croats might forget. Then in the 1960s, when Tito supposed the wounds had healed, the memorial centre was opened. But after all the school visits and lectures and film showings, Yugoslavia never came to terms with what happened here. The past remained unmastered and unforgiven.

If the new Croatian state, proclaimed in May 1990, made one central mistake on the road to war, it was its failure to publicly disavow the Ustashe state and what it did at Jasenovac. The President of free Croatia, Franjo Tudjman, fought the Ustashe as a young partisan, but in the euphoria of independence he tried to unite all of Croatia's tortured past into what was called a national synthesis. So he never came to Jasenovac. He never got down on his knees, as Willy Brandt did at Auschwitz. If he had done so, Serbs and Croats might have begun the process of ending the past, instead of living it over and over. Because Tudjman did not come here, Serbs in Croatia were manipulated by Belgrade and by their local leaders into believing that the new Croatia was the fascist Ustashe come again.

Serbs scoff when you say Tudjman should have atoned for Jasenovac. 'Are you crazy?' they say. His party was financed by Croatians abroad, in Toronto and Melbourne. And who were they? Old Ustashe.

But the problem of confronting the past runs deeper than that. The war-time Ustashe state was Croatia's first experience of independent nationhood. It has proved impossible for Croatian nationalists to disavow a nationhood that was fascist. Instead, Croatians evade the issue altogether, either by dismissing tales of

Ustashe atrocity as Serbian propaganda, or by attempting to airbrush atrocity into crime by playing statistical sleight of hand with the numbers who died here. Finally, it appears, some Croats have dealt with Jasenovac by trying to vandalize its remains.

It is always said that aggression begins in denial and that violence originates in guilt. A nation that cannot repudiate a fascist past may condemn itself to a fascist future. True enough. But there is another equally imprisoning mechanism at work. If your enemies call you a fascist enough times, you will begin to call yourself one too. Take your enemies' insult and turn it into a badge of pride. How many times in the weeks ahead do I meet Croats at checkpoints who say: 'They call us Ustashe. Well then, that is what we are.' And likewise, the Serbs. 'You call us Chetniks. Well that is what we are.' The two sides conspire in a downward spiral of mutually interacting self-degradation. And where does that spiral begin? In the most ordinary form of cowardice, the one every one of us knows only too well – telling lies about the past.

But that is not all. Jasenovac is not the whole suppressed truth either. It is not all there is to say about Croatia in war-time. If Croats cannot bear Jasenovac, it is not merely because of what was done in their name, but also because of the partiality of what is remembered. At Jasenovac, Tito's Yugoslavia remembered Croatians only as murderers, never as victims. Tito never built a memorial centre at any of the mass graves of the thousands of Croatians massacred as they fled before his communist partisans on the roads of north-eastern Croatia and Slovenia in May 1945. The guilt of Jasenovac became unbearable, not merely because it was great, but also because it was unjust. At Jasenovac you begin to discern the lie about the past which eventually destroyed Tito's Yugoslavia. The lie was that the Second World War was a national uprising against German occupation led by Tito's partisans. In reality, it was a civil war fought among Yugoslavs. Post-war Yugoslavia never had enough time to heal the wounds of that war.

Jasenovac is a place to make you ponder your inherited liberal pieties. Some-where in my childhood, I must have been taught that telling lies eventually makes you ill. When Václav Havel said that people need to live in truth, he also meant that nations cannot hope to hold together if they do not come to some common – and truthful – version of their past. But there are nations with pasts so hard to share together, that they need centuries for forgetting to do its work. To ask for truth, to ask for shared truth, might be to ask for too much. Yugoslavia might be such a case. Fifty years was not enough time to forget.

Whatever the case, it is hard to continue believing in the healing power of historical truth when you stand in the middle of a vandalized museum. Some dark spirit, stronger than truth, was at work here. And it is at work on the road from Jasenovac as you drive away. Towards Novska, you pass Serb house after Serb house, neatly dynamited, beside undisturbed Croat houses and gardens. When you turn towards Lipik, it is the turn of all the Croat houses to be dynamited or fire-bombed, next to their untouched Serb neighbours. Mile upon mile, the deadly logic of ethnic cleansing unfolds. In village after village, they have ripped open the scar tissue over their common wound.

CRY, GIRL, CRY

I am in central Croatia now, in the heart of what was once one of the most complex multi-ethnic communities in Europe, shared between a Croatian majority, a Serbian minority and several other groups – Germans, Italians and Hungarians – besides. The 1991 war tore these villages apart, and now they are divided between Croatian and Serbian sectors, with UN checkpoints in between.

On all the roads which lead north from the Highway of Brotherhood and Unity, there is a continuous swathe of devastation wherever you look. Roofless houses, with a cascade of roof tiles and roofbeams strewn about the deserted, weed filled rooms; fire edged window and door frames, brick walls pierced with tire-sized artillery blasts. Some houses have been raked by so much automatic weapons fire that the plaster has been completely torn away, leaving only the pitted brick, the tree trunks outside the houses wearing a glittering jacket of metal slugs. In the ditches, lie small Yugoslav Zastava cars, riddled with bullet fire, or twisted into rusted sculpture by a tank's treads.

At first the destruction appears to have no rhyme or reason. In some villages, not a wall has been left unsprayed with bullets, while in others, scarcely a house has been touched. After a while, you begin to work like an archaeologist, sifting through the clues to discern a pattern to what must have happened. There appear to be three typical forms of destruction. The most surgical form is dynamiting: the houses are collapsed in neat piles, with minimal damage to the houses next door. Families were driven out by their neighbours or by paramilitary militias and their homes were blown up. Many of these dynamited piles appear to have once been large, recently constructed houses, and it makes you wonder how many years of a man or woman's life as a gastarbeiter in a German car-plant went into this, only to see it fall like a pack of cards.

The second type of destruction appears to have been accomplished by artillery fire, from the Yugoslav National Army guns which punched round, tire-sized holes in Croatian village walls. The third type of destruction is fire-bombing, which leaves fire-marks on all windows, and which would have been the work of marauding paramilitaries on both sides.

Some houses were daubed by the Serbs with the slogan U, for Ustashe, which then marked them for ethnic cleansing. Others are marked with crudely and rapidly painted names of those who lived in them, as if, as they were abandoned, their inhabitants were hoping to remind the defenders that they belonged to the same side. I spent hours in these ruins, the dust in my throat, the sound of broken glass under my feet, deciphering the clues to the shape of catastrophe.

Never say ethnic cleansing is just racial hatred run wild, just Balkan madness. For there is a deep logic to it. By 1990, this part of Yugoslavia was a Hobbesian world. No one in these villages could be sure who would protect them. If they were Serbs and someone attacked them and they went to the Croatian police, would the Croats protect them? If they were Croats, in a Serbian village, could they be protected against a night-time attack from a Serbian paramilitary team, usually led by a former policeman? This is how ethnic cleansing began to acquire its logic. If you can't trust your neighbours, drive them out. If you can't live among them, live only among your own. This alone appeared to offer people security. This alone gave respite from the fear which leaped like a brush-fire from house to house.

The West has to make up its mind about the emerging order of ethnically cleansed micro-states which have taken the place of Yugoslavia. Nobody in the West wants to appear to be condoning ethnic cleansing, but every day, every hour, civilians are fleeing war zones, or being driven hence by men with guns, into the relative safety of their own ethnic enclaves. Ethnic apartheid may be an abomination, but for the more than two million refugees who have fled or been driven from their homes, apartheid is the only guarantee of safety they are prepared to trust. Civilian victims in the area are rightly indifferent to our scruples and our strictures about ethnic cantonment. For the West failed to save Sarajevo, where Muslim, Croat and Serb lived together in peace for centuries. It is asking the impossible to believe that ordinary people will trickle back to the multi-ethnic villages they have left behind, simply in order to vindicate our liberal principles.

As you travel through the zones of devastation in central Croatia, you also have the impression that you have fallen through some hole in time and are spinning backwards into the past. You are not in 1993, but in 1943. In Serb villages, old ladies in black scarves and black wool dresses watch you suspiciously as you pass; ribbed haycarts go by, driven by old men in their Second World War khaki forage caps. Out in their back gardens, women are bending over their hoes. On the roads, militiamen, wearing the red, white and blue shoulder badge of the Serbian Krajina, emerge from dugouts by the road, to stop the car and search you. Everyone is wary. Few will talk.

In one ruined farm, formerly inhabited by Croatians, I came upon an old Serbian couple camped out in the remains of an outbuilding. They were in their 80s, and they had been driven from their home in Daruvar, forty kilometres to the north, by the Croatians. The old man was sawing up a piece of charred wood for the stove. The old lady was tidying up their tiny room, with its bed, its cracked window, table, two cups and two chairs, and spotlessly swept floor. They had rebuilt the roof themselves, and they survived on what they got from neighbours and the Red Cross. We sit on a stump, in the middle of the ruins, with glass, brick and burnt roofbeams littered about, and when I ask them whether this war has been worse than the last one, the old lady replies, with bitter scorn, that this one has been much worse. 'In the last one, we all fought the Germans. This time, there was just betrayal.' Neighbour against neighbour, friend against friend. Can you ever live together again? They both shake their heads and look away.

When I ask them how they manage to survive, they suddenly seem to revive. 'God will arrange everything,' they both say, in unison, exchanging a cheerful glance across what must be fifty years of marriage. When I get up to leave, the old man takes my hand and holds it in a long, intense grip. His bright blue eyes stare deep into mine. 'Truth and national rights. That is all we want. Truth and national rights.'

A mile away, across another checkpoint, this time in the Croatian village of Lipik, I come across a man helping a team of six women in blue overalls stacking up the usable bricks from the rubble of a flattened house. It turns out that he is the owner of the house, and the women are from a municipal detachment sent out to repair damaged houses.

Tomislav Mareković is the man's name, Yup to his friends. Yup is the caretaker in the local hospital and a trainer of the local football team in his spare time. I suspect, without knowing for sure, that he also is a prominent local supporter of the HDZ, the ruling Croatian party. Why else, I reason, is his the only house I can find in Lipik where the rubble is being cleared by a municipal work detail?

He shows me where his kitchen was, where the television set used to be, where his couch stood. Now there is nothing left but the foundations and a mound of bricks which the women are stacking in piles after chippping away the mortar. Next door's house was untouched. Why? I ask. Serbs, he says. We always got on. Now, he says, they are in West Germany. And the house next door? My parents, he says laconically. Suddenly, he points out into the street. 'That is where they left my father. There, in the street, for three weeks, before someone buried the body. And my mother, they took her to a barn and set her on fire.'

Yugoslav army tanks, dug into the hills above Lipik, were pounding the town and, under directions from local Serbian paramilitaries, were targeting Croat houses. When Yup's house came under bombardment, he and his wife jumped in their car and fled to Zagreb, but his parents refused to come, thinking they would be safe. Days later, they were dragged out of their house by Serbian paramilitaries, possibly from the same village. They were shot and their bodies were burned. Yup tells me all this with a few sighs, a few pauses to light a cigarette, staring glumly into the distance. All the while, the women work silently around us, stacking bricks.

Yup declares a break and I sit down with the women at a trestle table in his tiny back garden. I want to know why the work detail is all female, and they all reply, with much laughter and winking: 'Because women are the best.' Left unsaid is the fact that so many Croatian males are away serving in the army. I tell them that I've noticed on the other side the Serbs aren't rebuilding. They're just living in the ruins, with their guns trained towards Croatia, waiting. 'They're not rebuilding,' says one lady, matter-of-factly, 'because they know they're done for.' Some of the other ladies nod, while others look down silently at the table.

Yup says, 'Three of you are Serbs, isn't that right?' And three of the women beside me nod and look back down at the table. In the silence, they leave it to me to figure out how it comes about that three Serbian women are helping to rebuild a Croat's house. It can only be because they were married to Croats, have lived here all their lives and find themselves now torn in two, as their village is. Then the Serbian woman beside me slowly begins to cry and a stillness descends over everyone. The Croatian women across the table look at her dispassionately, while she crumples into herself. 'Cry, girl, cry,' says one, and reaches over and takes her hand.

WARLORDS

Back in 1989, we thought the new world opened up by the breaching of the Berlin Wall would be ruled by philosopher kings, dissident heroes and shipyard electricians. We looked forward to a new order of nation states, released from the senile grip of the Soviets. We assumed that national self-determination had to mean freedom and that nationalism had to mean nation building. As usual we were wrong. We hoped for order. We got pandemonium. In the name of nationalism, dozens of viable nation states have been shattered beyond repair. In the name of state building, we have returned large portions of Europe to the pre-political chaos prior to the emergence of the modern state.

Large portions of the former Yugoslavia are now ruled by figures that have not been seen in Europe since late medieval times: the warlord. They appear wherever nation states disintegrate: in the Lebanon, Somalia, northern India, Armenia, Georgia, Ossetia, Cambodia, the former Yugoslavia. With their car-phones, faxes and exquisite personal weaponry, they look post-modern, but the reality is pure early medieval.

Their vehicle of choice is a four-wheel drive Cherokee Chief, with a policeman's blue light on the roof to flash when speeding through a checkpoint. They pack a pistol but they don't wave it about. They leave vulgar intimidation to the bodyguards in the back of the jeep, the ones with shades, designer jeans and Zastava machine pistols. They themselves dress in the leather jackets, floral ties and pressed corduroy trousers favoured by German television producers. They bear no resemblance whatever to Rambo. The ones I began meeting at the checkpoints on the roads leading off from the Highway of Brotherhood and Unity were short, stubby men who in a former life had been small-time hoods, small-town cops or both. Spend a day with them, touring their world, and you'd hardly know that most of them are serial killers.

Warlords not only dominate the war-zones, they also have worked their way to the heart of power in the authoritarian single party states of Croatia and Serbia alike.

War criminals are celebrities in the Balkans. They have seats in the Serbian parliament. One of them, Vojislav Šešelj, the self-styled Duke of the Serbian Chetniks, runs his own party as well as a full-time paramilitary unit. Another, Željko Raznjatović, aka Arkan, controls an 800-strong paramilitary unit called the Tigers, who raped and tortured their way through Eastern Slavonia in the Croatian war of 1991. This odious thug, on the run from an Interpol warrant for an attempted murder in Sweden, is a parliamentary deputy and operates a number of immensely profitable sanctions-busting businesses, including selling smuggled petrol for hard currency at petrol stations around Belgrade. Ever the post-modern Prince of Darkness, Arkan has launched himself into celebrity franchising. In Serbian farmhouses in Eastern Slavonia, the icon you are most likely to see beside an image of Saint Sava is a large coloured calendar, with a different picture of Arkan for every month of the year.

At anti-Milošević demonstrations in Belgrade, which I attended at the end of my journey, who should appear, cruising through the middle of the crowd in his Cherokee Chief, but this smiling killer in a smart sheepskin jacket, waving suavely to left and right, obviously revelling in his provocation of Belgrade's impotent peace party.

Croatians will tell you that the fact that Arkan is allowed to serve as a deputy in the Serbian parliament is proof that Serbia is a fascist regime. It is not. There are functioning opposition parties and newspapers, and, indeed, just as much democracy in Belgrade as there is in Zagreb. It is Djilas's characterization of Serbian politics – 'democracy with a tinge of banditism' – that best describes the way warlords have worked their way into the heart of the system.

There are warlords on the Croatian side too – if not in Zagreb, then in the front-line towns like Osijek, run by town council president and local party boss Branimir Glavaš. When you tour the town in Glavaš's jeep, it is like being with a spectacularly popular local politician in a small American town. He comes across a local wedding and the band serenades him. The bridegroom asks him to kiss the bride, the revellers hand him bottles to sample. It is hard to remember that this man is leader of the Glavaš Unit, a paramilitary group held responsible not merely for the defence of Osijek but for the cleansing of Serbian villages and for the murder of Croatian policemen who sought to maintain good relations with Serbs.

Glavaš flashes a policeman's badge at the police checkpoints, as well as a military pass at the front line. The limits of his power are as imprecise as they are pervasive. He has translated the nefarious glamour of the warlord into peacetime power, yet he assures you with a snap of his fingers that he could remobilize his paramilitaries overnight. Thirty kilometres away, across the front line in Serb-held Vukovar, there is Mr Kojić, the Serbian equivalent of Mr Glavaš. Same jeep, same courteous manner. Same guns.

The warlords are nationalists, but their convictions are uninteresting. They are technicians of violence, rather than ideologues. Earlier than everybody else, they understood that ethnic nationalism had delivered the ordinary people of the Balkans straight back to the pre-political state of nature where, as Hobbes predicted, life is nasty, brutish and short. In the state of nature, the man with a Zastava machine pistol and a Cherokee Chief is king. For he can provide the two commodities everybody here craves: security and vengeance.

Once the Yugoslav communist state began to spin apart into its constituent national particles, the key questions soon became: will the local Croat policemen protect me if I am a Serb? Will I keep my job in the soap factory if my new boss is a Serb or a Muslim? The answer to these questions was no, because no state remained to enforce the old inter-ethnic bargain. As a result, every individual rushed, pell-mell, to the next available source of protection – the warlord.

For the warlord not only offers protection. He offers a solution. He tells his people: if we cannot trust our neighbours, we must rid ourselves of them. If we cannot live together in a single state, we must create clean states of our own. The logic of ethnic cleansing is not just motivated by nationalist hatred. Cleansing is the warlord's coldly rational solution to the war of all against all. Rid yourself of your neighbours, the warlord says, and you no longer have to fear them. Live among your own, and you can live in peace. With me and my boys to protect you.

VUKOVAR

After dark in Vukovar, your car headlights range over pockmarked walls, roofless ruins and piles of rubble on both sides of the road. You do not stop at the bullet-shredded Stop signs because there are no cars at the crossroads. There must be people living here, because you occasionally see a solitary light gleaming from behind a shutter in one of the bombed-out tower blocks. But you see no one because no one ventures out after dark. Rats scuttle to and fro across the road to forage in the garbage. In the distance, you hear an occasional burst of small arms fire.

This ghost town was once a Habsburg episcopal seat on the Danube. In 1991 it became the Croatian Stalingrad. Throughout the autumn, the Croatian national guard defended it to the last street against the heaviest artillery bombardment seen in Europe since 1945. When the Serbian paramilitaries and the Yugoslav National Army finally 'liberated' the town in November 1991, at a cost of something like 9000 lives, there was nothing left to liberate but a devastated ruin.

The self-proclaimed Republic of Serbian Krajina has its eastern headquarters in Vukovar. Krajina means the military frontier. Serbian settlement in Croatia was established in the seventeenth century by the Austro-Hungarians as a buffer zone between them and the Ottomans. As the appointed defenders of European civilization against the Turks in the Balkans, the Serbs have always gone armed. The gun culture here is ancestral.

In the town square, a banner has been stretched over the road from one pulverized house to the other. It reads: 'Welcome to Vukovar, Year One.' But eighteen months after entering the town, the Serbs have done nothing to rebuild it. It should probably be left as it is. UNESCO could fence it off and declare it a European heritage site. What could be more European, after all, than our tradition of senseless nationalist warfare?

The Serbs have taken down the Croatian street signs and replaced them with Serb ones in cyrillic, but the Croatian signs are still stacked in the attic of the pulverized town museum, as if somewhere in their minds the Serbs expect the Croatian signs will one day go back up again.

In the museum attic, too, is a still more extraordinary sight: three bronze busts – Marx, Engels and Lenin – sitting on the main roofbeam, despatched there in the 1980s at the official death of communist ideology, and now revealed by the bombardment which blew away all the roof tiles and the false ceiling concealing the roofbeams. These three bronze busts were the only exhibit in the museum to have survived the siege intact.

While the responsibility for the destruction of Vukovar lies squarely with the tanks and artillery of the Yugoslav National Army who lobbed 150,000 shells into the place, the Croatians also appear to have dynamited parts of it as they withdrew, so that the Serbs would gain nothing but rubble for their pains. The pulverization of Vukovar made no military sense. When I asked a Serbian tank commander why they had done it, he shrugged his shoulders. 'War has many such tragedies ... Leningrad ... Stalingrad ...' But these were battles with a military objective. In a nationalist war, on the other hand, military objectives were driven by a desire to hurt, humiliate and punish. The JNA (Yugoslav National Army) could have bypassed Vukovar and sent its tank columns down the Highway of Brotherhood and Unity all the way to Zagreb. Instead, it sat on the other side of the Danube and pounded Vukovar into rubble, as if to say, with each outgoing shell, 'So you want to be independent, do you? This is what it will cost you, and what you will have at the end of it is nothing but ruins.'

It is hard not to think, as you stand in shattered graveyards, convents, churches and homes, that someone derived deep pleasure from all this destruction. All these ancient walls, all these crucifixes, church towers, ancient slate roofs, were demolished by people whose ideologies ceaselessly repeated that they were fighting to defend the holy and sacred past from desecration. In a way, the artillery expressed the essential nihilism of what people called conviction more honestly than all the nationalist pieties about fighting for the sake of the sacred motherland.

Some quite uncontrolled adolescent lust was at work here. The tank and artillery commanders could not have seen what they were hitting. It was all as abstract and as satisfying as playing the machines in a video arcade. It didn't even seem to bother the largely Serb commanders that a significant percentage of the population being bombed, perhaps as many as 20 per cent, were ethnic Serbs. Now many of them lie on the city's outskirts beneath one of the bare, nameless crosses in a mass grave.

The Serbs have inherited the ruins that they themselves have made. One might have expected regret or shame, or, failing that, some state of moral confusion about what they had done to the city. But nothing, not a syllable. Only a kind of embarrassed silence.

It was in Vukovar that I began to see how nationalism works as a moral vocabulary of self-exoneration. No one is responsible for anything but the other side. In the moral universe of pure nationalist delusion, all action is compelled by tragic necessity. Towns must be destroyed in order to liberate them. Hostages must be shot. Massacres must be undertaken. Why? Because the other side started it first. Because the other side are beasts and understand no language but violence and reprisal. And so on. Everyone in a nationalist war speaks in the language of fate, compulsion and moral abdication. Nowhere did this reach such a nadir as in Vukovar. The pistol toting hoodlums, holed up in the ruins of the Hotel Dunav, who came out and threatened to kill my translator, simply because he was a Hungarian; the Krajinan Information Minister who had no information that was not a lie; the Mayor of Vukovar, who went around the Vukovar hospital handing out Serbian flags to men whose legs ended at a bandaged stump – not one of these creatures ever expressed the slightest sense of shame, regret or puzzlement that the insensate prosecution of their cause had led to the ruination of their own city. For all of them, the responsibility was solely Croat.

Serbian Krajina calls itself a state, but is more like a feudal kingdom run by small-time warlords, called Deputy Minister This and Supreme Commander That, whose power depends on how many cars, weapons and men they can commandeer. You soon discover that their writ usually runs out at the next checkpoint.

Mr Kojić, the security boss of Vukovar and district, assures you he has the town under control, but there are three impact clusters on the bullet-proof windscreen of his Passat from a fire-fight with the local gangsters three nights before. There are guns everywhere: on the backs of old men bicycling out to guard duty on their village checkpoints; hanging from the belts of the militiamen who check your papers at the entrance to the town; behind the counter in the local bar. Everywhere in Krajina, the democracy of violence rules.

At night, the Serbs of Krajina sit in bunkers at the entrance of their villages with their guns trained down the lonely roads, waiting for the Croats to come at them. It's a village war, and the front line often runs right between two back gardens. One rainy night I went out to the front lines about thirty kilometres from Vukovar. With the faint glow of the Croat positions in Vinkovci clearly visible, I scuttled to the Serbian trenches under washing lines, over garden fences, past old discarded washbasins and newly hoed vegetable gardens. When I reached the safety of the Serb bunker, I could hear Croatian music from the other side, mixed with the grunting of Serbian pigs in the sty next door.

From their positions, the Serbs can see the homes they were forced to flee; they can see their neighbours in their gun-sights. One paramilitary called Chobi Chetnik, with a sign reading 'Serbia: Liberty or Death' on his battledress, got on the CB radio at two in the morning to taunt the Ustashe a hundred metres away. This is a war where the enemies went to school together, worked in the same haulage company, and now talk on the CB every night, laughing, taunting, telling jokes. Then they hang up, and try to line each other up in their gun-sights.

And so it goes, night after night, neither peace nor war, the two sides straining at the leash, taunting and testing each other, probing each other's positions with small arms fire and the occasional lob of a mortar or artillery shell.

The Serb positions are defended by ex-Yugoslav army officers, Dad's Army village volunteers and wild Chetnik paramilitaries. Without the UN, they know they would be quickly overrun. You can see their desperation in the way they drink, and in the listless fatalism that steals over their faces when the bravado of the bunker dies away.

The Croat forward lines, which I visited at Osijek, thirty kilometres from Vukovar, look altogether more impressive. They are dug in behind a stretch of dynamited motorway, and they seem to be both more disciplined and more belligerent than the Serbs. They believe the UN is ratifying the permanent occupation of a third of their country, and the men in their flak jackets, and helmets, wave their Zastava automatics in the direction of the Serbian lines and tell you the Croatian flag will soon be flying over Vukovar. More front-line bravado perhaps, but I left both sides feeling that the ceasefire in eastern Slavonia hangs by a thread.

The Serbs in their bunkers have a case which deserves to be heard. In Yugoslavia, they were a protected constitutional nation. In an independent Croatia, they were reduced to a national minority in a state with a genocidal past. Without a state of their own, the Serbs repeat over and over, they face extermination again. The Serbian war in Bosnia is designed to give them such a state, by providing a unified land corridor from Serbia proper, connecting up the Serbian lands in western, central and southern Croatia. Without such a corridor, the Croatian Serbs know they will not survive, and until such a corridor is secure, they live from day to day, in a state of armed paranoia. There is a currency and there is a flag, but there is no state in Krajina, merely a jungle. And they have no sure protector. For all their bravado, they know they cannot count on Milošević. If the price of their defence becomes too high for Serbia proper, the Krajinans know they will be sold down the river.

The Serbian case would be more convincing if they were less persuaded that the whole world, especially foreign journalists, are against them. After you have had your car commandeered by drunken paramilitaries, after you have been shot at and had your life threatened, a certain indifference to their cause tends to steal over you.

The war zones of Eastern Slavonia, and Vukovar in particular, leave behind an unforgettable impression of historical retrogression. Graveyards where Jews and Ruthenes, Germans, Croats and Serbs once were buried together now lie desecrated by the bombs of both sides. Elegant episcopal palaces and monasteries, delicately arcaded squares left behind by the Austro-Hungarians lie in ruins. Time has slid back through five centuries here. One of the richest and most civilized parts of Europe has returned to the barbarism of the late middle ages. Such law and order as there is is administered by warlords. There is little gasoline, so the villages have returned to the era before the motor car. Everyone goes about on foot. Old peasant women forage for fuel in the woods, because there is no heating oil. Food is scarce, because the men are too busy fighting to tend the fields. In the desolate wastes in front of the bombed out high-rise flats, survivors dig at the ground with hoes. Every man goes armed. No one ventures beyond the village. No one trusts anyone they have not known all their lives. Late twentieth-century nationalism has delivered one part of the European continent back to the time before the nation state, to the chaos of late feudal civil war.

A week spent in Serbian Krajina is a week spent inside a nationalist paranoia so total that when you finally cross the last Serbian checkpoint and turn on the radio, and find an aria from Puccini playing, and look out of your window and see the wet fields in the rain, you find yourself uncoiling like a tightly wound spring, absurdly surprised to discover that a world of innocent beauty still exists.

BELGRADE

On the Highway of Brotherhood and Unity, you never tell anybody where you've really come from or where you're really going. At the Croatian checkpoints, you say merely that you're going to the next Croatian town. At the Serb checkpoints, you smile, let them search your trunk, rummage through the dirty underwear in your luggage, offer them Marlboros, and tell them over and over that you are heading towards the bosom of Mother Serbia.

At the first toll booth on the Serbian side of the highway, you do not hand them the toll card you picked up at the Zagreb entrance. You say, instead, that you've come from the Serbian Krajina, and then you negotiate your toll fee in German marks. This is the only toll booth in Europe where, with laughter, exchange of cigarettes and displays of mocking disbelief at what they propose to charge you, you can barter your toll fee down to a reasonable sum.

About twenty-four kilometres from Belgrade, you see your first sign of the impact of Western sanctions: enormous queues of small Zastavas, Fiats, Renault 5s, stretching down the motorway from the service stations, and large crowds of men gathered around the empty pumps, waiting for the occasional delivery. They play cards, talk politics, sing along to a harmonica to pass the time, but when you come up to talk, and they discover that you are a Western writer, an angry knot of men soon surrounds you. A short, stubby man with a pork-pie hat on his head, mud-encrusted boots and the hands of a farmer pokes you in the chest and says: 'What the hell were we supposed to do with those Croats? Stand there and wait for them to cut our throats? And what do you do? You give us these sanctions. You call that fair?' And so it goes, with themes and variations, that soon have them blaming Churchill and the British for supporting Tito rather than Draža Mihai-lović. So apparently it is the fault of the British that Yugoslavia had fifty years of communism.

Their anger would be more threatening if it were not accompanied by a certain comic ritual. The men in the queue approach, say they don't want to have anything to do with a Westerner, turn on their heels, so that their friends can see what a splendid gesture of defiance they have made, and then they return anyway and start talking, pausing to let you take notes, peering over your shoulder to see how you write their names and so on. This, I learn in the days ahead, is part of the ritual style of Serbian nationalism itself. The dance has its opening quadrille: we won't talk, the West never understands; we despise you, you tell nothing but lies; then they start talking and never stop. Ask anybody a simple question and you get that tell-tale phrase: 'You have to understand our history ...' Twenty minutes later and you are still hearing about King Lazar, the Turks and the Battle of Kosovo. This deep conviction that no one understands them, coupled with the fervent, unstoppable desire to explain and justify themselves, seemed to define the style of every conversation I had in Belgrade.

Next morning, when I visit a bank queue, the same rituals repeat themselves. People violently and vehemently refuse to talk, only to start into a stream of Serbian self-justification that begins with their immemorial struggle against the Turks and concludes with their defence of Serbian Bosnia against the Muslim fundamentalists. Along the way, the invective sweeps up the anti-Serbian crimes of Churchill, Roosevelt, Stalin and Tito into a rhetorical flow as muddy as a spring torrent.

Bank queues are as fundamental a part of Belgrade life as the petrol queue. The economy is in a state of advanced hyper-inflation – running at 200 per cent per month. In the restaurants, the price stickers on the menus change overnight. The only reliable hedge against inflation is a hard currency account. Many private banks have opened for business and promise to pay 10 per cent per month on such accounts. How they manage to do so is a mystery. The rumour is that the private banks are deeply engaged in the nether world of smuggling, illegal oil imports from the Ukraine, arms-trading with Russia together with the laundering of Western drug money. Some of these banks have gone bust, and the fear is that if more of them do the Milošević regime itself might be swept away in the ensuing economic chaos.

So anxious are the small depositors about the fate of their accounts that many of them queue all night long in order to be sure to be able to withdraw their hard currency. These queues stretch hundreds of metres down the streets, a pushing, shoving mass of cold, deeply unhappy old-age pensioners, some of them weak with tiredness.

You might have thought such queues would be full of anti-Milošević grumbling. Belgrade, after all, never voted for him and has always resented its demotion from a world capital of the non-aligned movement, as it was under Tito, to an isolated, embargoed Balkan provincial capital. Yet, again, all the anger that might be directed at Milošević is directed at the West – at Churchill, at Mrs Thatcher for having supported the Croats, at the Americans for aiding the Bosnian Muslims, and so on.

DJILAS

He answers the door of his Belgrade flat himself. His hair is white now, and age has loosened the sharp, aquiline features I remembered from the book jacket of his *Conversations with Stalin*. He is 82, and seems stooped and frail as he leads me down the corridor to his study. He tells me which of the low green velvet armchairs to sit in and asks me whether I want tea or a drink. When I decline, he laughs and remembers the time he led a Yugoslav delegation to meet Stalin in 1944. The Russians offered them vodka, and when the Yugoslavs turned them down, the Russians shouted, 'What kind of people are you?' 'We were partisans,' says Milovan Djilas, with a thin, watchful smile. There is something of the puritanical partisan in him still.

Djilas was at Tito's side throughout the partisan guerilla campaigns against the German occupiers and their Serbian and Croat collaborators. Better than anyone else, he knows that the mutual loathings of 1993 all go back to the the massacres and counter-massacres among Yugoslavs between 1941 and 1945. As the last great partisan leader left alive, he is the last one who still remembers the Yugoslav dream that the next generations tore apart.

He tells me about setting off in an American Willys jeep in the summer of 1945, as Vice-President of the new Yugoslavia, to establish the border between Serbia and Croatia. 'I was a Montenegrin, after all,' he says with a smile, 'and so I was supposed to be impartial.' What principle, I ask him, did he use to decide which villages were to go to the Croats, which to the Serbs? 'The ethnic principle,' he says, and he describes how he counted up the ethnic percentages in each village along the border before deciding which ones would belong to Croatia, which to Serbia. This was the border the war was fought over, and to this day Serb nationalists accuse Djilas of selling out Serbian interests to the despised Croatians.

He was both a key architect and map-drawer of post-war Yugoslavia and the first communist dissident in Eastern Europe. He broke with Tito in 1953 for betraying the ideals of the partisan movement and for allowing the new communist state to be taken over by a new bureaucratic, privileged class. For this, Tito had him imprisoned for nine years. It was in prison that he learned his meticulous, heavily accented English, using a dictionary to translate Milton's *Paradise Lost* into Serbo-Croatian.

I expect him to blame his old enemy, Tito, for failing to understand ethnic nationalism, but he shakes his head vigorously. Tito's handling of nationalism could not be faulted. He gave each republic just enough autonomy to satisfy nationalist demands, without compromising the unity of Yugoslavia. His fundamental mistake was that he never managed a democratic succession. He never created the institutions and the state of mind necessary to make democracy work. The minute the communists began to disintegrate, Yugoslavia itself began to fall apart.

I ask him whether democracy and nationalism are compatible. In the Yugoslav case, could a democratic system have held the country together? Yes, he insists, gradual democratization, gradual relaxation of one-party rule, might have resulted in the kind of democratic culture which could have allowed the nationalisms of the region to share power together. And why didn't he democratize in time? 'Because he was both the master and the slave of the privileged communist class,' Djilas says, with the relish of a man who has lived to see his original heresy proclaimed the truth.

By failing to democratize in time, Tito threw away all of his achievements. In the end, the communists proved no more successful than the Austro-Hungarians or the Turks in mastering the region. 'We communists,' he says, 'were the last empire.'

How does he understand the nationalism that has torn his Yugoslavia apart? Balkan nationalism, he argues, was an imported Germanic ideology, which reached these regions only in the 1870s. Immediately, it had a fatal impact, tearing apart the complex ethnic tissue of peoples and nations who had grown together as neighbours over the centuries. He thinks of nationalism still, not as an intrinsic folk emotion, but as an alien virus, the work of city intellectuals who stirred up unlettered people and pushed a successful multi-ethnic experiment over the precipice. Few people I meet in Belgrade believe Milošević himself has any deep nationalist convictions. He merely knows that when he shouts from a podium, 'Nobody will ever beat the Serbs again!' they applaud him to the rafters.

The West's greatest mistake, Djilas then says, is that it has 'satanized' the Serbs. This comes as a surprise from someone constantly vilified in Serbian nationalist propaganda as a betrayer of Serbian interests. Yet Djilas is insistent: by placing exclusive blame on the Serbs for both the Croatian war of 1991 and the Bosnian war of 1993, the West has delivered the Serbian population into the hands of Milošević and the nationalists.

Thus far, the Balkan sorcerer, Milošević, has turned all of the brew of resentment towards the West to his own advantage. Sanctions are turning the day-long queue into a way of life for ordinary people, but the regime seems more secure than ever. Although Belgrade itself voted against Milošević in last autumn's elections, street demonstrations against the regime fizzle out almost as soon as they begin. Opposition parties are weak and divided, and even more nationalistic than Milošević. All in all, the scene is bleak confirmation of Djilas's essential point: a society with no democratic tradition has filled the post-communist void with persecution mania directed towards the West and delusions of grandeur directed at their fellow Serbs.

In Djilas's view, the Western 'satanization' of Serbia has also enabled Croatians and the Bosnian Muslims to lay claim to the role of blameless victim. Sanctions against Serbia were unavoidable, he admits, given the siege of Sarajevo, the occupation of a quarter of Croatia, and the concentration camps for Muslims. But this only convinces Croats and Muslims that they will not receive international sanctions for acts of revenge against the Serbs.

Djilas views this all with the olympian detachment of an old man, but there is one moment in our conversation when his detachment breaks down. 'We must be the only country in Europe,' he says with cold contempt, 'actively rehabilitating fascist collaborators.' He means the Croatian Ustashe, but also Serbian collaborators, the Chetniks, who fought with the Germans. The thought that everything he fought for has collapsed and everything he fought against fifty years ago has been restored to public honour momentarily clouds his face. He looks tired and dispirited. 'The Second World War is not over, not here anyway,' he says with a sigh.

TITO'S GRAVE

He liked greenhouses. So he built himself a greenhouse. He used to rest there, among the poinsettias and the cactuses, like an old lizard in the sun. Now they have buried him in the greenhouse, in front of his residence in Belgrade. There is a large white marble slab, with bronze lettering which reads Josip Broz Tito, 1892–1980.

No one much visits any more, and the place is neglected. On the day I visit it is raining, and rain is dripping from a broken skylight on to the Marshal's grave. Nobody cares.

On his birthday in 1945, some teenagers ran a relay race from Kragujevac to Belgrade and presented him with a baton. Every year of his reign, the 'youth' of Yugoslavia repeated that race, and at the end of it they presented the old dictator with the relay batons. His birthday became 'Youth Day'. Twenty thousand batons are kept in the museum next to his grave. Nobody visits the batons any more.

How quickly the legitimacy of power drains away. The batons were not ridiculous twenty years ago. The relay race meant something to people. Now it seems to belong to the rites of some vanished tribe.

What does one conclude? Dictators have no successors. Charisma is the most unstable of legitimacies. That much is obvious. But what about democracy? Was there ever, really, a chance of democracy here? The old lizard himself would have said: never, they will only tear themselves apart if you let them. From the hell where dead tyrants are sent, he would be surveying the inferno that followed his reign and he would be saying: I told you so. There must be a rule of iron. I was right. Djilas was wrong. After me came the deluge.

But nothing in what happened proves the dictator right. What was needed was more time – time for a people to forget, for old men to die and for their memories and their shame to die with them. Time for vengeance to seem ridiculous. Time for hatred to seem stupid. Time for the politics of honour and memory to be replaced by the politics of interest. Time, in other words, for what the dictator spent his life opposing: the banality of bourgeois politics.

In a culture which never had the time to experience the banality of bourgeois politics, nationalism became the vernacular in which democracy came to the ruins of Yugoslavia. Not real democracy, of course, but the manipulated plebiscitary democracy which ratifies one-man rule. In that kind of democracy, nationalism offers the immense appeal of a politics of permanent fever, of eternal exaltation. Instead of the banal politics of the real, instead of a political world which confronts the facts – the poverty, backwardness, stubborn second-rateness of ordinary Balkan existence – nationalism directs the mind to higher things. It offers the glorious politics of identity and self-affirmation. Instead of the interminable politics of interest and conciliation, there are enemies within and without to defeat; there is the immortal cause, the martyrs of the past and the present, to keep faith with. And it does not escape the attention of cynics and criminals that in this state of organized and permanent exaltation, there is no cynicism, no crime, no large or small brutality, which cannot be justified if the words 'nation', 'people', 'rights' and 'freedom' are suavely sprinkled over them.

And what about us?

Standing back from the disaster, one begins to see that Western failures to act in time were caused by something deeper than inattention, misinformation or misguided good intentions. The very principles behind our policies were in contradiction. In the light-headed euphoria of 1989, we announced our support for the right of national self-determination and for the territorial integrity of existing states, without realizing that the first principle contradicted the second. We insisted on the inviolability of frontiers, without being clear whether we also meant the frontiers within federal states like Yugoslavia.

Most of all, we allowed guilt over our imperial pasts to lead us to evade our responsibilities to define the terms of a post-imperial peace. Post-imperial societies felt guilty about condemning the nationalism of peoples who have been kept under imperial control. When the 'captive nations' – from the Baltic to the Balkans – demanded their freedom, we did not stop to consider the consequences. After Versailles, after Yalta, the collapse of the last empire in Europe offered us a third opportunity to define a durable peace and create a new order of nations in Europe. We could have ended the Cold War with a comprehensive territorial settlement, defining borders, guaranteeing minority-rights and adjudicating *between* rival claims to self-determination. So concerned were we to avoid playing the imperial policeman, so self-absorbed were we in the frantic late 1980s boom, that we allowed every local post-communist demagogue to exploit the rhetoric of self-determination and national rights to his own ends. The terrible new order of ethnically cleansed states in the former Yugoslavia is the monument to our follies, as much as it is to theirs.

AN OLD MAN'S WALLET

I am standing directly in front of the Moscow Hotel in downtown Belgrade in the middle of a listless, slowly disintegrating demonstration against the Milošević regime. A crowd of several hundred people has been there all morning and is slowly discovering that it is too small to make anything happen. In the middle of the crowd is an old man wearing a Chetnik hat. I go up and talk to him. He is in his 70s and he fought with Mihailović against Tito during the Second World War. Does he have sons, I ask him, and if so, have they seen fighting this time?

Calmly, he takes out his wallet and shows me three passport-size colour pictures: each of his sons, all young men in their 20s. Two are dead, killed on the front during the Croatian war. The third is in prison. Why? Because, the old man says with grim satisfaction, he took his vengeance. He found the killer of one of his brothers, and killed him. Then he takes out a small folded news clipping from a Croatian newspaper, and there is a passport-size photo of another young man's face. 'The bastard who killed my son. But we got him. We got him,' he says, neatly folding the picture of his son's assassin back into the wallet with the pictures of his sons.

From father to son, from son to son, there is no end to it, this form of love, this keeping faith between generations which is vengeance. In this village war where everyone knows each other, where an old man keeps the picture of his son's killer beside the picture of the son who avenged them both. There is no end, for when he dies, this old man knows, and it gives him grim satisfaction, there will be someone to do vengeance for him too.

GERMANY

EXPERIMENTS

A pair of twins is separated at birth. One is sent to a wealthy and permissive family; the other is raised in a poor, disciplinarian household. After forty-five years, the richer brother manages to trace his poorer sibling and invites him over to his suburban home. At first, they are delighted to be in each other's company and to rediscover, as it were, their lost half. Within an hour or so, however, they find each other's company irritating. The poor brother is aggravated by his rich brother's boisterous and aggressive laughter; the rich one is irritated by his brother's resigned and resentful silences. When the rich brother tells his version of why their parents abandoned them, the poorer brother, who had been told a different story, angrily denies it. Soon they are sitting in silence, both thinking it would have been better if they had never met. Beyond the accident of having the same neglectful parents, they seem to have nothing in common.

Then the wife of the rich man comes out on to the lawn of the splendid suburban house and offers her poor brother-in-law a drink. He observes that she has red hair like his own wife, and the same taste for pumps which display her brightly painted red toenails. Then he notices that, although his own garden is much smaller, there is a fountain, exactly like his, spilling water from the lips of a cupid into a shell-shaped basin. More confused than ever, he notices that his brother, lying back in a lawnchair drinking a beer, parts his thinning sandy-coloured hair in exactly the same way as he does, from the left ear over to the right. Finally, when the rich brother's son comes out to borrow the keys to the car, the poor brother discovers that he and his rich brother have chosen the same name for their sons.

Take a nation and divide it into two separate states. Ensure that these states embody opposing philosophies and forms of social organization. Attempt to guarantee that the inhabitants of the nation are told, repeatedly, that this experiment will be permanent. Place a wall between the two states and prevent, as far as possible, any communication between them. After forty-five years, remove the wall. Inform the population that the experiment is concluded and that henceforth they are a single nation once again. Will they still be one nation?

The question such an experiment is designed to answer – does the nation make the state, or does the state make the nation? – is like the question about the relative importance of environment and heredity in the making of individuals. It should be possible to ask people who have been subjected to the experiment – as one would ask twins separated at birth – whether they still recognize each other as brothers. They should be able to tell you. The experiment should be conclusive.

In November 1989, the German film-maker Wim Wenders was in the Australian desert, at a place called Turkey Creek, when word reached him that the Berlin Wall had come down. At first he did not believe the news. Then he felt anxiety. Would the tanks roll back in? Finally, he felt it was all unreal. He had to get some tangible proof that it was actually happening. Being a film director, he had to see some pictures.

The flying doctor in Turkey Creek happened to have a fax machine and Wenders asked a friend in Berlin to send him all the pictures he could cut out of the newspapers. Soon, the pictures began rolling off the fax machine, curling into the film director's hands. Being so far away in the Australian outback seemed to make these images more meaningful. They made him think of his father, who had died only a month before and who had thus been cheated of a moment which seemed to reconcile two German generations. The film director remembers that he shed tears, something he had not done for a very long time. 'Something wrong with the world was put together,' he remembers thinking. 'Something wrong inside myself was put together.'

All these faces of the people on top of the wall, tearing it down. They were so remarkable. They seemed more real than our faces; they seemed like faces from the films of the 1940s and 1950s. Why more real? I don't know exactly. Suffering makes people real. Maybe that is what it was. These people had been through more than we had, and that made them more real.

Volker Schlöndorff, German film-maker, 1989

I grew up being ashamed of Germany. But this was a time when I could feel something different. The simple fact is that there have not been many times in the last hundred years when Germans risked something for the sake of freedom and liberty.   Peter Schneider, German writer, 1989

In all the years of the Cold War, in all the years of cynicism and bitterness that have followed, there was only one night of unambiguous joy – when the Wall came down, and people streamed through, not daring to believe it, wondering whether they were dreaming and discovering that they were not. There was just that one night of pure happiness in the whole post-war history of Europe.

Nothing since has turned out as we hoped, and we have begun rewriting the history of our own emotions. We have all but forgotten that night, and if it still returns to our memories we ask ourselves why we could have ever treated ourselves to even one night of illusion. Why should we have had any hope at all? What fools we were.

THE PHOTO ALBUM

The German revolution of 1989 was centred in Leipzig, a city of 2 million people in Saxony, in the south-eastern corner of the DDR, the German Democratic Republic. That was where the biggest demonstrations against the old regime were held. They were silent, orderly affairs, begun at night, after everyone had finished work. Hundreds of thousands of people assembled and took up the whole of the avenues, making their way towards the Karl Marx Platz and the opera house. At first, in late September 1989, the placards only demanded 'Press Freedom' and 'Visa Freedom'. There were also timid banners which read 'Gorbi help us!'

In late September, the regime met the demonstrations with water cannons, massed police lines, shields, truncheons and dogs. Marchers were frogmarched away, their arms twisted behind their backs, and were tossed into the backs of the Volks Polizei wagons. But the demonstrations continued and the slogans began to move beyond the cautious demands formulated by the Lutheran opposition in the crypt of the Nikolaikirche. By mid-October 1989, the banners were reading 'We want reform!' 'We are the People!'

Since the regime had lasted by convincing individuals that they were alone, these demonstrations were an exercise in collective self-discovery. Night after night, the crowds would gather, and people would look around and discover how many people there were like them, stretching from one side of the street to the other, and as far back and as far ahead as one could see. And at last there were leaders prepared to risk something: the director of the Leipzig Opera, some Lutheran pastors and a comedian at the local cabaret. Other cities followed Leipzig's example and their citizens came out into the streets. The old regime wheedled, cajoled, barked and hectored, but nothing seemed to work any more. Obedience and resignation were mysteriously ebbing away. After the regime appealed for order on the television, more placards would appear in the crowd, saying 'No more speeches!' 'No more bla bla bla!' 'No more cosmetics!' 'It's time for surgery!'

It rained in October, but the people kept parading under umbrellas. They held vigils for reform and placed candles by the thousands at the walls of churches so that their wax ran together, fusing into translucent pools on the pavement. Meanwhile, photographers noticed that the expression on policemen's faces had changed. They posed for pictures in front of their squad cars and kept their batons in their belts, and as every day passed it became less and less clear who was in charge. At schools around Leipzig, teachers would tell students not to go to the demonstrations, and when students went anyway they would discover their own teachers marching beside them. Next morning, they would wink at each other in class.

By late October, the placards in Karl Marx Platz were reading 'The DDR belongs to the people, not the party.' And then, when the Wall came down on 9 November, the demonstrators discovered to their immense surprise that they had brought about a revolution without the loss of a single life. It was a revolution whose symbol, appropriately enough, was that eerie flag you saw in the crowds in Bulgaria and Romania too, with the hammer and sickle cut out of it, as one cuts holes for eyes in a bedsheet to make a ghost costume for children.

A state that has a flag with a hole in it is a state that no longer knows what it is. Some who waved that flag hoped that it would remain true to the colour red; others simply did not know what else to wave. But there were a few who began waving the flag of the other Germany, the one across the Wall.

A month after the Wall came down, there appeared in the Karl Marx Platz a new slogan, first on one hand-scribbled banner, then on a dozen, then on a thousand: 'Deutschland, einig Vaterland.' Germany, one fatherland. In the space of six weeks, the cry of 'We are the people!' had turned into the chant 'We are one people!'

Germany, one fatherland. The slogan now seems genuinely mysterious. One fatherland. What could this mean, after all? Is it a statement of fact? An expression of a wish? Or a puzzled question?

In a shop in the arcade beneath the old Rathaus in Leipzig, you can buy a photo album which records nearly every day of that period from September to December 1989. The most remarkable faces in the book are the ones that stare out of the crowds at the camera. In every single case, their faces are tight with fear. The fear has broken their smiles in half; it has stopped words halfway out of their mouths; it has snapped their gestures of defiance in two.

The fear is more than fear of arrest; more than the suspicion that the photographers are working for the police. It is historical fear, of the kind one might have seen on the barricades of Europe in 1848, the anxiety of a people who have taken a step into the unknown and do not know what will happen next. If all revolutions begin with that mysterious step into the unknown, the fear you see on these faces makes one wonder how they ever dared to take that first step. Yet, as you turn the pages of the album, as the demonstrations move into their second, third, fourth week, you can see this fear slowly begin to disappear. Faces unclench, gestures acquire defiance, laughter becomes full-throated. By November, the crowd no longer wonders what it has got itself into. Now it believes that history is marching alongside it. In their thousands, the people of Leipzig pour up the streets into Karl Marx Platz, laughing and waving at the cameras.

KARL MARX PLATZ

A tram drops me at Karl Marx Platz. A roadsweeper scratches in the gutters. Rain lashes the rearing copper horses in the empty fountain. All around me, empty, rainswept pavement. In the old newsreels of this square there were more fountains, with gas-lights and a massive opera house with a Corinthian portico beneath which the horse-drawn carriages would draw up. In the newsreels, men in trilbies with newspapers under their arms saunter up and down at the very tramstop where I am standing; a small girl sells violets; there is an organ grinder, a bearded beggar holds out his hand to passers-by and a man behind a barrow holds out a cone of newspaper filled with sunflower seeds. You can almost hear the rustle of the women's long dresses on the pavement. It is April 1913.

In the Leipzig bookshops, they sell a book of portraits of Leipzigers in year zero, 1945. The Allies had bombed the city, and acres of rubble stretched out on every side of Karl Marx Platz. From the photographs, they stare out at you, the 'rubble women' from the work details who cleared the square of debris and stacked the bricks in neat, hatched rows. Their aprons are torn; their hair is thick with dust; they wear overalls and work boots. There are roll-ups behind their ears and their raw hands hold bricks and hammers. They stare out at the future, as if they can see it more clearly than we can. Perhaps that was the moment – at the very beginning, in year zero – when the workers' state did seem like a wonderful dream.

It seems astonishing now that that there should ever have been a dream here and that anyone should ever have believed in it. The workers' state sent the tanks against the workers of Berlin as early as 1953. Even then it was obvious what this state really was. But there were rubble women and returning soldiers who wanted to keep faith with something, even when their leaders did not, and they did so until the end because it was too painful or too ridiculous to entertain the suspicion that your whole life could have been in vain.

The unbelievers and the disillusioned left for the West, and their departure left behind only a silence without an echo. Most of those who stayed did so without illusion, consoling themselves with the thought that, if it was bad in the DDR, it was worse in Poland, worse in Hungary, infinitely worse in Russia. The regime's legitimacy depended upon the reassurance offered by negative comparison.

In the 1960s, the DDR regime rebuilt the square in the concrete brutalism which so suited their political style. It dynamited a 300-year-old Baroque church in one corner of the square and built a thirty-storey steel skyscraper on the ruins.

Karl Marx Platz still survives as the public desert at the heart of a vanished regime. It is a monument to the DDR's terror of public space and human spontaneity – the sausage-sellers, pamphlet hawkers, artists, whores, teenage rebels – who might have spilled over it if given half a chance. But people do resign themselves to life in the desert. They are efficient with unfulfilled wishes: they simply strangle them. There were good concerts in the modern concert hall at one end of the Platz, and decent productions in the opera house, and you could tell yourself that you lived in a state which, whatever the coldness at its heart, did encourage a certain moral and aesthetic seriousness.

The glacier action of time was slowly creating two nations out of two states. Of course there was the Wall, and there were the images of West Germany that reached you on the television screen. But by the late 1980s, if you had not already left, you had pushed the memory of your twin brother and sister from your mind.

A vast structure of necessity – the imperial division of Europe – made this forgetting quite easy. In time the division of Germany came to seem eternal. Indeed, two generations grew up on either side of the Wall who actually feared what their nation might become if it were ever allowed to unite. The dream of a united Germany was not merely renounced; it was officially anathematized by the Ostpolitik pursued by both sides.

So when that great structure of imperial necessity began to tremble and shake above their heads, and the people of Leipzig took to the streets, they never imagined, for a second, that they would end up bringing down a state and bringing about the reunification of a nation. They never suspected that if they leaned, all together, against the locked door, it might suddenly swing open and tumble them into a strange new world.

After 1989, Karl Marx Platz was restored to its pre-1914 name of Augustus

Platz. The cold blue neon circle of Mercedes-Benz now floats above the insurance building opposite. There are even plans to dynamite the skyscraper and rebuild the vanished Baroque church stone by stone, from old photographs and ground plans. But some malignant shadow continues to set these plans at naught. Everywhere else old Leipzig is being tossed into a builder's skip, while Karl Marx Platz remains stubbornly unchanged. It is as if historical memory falters before the task of reclaiming such a desert. Karl Marx, a huge shaggy buffalo's head in soot-blackened bronze, continues to stare down at the square from the middle of a bas-relief of ardent workers over the entrance to the university building. Somehow he remains the presiding genius of this windswept place. He ceded his authority when the marchers filled it with their chants and banners, cries and hopes. Now it is a desert again. It is as if his ghost has reclaimed it.

CABARET

'It was great. It was a revolution. For one month, the revolution was in the hands of the Leipzigers. Then it was over. And now the people who made it don't have any power. But they are still there – the shop assistant, the librarian, the professor. They still want what I believe in.' Herr Böhnke pauses, looks embarrassed, rubs his thick hand over his forehead and down over his drooping moustache. 'It's a bit pathetic now, talking about what you believe. But I mean a Germany for the people.'

I'd found Gunther Böhnke drinking a beer at a round table at the back of the bar in a basement cabaret, down a narrow cobble-stoned street leading off the Karl Marx Platz. Herr Böhnke is the star of Academixer cabaret, and he talks to me in the methodical and precise English of the Cold War zones of Eastern Europe, the English untouched by vernacular contact, the language mastered entirely from a tape. By day, he translated children's books in a publishing house. By night, he was a cabaret artist. In the old days, cabaret artists were the licensed fools of an authoritarian state. Cabaret was where the whispered and unsaid could be spoken, fifteen metres underground, on a tiny stage in front of a faded grey velour curtain. In the old days, the theatre was sold out for ten years in advance. A cabaret artist used his own allocation of tickets as money: so many seats for so many sausages from his butcher. Nowadays, the tickets are too expensive for the locals; the seats are filled with parties of West Germans who come to laugh, uneasily, at jokes about themselves. Herr Böhnke personifies the Ossi – the East German – and satirizes the type. He is small and bald, wears an ill-fitting tweed jacket and a outsized East-bloc tie. His stomach sticks out through his shirt buttons and his melancholy face is a mixture of resignation and cunning.

His routine on stage is about the poor dumb East German who goes for a job interview with a West German personnel director. The Ossi blurts out that he never joined the party, thinking this is what is wanted, only to hear the Wessi reply, 'What was the matter with you? Where was your motivation?' All his jokes are like that, bitter reflections on a divide which ought not to be there: one people, one language, one nation, yet, after forty-five years in different states, barely able to recognize each other.

'They are nice people,' the new West German owner of Leipzig's oldest restaurant had told me over dinner before the cabaret. 'Nice people. Only they don't know how to work. I swear to you. I have had to start all over again. Teaching them to show up on time, ring up customers' bills properly, keep their hands out of the soup, I'm not in the restaurant business. I'm a social worker.' He had talked about his fellow Germans with the same affectionate condescension British colonial administrators used to adopt when discussing Tanganyikans.

Unification has not been the disquieting reunion of two lost twins on a suburban lawn, but a colonial occupation. The sound you hear when you wake up in Leipzig is the guts of old buildings – lathe, plaster, nails, window frames, boards – being tossed down those long, echoing plastic chutes into builders' skips. The façades are retained – there must be something to pin the Benetton sign on – but the guts of the city are being removed.

It is only to be expected, Herr Böhnke thinks, that when a social system collapses, those who were mostly its victims should be blamed for its failure. It is just the way of the world that a people who actually brought the regime down should now be dismissed as whining scroungers by the same West Germans who once sat in front of their television sets and applauded their civic courage.

As the German writer Peter Schneider used to say, the Wall was a mirror. Mirror, Mirror, on the wall, the West Germans asked, who is the fairest one of all? And the Mirror unfailingly replied: You are. For forty-five years, the division of a nation into two states offered both sides the necessary negative image of each other. Why should this end just because the Wall has come down? Why should this end just because everyone now lives in the same nation?

But something has changed in this game of mirrors. Before the revolution, the negative image in West Germany was the DDR, the state itself and its odious institutions. Now the negative image is the nation, the people themselves: their whining passivity. Now that the state has vanished, the people itself – the nation – are blamed for its ever having existed.

The blame, curiously enough, is often apportioned from the East German side. There is no shortage of former East Germans doing well in the West by loathing their former brothers and sisters. Thus the former DDR novelist Monika Maron: 'What I like least about my fellow ex-DDR citizens is their belief that the whole world owes them something, and that it particularly owes them their dignity. They seem to have forgotten that until three years ago they had not exactly looked after that dignity.' Hans Joachim Maatz, an East German psychiatrist, has written a book which tells the West German public that forty-five years of totalitarianism produced an East German personality structure characterized by 'repressed emotion, insecurity and latent aggression'. He goes on:

> The basic human right to be oneself, to have an opinion, to be understood and accepted as an individual were secured nowhere in that society ... Only those could live safely in this system who adjusted and sacrificed their spontaneous liveliness, their honesty, their ability to criticize, to the dull but relatively danger-free life of a subordinate.

Like all forms of psychological triteness, this must be true of someone. But then how did those insecure, neurotic, subordinated individuals – people like poor Herr Böhnke – find the nerve to bring down a whole regime? The negative image of the East German certainly flatters the narcissism of the West Germans, but it renders the history of unification incomprehensible.

Herr Böhnke is detached about the bitter comedy of his country's fate since 1989. 'After the Wall came down, our people went West and they came back with incredible stories. Over there, you could buy fresh lettuce and tomatoes in January. Can you imagine? And now that the supermarkets have arrived here, so can we. Only we can't afford them and our rents have gone up five times.'

He shrugs and smiles. 'When we walked around Leipzig in the rain in October, all we wanted was a little more democracy, a little more decency. Nobody wanted to be unificated.'

Unificated.

Nobody wanted cabaret to die, either, but now, says Herr Böhnke, you can see everything on German television. The satire there is sharper, the timing is faster. Who needs cabaret now? Herr Böhnke took his show on the road to the West and it did not do well. Too local, too Saxon, too provincial. He doesn't want the old days back, but as he looks about the dark, nicotine-stained walls of the bar where he has spent the best years of his life, at the posters of the old shows, at the chandelier above the table where the old Stasi microphone used to be hidden – 'Can you hear me, Boris? Am I speaking loud enough?' – it seems clear that the bell-jar of the dissident culture inside which his life once made sense, inside which, once upon a time, you could trade cabaret tickets for sausage from your butcher – all this is being 'unificated' too.

Academixer was where it used to happen in the 1980s. Now, in the 1990s, it happens at U-2, a discothèque in the basement of a grey office slab nearby. The music is from Munich; the beer is from Munich; the disc-jockey is from Munich; so are the pinball machines and the dry ice. It's a low-ceilinged place, and the sound ricochets off the walls and the rhythm comes up through the soles of your feet, and you find yourself slipping into a state of torpor. Girls dance alone on top of the amplifiers: toss, shake, thrust, toss, shake, thrust, their eyes closed, alone in the cavern of sound. Boys wander from pinball machine to pinball machine, from video game to video game, eyeing the girls. It's any discothèque, anywhere in the world, except that this low basement used to house the interrogation cellars of the secret police. Everyone knows this. It is no dark secret. The girls behind the bar will tell you about it and even point to some murals on the walls painted by former prisoners. Three years ago, it was an irresistible combination: the sadistic glamour of the Stasi meets the erotic glamour of the Munich discothèque. Getting into U-2 once gave entry into two forbidden worlds for the price of one. But the glamour of the forbidden is all gone: now it's just a disco, like any other. 'Alles ist cool,' the girl at the bar shouts in my ear, as the rhythm shakes the floor and the strobe lights turn her clear white face into a butterfly mask that dances up and floats away into the air.

In the DDR as a whole, there were half a million informers for the Stasi. The files that once were lodged in buildings like this contained billions of pieces of paper: whispered denunciations in cafés, hearsay in buses, cutting remarks from colleagues – a minutely indexed library of a whole society's malice and spite. But what could a person do? If they didn't contribute their quota of vicious gossip, they might find themselves down in the cells. The circle of incrimination became so wide that it is a wonder anyone was capable of recovering their civic courage. But some did. Those who didn't now keep making the same tired, self-exculpating gesture with their hands: 'It was my world. It was all I knew.'

What, exactly, is one to make of the fact that an interrogation centre has been turned into a discothèque? Should there be a memorial here, or a museum instead? The music is so loud that it wears down your middle-aged interiority and fills up every empty space inside:

> Feel the rhythm building
> It's the voice of passion
> Can't you feel it in the air?
> Free your mind and join us
> Oh oh passion, oh oh passion
> Can't you feel it everywhere?

'Coming to terms with the past' does not imply a serious working through of the past, the breaking of its spell through an act of clear consciousness. It suggests, rather, wishing to turn the page and, if possible, wiping it from memory.
T. Adorno, 'What Does Coming to Terms with the Past Mean?' (1959)

Ask yourself what the girl at the bar, mixing a daiquiri, or the boy with wet-look hair, wearing a Benetton 'Colours of the World' T-shirt, is supposed to make of the fact that people were beaten and interrogated here. Pull a solemn face? Is solemnity any more genuine a 'coming to terms with the past' than a fervent desire to forget about it altogether? I cannot ask such questions of the pair beside me at the bar, their faces a pair of dancing discs in the strobe light. How could they be expected to know what I was talking about? Honecker is already ancient history to them. This girl and boy were 13, maybe less, when his regime collapsed. 'It's not my problem,' I can hear them say. 'It's not *my* past.'

THE BATTLE OF NATIONS MEMORIAL

It resembles a vast Teutonic funeral pyre in soot-blackened granite, so that as the rough-cut stones rise into the air, they seem to be offering the body of some mighty warrior to the flames, except that on the flat bier at the very top of the monument there is nothing – no body to be committed to the sky – just a view from all sides of the city that has grown up around it. It is so large that it outranks any war memorial in Europe: a glowering pile of Wilhelmine stone, set off by itself, like the family's difficult relative, in a park on the outskirts of Leipzig. It is altogether an embarrassment, in its truculent bad taste, its stolid, vulgar monumentality. The rain streaks its heavy flanks and it seems to sneer: come on, try and dynamite me, you will fail. I am too large, I have been here too long. I will survive you all.

It was begun, soon after the unification of Germany in 1871, to commemorate the Battle of Nations in 1813, when a million soldiers, from Russia, Austria, Britain, France, Germany and Poland, fought for a day and decided the fate of Europe. Napoleon's defeat at day's end signalled the beginning of the end of his empire. It was the first time that Germans from the different princedoms had stood and fought together as Germans, and even though some Germans also fought on Napoleon's side, this battlefield can claim to be one of the places where the German nation was born. And it is this which was commemorated when the Kaiser, Wilhelm II, presided over the monument's final unveiling on the hundredth anniversary of the battle, in 1913.

One can imagine the flag-decked reviewing stand, the forest of imperial plumes, the glinting breastplates, the tight leggings flowing into high cavalry boots; the swords clinking against thighs, the hard imperial faces, the heels which click together in greeting, the helmeted heads which curtly nod to each other – all these marionettes conscious of being at the acme of a glory symbolized by the almighty pile that rose above their heads.

The sculptor who decorated the monument chose to flatter the Wilhelmine grandees by imagining them as Teutonic warriors. There is one such master image, in the frieze at the base of the monument, of St Michael as German knight, with a helmet which curves down to his cheekbones and eyes that stare into the predestined greatness of the German future. Around him writhe the symbols of the natural world: lions, tigers and dragons, all subdued to his will, and a long spotted snake which hisses and smiles. These creatures are charged with ambivalence: are they inner demons or the forces of evil? They seem to be both, because his gaze manages to be both haunted and resolute, both anguished and determined. To the left of St Michael, like leering monkeys, a pair of grinning death's heads mock his solemn gaze.

There is a famous poster from the 1930s of the Führer clad as a Teutonic warrior, in a shining breastplate, with a sword and helmet, astride a horse, raising high a blood-red banner. I had always supposed that Hitler and Goebbels had shown some inventiveness in their appropriation of the figures and images of German nationalism. I had always supposed, in fact, that this artistic inventiveness – to which Speer contributed his monuments and Riefenstahl her films – helps to explain the extraordinary enthusiasm the Nazis managed to generate in the population. Besides awe and fear, there was the shiver of being in the presence of the new.

But as artists of politics, they invented less than I had supposed. The entire erotic paraphernalia of Nazi appeal is already there in the Leipzig monument: the same helmets, the same snakes, the same Teutonic ardour, the same ludicrous cult of masculine hardness; the same erotically charged confusion about nature – is it to be life-giving force or carnal malignity? It is all there. Hitler was no artist of the political, simply an adept connoisseur of kitsch.

There is no nationalist art that is not kitsch, no patriotic creation that does not pantomime emotional sincerity. Why? Perhaps no art that is not personal can ever be genuinely sincere, and nationalist art, by definition, cannot be personal. Perhaps also a nationalist art cannot invent the new. It is chained to available tradition, or, failing that, chained to kitsch, in this case the dark Germanic forests of the Teutonic knights.

Hitler's appropriation of the Teutonic past merely exploited the fervent emotional insincerity of a nineteenth-century medieval pastiche. Both the original and the copy, therefore, imply a form of nationalism which, as Adorno puts it, cannot entirely believe in itself. The sheer massiveness of the monument is a confession of doubt, Hitler's imitation likewise. Both must intimidate in order to convince.

This bombastic imitation of the iconography of kitsch did not end with Hitler. The Hitler Youth, in neck scarves and lederhosen, used to hold torchlight parades to the monument, ending with a service of dedication to the Reich. In the photographs you can see the torches flickering in the reflection of the ornamental lake and the smoke rising in the fiery air. The DDR insisted that it had broken with the fascist and capitalist pasts alike. Yet the neck scarves and shorts of the Free German Youth told a different story, and the adolescent rite of passage, called Youth Consecration, in which massed voices shouted their allegiance to the new state, even copied the old sub-Wagnerian décor of torches, fiery smoke in the air, and eerie reflections in the ornamental pool.

'But what else do you expect?' Helmut Börner says, pushing his glasses back on to the bridge of his nose in a gesture that suggests that he is both cornered and angry. 'This was our world. This was all we knew.' Herr Börner is the curator of the museum next door to the monument. Does he think it odd that the DDR should have copied the scarves of the Hitler Youth? No, he says, I have got this wrong. 'In the case of the pioneers, in my time, I had a blue neckerchief. My father in his time had a black neckerchief.'

'But,' I say, 'they were still the same neckerchief.'

'Ah,' says Herr Börner, slipping away from me behind the glass cases which hold the French cuirassier's uniform, and the handful of grapeshot from the cannons, and the old muskets and a drum. 'It's a case of new wine in old bottles. The old bottles were perfectly good. My parents didn't chuck them away. They just changed the white wine for red.' He thinks about that for a moment. 'Yes, perhaps that's how it was.'

'But didn't the new wine get corrupted by the old bottles?'

He squints through his thick glasses, scratches his short red beard and retreats further behind another glass case in his museum. Then he asks me whether I have ever left my family and tried to start a new one. I say I haven't. 'Well, when you do, you don't tear down your old. You try to lead a new life, a different one, better in all ways from the old marriage which has failed.'

He points at a small water-colour in a frame inside one of the glass cases. It depicts a group of Leipzig women helping to load wounded soldiers on to a cart after the battle. 'It didn't matter at all whether they were French or Saxons or Prussians or Swedes or Austrians or Russians – they looked after them all,' he says quietly. 'Of course, you can't compare the kind of care they gave to what is available today. Thousands of them died, of typhoid, of nerve and wound fever, amputations were carried out, so terrible, we can't imagine it.'

Herr Börner would be much happier to spend the rest of his days in the year 1813. It would be much simpler, and I can sympathize with him. Who wants to explain how a party member copes with the collapse of his world?

'I am one month older than the republic,' he says, in his quiet, musing, indirect way. 'I was born in September 1949. So I grew up in this period, this country, in this society. It was my world.' The regime let him burrow into the safety of the distant past and insisted only that his exhibits emphasize the historic friendship of the Russian and German troops, forged at Leipzig. This was easy to do, because they had fought on the same side. There were some display cases of Soviet uniforms to bring this point home to the present, but they took up too much space, and he got permission in 1988 to do away with them. He sees no reason to pretend that he was not in the party. He still hopes that history will judge the

DDR kindly. It was more equal than the society which is taking shape around him. And it lived in peace. No troops from the DDR ever took part in combat. Not even in Czechoslovakia, in 1968? I ask. No, no, he insists, logistical support perhaps, but combat troops never.

He wishes history would judge the DDR dispassionately. But he knows that history judges no one. There will be no reckoning at all. What will happen has already begun – every single trace of the DDR regime is being shovelled into a skip, so that in ten years a new generation will scarcely believe it ever existed.

I find myself thinking that there ought to be a museum to the DDR, full of Trabis and Wartburg cars, hammers and sickles cut down from the pediments of buildings, photographs of the sporting heroes, Erich Honecker's trilby, some Stasi files; hidden microphones; re-created interrogation cells; a full-scale party hunting lodge. Herr Börner smiles. Museums are always archives of success, he says, shrines to victors. But there should be museums of error, I say, especially to errors that ruined lives. The trouble is, he says, who would want to visit one?

This effacement of the DDR, Herr Börner knows, is very German. Every fifty years, the nation's past is rewritten, and the lives that were lived under other conditions are suddenly stripped of all their sense. As it was with Herr Börner's father – a schoolteacher under the Nazis – so it will be with Herr Börner himself. It is only human, he says, for people to want to repress the past. 'It's the same perhaps as in private life – when something has gone wrong – where you have been very disappointed, you want to shut it off, draw a line under it and not be reminded of it.' Very human indeed, although one wonders whether nations should allow themselves the forgetting that individuals do.

Herr Börner is resigned to losing his job when the purification of party members like himself reaches the dusty corner office of the museum where he works. In the new conditions, he imagines he will live much as he has always done, by trusting only 'a few people in one's most intimate circles on whom one can depend – with whom one can be happy'. East Germans ceaselessly lament the privatization of life that has arrived with capitalism ('All anybody buys these days is locks for their front doors'). The truth is, it will only reinforce the existing privatization of life under socialism.

Herr Börner also knows that what will happen to him will be mild compared to what happened to his father. In 1945, thousands of Nazis were tried by Soviet military court martial and shot. His own father did four years in a Soviet camp and considered himself lucky to have escaped alive. Since the revolution of 1989, the purification of the past has not cost a single life. That is something, Herr Börner says. We Germans do not always have to repeat our mistakes.

What puzzles him most is why he allowed himself to believe that the risks of thinking for himself were so much greater than they actually were. That is what he most regrets. 'I certainly could have been braver, because we certainly were afraid, had fears, which it turns out today were unfounded. We had imposed a form of self-censorship on ourselves, that needn't have been so.' When he says this, the reflection of his face in the glass cabinets of uniforms, muskets, ambulance wagons, drums and little water-colours, suddenly looks mournful and perplexed, as if he had stumbled, too late, on the secret of the regime that held him so easily in its grip.

He shows me out of the museum, and we stand with the shadow of the Battle of Nations monument slanting over both of us. I ask him whether it doesn't symbolize a certain idea of Germany. He laughs. 'We didn't speak of Germany in the DDR.' Germany was the forbidden subject. Identification was with the state, with socialism, with fraternity towards the great Soviet motherland, but not with Deutschland, not with the Volk, not with the ancestral memories – those reactionary capitalist fabrications – symbolized by the brooding Teutonic St Michael.

Then Herr Börner smiles and makes a little joke. 'I'm glad,' he says, 'that the DDR never built its own Battle of Nations memorial, never tried to build its idea of Germany in stone.'

'Why not?'

'Can you imagine what it would have been like?' he says, suddenly venturing out into the bright light of a free thought. 'It would have been a concrete bunker.' He laughs again. 'Yes, a concrete bunker. That's all the DDR would have left behind.'

LIVING UNDER
DEMOCRACY

In the old days, the relative well-being of the East Germans under socialism provided West Germans with an opportunity for German narcissism. The fact that East Germany was the most successful socialist economy seemed to prove that the German virtues could even prevail over Bolshevik nonsense like the planned economy. Nation, in other words, was stronger than state.

Down came the Wall, in came the West German industrialists. They toured the East German factories; looked carefully at the machines, made inventories of plants, buildings, raw materials; logged worker productivity per hour and so on. They returned to head office in Stuttgart, Frankfurt and Munich with worried faces. The East was a disaster zone.

There seemed only one thing to do: blow it all up and start over again. And that included the workers. They would have to relearn all the German virtues: good time-keeping, cleanliness, application, hard work. Moral of the story? States make nations; socialism deforms national character; regimes can ruin a people, even the Germans.

Karla Schindler wears her brown hair cut in a short, mannish bob, which shows off her stylish hoop earrings. She is in her early 50s, and she remembers the day she joined the Leipzig Cotton Spinning Factory: 1 September 1953. Just like her mother before her and her daughter after her. What she has to show for forty years' work is a pair of certificates, from a grateful socialist management, decorated with that symbol of the DDR, the hammer, the sickle and, coldest of all, the scientific protractor. She also has a stubborn and persistent cough, brought on by forty years of working on the cotton machines, breathing in a haze of cotton filaments so dense that sometimes she couldn't see the worker next to her.

She ought to hate this vast, ramshackle, nineteenth-century warren of barracks and sheds, yet she bustles around it, chatting to the man on the forklift, kidding about with the nightwatchman, sharing a confidence with one of the machine-room girls. 'Why should I hate this? It was my life. It still is.' Frau Schindler is the factory representative on the Treuhand – the organization which is privatizing or shutting down the East German industrial sector. The West Germans want to close the factory down. Frau Schindler is fighting to save it. 'There was a Jewish gentleman from the family who used to own it in the old days. He is interested in it,' she says hopefully, as she shows me into the first machine room. It's an old industrial inferno, and everything in it – the walls, the turquoise-blue machines, the cages full of bales of cotton – is encrusted with white cotton filaments. The air is a dark brown suspension of cotton filaments and dust lit by thin bars of light from the smeared windows. One old man is feeding raw cotton into a separator, which pulls it apart into skeins. Frau Schindler digs her hands disparagingly into a bale. 'From Uzbekistan. Soviet. Hopeless.' That was how it was here: cheap, poor-quality cotton from the Asian provinces of the Soviet empire was sent to be transformed, by industrious Germans, into cheap spun cotton for the poor housewives of Cracow, or Budapest, or Leipzig. It can't go on, and Frau Schindler knows it. Without decent raw materials and new machines, this old man will be out of a job in months.

Leipziger Spinnerei is a monument to a certain utopia of labour, a certain belonging and comradeship, which, whatever else was false about socialism, was true enough for someone like Frau Schindler. Not that she ever believed all of it. There was a brigade system, and brigades were supposed to compete with each other to fulfil the production norms. At one door to the spinning rooms, we come across an old sign which reads: 'The Friendship between Peoples Brigade.' Meaning, of course, the eternal socialist friendship between the Russian and German peoples. 'What about this?' I ask her, and she raises an eyebrow, as if to say, are you kidding?

In the spinning rooms, two or three perspiring girls in light, see-through frocks, which reveal their white underwear beneath, slap to and fro in thongs, tossing full bobbins into waist-high red bins, putting fresh bobbins on, retying the thread. Frau Schindler leans in close to hear their complaints about a new type of linen thread which is giving them trouble. She doesn't need to tell them their jobs hang by threads as thin as the ones they cut with their teeth. Room after room, floor after floor of the old mill are now shut, the machines covered with plastic, dust gathering on the floor.

Upstairs, in the union office, with its straggly potted plant and its faded poster depicting the tourist delights of Bulgarian beaches, she tells me the Treuhand puts her between the devil and the deep blue sea. They tell her they are going to try to save the factory. In return she has to fire most of the people.

Still, she insists, things are better now. She can earn Deutschmarks, she can travel to West Germany. 'It's amazing,' she says wistfully, as if talking about some island in Tahiti, 'how clean the air is over there.'

I tell her I've been hearing this curious phrase from people I talk to. We used to live under fascism, they say, then we lived under communism, and now, they say, we live 'under' democracy. Isn't that an odd way to talk about democracy, as if it were just another regime you had to submit to?

She smiles and shrugs. 'In the old days, the director used to preach socialism in a big way. It was brigades this, and brigades that. And now it's the Free Market Economy. He's gone the whole 180 degrees.' But she isn't surprised or indignant about this. 'We used to call it swimming along with the tide.'

'And now,' I say, 'you're learning to swim on your own.'

'Yes, now I'm learning to swim on my own.' Then she blushes. 'I talk in public now. Yes, I do.' She was at a conference about the future of her industry. 'I heard our Prime Minister here in Saxony going on and on about the textile industry this and the textile industry that, and I thought to myself, I ought to make him see what things really are like in the works.' So in the break after his speech, she had a couple of brandies, and then, when the conference reconvened, she stood up and spoke her mind. 'That was the first time I had ever been brave enough to speak.' She looks over at me, smiles bashfully and shrugs again, surprised at what has happened to her. 'Now I'll speak anywhere, even in the Market Square.' Frau Schindler, at least, is not living 'under' democracy, but 'in' it for the first time.

BEING A GOOD GERMAN

In the old days it was called the Dimitrov school, and there was a statue to the Bulgarian communist who was tried for the Reichstag fire in 1934. There was even one of those socialist realist statues of Dimitrov in the school yard, but it has been toppled and nothing has been put in its place. Since the revolution, it has been renamed Reklamschule, after Reklam, a free-thinking publishing house suppressed both by the Nazis and by the DDR.

I am in the students' room in the basement, new since the revolution, one wall of which is daubed, in English, 'Hey, teacher! Leave those kids alone!' Martin

Moschek is 17, and he is telling me what the lessons used to be like in the old days.

'For example, in maths we had to work out things like: Cuba is attacked by the imperialists and five men are stationed at an anti-aircraft rocket station. We had to figure out the parabola of the missile's trajectory if it was going to hit the imperialists. That kind of thing.' He shakes his mop of curly hair at the thought of it. 'At the time, we didn't notice anything strange.'

Martin's father was a Lutheran pastor, and so Martin grew up halfway inside the ideological bell-jar of the regime, halfway out. Looking back, he cannot tell how many of his fellow students believed what they were told, or just went into silent internal emigration. It does seem unbelievable to him, looking back, that students were so obedient. He smiles cheerfully, and says in his quiet, formal, slightly pedantic way, 'It is recognized a bit more that school can't be school without the pupils.' Hence the wit and wisdom of a British rock-and-roll band daubed on the wall behind him.

Martin has a smooth, angelic face framed by curls, as in a drawing by Dürer, with the deep inwardness of German Lutherans in his soft, thoughtful way of speaking. I ask him what nationalism meant in the old days.

'I was proud to be a citizen of the DDR and I was proud of my fatherland and we always associated fatherland with the DDR – there was no "Germany".'

Herr Börner had said much the same. 'Germany' was a discredited phantom for anyone who grew up in the DDR, a figure of speech used only – or so the DDR television said – in revanchist rants in Bavarian beer halls. In any event, the old Germany of 1939 – the one which stretched far into present-day Poland and had swallowed up Czechoslovakia – had been smashed by the heroic Soviet army. It was gone for ever, buried beneath the joint Allied–Soviet occupation. A socialist state would create a German whose attachment was to socialism itself, to the institutions of the workers' movement, to its symbols, that sharp and cold scientist's projector.

It did not escape the elite, however, that loyalty to the state could be enriched if certain national symbols were revived and refurbished. In the 1970s its propaganda ministry organized a carefully circumscribed appropriation of traditional German heroes. The Luther who had defied the German princes was allowed into the pantheon, while the Luther who had screamed for the German princes to put down the peasants' revolt of 1525 was carefully airbrushed out of the picture. The military martinet Frederick the Great received official veneration from a regime now more interested in being martinets than in being socialists. As with Milošević of Serbia, Ceauçescu in Romania or Husák of Czechoslovakia, Honecker in Germany turned to nationalism to mask the senility of his regime.

Too late, too late. In November 1989, the people decided that they, not the state, were the true nation.

So what is a 17-year-old East German to make now of the concept of the

German nation? Martin thinks for a long time and then says softly, 'If you say you're a nationalist now, then it's clear – at least for me – that you're saying you're proud of your country – which in itself is not a bad thing. The problem is that it doesn't stop there. It goes on so far that some people around here say the reunification is not complete – the Polish territories in the east and the Sudeten-land are still waiting. That sounds an alarm bell inside me.'

He thinks some more, and then says, 'It all comes down to violence. If someone says he is proud of Germany and persuades me without violence, that's fine. Unfortunately, that is rare nowadays in Germany.'

Martin and I are crossing a narrow footbridge over a canal at dusk on the outskirts of Leipzig. I suddenly notice dark men passing us on the bridge, North Africans, Pakistanis, Somalis, in pairs, with plastic shopping bags in their hands, their jacket collars pulled up against the cold. They are the first non-white faces I have seen in Leipzig. Like most of Eastern Europe, East Germany is overwhelmingly white. Of all the surprises of reunification, from the East German point of view, the most considerable is racial. Cities like Frankfurt are 30 per cent foreign-born. In every crowd, there is a sea of faces such as these. In Leipzig, they are novel, strange, alien. They are on this bridge, because it is the way home, and home is an asylum hostel, a cluster of portakabins, set down behind a thin wire fence in a gravel yard adjacent to the Berlin–Leipzig motorway.

We get talking in French to some young Algerians. They have bounced around Europe, looking for work, and they've applied for asylum here, and are waiting to have their applications processed. But it's a miserable wait. The portakabins, they say, are cold and draughty; and at night they lie on their bunks, smoking cigarettes and waiting for the Nazis to attack.

Martin nods agreement. They are not exaggerating. He was there, with a friend from school, two weeks before, when the skins first appeared on the bridge and marched on the hostel. They had knives and baseball bats, and the police sitting in a Volkswagen bus on the other side of the bridge did nothing to stop them. So Martin and his friend tried to prevent the skins from crossing the bridge. They did their best, these two decent teenage boys, who hadn't thought to carry any arms, who hadn't the first idea how to fight, and who thought that, just by standing bravely, they could turn a pack of skinheads around.

Martin smiles ruefully, like someone rubbing an old bruise. 'We were kicked and beaten up and they tried to chuck us in the canal,' but the police finally jumped out of their cars and chased the skins away. Martin leans on the railing of the bridge and looks across at the portakabins. I ask him why he thought he should get involved. The skins mean business, they are armed, it's no place for a teenager. He thinks about this, and says that he knows – because his father told him – about the Weimar days of the 1920s when a cycle of violence between left and right escalated until it got completely out of hand. Then he says, staring at the dark figures sitting in the open doorways of the portakabins, smoking cigarettes, 'Look, I just wanted to show that there are still some people who stand up for them around here.' He thinks some more, and then he says, 'I wanted the skins to know that if they came for these people again, they would have to get past a German.'

LEO AND THE LEECH

Leo has a fresh scar, running across his forehead and down his right cheek, from a fight at a taxi stand a few nights before, and some other scars, at his hairline and on his arms, from his years in East German children's homes and prisons. He has the word 'Skinhead' in English tattooed along one forearm, and on the other arm a tattoo of an Iron Cross and a map of the Germany of 1937, which stretched halfway across Poland. His sweatshirt reads 'FAP': Frei Arbeiter Partei. 'They're the only party that sticks up for workers,' he says. 'All the rest of the parties are shit.'

Leo isn't unemployed, and he would be contemptuous if I were to say that neo-Nazism is created by unemployment in East Germany. For Leo, neo-Nazism is a creed and a way of life, perfectly compatible with a steady job. After all, the best thing about Germans, he says, is that they know how to work. He is such a good German he has let his hair grow to a respectable brush cut in order to keep his job as an assembler of flat-pack furniture kits for a small West German firm. Today is his day off, and he and his mate, a jug-eared 16-year-old secondary school student named Leech, are drinking 'diesels', pints of beer mixed with cherry liqueur, in Leo's flat in a working-class block in north Leipzig.

What is happening here – a foreign writer talking to neo-Nazis – is a well-worn ritual. I provide them with the oxygen of publicity. They provide me with vivid and unpleasant copy. I ask them the standard questions and they provide the standard snarls in reply. Auschwitz? Never happened. Just a lie to blacken Germany's name. 'All that crap about gassing people. It never happened.' They told us about it in school, but you were a mug if you believed anything teachers told you. Is there nothing about Germany that makes you feel ashamed? Nothing. Nations start wars, nations lose them. So what? Ritual completed, I am supposed to say that people like him represent the cancer eating away at the heart of a fragile German democracy.

This is true enough. But there is more to say. For a start, take Leech's braces. They are decorated with Union Jacks. It is something of an embarrassment to good Germans like Leo and Leech to admit how much they owe to the Brits. But that is how it is. Neo-Nazism may be waning in Britain, but skin culture – the racism, the haircut, the music – is sweeping from the Polish–German border of the old DDR right through to Frankfurt. Skin culture may just be Britain's most enduring contribution to Germany and the new Europe.

Listening to Leo, I try to figure out why he is the only German I've met in Leipzig who is fiercely proud of his country. That is what makes him alarming to me, not his scars, not his macho talk, not the cosh he keeps by the door. If you see the world from his point of view, he comes from the only country in Europe that isn't allowed to feel good about itself. In the DDR they taught him nationalism equals fascism. In West Germany they said the nation must atone for its sins and they set about building a post-nationalist identity based on the Deutschmark. Leo may just be what a country gets when it loses peaceful ways of being proud about itself, when the language of national pride is forced underground, when patriotism is hijacked by criminals.

Leo also represents the return of the repressed. In West Germany most people are reconciled to the borders imposed on them by defeat in 1945. Not so in East Germany. Leo's mother was born in Upper Silesia, in a German province of what is now Poland. Leo's father had a farm, 'an estate' so he says, in Upper Silesia. Leo grew up hearing the story of how the family were dive-bombed by the Russians and flung themselves into ditches to survive, as the Russians drove them into Leipzig in the spring of 1945. When I ask Leo whether he wants to go back to Upper Silesia to visit, he says, 'Not as a tourist, never. Only with a German flag.'

But didn't Kohl sign a treaty accepting the border with Poland? Leo takes a contemptuous pull on his Marlboro. No politician can swindle the Germans out of their land, he says.

Had he not grown up being lied to by a workers' state, Leo might have been a good socialist. He is fiercely proud of being a worker, and what he hated most about the old days was the way the party bosses made the language of class solidarity into a sick justification of their privilege. Being a skin in Honecker's regime was not just a badge of nationalist defiance. It was also a way of fighting, he says fiercely, for real German workers.

Leo did two years – 'my wasted years' – in one of Honecker's prisons for trying to escape to the West. After reunification, Leo claimed compensation as a political prisoner. Giving 10,000 marks in compensation to a skinhead who'd cheerfully set the constitution alight is another irony of Germany's well-meaning democracy. But gestures like that have no chance of winning Leo over. For democracy is not a value to him, just another regime, like Honecker's, like Hitler's before him. He lived 'under' socialism, and he will live 'under' democracy, and he respects neither.

Under socialism, at least there was comradeship. 'Under communism, well, perhaps there were thirty or forty skins here in Leipzig, and we all stuck together, and if one of us didn't have any money, like, then that wasn't important, the others helped out so's we could all drink, and now, well, we're all counting every penny. It's terrible.'

It isn't a justification of Leo to say he is in revolt against the mental residue of passivity and lies left behind in people's heads by a corrupted workers' state, or that the new unification has left him more homeless than ever. Explaining Leo isn't justifying him. It is just that he looks out of his window at the crumbling flats, at the rusting Trabis, at his wasted, ruined homeland, and he wants to smash someone's face in. 'Home,' he says, bitterly. 'This isn't home, this is just misery.'

If he were in Los Angeles or Liverpool, he would be just another teenage gang leader. The nightmare of the new Germany is that its teenage gangs talk politics. It may be reassuring that they have invented so little, that their rhetoric and political imagination are so derivative. Hitler was dangerous because he appeared to be new. These teenagers, wearing 'Hitler: The European Tour' T-shirts, lack their own Goebbels, their own Riefenstahl or Speer. No middle-class post-modern smoothies in pigtails and double-breasted suits have attached them-selves to these gangs to work on the marketing or the image. Without marketing, without the glamour of which middle-class nihilists are the masters, Leo can be contained. Poor Leo, he is so much of a worker that he despises me and middle-class smoothies of all kinds. If he were more ingratiating, he might know how to use me. If he were more cynical, he might be truly dangerous.

As it is, he is dangerous enough. Leo knows that when he and Leech torch an asylum hostel they have more leverage over German politics than a hundred speeches in Parliament. His contempt for these speeches – appealing for toler-ance, condemning violence, preaching reconciliation – is entirely understand-able. He knows weakness when he sees it.

What is German democracy doing about Leo? Besides official rallies against racism, and courses on multiculturalism in the schools, throughout the former East Germany, the government is spending money on a public-relations cam-paign. The central image is a poster, showing a sea of red, gold and black German flags, with the caption: 'This is the colour of tolerance and respect for human dignity.' This remains the burden of being German: you still have to remind people that being proud of yourself doesn't require you to hate others. The poster fights for visibility among the ads for cars and beer. For all its surface gloss and sophistication, the poster amounts to a cry for help. And what does Leo think? He smiles contemptuously and shakes his head. He knows the poster is saying: right now, Leo is winning.

INTERLUDE ON THE HISTORY OF GERMAN NATIONALISM

Ethnic nationalism was the invention of the German Romantic intelligentsia during the period of the Napoleonic invasion of the German princedoms, between 1792 and 1813. The German intellectuals rose up against the French Enlightenment's vision of political society as a society of contractual equals, and they exalted Germanness as the universal culture of feeling against the cold and mechanical individualism of the French. In so doing, figures like Novalis, Schiller, Fichte and Müller self-consciously constituted themselves as the true voice of the nation. Yet their nationalist creed, intended to defend the established order against the French, then unleashed aspirations for unification and change which dissolved the status hierarchy and the German princedoms.

For the Romantics, the new principle of social authority was to be the Volk, a highly romanticized and abstract image of the German people. The Volk was the decisive ethnic twist given to the French idea of *la nation*. This Volk – simple, clean, pure, ardently communitarian – was the happy projection of an unhappy intelligentsia, seeking the emotional belonging denied them in real life.

In France, Britain and America nationalism served as a modernizing ideology. Among the Romantics, it became an anti-modernist creed, expressing their envy and resentment at the emergence of a secular democracy in France. Romantic nationalism became a flight from individualism and from individual rights, towards a vision of society in which the individual achieved inner freedom through an intense experience of belonging to the Volk.

It is a convention of German historiography to trace the malignant German nationalism of Hitler to the apparently innocent emotionalism of the German Romantics, yet how, exactly, does one derive Hitler from Herder? At least from the Herder who famously remarked, 'So at bottom all comparison is out of place. Every nation has its centre of happiness within itself'? Hitler's expansionary and aggressive nationalism was a universalizing creed. Germany was to be the standard of comparison for all. This is exactly what Herder's historicizing and relativizing idea of national consciousness denied.

Nor should the genocidal results under Hitler lead us to rewrite the history of Volkisch nationalism backwards, as an obsessional attempt to define the Volk in excluding the Jew. In fact, anti-Semitism did not become central to German nationalism until after 1871, and when it did so, the influence of Anglo-Saxon anti-Semitism (Austen Chamberlain), French eugenics and American neo-Darwinism was just as important as native German currents of opinion.

Moreover, the Jews are only one of the groups which German nationalism seized upon as its defining Other. After the French Revolution, it was the French. After 1871, it was the Slavs.

The Germans had always been preoccupied by their eastern border with the Slavic nations. The huge eastward migration of Germans to the Slavic border marches of the Holy Roman empire left Germans convinced of their own ethnic distinctiveness. The large German communities in the East retained their language, religion and culture, and while in practice much Slavic-German assimilation did take place, the decisive fact for national self-understanding was the assimilation that did not occur. The Slavic borderlands to the east led the German heartland to define itself as an ethnically distinct frontier state, in a way that has no parallel in France.

As the Slavs themselves learned ethnic nationalism from the Germans, the Germans in turn took fright at the projects of national unification – Poles, Czechs and Hungarians – on their eastern borders. Such fears of the east were containable only so long as the two German empires, Hohenzollern and Habsburg, kept the emerging Slavic nations in check. Once these empires disintegrated in 1918 and a new Slavic empire, led by Lenin and then by Stalin, emerged on the borders of a weakened Germany, the old German fear of Slavic barbarism revived. These fears were adroitly articulated by Hitler, a man who had grown up in the multi-ethnic melting pot of imperial Vienna, and who had come to loathe its dense multi-ethnicity as an affront to the natural superiority of the German people.

Even when one has drawn attention to the millennial German fear of the Slavs, and their deeply imbedded hatred of the Jews, it is a form of kitsch to claim, as some recent historians have done, that 'Germany was ready for the Holocaust from the moment German national identity existed'. This has no more content than the proposition that, from the moment modernity existed, with its railways and gas ovens, the Holocaust was ready to happen.

The real problem is how to explain why an ethnic definition of the German nation saw off all available competition. For competition there always was. The Frankfurt Parliament, convened after the 1848 revolution which swept away the German princelings, even went so far as to accord German citizenship, not merely to those who were ethnically German, but 'to all those living in Germany ... even if they are not so by birth or language'. It was to such traditions, even though they were swept away, that post-war Germany turned in trying to define an acceptable image of itself.

Besides an explicitly liberal and civic tradition, there was also what might be called 'state nationalism'. This form of nationalism provided the ideological impetus for the Stein–Hardenberg reforms in Prussia after the Napoleonic defeats, and then for the unification project of Bismarck which culminated in 1871. Unlike the reactionary ethnic nationalism of the Romantics, 'state nationalism' had a strongly modernizing impetus. It sought above all to forge a nation state, not by calling up the romance of the Volk, but by creating collective civic attachment to the institutions of the Reich. Hitler's demonic achievement was to force together Reichsnational and Volksnational consciousness into the ideology of German totalitarianism.

The other competition to ethnic nationalism was provided by German social democracy, the strongest workers' movement in Europe before 1914, and one marked by a strongly internationalist and anti-nationalist consciousness. The social democratic tradition was persistently, if unsuccessfully, opposed to ethnic particularism, and its residue remained alive in the socialist ideology of the DDR.

On the one hand the parties with workers' support refused to speak the language of the nation, believing it to be chauvinist, bourgeois and reactionary. On the other hand traditional German conservatism failed to create support for constitutional nationalism among the German workers. Into this void stepped Hitler. The disastrous failure of both the left and the German right to anchor support for constitutional, civic nationalism among the German working class left the way open for Hitler to wean them onto ethnic nationalism of an especially virulent kind. He was the first German politician to turn nationalism into a popular mass movement. His politics of resentment, directed at the victorious allies held responsible for the punitive peace of Versailles and at the Jewish conspiracy held responsible for the Great Depression, shrewdly categorized the Volk as noble victim. A disoriented and defeated people turned to Hitler because his nationalism flattered them, caressed their uncertainties away and made them believe someone else was to blame for their sufferings. Nationalism offered party believers a politics of intoxication, a heady state of permanent indignation, exaltation and occasional violence which offered escape from the normal tedium of ordinary life.

Neither German liberalism nor German social democracy proved strong enough to stop Hitler, but if one writes them out of the story the history of German nationalism becomes one long, grim and featureless march towards him. Moreover, if you exclude the German liberal and social democratic traditions from the story, you cannot explain the post-war revival of a liberal and social democratic conscience. You cannot explain, in other words, the very fact of forty-five years of democracy in the federal republic. What is the moral of this story? German history is not its fate. The future is not the prisoner of the past. Only nationalists believe so.

THE MEDUSA
RESTAURANT AND THE
CAFÉ VOLTAIRE

Leipzig and Frankfurt airports are only forty-five minutes flying time apart. The cities are of roughly the same size; both have huge international trade fairs; they are twinned with each other, which means that, since unification, Frankfurt officials travel to Leipzig to tell them how to run their city. But if they are twins, you cannot tell it from their airports. In Leipzig, there are two gates, three planes, a bar, a couple of ticket counters, a rent-a-car agency, and that's it. In Frankfurt Airport, I lose count of the number of gates at 100. I lose count of the bars, restaurants, clothes shops, porn cinemas, newsagents, book stores, rent-a-car agencies. It is not so much an airport as a marble and glass souk at the hub of the new Europe. Huge aircraft nose up to the windows of the departure lounges and peer in upon the waiting passengers like whales in an aquarium. You can imagine what impression Frankfurt Airport must have made upon Frau Schindler,

Herr Börner or Herr Böhnke, when they arrived with their cardboard suitcases off the plane from Leipzig for the first time. The stewardesses with clipboards under their arms click by on the marble; businessmen with suitbags on their backs dash past, heading for the taxi rank; in the blur of movement, you can sometimes make out a small island of stillness: an East German couple, holding on to their children, gazing about them, baffled, motionless and unnoticed. Around them, the cash registers ping, tills open and slam, cameras and computers, personal organizers and walkmen slowly rotate on the turning stands inside their glass cases, enticing and out of reach.

In fifteen years, will it still be possible to tell an East German and a West German apart? Will each be tanned, speak the same American English, wear the same crushed-linen suits, look as tired and harassed as these German businessmen running to the taxi stand after a week on the road? Will the market end up making one nation out of two states? Perhaps. But memory is stubborn and unreconciled. There may be one Germany in fifteen years, but there will be two German memories for much longer than that

On a wall-mounted television in the bar of my hotel in Frankfurt, I catch the eight o'clock news.

Caption: 'Three Deaths in Arson Attack.'

'Violent extremists who apparently emanate from the right-wing extremist scene killed three people in the night. The criminals set fire to two houses in Mölln in Schleswig-Holstein, which were occupied mainly by Turkish families. One woman and two girls died as a result of the flames.

'In two telephone calls to the police, the arsonist signed off with "Heil Hitler".'

On the screen, I see dazed fire-fighters, their yellow jackets wet with water, and their eyes red with smoke, leaving the gutted two-storey brick house, carrying a small, shiny, green coffin.

'One of those who died was a ten-year-old girl. The mother had been living in Mölln for more than twenty years. Her ten-year-old grand-daughter was actually born there.'

On the screen I hear Chancellor Kohl say, 'What is manifesting itself here is a kind of brutality which is totally incomprehensible for any human sensibility.' Then he says something strange. 'I should also like to express most particularly my sympathy for our Turkish fellow citizens, both male and female, at this moment who have been living amongst us for many years.'

Fellow citizens. It is a curious lapse. Everyone knows that Turks may be born in West Germany, work there all their lives, pay taxes. But they cannot become citizens.

At the Medusa, in Frankfurt's Sachsenhausen district, the Turkish musicians are picking out melodies on a lute, tambourine, lyre and zither. Men are dancing with men, women with women, weaving among the tables, into the passages of this whitewashed labyrinth below the streets, while the waiters ford the seething dance floor, carrying trays of beer and kebab and Turkish salad.

Huseyn and Zu, in their 20s, both speak faultless German. They came here from Turkey as children. Germany is all they know. Zu could, as they say, 'pass for German': she has teased blonde hair and light skin, and having worked for American Express she speaks that strange American English which is the second language of Frankfurt, that English which actually declares: 'I'm not just a German. I'm a European.'

Huseyn holds her hand; she strokes his cheek at his beard-line. I can tell they'd rather not talk about the Nazi attack at Mölln. They'd like to push it away, for another night, so that they can listen to the zither and dance and forget about how it really is, out there in the streets. For the real issue for them is not anger or fear – though there is that in abundance. 'When I hear Kohl express his regrets, it's enough to make me explode,' Huseyn mutters. The real issue is where they belong now, whether they can belong anywhere. 'I don't know where to go,' Huseyn says. 'I grew up here, I speak German. I love Turkey, but I'm not at home there any more.' Then he adds, 'But I'm always thinking about going back.' He reaches over and takes Zu's hand again.

In Germany, they can be seen together in the street. They can't live together, because their parents won't allow it, but there is an understanding uncle, and sometimes he lets them use his place for the night. Huseyn and Zu smile bashfully. Now, in Turkey, Zu says, playing with her beer mat, 'that would be out of the question for me. Not for him, but for me.'

Even if Huseyn does get citizenship here eventually, he doubts that it will make much difference. 'What am I supposed to do with a passport?' he says bitterly. 'Hang it around my neck?' Will a passport make people stop calling him a dirty Turk? Will a passport make German workers share a cigarette with him on the factory floor? He has a Turkish face, and the formal rights conferred by a passport will not change the looks he gets from Germans. One day, Huseyn might belong to the German state, but never to the German nation.

The next morning it is raining in the playground of a local Frankfurt school. The children and their parents are kneeling on the pavement finishing their signs, which are running a bit in the rain. The signs and placards have been written by the children and they say things like 'The Foreigners are my Friend' and 'We are all Turks'. There are perhaps 150 teachers, parents and children, and they set off from the playground for a march through their neighbourhood.

We are making a gesture, I tell myself, as I join in the march through the rainy streets of this suburb, beside all these children, with their hopeful, innocent faces, holding up these rain-streaked placards with their decent sentiments. We will not count ourselves among the silent majority. We will not be counted among those who did nothing. The question, of course, is not whether decent Germans are prepared to stand up. In the weeks and months, millions stand up and march. But what exactly does it signify, this innocent and honourable form of moral narcissism? It says: I am ashamed of my country, but I am not responsible for its worst acts. So as we march, we dissociate ourselves from Mölln, from Rostock, from Solingen, from the list of towns that now have acquired their association with flames in the night, with torches, with flick-knives and screams, and the stamp of boots.

In the crowd I fall in with a middle-aged, balding engineer walking hand in hand with his daughter. I tell him I've just been in Leipzig. 'Just back from the east, are you? I was there for six months myself. What a shithouse. Hopeless. Nobody does a decent day's work. We're going to have to start again. They're shiftless, hopeless. Never stop whining.' He shudders. 'Glad to be home,' he says, squeezing his daughter's hand. Of course, he would never think of saying about the Turks what he says so casually about his fellow Germans. Curious people, who like each other so little.

As the little demonstration wends its way through the streets, past silent spectators whose faces do not register what they think of the banners, I get to talking to a young woman, named Sabine, whose children, she explains, are as yet too young to attend the school. So why is she here, then? She has a long, tanned, beautiful face, sharp blue eyes, and wears her hair in an auburn and golden braid down her back. She has a delicate, mournful distance to her as she speaks. 'I'm not sure. Just to be here. Just so I'm not sitting at home.' Then she pulls her long black coat around her shoulders and shivers. 'There is so much ugliness in this society now. So much hatred.' And then, with anguish in her voice, she says, 'I cannot keep it away from my children. I want to. But I cannot.' We walk for a long time in silence, and then she stops and strokes rain from her hair, and says, as if finding the words for why she is here at last, 'I'm afraid. For the first time in Germany, I am afraid.'

One third of the population of Frankfurt is foreign-born: Yugoslavs, Turks, Spaniards, Greeks, Italians, and 140 smaller nationalities. They have no citizen-ship rights: they cannot vote or hold civil service jobs, and their status – even if they happen to be born in Germany – is always temporary.

Rosa Wolf explains these facts to me in the bar at the Café Voltaire, in downtown Frankfurt. She works for the city government's multiculturalism bureau, and she is not sure whether anything her office has done is capable of stemming the rising tide of xenophobia in her city. Moreover, if the right-wing win the next local elections, they are likely to close down her office. Already, one of the local CDU politicians has written an article linking asylum seekers with drug pushing and welfare fraud. She called publicly for him to be charged with racial incitement, and the mayor disciplined her for violating her civil servant's political neutrality. Rosa is cheerful, undogmatic and unrepentant.

We turn out to have a lot in common. Both of us are children of the 1960s, who have lived long enough to see the icons of our youth turned into museum pieces. The Café Voltaire was once a centre of Frankfurt's left-wing counter-culture. Now it hosts book launches for Frankfurt publishers. Then it was where the feverish demonstrations against American bases were planned. Now the painted mural of Rosa Luxemburg and Friedrich Engels and Karl Marx, behind us on the bar, seems a vaguely pathetic monument to lost illusion.

'We wanted to change German society,' she says, with a rueful look, as if aware how odd such thoughts must seem now. 'We wanted to make it less obedient. The trouble was that we succeeded.' In wry detail, she catalogues her own difficulties with her children. Parents from 1968 often find their words coming back to haunt them. I had heard nothing about this revolt against obedience in Leipzig, of course. It is just another part of post-war German history that the two Germanies never actually shared.

'We denounced our parents as fascists. We moved out of the house. It was very painful, but we thought, in spite of everything, we would create a new kind of identity for ourselves.'

The revolt against obedience, she goes on, was all very well. The problem was that it led, in the 1970s, to the dismantling of the old system of juvenile punishment. 'So now these sixteen-year-olds in Mölln, Rostock and Solingen fire-bomb an asylum hostel or an immigrant's house and there's no punishment. They just laugh at the police.'

She is ruefully aware, now, that the revolt against obedience was a revolt against the German past, but not a real encounter with it. 'We were too optimistic. We didn't work on the past.'

We both ponder in silence on what it might mean to 'work on' the past. Freud says somewhere that there is knowing and there is knowing and they are not the same. Meaning: you can confront something in your head, without confronting it in your heart, your guts. Working through something is what therapy is all about: moving knowledge from your head to your body, from intention to action. But no one knows what the equivalent of therapy for a nation might be. No one knows how a nation works its way towards that deeper knowing.

What Rosa realizes is that reunification marked the end of something much more than a beginning, and that the whole of German society is still struggling to come to terms with this ending.

'Anyone who grew up after the war thought this life would go on for ever. You know, that clean, organized Germany, that Germany which believed that everything could be organized. Since 1989 we have entered the real world. We are coming to the end of the growth of our economy. With the Wall coming down, we are coming to the end of feeling secure in our little garden. We know something has ended for good.'

With something ending, the past returns, but not as one might expect or wish. Rosa throws her arms up in a gesture of amused irritation. 'There are all these Germans now who say, "For forty years we had to be quiet. For forty years we had to make a humble impression. Now at last we can say we're Germans." And then they say, "And besides, we were born too late. We have nothing to hide." ' She laughs, at them, at herself for ever believing that the 'revolt against obedience' would silence that old Germany for ever.

'We made a mistake,' she says suddenly. 'We never talked about the nation. We thought we were beyond the nation.' And she gestures ironically at the mural of Rosa and Karl and Friedrich behind her. 'We were internationalists, remember?

'You made a mistake too,' meaning Germany's neighbours. 'We were not allowed to work on our past, to come to terms with it, as a nation should.'

I say, 'What you mean is that the rest of the world never allowed Germans to be proud of what they could be proud of.'

'Exactly,' she says, surprised that, twenty-five years after the revolution against obedience, twenty-five years after thinking the 'nation' was a category for fools and revanchists, she has come to such a conclusion.

HERR K'S WHITE HORSE

The key task should be to regain one's self-confidence. I define this population as a wounded nation ... My feeling is that this population will only be at ease when it has regained its natural self-esteem as a nation. When you take away an individual's self-esteem, they are deeply damaged, and this is likely to be true of nations.

Elisabeth Noelle-Neumann, public opinion researcher, Germany, 1992

'Why are we the only people in Europe that cannot be allowed to be proud of ourselves?' Herr K. asks me bitterly. The question – I have heard it a dozen times around Frankfurt already – hangs in the air between us. We are in his bungalow in a village outside Frankfurt, and he glares at me, as if I am to blame for the fact that he is not allowed to be proud to be German. The trouble is, I haven't said a word.

Then he gets up and says brightly, 'Would you like to see my horse?' Herr K. loves his horse, a white Arab stallion he keeps in a paddock behind his house in a dormitory village north of Frankfurt. His love for his horse – romantic, extreme and innocent – is rather like his love of Germany.

He mounts his steed bareback and tells me how he grew up reading Karl Mai's pulp fiction about German-speaking cowboys riding the range. 'My horse,' he says, 'is my dream come true,' and then he gallops away. He would like to be a cowboy and he would like this to be a German-speaking Wild West. Unfortunately, he is a balding 53-year-old, a retired prison officer, and this is a small muddy field fenced on all sides. Instead of galloping off into the sunset, he rides disconsolately back to talk to me.

Like most Germans his age, he tells me proudly that he belongs to the first German generation lucky enough to have been born too late. Too late for what? I ask. Too late to be guilty of anything, he replies, with a mirthless chuckle.

He just remembers the red glow of burning Berlin in the winter of 1945. As the Russians moved into the city, he and his mother fled to this village in the verdant hills north of Frankfurt. Now, after twenty-five years in the prison service, he is standing as a candidate for the right-wing Republikaners in the round of municipal elections to be held in Hesse. German politics is being driven right-wards, and the people driving it in that direction are men like Herr K. He knows he will be elected: he is a good politician, he can feel the wind turning his way.

'Ignatieff, Ignatieff,' he muses, as we sit together over a beer in his village restaurant. 'What kind of name is that?' I tell him what kind of name it is. No offence, he goes on, but Slavs just don't know how to work. Look at the disaster they've made of Russia. Was it the people or was it the system? I counter. Definitely the people, he replies. If only they had the German virtues.

'We are a clean people, a self-respecting and independent people,' he says, and he is rightly proud of the suburban bungalow he and his wife have built with their own hands. The house, with its heavy nature paintings on the walls ('from my ancestors' he says), and its Brockhaus encyclopedia and collected works of Schiller and Goethe in the bookcases, is a humble bourgeois monument to a certain idea of Germany.

Ten kilometres away from Herr K's immaculate villa is a tent city for asylum seekers. He drives there, and we stand outside the fence and look at the rows of tents, the board walks in the mud, and a pair of sad Africans giving each other a haircut in the rain. Herr K. particularly wants me to know that German women, in need of pin money, come here to do the cleaning. Can you imagine it? he says. A black man knocking his cigarette ash on the floor and a German woman on her knees sweeping it up. No, this cannot go on.

Then his bonhomie returns and his shoulders shake with his strange mirthless laughter, and he says that the asylum law is a 'typical piece of German megalomania'. What other country would dream of making itself the world's welfare officer?

He is remarkably cheerful for someone who believes the German way of life is under attack. He should be, for he knows his party cannot lose. The constitutional right of asylum has been abridged, and the Republikaner have taken the credit for saying out loud what other parties only said under their breath.

Yet tightening up the asylum process, Herr K. says, will not get to the root of the problem. The real issue is that Germans no longer feel at home in their own country. Thirty per cent of the population of Frankfurt is foreign. Why do you think I live in the countryside he says.

Multiculturalism is the problem. We will have no culture at all if we go on 'in this way'.

But Turks in your country speak German, live in a German way. Why can't you admit them as citizens?

'We are Germans. They are Turks.'

Racism is too simple a word for Herr K's view of the world. A racist usually has some fantasy about the way 'they' smell, or the way 'they' cook. Herr K. doesn't seem prey to any phobias. Ethnic essentialism is a fancier term for his position, and perhaps more accurate. He believes that being German defines the limits of what he can possibly know, understand or sympathize with. Herr K. is hardly alone. All week long I met liberal Germans who would not be seen dead with the likes of Herr K., for mixed reasons of social snobbery and political conviction, who nevertheless spoke Herr K's language. They all feel that the liberal German conscience has reached its hour of truth with the asylum crisis. 'This cannot go on,' they all said to me. 'We will end up not knowing who we are.'

Herr K. will not allow me to suggest that the Republikaner have been assid-uously fanning the flames of a violence they are then at pains to condemn. Blame the violence on the movies and video culture, on the loss of moral values in our youth. Don't blame it on me. Or on my history.

Why should Germans take the blame for these attacks? Why can't you let us be at peace with ourselves, Herr K. asks me again, as if I am the source of his guilt or the means of his absolution.

It strikes me that it would be nice for Germans to like themselves and like their nation, so long as they accept the Germany that actually exists, the Germany of the post-1945 borders, the Germany that is home to millions of foreigners. The problem with Herr K. is not that he is a nationalist, but that he is a German nationalist who actually despises the Germany he lives in.

He wants a Germany for the Germans, when there are already 6 million foreigners here. He wants a Germany that is law-abiding, clean, orderly, where women stay at home, where the television does not preach sex and violence to its adolescents. It is a Germany, in other words, in which not just the 1930s, but the 1960s never happened. It is a Germany, he keeps saying, that is at home with itself, at peace with itself. ('How do you say it in English?' He searches for the word. 'Ah, yes, "serene".')

A serene Germany is a fantasy land out of the Karl Mai stories he heard in his childhood. In his political daydreams, he is riding his white stallion through the pure and empty fields of a Germany which, if it ever existed, does not exist now, and cannot be brought into existence except at the price of other people's liberties and some Turkish blood.

HEIMAT

Every night at Frankfurt Airport, you can watch them coming off the flight from Moscow and taking their first dazed steps into the promised land. The stout, impassive women wear sturdy winter boots and wear floral headscarves. If they smile, you see two rows of brass teeth. The men in sheepskin hats and winter coats busy themselves with their bundles and look as if they need a vodka. Pale children, in shell suits and cheap anoraks, cling anxiously to their mothers. As the West German businessmen elbow past them to the taxi stand, these families walk into what they are told is freedom with the stunned gait of sleepwalkers.

As they board the buses taking them to transit camps, the language you hear them whisper to each other is Russian. But if you approach them, the embarrassed ones lapse into silence and the canny ones tell you loudly, '*Ich bin Deutsch.*' Even though safely through passport control, they half suspect you must be some kind of cop about to bundle them back on the plane for not being as German as they claim to be.

These families are among the most puzzling of the many streams of migration pouring through the gates of Europe. They are ethnic Germans flooding back – at a rate of 100,000 a year – from every quarter of the ruined empire in the east.

Germany is one of only two modern states that allow their scattered tribes a right of return. The other state, of course, is Israel. Two nations, who believe that nationality is in the blood, are in the process of discovering that the blood tie can be thin indeed.

'They have to be taught to flush the toilet,' a German social worker told me in a settlement house for Russian Germans in the Frankfurt suburbs. Families who have never known indoor toilets, showers or private baths have to be gently reintroduced to the classical North German Protestant equation between cleanliness and virtue.

In the dining hall of the settlement house, I watched a traffic policeman patiently telling a group of 60- to 70-year-olds how to cross the street at the traffic lights. They listened as impassively as if they were still at a party or factory lecture. The policeman got them to their feet, and they practised moving their heads right, then left, then right again, so that when they cross the street they will not be mowed down by the BMWs of their prosperous hosts.

Such a scene brings you face to face with the mystery of ethnicity. These people look Russian, and their habits and mentality are Soviet. Their ancestors left Germany 300 years ago to settle and colonize the eastern Slavic border regions beyond the then Holy Roman Empire. Intermarriage has thinned the tie that binds to vanishing point. Yet if you ask them where their Heimat is, they look around the cramped rooms of their Frankfurt hostel, and they say proudly, 'Here.' For the eldest among them, they are coming home to die.

'It was always my dream to die here,' Olga Oschetzki says, her big Russian peasant's hands folded on the linoleum tablecloth in front of her. The German she speaks is a beautiful antique. It has been preserved in her family like an ancestral linen tablecloth. She is proud that she never lost her language, even though Stalin shot all the German schoolteachers in the Zhitomir district of the Ukraine in 1937 and deported her to Siberia after the war for having collaborated with the Wehrmacht. When I venture to suggest that some might think her more Russian than German, she flashes angry blue eyes at me. 'I know who I am,' she says.

The ethnic Germans are one of those rare migrations where grandparents are leading their children and grandchildren home. The grandparents have kept their German, but their children have lost it. Most Germans probably wish their Russian brethren had stayed where they were, but they also know that, if they had not allowed them to come, there might, in another generation, be no Germans left to bring home.

The Heimat Olga and her daughter dreamed of bears no relation to the one they are venturing out to explore. They are surprised by everything, by the twenty kinds of soap in the stores, for example, and by the brutal speed of the traffic. Most of all, they are surprised by all the foreigners. 'I thought I was coming to Germany,' said Olga's daughter. 'Instead, it's Turkey,' she says, wrinkling her nose in dismay. She says this in Russian because she speaks no German.

FINAL THOUGHTS

In guilt and reparation for its ethnic nationalist past, the German constitution enshrined a commitment to grant asylum to all victims of political persecution, only to find it could not keep its promise to its own conscience. It is not the number of asylum seekers that constitutes the problem. It is also that post-war liberal Germany saw itself so much as a post-nationalist or even anti-nationalist state that it found itself incapable of defining clear national interests in relation to international migration. Thus, for German liberals like Rosa Wolf, the asylum crisis is the first moment in the post-war period where they feel forced to renounce the utopia of a post-nationalist state and think more soberly of Germany's national interest. Even for liberals, in other words, some nationalist discourse is unavoidable. They have to talk about quotas, limits, repatriations, putting the German unemployed first. All of this would be natural enough, were such a language not disgraced by its associations with the Right.

Yet the times are no less disobliging to the German Right. The arrival of a multicultural society in Germany's cities makes it absurd to think of the Germans as a mono-ethnic Volk, and the persistent divide between East and West Germans must make anyone wonder just what the identity of the Volk actually consists in.

Despite these violent incursions of reality into the fantasy of German identity, the legal instruments which define German identity remain defined by the ethnic nationalist past. The criterion of citizenship remains one of ethnic descent on the basis of *jus sanguinis*. The resulting contradiction between reality and ethnic fantasy produces manifest unreason. To most outsiders, and to many Germans, it seems absurd that a Turk, born and brought up in Germany, should be unable to become a citizen, while a German from Siberia, with no history of residence in the country and little language competence, should be entitled to citizenship and to extensive settlement assistance.

The absurdity of German citizenship law is forcing conservative Germans to confront the incoherence, in a modern multicultural world, of grounding national identity in the Volk. At the same time, liberal Germans are discovering that a post-national identity built on guilt and reparation is not enough. It is as if both sides are slowly being pushed, by the force of reality, into abandoning a utopia, in the one case, of a Germany for the Germans, in the other, of a Germany open to the whole world.

At the same time, Germany is at last, with unification, passing from the stage of being a hungry nation to being a sated one. Its borders are settled; its lost peoples are coming home. Its task now is not, as some liberals suppose, to pass beyond nationalism altogether and move into bland Europeanism, but instead to move from the ethnic nationalism of its past to the civic nationalism of a possible future. This could be the moment, in other words, to bury the idea of the German Volk for ever. In practical terms, this would mean moving away from identification with the nation towards identification with the state, i.e. away from a citizenship based on the fiction of ethnic identity towards one based on allegiance to the values of democracy.

The chief obstacle to this enterprise lies not with the ethnic minorities themselves, but with conservatives who dream of a Germany that has never existed and with liberals who suppose that patriotism is for fools.

The result is an impasse, a political and cultural void where a believable image of Germany ought to be found. In this void where a nation ought to be, there is only the state, and it lacks the will to do what any state must do, which is to conserve its monopoly of the means of violence. Every day that this impasse persists, every day that the state's authority weakens, Leo, Leech and his friends grow stronger.

I board my plane for London, wondering at the irony that the Germans, who invented the idea of ethnic nationalism, should actually like themselves so little. What would it be like, I wonder, for a German to be genuinely at peace with his nation? To love it for what it is, not for what it might be, to love it with all its history, all its tragedy, all its violence? What might that nationalism be like? Is such a love possible?

1 Building the Highway of Brotherhood and Unity, linking Zagreb and Belgrade, 1950.

2 Croatian villagers stopping Yugoslav National Army tanks, 1991.

5   The Berlin Wall comes down, November 1989.

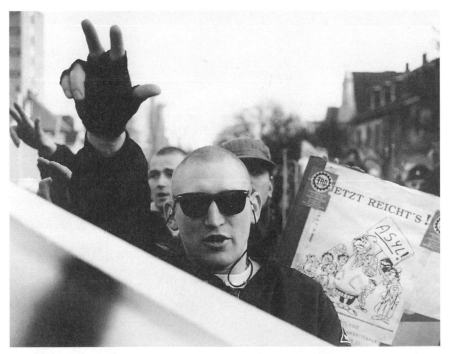

7   The face of German neo-Fascism: the FAP (Free Workers Party) takes to the streets.

8   East German assembly line in the 1980s: 'You pretend to pay us
and we pretend to work.'

LEFT 6   A Turkish family dies in a firebomb attack in Mölln, November 1992.

10   Russian Orthodox priest
and his wife, Kroupodernitsa, 1992.

9   Religious freedom returns to the
Ukraine: a woman weeps at the first
Uniate Catholic service in Lvov since 1946.

11   The faces of the Empire: Black Sea fleet sailor at Sevastopol.

12   The heroes of socialist labour in revolt: Donetsk miners on strike.

3

UKRAINE

WINE BOTTLES
AND SOAP

On the flight from Vienna to Kiev, I find myself examining a small plastic bottle of Austrian table wine served with my airline meal. Archaeologists say you can infer the shape of a whole civilization from the smallest trinket. My little wine bottle is capitalism epitomized: efficient, cosmopolitan, without distinction.

Beneath me the rug of the Hungarian plain crumples up into the Carpathian mountains and we enter Ukrainian air space. I have been across the border many times. My sudden attention to the flotsam of capitalist life is a sign that I am reluctant to leave this world behind.

What will I choose, as the tiny symbol that stands for the whole magnificent, dreadful, failed attempt to imagine an alternative to capitalism?

As we begin our descent into Kiev, I decide it will be the soap: the tiny pink bars with crenellations that await me in what I know will be the dank, evil-smelling bathroom of my Kiev hotel room, lit by the smeared light of a 40-watt bulb. This soap, which appears to be made from the renderings of some animal, which has no odour and no discernible cleansing power, is produced in hundreds of millions of bars, all the same, for every dreary hotel room on every interminable echoing corridor of every hotel in a once vast, now collapsed empire. A civilization's largest yearnings are expressed in those little bars of soap: for equality, for an end to a society where some have fragrant soaps in sculpted soap dishes and others have no soap at all; the ban on pleasure, on the very possibility of idle soaping in a foamy bath; finally, the baffling inefficiency: this hard, plain little bar of soap never in fact cleans you.

Thinking about soap bars and plastic wine bottles, I decamp from the plane and join the double lines of men in suits and briefcases queuing up for their Ukrainian visas. Every single person in the line is male; every one is on business. These are the new post-imperial type you see everywhere in Eastern Europe, who all speak such a strange English esperanto to each other that you wonder whether they have a native tongue of their own. The man ahead of me turns out to be a Russian *émigré* based in Vienna who works for an American chemical company. Which one? Dow Chemical. A name to conjure with. The makers of napalm. I once sat in on the steps of a university job centre to prevent Dow Chemical from recruiting young men like this to join their company as sales reps. What is he selling? Fertilizers. To whom? He smiles. In the old days of the empire, he explains, all our business was through Moscow, and we had one purchaser. You wined him, you dined him and at the end of the bargaining you got your price. Now, he smiles again, we have to do business, republic by republic. There are a lot more people to entertain. A lot more to bribe? I wonder. Do you have any small customers here? Yes, a few farmers. A few collective farms. They have assets – and I think of the vast flat black-soil country I have seen south of Kiev. But they are all so short of foreign exchange. A British businessman, a wide boy with seven suitcases of soccer kit he hopes to unload before

his return flight tomorrow night, overhears us and agrees. Plenty of business opportunities, provided you bribe everyone you come near.

Throughout Eastern Europe, these are the men of whom everyday miracles are expected. They are the ones who will provide the soap which will smell decent and actually clean you. These are the ones who will make the phones work, who will market wine in the small plastic flat-sided bottles. Everything else has been tried: the command economy's armoury of terror and menaces is bare; social democracy is too Swedish, too distant to be plausible. There is no one else to turn to but these men with briefcases.

Each well-dressed, well-coiffed male disappears through passport control and dissolves into the mass of people in the airport lobby, like sharp drops of ink dispersing in a large tank of water. In the next three weeks, I see Western businessmen in only two of the biggest Kiev hotels. Hundreds of them arrive daily, yet such is the size of the country, and of its problems, that they seem to vanish leaving scarcely a trace behind.

The customs declaration, I notice, is the same old Soviet form. I declare how much currency I am carrying, 'in figures and in numbers', whether I am carrying weapons, 'objects of art', books or medicines. The new nation hasn't got around to printing new ones, so, in the mean-time, the dull momentum of imperial bureaucracy continues to grind on.

By peeking over someone's shoulder, I discover that even the Ukrainian passport is the old Soviet document with Ukrainian in a ragged ink stamp on the spot reserved for 'Nationality'. Ukrainians have been told they will have their own passport and their own money. Till then, they make do with a transitional non-convertible currency called the kupon, still pegged to the Russian rouble, and like the rouble depreciating at something like 20 per cent a month. Like all the countries of Eastern Europe, the whole society is engaged in a frantic search for hard, convertible currencies as a hedge against the slow collapse of their own. At the visa window, Ukrainian officials are writing out visa forms as quickly as they can manage, palming businessmen's 50-dollar bills into cash boxes. All around me, the first impressions of Ukrainian independence are of decline and decay, broken panes of glass, smeared windows, cigarette butts all over the floor, the dim half-light from low wattage bulbs, policemen in new green uniforms, smoking, fingering Kalashnikovs. What, I ask myself, am I doing in this god-forsaken place?

This is the largest successor state of the fifteen that have emerged from the ruins of the twentieth century's greatest empire. I've come here to find out what real difference it makes to have a nation of your own. Does it get ordinary people proper soap, for example? Ukraine is the largest new state to be created in Europe this century: 52 million people, in a territory the size of France. A nation with an army of 600,000 men; the legatee of an imperial arsenal which makes it the third nuclear power in the world; the sixth largest naval power by virtue of its claim to part of the Black Sea fleet moored in Sevastopol; a nation of enormous natural wealth ranging from the coal and steel of the Donetsk basin to the agricultural abundance of the black soil lands.

I have reasons to take the Ukraine seriously indeed. But, to be honest, I'm having trouble. Ukrainian independence conjures up images of peasant embroidered shirts, the nasal whine of ethnic instruments, phoney Cossacks in cloaks and boots, nasty anti-Semites.

From my childhood in Canada, I remember expatriate Ukrainian nationalists demonstrating in the snow outside ballet performances by the Bolshoi in Toronto. 'Free the captive nations!' they chanted. In 1960, they seemed strange and pathetic, chanting in the snow, haranguing people who just wanted to see ballet and to hell with the politics. They seemed fanatical too, unreasonable. Hadn't they looked at the map? How did they think Ukraine could ever be free?

Yet the tendentious fanatics who refused to look at maps, who refused to accept that Soviet power would last an eternity, got it right, and the rest of us were wrong.

Clearing customs, I feel like declaring my basic prejudices on arrival. Isn't nationalism just an exercise in kitsch, in fervent emotional insincerity? Especially so in the Ukraine. It has been part of Russia for centuries. They now have a state, but are they really a nation? Into this inauthentic void streams nationalist emotionalism, striving to convince Ukrainians that there always was a Ukrainian nation, that it has been suppressed for centuries; that it has at last found its freedom, and so on. The reality is different. Some Ukrainians – especially those who joined the party – did well out of the empire. For most of the last fifty years, the party was not wrong when it dismissed nationalist feeling here as weak, marginal and easily suppressed. The glasnost era did see an awakening of nationalist feeling, and in the western Ukraine it blossomed into a genuinely broad-based national movement. But elsewhere, in the more russified parts of the eastern Ukraine, there was no upsurge of demands for independence.

When independence did come, in the wake of the failed coup in Moscow in August 1991, it did not represent – as it did in the Baltic – the culmination of years of nationalist agitation. It happened because the local party boss, Leonid Kravchuk, saw that, without firing a shot, he could slip away from the empire and set himself up as the leader of a nation state. And so he remains, presiding over an apparatus still run by ex-party people. The Ukraine might not necessarily be a story about nationalism at all, perhaps only a story about how a leopard tries to convince you he has changed his spots.

Glumly, I prepare myself for what I fear may be in store: city-dwelling intellectuals lyricizing about peasant roots they have long since left behind; party apparatchiks conjuring up retrospective indignation at the Soviet suppression of things Ukrainian; fanatics trying to convince themselves that independence will solve all economic problems; and a few old fascists telling me that with a name like mine – Russian isn't it? – I don't belong here.

But I do. The first thirty years of my Russian grandfather's life were spent in the Ukraine, attending the lyceum in Odessa, holidaying in the Crimea, then farming on his father's estates in the central Ukraine, in a village called Kroupodernitsa. He became the head of the Kiev district council, the *zemstvo*, and then, after the revolution of 1905, was appointed as the civilian governor of Kiev region. My grandmother thought their years in the big house in the Lipki, Kiev's linden-shaded residential quarter, were the happiest of their married life. My grandfather spoke the language and, to the end of his life in exile, sang Ukrainian songs and signed his letters to his sons, not with the Russian word for father, but with the Ukrainian word, *batko*.

For my grandparents, Kiev was more than a Russian town. It was the birthplace of Russian national identity itself. Russian Orthodox Christianity began in

987, when the ruler of Kievan Rus was baptized into the Christian religion. Now, unbelievably, it was the capital of a new independent state.

My difficulty in taking Ukraine seriously goes deeper than just my cosmopolitan suspicion of nationalists everywhere. Somewhere inside, I'm also what Ukrainians would call a Great Russian, and there is just a trace of old Russian disdain for these 'little Russians'.

THE DOLLAR ZONE

Kreschatik is the curving boulevard where Kiev strolls at night beneath the trees. In the metro station concourse below, a jazz band is playing, a mime troupe is improvising, ten drunks are begging and weeping, three old ladies are selling flowers, one woman in a white coat is avilable to weigh you at her weighing machine; one man sells posters of Samantha Fox in a wet T-shirt from one kiosk, and the formerly banned history of the anti-communist bandit guerillas from another. All of this, from Samantha Fox to the jazz band, is as it was before independence. What is new are the money changers. Young men in leather jackets cruise up and down the metro concourses and up on to the sidewalk with small, imitation dollar bills clipped to their lapels, or just the dollar sign, or sometimes the rouble. The other new feature of post-independence Ukraine is the special militia, armed with revolvers, knives and rubber batons. They strut up and down, ignoring the money changers who ply their trade on every corner.

Here the hard currency, the money of choice, the power that defines nearly all striving from the President to the hotel bed-makers, is the American dollar.

The dollar divides the society into two zones: the dollar zone and the rouble or kupon zone. In one, the domain of plenty: peroxide-blonde women, food and technology; in the other, the domain of shortages, queues, bad temper and the old days. The dollar zone is the hard currency shop, the joint venture, the hotel bar, the casino, the brothel. In the dollar zone, if you make a phone call home – using an American satellite line with a Dallas-based operator – the connection is instantaneous, but it costs you between 9 and 15 dollars a minute. In the kupon zone, it can take hours or days to get an international line, and the cost of the call is 9–15 dollars an hour. In the dollar zone, there are no shortages. At the Apollon restaurant, in a street off the Kreschatik, you are in the dollar zone. It is a Swiss-Ukrainian joint venture. Almost everything, from the frozen pasta to the beer, from the tablecloths to the kitchen dishwasher, is flown in from Switzerland. Apart from bread and butter, the restaurant buys nothing from local suppliers, because, says the Ukrainian manager with a shrug, 'We have too many problems.' You can't eat a Russian dish here. It is a Swiss version of Italian pasta that is on offer, washed down with German beer. It's one of those little outposts of the capitalist no-man's land, establishing itself in the grey East. The old zones of party privilege, policed by state security, are now replaced by new zones of privilege, where there may be no policemen on the door, but where access is barred to anyone who does not come with a credit card or a wallet full of dollars.

At the Apollo I meet Christia Freeland, who writes for the *Financial Times* and *The Economist* in Kiev. She's a Canadian Ukrainian from a farming family in the Peace River country of northern Alberta, one of thousands of those second-generation Ukrainian Canadians who were raised to dream about an independent Ukraine by their exiled parents and now have come back to live and work in the reality of independence. It is common, she says, for Canadian Ukrainians to think of themselves as the true Ukrainians, the ones who kept the faith while among the actual Ukrainians the compulsion and fatalism of the communist system was working its way into their bones. The Ukrainian Canadians return 'home' expecting a fervently nationalist and religious people, and find instead phlegmatic, ironic, sober and fatalistic Soviet souls. Independence requires a new human type, but, she says, with an equal measure of affection and irritation, it will be a long time coming.

Independence, moreover, has done nothing for the economy. Inflation is rocketing, production is plummeting, there are real shortages everywhere. Most people in Kiev actually get by through knowing someone in the countryside who can supply them with potatoes, or by cultivating their own allotment. The government is afraid to embark on market reforms, for the good reason that market freedoms might eventually dislodge them. Democracy is more apparent than real. The President rules by decree: everything from Kievan food supply to foreign trade policy is decided by him. There is no organized party opposition in parliament; democratic debate is weak. The old elite is still in power, parroting nationalist rhetoric, in practice holding on like grim death, waiting for something to turn up. I haven't been here three hours, and already it looks as if national independence has been a disaster.

So what would you do? I ask her. She reels off a list: land to the peasants, radical market reform, convertibility of the kupon, and then, with a ruthless laugh, she says, 'Let's see what happens.' What will happen, the Ukrainians fear, is what has been happening in Russia: ever deepening chaos.

No one knows exactly how to convert a failed command economy into a liberal market society. No one can afford easy confidence about the advantages of Western shock therapy. I find myself thinking about what that astute historian of nationalism Eric Hobsbawm had told me before leaving London. 'We have nothing to teach these people. None of our lessons are applicable. Free-market snake oil won't work. Democracy won't necessarily work. Nothing we export is necessarily going to work. They are all going to have to find their own way.' It is not that Eastern Europe is hopeless. It is merely that the capitalist triumphalism, which assumes that what works for us must inevitably work for them, will be found wanting. Western liberal market societies cannot be exported in the same way that you can export the frozen pasta, dishwasher and place mats of the Apollon. The fallacy is to suppose that we live in one world, with one solution to all available problems. There may not be a viable systemic alternative to capitalism. But that does not mean that capitalism is the only answer in this world. It looks to me, on the first night, that he is right. And it still looks that way, three weeks later, when I leave.

On the way back from Apollon, I follow the Kreschatik in the dark, past the curving four-storey apartment blocks, late Stalin style, erected along either side of the boulevard to replace those destroyed in the fighting for the city in 1943. There is a burly confidence in these buildings, a ruthless civic grandeur in late Stalinism. Every building is still adorned with a hammer and sickle, or the granite standards of the battle regiments of the Great Patriotic War. These buildings represent the high-water mark of empire, an architecture of intimidation, the embodiment of pure power. The pediments, the massive granite out of which they are hewn, proclaim: look on my works ye mighty and despair. They were supposed to imply: we will be here for ever. In reality, the empire was to last only forty years more.

As I pass the Kiev Soviet, site of the city government, I notice that the entire front façade, hammer and sickle and all, has fallen into the street and lies in rubble and ruin behind a wooden hoarding, leaving it a building without a face.

A GENTLE NATIONALIST

Next day I return to the Kiev City Hall to meet one of the quiet heroes of the Ukrainian independence movement, Mikola Horbal, now a sober-suited, middle-aged deputy in the Kiev municipal parliament.

If you are a Ukrainian nationalist you could be forgiven for a sense of disillusion these days. Horbal went to prison in the 1970s and 1980s for demanding the right to speak his own language and to worship in the Uniate church (the Catholic Orthodoxy practised in western Ukraine), and now he has a state of his own, and the people running it are the people who put him in prison.

But that is not how Mikola Horbal sees it. He was, by his own description, 'an everyday Soviet teacher and a musician', whose music, he says wryly, 'did not happen to proclaim communism'. The KGB held his songs in such esteem that they gave him five years in prison, followed by two years of exile. They put him to work cutting stones with a jack hammer in a quarry, and that soon put paid to his fingers. He has never played an instrument since. His jailers could not understand him. Sober materialists that they were, they asked him, 'You have everything in Kiev, even a flat, why are you making trouble?'

Because he grew up in a religious family in the western Ukraine. Because denial of his language rights seemed an issue of conscience to him. Because he wishes to be an honourable man. He is not sure why this was evident to him and not to others. 'When you are not allowed to speak your language, and are persecuted for it, then you have to go prison.' Prison, he now says, perhaps with the nostalgia of hindsight, was the making of him. Before he went to prison, he had never questioned the idea that the empire was one great family of peoples. He met other nationalist figures and through them came to retrace the Ukrainian via dolorosa through the Soviet period: the famines of the 1920s and 1930s, the forced collectivization which destroyed Ukrainian peasant agriculture, as well as the liquidation of most of the Ukrainian intelligentsia. Much later, in 1990, when he took his first visit to Ukrainian communities abroad in the USA, he came back convinced that Ukrainians will always – whether they be in the prison house of the Soviet system, or in the soft, assimilative freedom of the capitalist world – remain Ukrainian.

We are not a nation state yet, he concedes. We have to build one, with a consciousness of our own history and distinctiveness. And then he corrects himself. We do not have to build this nation. It will build itself.

Horbal's is the most ecumenical of nationalisms. Of course Russians who want to become Ukrainians will be welcome in the new state. 'One Russian defending the interests of Ukraine is more dear to us than a Ukrainian who does the same, for that is expected of him.' He does not hate the Russians for imprisoning him, for they were perhaps the empire's greatest victims.

What kind of nationalism is this? Horbal denies he is a nationalist. 'Nationalism that causes the humiliation of other nations is simply chauvinism.' A patriot then? Yes a patriot. A man who admits that the sight of the Ukrainian army marching in uniform for the first time on the Independence Day parade moved him deeply.

But the very communists who imprisoned him are still in power. 'I do not hate them. The communist who is still in power shall have two sandwiches and I shall have only one. But he shall never have three.' Yes, he says with an engaging, quiet smile, 'I should hate Kravchuk.' When Horbal was in prison, Kravchuk was party ideology chief, responsible for the condemnation of nationalists like Horbal as ideological fascists. Now Kravchuk dons a Ukrainian peasant shirt when he makes public appearances and nationalist discourse has become his native tongue. 'I should hate him, but I don't. When I see him at the United Nations, speaking for the Ukraine, I feel proud of my country.'

THE PRESIDENT

When you go to see the President, in his office in the leafy heights of Lipki, security keeps you waiting at the bottom of a huge wide flight of marble, red-carpeted stairs. Men in suits with earpieces keep you under surveillance. It is all very Soviet, with one comic and jarring difference. By the door, refusing to budge, unintimidated by the heavy men in suits, stand three old peasant ladies, clutching papers in their hands, demanding to see the President as if this were the middle ages and he were not the master of a modern nuclear state, but the booted, robed Good Old Tzar of old.

Finally, I get the nod from the men with earpieces and ascend the carpeted stairs to the President's office. Everything about the place brings back the bare sobriety of Soviet-style power, the empty marbled corridor, the long, vanishing red carpet, the heavy padded doors off to each side, the silent shining room adjacent to the President's office where I am to hold the interview. What else should I expect? Is there a Ukrainian style of power? Of course not. There is only the Soviet, just as for the Gallic and Teutonic chiefs who succeeded the Romans the available models of authority were a Roman breastplate, a fasces, a toga.

The President is a solidly built, immaculately groomed, white-haired man in his late 50s, urbane, relaxed, not noticeably drawn or harassed, the very picture of a confident Soviet official of the Gorbachev era. He seems to have a sense of humour, seems to relish authority and office, seems to believe it is an easy matter to deal with foreign journalists.

He incarnates the ambiguity of Ukrainian independence – a western Ukrainian by origin, fluent Ukrainian speaker, who rose within the party hierarchy through the 1970s and 1980s, became party boss in the late Gorbachev era, and then, with fine sense of timing, declared independence, using the rhetoric of the nationalists he had arrested only years before.

I ask him to explain how a communist becomes a nationalist. He gives me his most engaging smile, the one that says, I am being perfectly frank with you. 'This puzzles not only you, but also people here and abroad. But is my behaviour exceptional in history? There are plenty of examples of where a person has lived in a certain system, within certain co-ordinates, and has gone on to lead the rebellion against this system.'

He now says he always knew the formal autonomy of the Ukraine within the Soviet federal structure was a sham. He knew that Soviet collectivization had decimated the Ukraine in the 1930s and that Stalin had murdered the flower of the Ukrainian Communist Party. 'I saw it all with my own eyes.'

But, I say, many believers in independence are disillusioned. So many from the old apparatus are still in power. Here, his eyes narrow. He ceases to be urbane and amused. 'You are misinformed.' The only people available at independence who knew, as he puts it, 'the art of governing', were the 3.5 million members of the Communist Party. We will bring on new people, but they need to be educated and trained. And besides, he says, what is so bad about the communists? Some are more democratically inclined than the so-called democratic opposition.

He assures me that he does not want an ethnically based national state in the

Ukraine. He has invited ethnic Germans to settle in the Ukraine; he wants to reassure the 11 million Russian minority that their language rights are secure. On this I believe him, for the simple reason that any other policy would lead to civil war.

But won't you get a civil war anyway if the economy continues to spin downwards? There, he agrees. 'The most important thing is to avoid deepening economic crisis which could lead to an explosion which in turn could lead to explosions in other spheres.'

THE STATUE AND
THE CAVES

The next morning, I strap myself into the seat of a Soviet helicopter for a flight over the city. Down below, the mighty Dnieper River has a lustrous green colour. Ninety miles north of here is the malediction of Chernobyl, still spilling contaminated water into the big river below me. Nothing did more to hasten Ukrainian disillusion with empire than the Chernobyl disaster; no other single event of the 1980s did more to win support for the nationalist cause.

Suddenly there is another malignant reminder of Soviet civilization looming right in front of us, a gigantic silver statue of a frowning Amazon in metal robes, sword aloft in one muscular fist, shield in the other, a staggeringly large figure – equal in size to the Statue of Liberty – made of glistening aluminium and appearing to be perspiring with martial effort.

She is Mother Russia, guarding the Gates of Kiev, facing west to repel intruders, a monument to the Great Patriotic War and to the soldiers who died retaking Kiev from the Germans in 1943.

This vast aluminium matron was erected, not in the first flush of victory, but in 1980, as part of the senescent Brehznev regime's attempt to manufacture patriotic ardour. The memory of the war was, more than anything else, what held the empire together. The parades, march-pasts, speeches and holidays of Soviet institutional life all took the war memorial as their focal point. Soviet brides and bridegrooms laid their wreaths on the tombs of the war dead. As the memory of war receded, giant aluminium matrons went up in the 'hero cities' of the Second World War, to maintain and manipulate popular memory. The message of such monuments was unsubtle: the party saved the empire and the peoples of the empire sacrificed themselves as one.

As the helicopter whirls me around, I want to land and walk up to the top, like in the Statue of Liberty, and stare out at the world through her eyes. Isn't there some observation post inside her head? It can't be done, the nervous keeper of the shrine tells me. The observation tower has had to be closed. Even though she was officially opened in 1980, she's so poorly constructed and her structural iron is rusting away so rapidly, she's liable to fall over.

She is meant to symbolize imperial unity in the war-time cause, but here in the Ukraine the war was closer to a civil war than a united patriotic outpouring. When the Germans poured across Ukraine's western border in June 1941, they were greeted as liberators by millions of western Ukrainians. For them, the war was an opportunity to escape the prison house. Western Ukrainian nationalists at first thought the Germans would allow them to set up their own state. Bandera and Melnyk, Ukrainian nationalists in exile, returned with the advancing Wehrmacht, fervently proclaiming their belief in the new order in Europe in the hope that the Germans would reward them with a client state. Too late they discovered that the Germans regarded them as a slave race, fit only for subjugation. Ukrainian nationalists found themselves caught between the German occupiers and the Red Army, sometimes fighting both at once. When the Soviets conquered the western Ukraine at the end of the war, some of the fiercest opposition came from Ukrainian nationalist partisans. They kept fighting until the early 1950s. All of this history is neatly suppressed by this statue.

The helicopter wheels away from the Motherland statue and passes over the golden domes of the Kievan monastery. In Soviet times, the Kievan skyline offered a scene of symbolic competition between two religions – the cult of the war dead and the old faith of the poor and excluded. Kiev is the fountain of all Russian Orthodoxy, for it was the Kievan Prince Vladimir who in 987 married the daughter of the Byzantine emperor in Constantinople and at the same time converted, along with all of his subjects, to the Orthodox religion.

Monks had lived in caves on these bluffs before Vladimir's conversion, and their remains, embalmed in coffins lodged in niches in a deep underground network of passageways, had become a site of pilgrimage for Orthodox believers. Since Ukrainian independence these saints are on what for Russians is foreign soil. Worse, a Ukrainian Orthodox church is seeking to wrest exclusive jurisdiction over them from the Russian patriarch. For Ukrainians, the monastery consecrates the site of the first beginning of Ukrainian national consciousness; for Russians, Kievan Rus is the beginning of the Russian national experience. The 'loss' of the Ukraine is thus, from the Russian point of view, not merely the loss of a province, but of its own symbolic beginnings.

When I make my descent into the caves beneath the monastery, it is dark and cold, and the doors have long since been closed on the tourists. At the bottom of a long flight of wooden plank steps, there is a small light blue antechamber, lit by a single oil lamp in front of an icon in an upper corner of the ceiling. In the faint light, I almost trip over what I take to be a bundle of rags on the stone floor. Stepping over it, I see that it is an old couple curled up against each other, beneath their ragged coats, lying together on a piece of cardboard to ward off the damp. They are sleeping or resting on their sides with their hands under their heads, for neither has a pillow. The old woman is wearing her kerchief, the man an old flat cap, and they sleep together in spoon position. As I discover them, I turn and see that there are several old couples asleep on the floor, and two others sitting on a bench in the near darkness beneath the icon. Leaving the antechamber and resuming my descent, I come across more of these silent old couples sleeping on the stairs, propped up against a banister, bundled up against the biting cold, almost inert, as if dead. These are pilgrims, old people whom the church allows to sleep here night after night in the sub-zero cold close to the saints.

The final door to the caves is guarded by a tiny old lady in a Ukrainian shawl and headscarf, a thick coat and slippers, who gets up from her bed behind the huge warm Dutch stove to unlock the door and let me in. She watches me suspiciously as I light my candle, and shadows me as I wander through the maze of tunnels. I lose my way down blind alleys, run up against locked doors, in a damp darkness lit only by my candle and the flames in icon lamps. In niches dug into the tunnel walls are the burnished wooden coffins and stone sarcophagi of the saints. But the coffins and sarcophagi are open, and in the dim light of the icon lamps their faces are shrouded, but in several I make out the withered brown claw of a hand clutching the vestments of burial. The dead do not return to dust here; the atmosphere and the properties of the earth preserve their hands, brown-black claws, with long nails. The old woman is suddenly behind me, watching to make sure I do not reach out and touch. Her life is spent here, deep in the earth, lying behind the stove, watching suspiciously over the saints. Something about this cult of the dead, this loving preservation of bodies which ought to have turned to dust, this association between faith and death, makes me nauseous. Two nations, two languages, two histories originate in this dark maze underneath the monastery. But all I want is to get out. I need to climb those stairs, over those sleeping bodies if need be, in any case as fast as I can. I need light. I need air.

THE FAMILY GRAVES

About two hours south-west of Kiev, by the River Ross, in the district of Vinnitsa, among the undulating expanse of sugar-beet fields, there is the small village where my great-grandfather bought an estate in the 1860s while he was Russian ambassador to Constantinople. In 1908 he died there; in 1917, before the revolution could dispossess her, his wife died too. They are both buried in the crypt of the church. No one from my family has been back here since February 1917. The road gives out some miles away and our bus struggles over the rutted, cobbled farm road that winds through the featureless, flat beet fields. Darkness falls. Past a town called Pogribisce, we pass a huge sugar-beet factory, working in the dark, sending up plumes of steam into the cold night air. Then, as the headlight beams pick objects out in the dark, I begin to have an eerie sense of familiarity. I've been looking at photographs of the place since childhood. There is the long, low, flat stone barn by the railway line. This must be the road grandfather took every morning in the trap when he went out to the railway siding to collect the Moscow papers off the Moscow–Odessa express. And this must be the church, its dome and cross, lit up in expectation of our arrival, poking up above the trees by the river bank, just as it looked in the Box Brownie photographs taken of it by my father's English nanny.

We stop by the churchyard gate. Not a sound. The emptiness of the country-side at night. No streetlights, just the black dome of the sky and a few stars. There are a couple of small brick cottages behind us, their lighted windows visible above faded picket fences, but we do not know which one to approach. Eventually a lorry driver from the collective farm stops and picks us up, my translator and I, and drops us off, in front of a blue and white brick house, covered with vines and plants, at the end of a dirt road in the dark. He bangs on the door, and after many minutes the priest emerges, pulling his black cassock around his stomach, smoothing out his beard with his fingers and muttering about the lateness of the hour and the rudeness of strangers. His wife, kerchiefed, bustling about, brim-ming with energy, leads us back down the path in the dark to a *hata*, where we will sleep. A room for the woman, meaning my translator, she says; this one for the men, she says, meaning me, plumping up the beds she has ranged against the wall; and a good fire, she says, banging on the coal stove which heats a Dutch oven which runs the length of the room. She lights the lamps in front of the icons in the corner of the room, crosses herself and bustles about in the kitchen, clattering in and out bearing tea and a soup tureen full of potatoes, and her jars of pickled tomatoes and onions and cucumbers, several bottles of vodka and some cognac. The priest returns and I ask him to bless the food, which he does in song, joined in with a high quaver from his wife, both of them crossing themselves unceasingly.

We eat together on a trestle table in the centre of the room, beneath a single light bulb. They keep stealing glances at me, the priest and his wife: is this really the Count's grandson? Why doesn't he speak Russian? Is he a believer?

When they came to the parish in the 1950s, they said, the church was boarded up and the machine shop for the collective farm stood in the churchyard. When they tried to get the machine shop out of the churchyard the priest was arrested, his wife says. But we are still here, he says phlegmatically, chewing on a piece of black bread. Thirty-five years. We restored everything. We have kept your graves. We have not forgotten, they say, quietly and undemonstratively, perhaps wondering to themselves why exactly I am worthy of this unrewarded devotion.

What has independence meant for them? I ask, over the vodka and cognac. The priest and his wife share glances. A Ukrainian Church, with the tacit blessing of the state, is demanding to take over all the Russian Orthodox churches in the Ukraine, and will require services to be sung in Ukrainian. The priest himself trained in the Russian seminary, yet he speaks Ukrainian to his parishioners. But the service can only be in Church Slavonic, and the only Church authority he is prepared to recognize is the ancient one that flows from the Bishops of Moscow and Constantinople, not some upstart in Kiev. Already, there are fights at church doors all over the Ukraine, between defenders of the old faith and the new nationalist Church. Their son is choirmaster of the cathedral in Vinnitsa, the big town nearby. The new Kievan bishop has come to Vinnitsa to demand the handover of the cathedral. The son is prepared to fight. 'People will be killed,' the priest's wife says gloomily.

The next morning I am at the well, winding up the water to wash in and make the tea. Village children pass by with satchels on their backs on the way to the school on the hill. Women in bedroom slippers and wrapped up against the cold scratch about in their back gardens, hanging out washing, cutting off the head of a cabbage, shooing geese away. A horse-cart clops by with two farm workers sitting in the hay with their legs bouncing over the side. An ancient woman, bent and crooked, straggles by, leaning heavily on a stick.

The atmosphere is heavy with desolation. It is not merely that people are old and poor and that the village is depopulated. It is that so many of the faces have the stunned and defeated air of survivors.

No one wants to work now, the head of the collective farm tells me later. Why don't you give them the land? I ask. Who do I give it to? Who has the capital? Look at these fields. He spreads his hands out to the huge, featureless fields of beet. What he implies is crucial: if agriculture is the backbone of new Ukraine, who will save it now? Where are the peasants? Where are the small farmers? The director of the collective farm takes me down to the river, near the church, to have a look at the *kolkhoz* flour mill. Erected in 1886, it says over the front door, at the same time as the church, and inside I find all the machinery great-grandfather imported from Leipzig and Dresden, still working, with hammered bits of Soviet tin and iron replacing those parts that have worn out. I watch as women in flour-covered kerchiefs pour sacks of grain into the old machines and watch the fine cone of white flour emerge beneath. I move the flour dust away from one of the labels: 'Leipzig, 1886'. 'Still the best flour mill in the region,' the head of the collective farm says.

I cannot shake off the sensation that these people are the survivors of a great catastrophe. From the family album, and the pictures taken by the English nanny, I know some of the names of the peasants who used to live here in my grandfather's time. Their names are inscribed in white ink beneath their pictures: full-bearded Sessoueff, the estate steward, with his ample wife and their seven children. Rudnitsky, the sly-looking head of the stables. What had happened to them all at the Revolution? In the churchyard, I found the grave of Sessoueff, buried next to the family vault. And his children? All 'repressed' in the 1930s. And Rudnitsky? Repressed too. Why? The priest shrugs his shoulders. They were *kulaks*, rich peasants, grain hoarders, money lenders, enemies of the state, two victims, among Stalin's hecatomb.

Walking along the empty, dusty tracks of Kroupodernitsa towards the big house, past some cottages in brick with tin roofs, past others still wattle daub and thatched, as they were in the nanny's photographs, I sense the reasons for the sadness that hangs over this place like a shroud. Something like 3 million Ukrainians died of hunger between 1931 and 1932. A further million were killed during the collectivization of agriculture and the purges of intellectuals and party officials later in the decade. An additional 2–3 million Ukrainians were deported to Siberia. The peasant culture of small farmers and labourers that my grandfather grew up among was exterminated. This was when the great fear came. And it never left. It remains in the eyes of the old women who stare at me over the picket fences of their kitchen gardens as I make my way up the muddy track to my great-grandfather's house.

It is on high ground, looking down on the village, a capacious two-storey mansion, in white stucco, with a ceremonial front porch, before which the family brougham used to draw up when the family arrived to spend the summers. The ceremonial gardens have long since gone. One wing burned down, another is in ruins. But it is still recognizable from the old family photographs.

The teachers greet me on the steps. A girl in a peasant costume and Ukrainian headdress, made of purple and pink plastic flowers, curtseys and presents me with a round loaf of bread, decorated with pastry leaves and a pastry sheaf of grain, and a small bowl of rock salt. Thus was my grandmother greeted when she came here, as my grandfather's bride, in 1902. From cottage to cottage they went, and each peasant family presented them with bread and salt. Now it is my turn, but I do not know what to do – my translator whispers that I must take a piece of bread and dip it in the salt and eat. Instead, I bow, in embarrassment.

They lead me through a house which my aging uncles in exile in Canada can still remember room by room, corridor by corridor. I feel I am sleepwalking through their memories. I walk across thick plank floors, pass through long low corridors, with children clattering behind me. I hear the school director tell me, pointing, that it was there, just there, at the bottom of those stairs, that my great-grandfather died, one morning in 1908. How he knows this he does not say. The house seems to relay its mythology, some of it untrustworthy. Is it true, the principal wants to know, that Honoré de Balzac spent a night here? He leads me into a long room, with a raised platform at the end, which might have been a stage for family theatricals or recitals. Now it is hung with pictures of Soviet pioneer heroes of the Great Patriotic War, and I am asked to give a little speech. I tell the children that I am the great-grandson of the man who built this house. I present them with copies of my family album's photographs. They stare at them and at me with awe and disbelief.

No one knows exactly what happened after the Revolution here. My grandfather's sister, Aunt Mika, who ran a dispensary in the village, stayed on, and then was spirited away to Kiev where she went into a nunnery. Everyone says, without ceasing, how all the children in the village were my family's godchildren, how Aunt Mika looked after them. This is true. It is also true that the house must have been put to the sack. Not a stick of furniture, not a picture, not a samovar, not a spoon remains, although one old man comes up holding a faded photo of my great-grandfather at the end of his days, wearing his old general's greatcoat, leaning on his wife's arm, rheumy, tired, his moustaches untrimmed and drooping, slippers on his feet in the ornamental garden. By the 1930s it was a dwelling house for many families; after the war an orphanage, now a school. In one room, 8- and 9-year-old children are singing Ukrainian patriotic songs, mournful, violent songs about the Cossack warriors who will overthrow Moscow's yoke:

The riflemen of the Sich come into the fray of this bloody dance
To free their Ukrainian brothers from Moscow's chains.
We'll cast off Moscow's chains
And in our illustrious Ukraine we'll make merry.

In one room the children are learning the Ukrainian alphabet, while in another there is a folk museum of the Ukrainian peasant past: a wooden spinning wheel, a wooden rake, a blackened iron samovar, the obligatory picture of Taras Shevchenko, the national poet. The rough plank floor is strewn with fragrant grasses. But there is so little left: the historical remains are so poor. The disaster of famine and forced collectivization has stripped the peasant past bare.

So I learn that a new Ukraine is being made in the house of my great-grandfather. The children learn about Shevchenko, as they once learned about Pushkin; they learn about throwing off Moscow's yoke as they once learned about the heroic Soviet achievements of Yuri Gagarin; they run their hands over the broken spinning wheel that is all that is left of the peasant culture of these parts.

Then to the church, where the bell is tolling and the parishioners are assembling for a special *pannihida* in memory of our ancestors. The priest's son has come from Vinnitsa with his choir. The priest's wife lights the thirty candles on the candelabra and hoists it skyward. The walls are bright with newly completed paintings of saints and holy scenes. I stand to the side with the choir. At the back, a large cluster of old men and women, crossing and recrossing themselves.

There had been suffocation in the maze beneath the monastery. Now another feeling began to steal over me, a feeling that, like it or not, this was where my family story began, this was where my graves were. Like a tunneller, I had gone through suffocation, and I had tunnelled myself back to at least one of my belongings. I could say to myself: the half-seen track of my past does have its start, and I can return to it. The choir sings, the priest names my father, mother, grandfather, grandmother, the names, some of them Anglo-Saxon, peeking through the seams of his prayers, the choir and their voices singing, the sound filling this church my great-grandfather built.

Afterwards, the priest asks me to speak to his parishioners. And I do, with Lena, the translator, to help me, explaining who I am, thanking them for coming. They stare and stare, and then they come closer. Old women are crying. They take my hand, kiss it. They explain, through broken teeth, that they have walked for miles to be here, they remember, they remember. How Aunt Mika, my grandfather's sister, ran the dispensary. How well the choir sang when my grandfather conducted it. How strict my great-grandmother was when you waited on table. How they brought mushrooms to the kitchen door, how they collected strawberries and how they were rendered down in tubs in the pantry. It is impossible to catch these stories, to hold them. Everyone is talking at once, crying, the women clutching my sleeves. They push pieces of paper into my hand. My grandfather served in your stables and went to Canada. We think he went to see your grandfather there. Do you know? No, I don't know. Threads of connection are established, then broken, across seventy years. They are all weeping, clutching at me, crying hopelessly for the past, seeing the young kerchiefed girls they were before the horror began. One old woman, bent nearly double, slumps against a bench at the back of the church, crying on her own, her mouth a black, stump-filled hole of lamentation.

The priest shoos them away, and leads me out of the church into the crypt, a low damp flag-stoned space, with icons ranged along the back wall. In the gloom, against the far wall, I can see piles of lumber. One by one the icon lamps are lit, and in their glow I make out three granite graves. In the centre, my great-grandfather's, with his military rank, and the names of the treaties he had negotiated in the Tzar's name embossed on the side. On either side, the grave of his daughter, my grandfather's sister, who died in a hospital train of typhus tending the wounded in 1915; and beside her, my great-grandmother. The priest points out on the white marble of my great-grandfather's grave the cuts in the stone from the butcher's knife. This was a slaughterhouse in the 1930s. I run my hands across these black slices in the marble. We stand and sing the *viechnaya pamyat*, the hymn of memory, the priest blesses the graves, and then they leave me alone, with a candle.

Nations and graves. Graves and nations. Land is sacred because it is where your ancestors lie. Ancestors must be remembered because human life is a small and trivial thing without the anchoring of the past. Land is worth dying for, because strangers will profane the graves. The graves were profaned. The butchers slaughtered on top of the marble. A person would fight to stop this if he could.

Looking back, I see that time in the crypt as a moment when I began to change, when some element of respect for the national project began to creep into my feelings, when I understood why land and graves matter and why the nations matter which protect both.

LVOV

After saying goodbye to the priest and his wife, his son and the choir, we set off for Lvov in the western Ukraine. As the hours pass, the countryside changes, from the flat, black-soil lands of the plain to the rolling and more prosperous villages of the Carpathian foothills. I eat the remains of a boiled duck, the collective farm's parting present to us, and a biteful of the ceremonial greeting loaf from the school. I fall asleep, and wake to the sound of the bus clattering over Habsburg cobblestones.

The Russians call it Lvov. Under the Habsburgs, it was known as Lemberg. To the Jews of the poverty-stricken nineteenth-century Galician stetl, it was their Jerusalem. Ukrainians know it as Lviv. It is one of those fated places in Europe where imperial borders have always met, peoples have clashed and nations have been born. Now it is witnessing the painfully slow birth of the Ukraine.

The sound of the trams grinding and rasping their way through the cobbled crooked streets makes you think of Vienna. The green copper Baroque spires make you think of Prague. But the tired, worn people in the bread shop, their faces lit by the bleary light of a 40-watt bulb, could only be where they are: foraging for food amid the ruins of the Soviet empire. Lvov is a kind of Habsburg Pompeii, perfectly preserved beneath the dust and ash of the Soviet volcano.

Lvov has always been the cradle of Ukrainian independence, perhaps because it once was, not a Ukrainian city, but a Jewish and Polish one, and so the Ukrainian minority had to develop an ideology to be heard above the competing din of other people's.

The city was always the least russified, least sovietized part of the Ukraine. Until 1918, the double eagle of Austro-Hungary graced the top of municipal buildings. Between 1918 and 1939 it was ruled by the Poles, and you can still see the Polish street signs just above the new Ukrainian ones. The Hitler–Stalin pact of 1939 handed Lvov to the Soviets, but the invading German army – supported by some Ukrainain nationalist paramilitaries – drove them out. The Soviet army retook the city in 1945, and it was not until 1956 that the last resistance from Ukrainian nationalist guerilla bands was wiped out. Grizzled survivors of those bands now walk the streets, wearing their old forage caps.

In the more russified eastern Ukraine, Soviet rule could count on some popular support. In the western Ukraine, the Soviets ruled as an army of occupation. The Uniate Catholics were banned, their churches were closed and their leaders imprisoned. Nationalism was defined as fascism, and nationalist families were deported. But it was the western Ukrainian nationalist myth – often nurtured in exile – which is now attempting to make itself the official nationalism of a whole state.

When the late 1980s brought glasnost and perestroika, the repressed force of nationalism returned with a vengeance. The western Ukraine was convulsed with student demonstrations, strikes and religious processions. The mistake which cost Gorbachev his empire was to believe a new Soviet man had been created here. He was to discover just how bitter, enduring and unforgiving national memory can be – in the Baltic, in Georgia, and here in Lvov.

As in Czechoslovakia, Poland and Hungary, nationalism and national revival here mean returning to Europe. Returning to Europe means pulling your nation, like a battered horse and cart, from the muddy ditch that is the Soviet system.

We are Europeans, the waiter tells me in the National Hotel in Lvov's main square. We are Europeans, a Ukrainian MP who once did six years in Siberia, tells me in her tiny, three-room apartment with a statue of a Cossack on her piano and a Ukrainian picture of the Crucifixion on the wall. Being a European here means not being Russian. It means being an individual, taking responsibility, standing up for yourself, all the characteristics the western Ukrainians passionately believe are absent in the Russians.

Being European also means being Catholic. In the western Ukraine, nationalism is a political religion. Since 1596, western Ukraine has had a faith all its own, the Uniate Church, a hybrid of Polish Catholicism and Russian Orthodoxy. The service sounds Russian Orthodox to me, but I didn't dare say that to a Uniate nationalist. The last thing they will admit to is owing anything to the religious traditions of the Russians. When I asked the Ukrainian MP why she continues to hate the Russians, she shrugged, smiled, and said that if you love something – your country – you also have to hate its enemies.

Now is the Uniate faith's hour of glory. In August 1992 they brought home the body of their leader, Cardinal Slipe, who died in exile in Rome. They have reclaimed St George's Cathedral from the Russian Orthodox, and the gilt on the Baroque cupids and the altar screen shines with new radiance. On Sunday, the church is packed with bare-headed men and kerchiefed women of all ages, and when they join the choir in the Alleluia, the sound floats above 700 heads, like a gently billowing canopy.

Standing among men and women who do not hide the intensity of their feelings, it becomes clear what nationalism really is: the dream that a whole nation could be like a congregation; singing the same hymns, listening to the same gospel, sharing the same emotions, linked not only to each other, but to the dead buried beneath their feet.

Every Sunday they dream, and on Monday they return to the sour reality of the queues outside the shops. The promised land is far away here. Independence is a year old, and it will take a generation before the Soviet system is lifted off people's backs. A generation? A tram driver I talk to laughs and shrugs. Two generations, maybe three. The tragedy for those who fought for Ukrainian independence is that they may never live to see the promised land.

The 'dull compulsion of everyday life', as Marx called it, grinds on here. It will exert its compulsion for a long time to come. The nationalists and democrats who fought to bring it down are just realizing that what people here so touchingly call the 'spiritual' benefits of independence are relatively easy to come by. It is getting the phones to work, the food to come to market, the toilets to flush properly which is the hard part of building a nation.

For the moment, everyone knows what the 'spiritual' benefits of independence are. When I ask my tram driver friend what he means by spiritual, he smiles. 'You can kiss your girlfriend in the streets, drink beer in the park, and cross yourself in church.'

It is impossible to be cynical about freedom when you see it in the faces of the young couples who come to hear the Gadukin Brothers, Lvov's best rock-and-roll band, play a free concert in front of the magnificent Austro-Hungarian opera house in the centre of the square. The crowd is wearing a wild array of costumes and funny faces, decked with old Soviet army hats, decorated with the blue and yellow ribbons of independence; a girl walks by with a toy pistol inside a militiaman's holster; nobody is imitating the West here. They are doing their own strange Galician, Carpathian thing, and the Gadukin Brothers up on stage are saying what is on everybody's mind. Through the guitars and drums, you can hear Brother Gadukin sing:

The old red cart went into the ditch
Lenin was the driver
Now the cart is blue and yellow
And no one knows where it is going.

CRIMEA

From Lvov, I travelled overnight by train to Odessa. As with Lvov, Odessa in the nineteenth century wasn't a Ukrainian city at all. Ukrainians were peasants mostly, while a southern port town like Odessa belonged to the Russian navy, the Jewish gangsters and merchants who figure in Isaac Babel's Odessa stories, and the Greek, Turkish, Bessarabian and Romanian merchants who dominated the Black Sea trade in wine and grain. Seventy years of Soviet power, plus German occupation and extermination, have silenced the ethnic babble of old Odessa. Now the Ukrainians have it all to themselves.

We spent all night on the quay at the foot of the Odessa steps waiting for the ferry to leave for the Crimea. No fuel, the ship's purser told me, shrugging his shoulders. As we waited, the decks filled with Azeris and Armenians, Crimean Tartars and Russian families going on holiday, and from the stern of the berthed ferry you could see the steps, like a bolt of black cloth rolled down the heights to the shore.

This is where the baby carriage started to roll in Eisenstein's *Battleship Potemkin*. After independence, a French producer screened the film on the steps themselves and Odessans came out to watch. They hated the film, chiefly for the portrayal of the Cossacks sent to disperse the crowd. Cossacks are heroes to Ukrainians, and on every festive occasion in the Ukraine, you meet fancy-dress Cossacks, in boots and sheepskin hats and capes, with daggers in their belts. That is what independence can do for you: a great film Ukrainians once loved now just seems like a low piece of Soviet propaganda.

I went to bed on the ferry, fully expecting to wake by the Odessa steps again, but, *mirabile dictu*, fuel was found, the ferry sailed and I woke next day to the sight of the Crimean cliffs and the villas and gardens of Yalta stretching up the terraced hillsides. A bus took us along the Crimea coast road that night, past the villa of Foros, where Gorbachev had been placed under house arrest during the August 1991 coup. This whole ravishing southern ledge of Europe, with its cliffs plunging into the sea, was once the preserve of the Moscow elite. No more. The rumour has it that Foros is now used by the Kravchuk family.

The bus brought us to a stop at a roadblock in the dark, sixteen kilometres from Sevastopol. Hushed parleys ensued between translators, minders and the Russian military police. We were to be the first foreigners ever allowed to spend the night in Sevastopol, home base of the Black Sea fleet.

The next morning we find a ferry man in the harbour prepared to take us out for a look. As the captain pilots the ferry-boat *Saturn* into the fingers of Inkerman inlet, I catch my first glimpse of an awesome sight: the Russian Black Sea fleet riding at anchor. The ferry gets in so close its wake tickles their mooring chains, and an endless line of vast grey hulls, some as high as a five-storey house, loom up and pass by over my head. The pages of *Jane's Fighting Ships*, read in childhood, seem to fly by in the bright harbour air: frigates, corvettes, navy tugs, troop ships, landing craft, hospital ships, frigates, minesweepers, destroyers and cruisers. Some are 200 metres long. Their masts bristle with communication aerials and satellite dishes, and their decks are crowded with missiles, anti-aircraft guns, torpedoes and attack helicopters. I try counting them all and lose track after sixty. After an hour's sweep through the many-fingered inlets of Sevastopol harbour, I've still seen only about a third of the fleet.

A graveyard for ships, a Ukrainian friend sniffs disdainfully as we pass them in review. If not a graveyard, then a retirement home. Some of the older ships resemble a line of sea-front codgers in deckchairs. But not all the ships are decrepit. The *Slava*, an 11,000-tonne cruiser barely eleven years old, displays its fangs in the morning sunlight and strains at its anchor chain like an attack dog on its leash.

The Black Sea fleet may be a wasting asset but it is still the twelfth largest naval force in the world, and its 337 ships comprise one third of the total Russian fleet. The deadliest components – the nuclear submarines and the aircraft carriers – are moored elsewhere, in Murmansk and Vladivostok. Yet the Sevastopol fleet still has the force to make Russia a power to be reckoned with throughout the Mediterranean basin, in the Middle East, North Africa and southern Europe. Anyone tempted to write off the Russians as a military power should take a ride on the Inkerman ferry.

The problem for the Russians is that Sevastopol is now in a foreign country. Ukraine claims the base and a portion of the ships, and bitter negotiations between President Yeltsin of Russia and President Kravchuk over a division of the spoils have only produced an agreement to put off the carve-up of the fleet for another three years.

To anyone with a military mind, the situation of the Black Sea fleet is unthinkable. Two states want to run their flags up over it; two admirals compete to give it orders; one of the ships has already bolted to Odessa and run up the Ukrainian flag; and the fleet's future officers, the cadets in the naval academies, were given a vote as to which flag to serve when they graduate. Eighty per cent chose to serve the Ukraine, though as yet the new state has only one coast-guard cutter to its name. No one on board these mighty ships actually knows who will be giving them the orders in a year's time.

In the anteroom of the commander of the fleet, Admiral Kasatonov, his orderlies weren't taking their extraordinary situation too seriously. Captains and commanders, lieutenants and young ratings were all clustered around the television set outside the admiral's office, glued to the smash-hit Mexican soap opera *Even the Rich Shed Tears*.

A worried-looking man in his late 50s, who runs his hands anxiously through wisps of grey hair, Admiral Kasatonov directs his rusting war machine from a bank of a dozen telephones on his desk and a large Compaq computer with a mouse. Looming behind his chair is a portrait of the man who made Russia a Black Sea power, Emperor Peter the Great. The message could not be clearer: Russia is the sole heir of the Russian and Soviet imperial naval tradition. Ukrainians, be warned.

When interviewed, he was all smiling platitudes, briefed by his chiefs in Moscow to say nothing that would add fuel to the fire. The two countries, he assured me in the most emollient way, had the same strategic interests in the Black Sea. He was just a simple military man, who wanted to leave the matter to politicians, who were bound to work out an agreement. But, I persisted, how did he feel, being the commander of a huge fleet whose home base was now on foreign soil? 'What do you mean foreign?' he cut in immediately. 'Just because political formulas change, it doesn't mean that anything essential has changed.' In at least one imperial mind, the idea that Ukraine is independent has not actually taken root.

The same feeling that the empire was still alive and well persisted when I spent the rest of the morning on board one of the Admiral's frigates, the *Ladni*. In the dusty shelves of the captain's cabin, I found that essential navigational aid, Lenin's Collected Works. The captain mustered four sailors for me to interview – a Ukrainian miner's son, two scared boys from Azerbaijan and a Tajik from the fastnesses of Central Asia. They had all been choreographed to say that the fleet was like the empire, one big happy family of nations. When the officers were manoeuvred out of earshot behind a gun turret, the sailors were more forthright. We want to serve the Azerbaijan navy on the Caspian, whispered the Azeri. As for the Tajik, he just wanted to get back to Central Asia as fast as his legs would carry him.

When I came ashore I watched conscript sailors on the dockside shovelling potatoes into buckets and then carrying them, laboriously, up the gangway to the ship's kitchens. Their uniforms were dirty, their complexions were sallow, and their dinner was not going to consist of much more than these same potatoes. Against the background of the unending downward spiral of the two economies, Russia and Ukraine's dispute over the fleet resembles a quarrel between a pair of muddy beggars fighting over the possession of some spuds.

An empire of paupers impoverished its people for seventy years to put a fleet like this in the water in order to scare us. Now nemesis has arrived. It can barely afford to keep up the huge rusting asset riding at anchor here. The Russians still have the power to scare us, but that power is steadily sinking below the waves of economic disintegration. The thought of the sacrifices demanded of the population to keep this fleet riding at anchor left me feeling coldly furious.

That is why the sharpest memory of Sevastopol is not the grey hulls riding at anchor, but a solitary figure resting against the wall of my hotel in the bitterly cold morning I left. She was in her 60s, wore her hair as educated older women do here, in a chignon, and she was wearing the remains of a woollen dress and a cardigan. She might have been a captain's widow, and that is certainly the title of the short story Chekhov could have written about her. For she had no shoes, and her face was chapped and red from sleeping rough, and she lay against the wall of the hotel, too exhausted to move further, weeping tears of pure desolation, amid the broken beer bottles the sailors had left from the night before.

THE TARTARS

The Crimea is the most contested ground in the Ukraine. If Russians are ever likely to fight Ukrainians, it might be here. Ethnic Russians outnumber

Ukrainians in the peninsula; all are stridently aware that the Crimea was ceded by Stalin's successors to the Ukraine only in 1954. There are Russian separatists here, with a party of their own in the local parliament in Simferopol, who want to declare UDI from the Ukraine and seek to restore the republic's status as an autonomous republic, which it enjoyed before the Second World War. Yet although Ukrainians may be outnumbered, they have the whip hand, for all of Crimean power and water comes from the Ukraine. A Russian separatist republic here could be strangled at birth.

Not so easily strangled are the aspirations of the peninsula's oldest inhabitants, the Crimean Tartars, a Muslim people who have been indigenous to the hills of Crimea for a thousand years. In 1942, as the German armies advanced on the Black Sea, Stalin ordered the deportation of the Crimean Tartars *en masse* and had them resettled in Soviet Central Asia. In the early years of Gorbachev, they were the first ethnic group in the old empire to stage a sit-in in Red Square, demanding justice and repatriation. They are now returning in their thousands to settle the hillsides around Bachiseray, their ancestral capital.

Pushkin came here in the 1820s and wrote a poem about the fountains in the palace of the Tartar Khans. The sounds of falling water are in every room. The Soviet guide book tells you about Pushkin, of course, but not a word about the deportation of the people.

On a bare hillside outside Bachiseray, we found a Tartar village, a straggling collection of half-finished breeze-block cottages, surrounded by building materials, in the middle of an abandoned beet field. Seeing us, a woman in a light blue housecoat beckoned to us to come in, and as we did she pointed with pride to a dark green tar-paper shack: our home before we built this, she explains, telling me to leave my shoes at the door.

Now a family of seven lives in the ground floor of what will be a three-storey house, very properly whitewashed and plastered inside, with linoleum on the floor over concrete, and two gigantic TV sets looming over the dinner table.

I had expected a dark-haired, dark-skinned Asiatic people, but most of them have no recognizable ethnic similarity. Some of the men are dark, heavy-bearded and stocky, but others are light-haired, light skinned, look typically Russian and speak Russian fluently. One young woman, sitting by the door, with a thin, pale face, says she was born in Central Asia, can hardly speak Tartar, but her parents were and she is.

They all talk at once. We gave up everything – houses, jobs, gardens – in Central Asia to come here. And now look. A house. And some rows of tomatoes and maize planted in brown topsoil they scrape from roadworks nearby. There is an outhouse among the tomatoes. No running water. It comes in a truck once a week. But there is electricity, and they heat water and grind coffee and serve us dark black Turkish coffee in neat cups, accompanied by honey brought by a relative from Novorrosiysk who keeps bees.

The father is a grizzled man in his 60s in a flat cap, with four or five days of greying beard on his face, scars on his right temple. His wife says, much to his embarrassment, strip him, see him naked, you would see scars everywhere; she laughs and shows her gold teeth. She is wearing a flowered housecoat and ankle-length white socks. The women are formidable, the men sadder, more broken; one lurks at the edge of the conversation, with a thin wasted face, weeping tears, looking away, like an orphan.

I tell him I am the child of people who had to go into exile. We made a new life. Why did they refuse the new life in Central Asia? The father says, 'Only a person who has no mother knows what a mother is, only a person without land knows what land means.'

And the young women with the children chime in: you could go to Canada and start a new life and no one cared if you were Russian, but when we went to Central Asia, they abused and humiliated us just for being Tartars.

And a young man says, 'We were called enemies of the people; half of our people died in deportation; they took the women and children and dumped them in Uzbekistan and they took the men and sent them off to die in the war.'

What do you want? I ask. Your old houses back? No, the woman tells me. I know where my house is. It is in a village a few kilometres away. A Ukrainian lives there now. I don't want to make them go away, like I did. I just want land on which I can build a house and live. And they call us squatters.

What do you want politically? We want a Crimean Tartar Republic. We want what we had until 1939 – the status of an autonomous republic. We don't want to drive out the Russians or the Ukrainians, but we want our own tongue recognized as an official language; and we want to control our schools and our communities and have this whole Crimea recognized by name as the Tartar homeland. We do not want a territorial nation; we want an ethnic nation, one of them tells me.

The lady in the housecoat takes out a crumbling brown piece of paper and passes it across the table. It is her birth certificate, from Stalin's time, from the days of the Crimean autonomous republic of the early 1930s, and what she wants me to notice is that it is written in two languages, Russian and Tartar. 'That is what we want,' she says, crossing her arms. 'What we had before.'

They take me outside and show me the village. A crowd gathers as we go, down a long rutted track with new houses rising on either side, and men waist deep in foundation work put aside their shovels and come up to talk. I ask one of them, who comes out of a trench where he has been digging, whether he will ever allow his people to be deported again. We are a small people, he says, and bigger ones will always do with us what they want. But I am not leaving this place. They will have to kill me first.

A young man, in a faded yellow army jacket, an army cap and a pipe, moustached, perhaps 25, says that when he was a child in Uzbekistan, his parents used to sneak back here to Bachiseray, when it was still forbidden, and they would scoop up some soil from where we were standing and take it back to where they lived. 'And we prayed over this soil and wept over it too.'

I ask the grizzled old man why this particular piece of land means so much and he says, 'This is a sacred place for us. My grandfather, my father, were born here and died here. If I had not pushed my children to return, who would have done it? We would have lost our nation, our culture. We have to piece together, brick by brick, our heritage and culture. Believe me. Otherwise, everything was doomed to be destroyed.'

I fall silent, and watch an old lady in a kerchief eating sunflower seeds cradled in her hand, the old man with the white scarf wiping his eyes; tears also streaming down the face of the old man who has been asked what this land means to him, all silent, staring at this unpromising, rainy hillside, so barren that they have to import topsoil in order to make something grow, a bare hillside overrun by powerlines, piles of building sand and bricks everywhere, and holes in the ground and cats and children running about.

An old woman, in a red sweater and jean skirt with a kerchief around her head and a healthy red complexion, golden teeth, suddenly says, 'I am sixty-three, look at me, why should I give up my house, my work, everything to come out here with nothing and start all over again? Why should I do this, except to be among my people on my own soil and give my children what I never had myself: a home in my own land.'

The young woman behind her listens, and says she is grateful for the old people who kept the nation alive during the darkest time. 'We don't get any money from the government; we don't get anything from anybody. When our people arrive they sleep in our houses; we have twenty-five people sleeping in our places at times. We are not going to wait for anything. We are going to build with our own hands.'

I've never encountered anything like this, a people for whom land has such a sacramental importance. In their discipline and dignity and fierceness they are like Israeli pioneers in the 1930s or the 1940s. What is self-evident to them is the connection between nationhood – narod – and personal dignity. Without nationhood, people sneer at you on the bus; people jeer at you for what you are. It is not enough to be a people. In order to have respect, you must have a nation.

When I ask them why they have survived, they say we must have some gift for it. Plus, we do not marry outside the Tartars. Big peoples can afford intermarriage. We have to have strict rules. And so we have strong families, and respect for our elders is the way we maintain strength and continuity in our traditions. Yet it is obvious from the faces that they have been intermarrying with Russians and Ukrainians for centuries.

I ask them whether they are going to build a mosque in the village. Of course, they all reply, and point up the hill to the place where, according to the plan, it is going to be. Again, in Muslim Central Asia they had freedom of religion, and were surrounded by co-religionists. It made no difference. It was their land they wanted back.

For them an independent Ukraine is more or less irrelevant. The crime was committed by the Soviet Union. They don't really care whether the Ukraine is an independent state or not. What matters intensely is getting the Crimea returned to its status as an autonomous Tartar republic.

I fear the Ukrainian nationalists may be as deaf to Crimean Tartar demands as Russian dissidents were when asked to identify with Ukrainian autonomist demands in the 1970s. Is the Ukraine going to be able to accept a state within a state? Nothing less will satisfy the Crimean Tartars.

KING KONG

From Crimea, I journeyed eastwards to Donetsk, the heart of the Ukrainian coal and steel industry. The Tartars are not the only ethnic group demanding autonomy within the new Ukraine. Many Russian miners and steelworkers in the Donetsk region also are demanding autonomy, to protect their language and education rights.

Donetsk is home of Stakhanov, the coalminer of the 1930s whose heroic and inhuman feats of production at the coalface became central to the productivist iconography of Soviet man. Through the 1980s, coalminers remained the aristocracy of Soviet labour, but with the steady erosion of their wage differentials with other workers in the Gorbachev era, they launched a wave of strikes which helped to weaken Gorbachev's support among the industrial working class. Then, in August 1991, they suddenly found themselves in another country. Once again, they took to the streets, and their demonstrations protesting the decline in their standard of living have been a persistent challenge to the Kravchuk government.

At one of those demonstrations in Kiev in front of the Supreme Soviet, I had waded into a crowd of miners, in their helmets and boots and thick felt jackets. I soon made contact with a huge miner, Vladimir Kolpakov, from Red Star Mine Number 6, Donetsk. Vladimir is a full-bearded, full-bellied giant, known to his mates as King Kong. He was the most voluble of the demonstrators, and when I got to Donetsk I rang him up. His wife told me he was down the mine, so I went out to the mine to find him.

It is a small mine, a hundred years old, employing about 250 men who all know, as they stand outside the dressing rooms taking their last drags on their cigarettes before suiting up for the trip down into the cages, that the place is on its last legs. They tramp off to the cages in their coal-blackened work clothes, beneath a now redundant portrait of Lenin.

The pit head is run by women, wrapped up tightly in scarves and woollen jackets against the freezing damp. They were curiously stylish, these chunky female characters with compact bodies, nicely made up, their mouths full of gold teeth. They slung the coal trucks out of the cages, slammed the doors shut with brisk brutality and operated the antiquated lifts and telephone systems. King Kong, I was told, would be up at the end of his shift. One of the mine ladies took me by the arm and led me to their tea room behind the lift cages, a cosy spot with wooden benches set close to the big heating pipes, and decorated with pictures of Western film stars of the 1950s. There, beneath pictures of Doris Day and Audrey Hepburn, these women drank their tea and joked about me. It was a touching place – infernal, yes, out of Zola, yes, but also dignified somehow. I could feel their camaraderie, their shared sense of danger, even a kind of gaiety.

King Kong finally appeared at the back of the lift, grinning like an enormous dirty raccoon, his face black with coal, his helmet and work clothes dripping wet from the constant stream of water in the shaft. I asked him whether I could go down with him on the next shift and he said: Out of the question. Far too dangerous.

After showering and dressing, he still looked like a giant raccoon, with the coal dust rimming his eyes. He took out his cigarettes, spat out some phlegm and lit up. What about your lungs? I ask him. He shrugs and grins. We have check-ups every year. Besides, he says, with a laugh, 'You just don't feel you've done any work unless you end the day with a cigarette.'

We went back to his flat, four bare rooms on the eighth floor of a co-operative block built by the miners themselves. He pours the vodka and shows me around the flat, which is considerably bigger than those inhabited by deputies in parliament. The miners were indeed the elite of Soviet labour.

But they are an elite fallen on hard times. Inflation is eating away at their monthly pay cheques, and food – in this, the former breadbasket of the empire – is expensive and hard to come by. 'A box of matches used to cost one copec,' he says indignantly, 'and now it costs one rouble and fifty copecs. A loaf of bread used to cost twenty-two copecs and now it costs seven roubles.' Pensioners have been left to their fate.

Instead of dealing with these problems, Vladimir suddenly thunders, the nationalists – meaning the Ukrainians – are spending their time in parliament passing laws to change the signs from Russian to Ukrainian and altering the speaking clock on the telephone to Ukrainian.

But, I counter, the nationalist argument is that it is Russian control of the economy which has kept Ukraine back. If the country could cut loose from Moscow, it would soon be prosperous. Vladimir is contemptuous. 'How can Ukraine exist without Russia? Ukraine has no gas or oil, and there is very little wood left. Can Ukraine live without all these? Sugar has all been sent to Russia.

Nothing is left. Next to us lives a very strong neighbour. We have always been together.'

Like millions of Russians in the Ukraine, he simply cannot get over his amazement that he lives in a foreign country, and that, whereas he once travelled freely there – working in the Vladivostok region, going to see his parents in Perm – now he can't, because he can't afford the rouble–kupon conversion rate. Where the nationalist agenda is not irrelevant, it is actively threatening to Vladimir and his wife. 'Little by little,' he says, 'they are ousting the Russian language.' We always got on well in the Donetsk, he says, not just Ukrainians and Russians but all the nationalities, Jews, Armenians, everyone who lived here.

Mind you, he has nothing against Ukrainian. His wife is Ukrainian and they both speak the language. They don't mind if their son is given Ukrainian classes every day, where he learns to stumble his way through one of Shevchenko's national epics.

If you press him, he admits 'the whole structure' of the former Soviet Union 'was wrong'. 'Sooner or later it was bound to fall apart. Moscow was in charge of everything, and it all came to the point when every republic wanted to break away.'

If so, isn't there some gain in independence? You are free to speak to a foreign writer like me, have him back in your home. You can say what you want in public without being arrested by the police. Yes, his wife says shyly, 'I never thought British people would come to my house.' But Vladimir is still dismissive. He's been on those demonstrations to Kiev. He feels they do no good. 'Yes, I can walk down the street crying "Down with Kravchuk". But nothing has really changed.' If independence has made many Ukrainians feel freer, that is not the case with the Russians inside the Ukraine.

At this stage of the journey, I hate the Ukraine. It is raining. There is no heat in the rooms in the Hotel Ukraine in Donetsk, there hasn't been hot water for days, the bathrooms are disgusting and the one light bulb in the room gives off a weak, yellow smear of light. Everything smells of diesel, wet rags, coal, alcohol, cigarette ends, and body odour. The lobby of the hotel is full of slot machines, and wet teenagers are spending the afternoon there. Various criminals from various southern regions of the ex empire are doing business in the lobby, handing each other plastic bags, counting out cash, sucking on cigarettes. There are a lot of languages being spoken fast and I don't hear any Russian. A burly man carrying a large suitcase enters with bodyguards, approaches the hotel manager. Negotiations ensue, wads of kupons change hands, and the burly man turns to depart, leaving the suitcase behind. I see the hotel cashier open it: chock-full of flesh-coloured condoms.

Waiting by the hotel door, I see a small boy, his blond hair wet from the rain, his sandalled feet sopping, going up to each businessman in the lobby with his hand out. A few absently drop coins into his hand. I watch him slink out of the lobby and disappear into the night.

Being a nation means creating your own way of life. What way of life is this? I could be in any hotel in any part of the empire. The dull, inert compulsion of Soviet existence persists. The windows are never cleaned. The potted palms in the lobby get dustier; the sullen old men at the door push the prostitutes back into the street; the stair carpets are holed; the wallpaper is peeling off; the cashier's office is never open; the gift-shop girl stands, nearly motionless, for hours in front of the little cabinet full of Ukrainian trinkets made of lacquered wood.

THE YOKE

There is a monument in Kiev, a vast steel arch erected to symbolize the eternal friendship of the Soviet and Ukrainian peoples. On my last morning in the Ukraine I pay a cold visit to the place. Beneath the arch are two gigantic heroes of socialist labour, one Ukrainian, one Russian, striding side by side. Also beneath the statue is a stone figure representing Bogdan Khmelnitsky, Cossack warrior king of the 1650s, who threw the Poles out of the western Ukraine and created the first unified Ukrainian Cossack kingdom on both sides of the Dnieper, only to end up putting himself under the suzerainty of the Duchy of Moscow. Khmelnitsky symbolizes all the ambivalence of the Ukrainian tradition, on the one hand fighting against the Polish oppressor, on the other hand submitting to the Moscow yoke. That yoke is still on the Ukrainian people, but not in the manner described by most Ukrainian nationalists, for whom it is a matter now of dependence on Soviet oil, on the rouble zone, on Yeltsin's machinations within the CIS. The yoke they wear but do not talk about is the whole weight of Soviet civilization, and the full weight of it is only to be measured in its totality, in the details: the lifts that do not work, the buses held together by bits of wire and string, the windows smeared with dirt everywhere, the casual brutality of all officialdom, the constant humiliation of workers in a workers' state – forcing a woman to earn her living in one hotel I visited by handing out pieces of toilet paper to every man who entered the downstairs hotel toilet.

You come away from the Ukraine believing that all the rhetoric about nationhood, about the return to Europe, is very distant from the quotidian reality, the vast pile of stone and rubble that must be moved out of Ukraine's past, before it can slowly recover a way of life that is really its own. And nobody knows what that life would be, for there is no visible alternative. Everyone alive now has known only the Soviet way of life. Behind them lies only the nostalgic paradise of pre-revolutionary peasant Ukraine, the lost world now caricatured in the hotel handicraft shops; beyond their borders lies the impossible world of the capitalist West. Impossible, because it is easy to import video cassettes and blue jeans and condoms and hard currency restaurants, but so much more difficult to import Western habits of mind and reconcile them with a Ukrainian way of life, to fuse them with a vision of belonging to the here-and-now. There is a devastating innocence in nationalists' faith in independence. Freedom itself is never the end of the road – only the beginning.

Q U E B E C

THE
FRENCHIES

There were Frenchies hiding in the cemetery, we were sure of that. They were tough Catholic kids and they had slingshots. We all knew they were there, hiding behind the gravestones, waiting to get us. The cemetery was up on the hill above Juliana Road where we lived, and I knew that I shouldn't ever go up there on my bike alone. Everyone at school knew that they pulled kids off their bikes and rode away on their wheels. They were bad kids, it was common knowledge.

Once, we English kids on Juliana got up the courage to lead an expedition into the cemetery. We planned it like a military raid, like General Wolfe sneaking up on the French at Quebec in 1759. We armed ourselves – my pockets were full of the sharp stones the gravel truck dumped on our street – and we fanned out at the base of the cliff leading up to the cemetery, and we advanced from headstone to headstone, right up to the top, just like we had seen it done by the Indians in the US cavalry movies on television. They were bigger than us, that was all we knew, big ignorant boys who spoke nothing but French and used real ball bearings in their slingshots. You could tell they did, because the ball bearings left neat round indentations on the Stop signs at the crossings in the cemetery road.

I was 8 at the time, and I was excited that the older kids on Juliana had let me join the raid. I made a point of how small I was, and how I could get ahead of them, hide behind the gravestones and act like a scout. That was what I did. I was the first to reach the top of the cemetery hill. It was so quiet up there, hiding among the gravestones of the Camerons and Frasers, McDonalds and Robertsons, heaved up into crooked positions by the frost, and above my head, the sound of the autumn maples rustling in the wind. The others were some time making it to the top, so I waited for them, crouched behind a gravestone, keeping watch for the Frenchies, who were supposed to be preparing an ambush for us on the other side of the crematorium. I could hear the English boys sneaking up behind me, taking their positions, and I knew they would be asking me where we should move next, to get closer to the Frenchies. And I knew that I was going to have to say, as I felt the stillness and emptiness of the graveyard all around me, that there were no Frenchies there at all. It was obvious. I am not saying they didn't exist. They were there, all right. It is just that none of us could see them. And we never did.

IMAGINED COMMUNITY

You can never know the strangers who make up a nation with you. So you imagine what it is that you have in common and in this shared imagining, strangers become citizens, that is, people who share both the same rights and the same image of the place they live in. A nation, therefore, is an imagined community. Yet these imaginings never exactly overlap, are never exactly shared. As I look back now, at the Canada I thought we had in common, it strikes me that English and French never did imagine it the same way. The myth I grew up believing was that Canada was a partnership between two peoples, two languages, two histories and two traditions. I believed this, yet I never actually met any Quebecois when I was growing up, although Ottawa, where I lived, was just across the river from Quebec. When I went to Quebec, I went to the Eastern Townships, to the English-speaking part, to a house where my Russian grandparents had lived.

The Canada I thought I belonged to was, believe it or not, an example to the rest of the world. We were a binational, bi-ethnic federal community, living proof that different races, different languages could live together within the framework of a single state. In my imaginings, I turned that dull but intricate contrivance, Canadian federalism, into a moral beacon to the whole benighted world. I had no idea, for example, that what for me was a family romance was, for the other partner, a loveless marriage. As for what came to be known as the First Nations, the native peoples, they didn't figure in my equation of the country at all.

It seems extraordinary, in retrospect,that I should have supposed that we – the Quebecois and I – actually knew each other well enough to constitute any kind of community at all. That childhood memory of the cemetery was actually closer to the truth. Yet is it actually a memory of mine or a fantasy? I had better confess now that I didn't always remember it as I have told it now. For years, I thought I had actually fought the Frenchies. I believed I had seen the big rough French boys, storming down from the heights of the cemetery, chasing us back into Juliana Road with a hail of ball bearings. Now I am quite sure: we never even saw them. They were phantoms to me, as I was to them, and phantoms they have remained.

NATIONALISM AND FEDERALISM

Nationalism is a doctrine which holds (1) that the world's peoples are divided into nations, (2) that these nations should have the right of self-determination, and (3) that full self-determination requires statehood.

Federalism is not a political ideology. It is just a particular way of sharing political power among different peoples within a state. But it is nationalism's political antithesis. Those who believe in federalism hold that different peoples do not need states of their own in order to enjoy self-determination. Peoples who share traditions, geography or common economic space may agree to share a single state, while retaining substantial degrees of self-government over matters essential to their identity as peoples. Federalism is a politics which seeks to reconcile two competing principles: the ethnic principle, according to which people wished to be ruled by their own; with the civic principle, according to which strangers wish to come together to form a community of equals, based not on ethnicity but on citizenship.

The federal states in the world – Canada, Czechoslovakia, Yugoslavia, Belgium, India, the former USSR – have sought to use federal forms of government to arrive at a balance between the ethnic and the civic principle. I am as much a child of a federalist Canada as Salman Rushdie is a child of the India created at midnight, 1947. In both cases, we grew up imagining that we lived in a political community that had found a way to rise 'above' racial and religious tribalism. The Cold War myth that the modern world had moved 'beyond' nationalism depended on the viability of these federalist experiments.

That Cold War landscape 'beyond' nationalism is now unrecognizable. All federal states are in trouble: divorce between Czechs and Slovaks in Czechoslovakia; civil war in Yugoslavia; separatist revolts in India; ethnic warfare in Sri Lanka; the collapse of the federal structure of the USSR; the fragmentation of Belgium; and, since 1963, the rise of separatism in Quebec.

It all began in 1963 when a bomb was left in a letterbox in Westmount, the English-speaking quarter of Montreal. For every English Canadian of my generation, the grainy newsreel of that letterbox, with the policemen running towards it, too late, and the dusty blur of the explosion that followed, marks the beginning of the end of a certain idea of Canada. It was an idea encapsulated by the leafy Westmount street itself. In the newsreel, you can see what a normal, average Canadian street it is – the lawns, the maple trees dappling the light on the sidewalks, that letterbox. It is the picture of the Canada I grew up in: suburban, dull perhaps, but innocent of bitterness and tragedy. When that letter box detonated and when by the end of a decade, an elected Canadian politician had been kidnapped, murdered and his body found in the trunk of a car, the Canada I grew up in began to die. Quebec terrorism was no more typical of Quebec nationalism than IRA terrorism is typical of Irish nationalism. But the idea that there were Quebecois, however few, who hated Canada so much that they would kill in order to destroy it made every English Canadian come awake from the happy daze of the family romance.

I came of age, politically, in a Canada that began arguing about whether it could survive and has been arguing about it ever since. At first the argument was in one dimension – between Quebec and the rest of Canada. Soon, a second dimension was added, with the resurfacing alienation of the Western provinces; and the third dimension arrived in the 1970s, with the emergence of aboriginal rights and their claims to self-determination over huge areas of the Canadian northland. Negotiations in one dimension are complicated enough. When three dimensions are involved, the professionals have to take over. The debate about the national future was confiscated by the political elite, by the experts in constitutional plumbing, and thirty years of our national life have gone by in an atmosphere of political crisis. The crisis remains unresolved. Someone of my generation has spent their entire adult political life wondering whether the country either can or deserves to survive. At this hour, nobody can be exactly sure whether it will.

Other people besides Canadians should be concerned if Canada dies. If federalism can't work in my Canada, it probably can't work anywhere. Canada has the resources to appease the economic resentments that nationalism feeds upon. As a parliamentary democracy, it has a political culture in which nationalist demands can be conciliated by argument rather than repressed by force. Federalism has not failed: the country is still together; but the cost of conciliating nationalism has been a thirty-year stalemate at the heart of the nation's institutions.

The nub of the quarrel is simpler than the infinite complexity of the constitutional negotiations makes it seem. Six million French-speaking North Americans – les Québécois – think of themselves not just as a people, with a language, history and tradition of their own, but as a nation, that is, as a people with a political personality and a right to self-government. They have conceived of themselves in this way, not just since the Quiet Revolution of the 1960s, but ever since Canadian Confederation, in 1867. The word 'nation' has always figured prominently in their public language. In Quebec, for example, unlike any other Canadian province, the provincial assembly is called L'Assemblée Nationale.

The Canadian federation's essential problem has always been that francophone Quebecois identify Quebec as their nation, and Canada as their state, while English-speaking Canadians identify Canada both as their nation and as their state. So long, however, as Quebec believed that it needed the rest of Canada for its own survival, this asymmetry did not prove fatal. Since 1960, however, Quebec has used its powers within the federal system to become a state within a state and to develop its own economy. Quebec has never needed Canada as a nation. Now it is asking itself whether it even needs it as a state.

Age 8, I had scaled cemetery hill in Rockcliffe in search of an enemy who turned out to vanish among the maples. Now, in my 40s, I set off into Quebec, to come face to face, not just with the Quebecois, but with the illusions, the phantoms, which shaped my imagined Canada. I should not have been surprised to discover that they did not imagine Canada as I had done, but I was. The embarrassing fact is that, in the twenty years I lived in Canada, I never travelled in francophone Quebec – I had been to Montreal many times, and just as often to the English communities in the Eastern Townships, but I had never been to Trois-Rivières, never to the Quebec northland, never to the heartland of the French reality in North America. This was in every sense not a return, but a voyage of discovery.

STATE AND NATION

Sixteen hundred kilometres north of Montreal, in a granite cliff-face, a large cantilevered metal door, coloured bright red, slowly begins to rise. The four-wheel drive enters a long descending tunnel, cut out of the rock, and the metal door closes, sealing off the tunnel from the arctic air. At the security checkpoint, the guards check the vehicle and wave it past. After a kilometre, dead slow, the vehicle stops at another, much smaller door.

You are not prepared for what you see when the small door opens. You step into a space as vast as a cathedral, only it is underground, and the walls are quarried out of granite, and the ceiling lights stretch away to the vanishing point, and there are low green instrument panels on one wall as far as the eye can see. Somewhere close by, vast turbines are turning. The floor shakes. The air is charged with a steady throbbing hum. Somebody must be in charge here. There must be a control room somewhere. As you walk through, there are signs of men at work – abandoned golf carts and several mobile tool kits on wheels – but you meet nobody. In this echoing, cavernous space, you are alone.

LG-2 it is called. La Grande Two. The biggest underground powerhouse in the world. Cost: 2.8 billion Canadian dollars. Beneath the floor are ten turbines, driven by the waters of La Grande River. It is seven-fifteen. In Montreal, kettles are being switched on in ten thousand kitchens, heat is being turned up at a hundred thousand thermostats, and in bedrooms from Westmount to Outremont, girls are running their hairdryers. Peak-load time, the guide says. The water is roaring beneath our feet, the turbines are whirring. There is enough power here to heat and light a city of two million.

I ask my guide what she feels. 'Proud,' she says, blushing slightly. Proud that her people had the know-how to dam the river, build the turbines, cut the powerhouse out of this rock. Proud of Quebec.

LG-2 has mythic status in the making of modern Quebec. It stands as the happy ending of a nationalist romance which goes something like this. We were a backward society once. The Anglos of Montreal ran everything. The priests were in charge. Our families were too large. We were poor. We were down on the farm. Not any more. We have come of age. We are proud.

We are masters in our own house now, and LG-2 proves it. With cheap electricity, we can build our own economy. We can export power to the Americans. We can pay our way in the world.

Quebec's nationalization of its hydro-electric resources in 1962 was the first major economic step in its drive to become a state within a state in Canadian confederation. Hydro is as important a constituent of Quebec's national pride as the Aswan Dam was to Nasser's Egypt, as the Kayser aluminium smelter was to Kwame Nkrumah's Ghana. The nationalization of Hydro set in chain the province's economic emancipation. There is now a host of major Quebec economic institutions, entirely independent of Canadian or American ownership. There is the Caisse de Dépôt et de Placement, another key institution of Quebec economic independence, which invests the funds deposited into Quebec's provincial pension fund. It is now the fifth largest pool of investment capital in North America. And then there are the investment funds amassed by co-operative savings banks like Caisse Desjardins, with assets in excess of 45 billion Canadian dollars, and mighty private companies, like Bombardier, which makes skidoos and public transport systems.

From an English Canadian point of view, the irony is that these developments, which make Quebecois feel they need Canada less, might just as plausibly have made them feel they need it more. For Quebec's state capitalism follows a deeply Canadian pattern. Given the small size of the domestic market and the huge size of the country, Canadian government and its business class have always had to work in tandem to develop the nation's infrastructure and resources. Public corporations – from the railways to the airlines to the Canadian Broadcasting Corporation to Hydro-Québec – have always played a more important role in Canadian development than in America. The result of 125 years of state capitalism à la Canadienne has been the emergence of a public culture which is pragmatic, social democratic and left of centre, in Quebec and English Canada alike.

Instead of leading to any discovery of what it has in common with the rest of Canada, Quebec's economic coming of age has confirmed a sense that it can go it alone. As the Quebec business elite has entered, first the North American and then the global market, they have come to look on the Canadian market, and their cultural and political links with the English Canadian business class, as a historical left-over, a relic of a time when they, as Quebecois, were the hewers of wood and drawers of water.

In Montreal, I went to see Claude Béland, one of the men who not only runs the Quebec economy but symbolizes its increasing confidence in the independence option. From an office on the fortieth floor of the Complexe Desjardins, he directs the $40 billion investment fund accumulated by the small savers and investors who bank with the Desjardins savings, loan and credit company. Two generations ago, a man like Claude Béland would not have existed. A Quebecois might have worked as a senior accountant for the English Canadian banking and security houses which ran the Canadian market from Peel Street in Montreal. But a Quebecois would never have had the corner office on the top of a tower, with a view over the ice-bound St Lawrence and his finger on $40 billion worth of investment funds.

Thirty years ago, he says, Desjardins borrowed and invested entirely within the Canadian market. Now, more than half of their business is overseas. Quebec has taken up its place at the big table of international finance.

Claude Béland looks like a North American bank president: silver-haired, immaculately suited in sober blue, with a fluent English which he uses to take calls from fellow bank presidents in Chicago, New York, Los Angeles and London. Yet what other major North American bank president's native tongue is French? What other North American bank president is a nationalist?

He wasn't to begin with. Like the cautious accountant that he is, he thought sovereignty was too risky an option in the 1970s and early 1980s. Now, he has changed his mind. Why?

'Well, because a state is the only way to protect the identity of a people, you know. Identity I define as the harmony between your values and your actions. In other words, you know who you are and you want to protect that ... and be recognized for that.'

It seems odd to me that a bank president should be talking about such metaphysical entities as identity, so I ask him whether statehood matters because it confers identity or because it completes an economic emancipation. Which is it, the pocket book or the soul? Béland doesn't want to have to choose. Independence, he says, is about both dimensions. We have one layer of government too many. Quebec is like a company 'with two finance managers, two marketing directors, two vice-presidents for resources'. We only need one of each, and we want them to be Quebecois. I asked him whether he was worried about Quebec's place in the coming North American Free Trade Area, linking Canada, the United States and Mexico. Anxieties about cultural and economic survival are endemic in English Canada. But not among Claude Béland's circle. 'No, people do business with us, not because of our politics, but because we are good buyers, and we make good products.'

As the president's public relations people show me out, down the long broad-loomed corridor in the executive suite, I find myself puzzling over the paradox that, as men like Béland join the global economy as players, they become more, not less interested, in national sovereignty for a little corner of the globe called Quebec. I had assumed that global players ceased to care about nations. I was wrong. Here was a man, in other words, who believed that the coming of continental free trade and globalization of capital markets strengthened, rather than weakened, the case for a sovereign Quebec.

English Canada looks at Quebec's economic development since 1960 – symbolized by a man like Claude Béland – and says, 'If you can do all this within Canada, why not stay?' Canada is already the most decentralized federation in the world. Quebec looks at its own transformation and says: 'Why do we need to?'

NATIONALISM AND THE
FOLKLORE OF
BACKWARDNESS

There is a further paradox here. Once upon a time, English Canadian domination of the Quebec economy was blamed, by nationalists, for the province's relative economic backwardness. You might expect economic nationalism to ebb as economic backwardness is overcome. Not so – at least if Quebec is any guide. Here is a people who have caught up economically in two generations. They no longer feel dominated by the Anglo-Canadian elite of Montreal. If you ask when they last were made to feel ashamed to speak French, they have to go back to their father and mother's times, or to their childhood, when Ritz Carlton Bar on Sherbrooke Street or the T. Eaton department store would not serve you unless you spoke English. These memories are no longer personal: they are from the mythic bad old days. One would expect that nationalist feeling would ebb as personal memory dissolves into myth. If anything, the contrary has been the case.

Isaiah Berlin once likened nationalism to a bent twig, which, if held down, will snap back with redoubled force once released. The twig in Quebec has long since been released, yet its force is far from spent. What does this mean? First that grievances do not cease to be actual, just because they are in the past. Collective myth has no need of personal memory or experience to retain its force. The English conquered Quebec 234 years ago. On the Plains of Abraham, in Quebec

City, where the battle was fought, nowadays children play with their sleighs and the Carnaval de Québec spills its horn-tooting, beer-drinking crowds all over its slopes. The Conquest is ancient history. No matter. Quebec nationalists still describe the nationalist project as 'la reconquête de la conquête': the reconquest of the conquest. Yet the plain fact is that Quebec nationalism has mythologized a nation's defeat at the very moment Quebec finally overcame it.

Nor is this the only paradox. Quebec nationalists insist on the cultural and social distinctiveness of their society at exactly the moment it is losing so much of what made it distinctive. In the 1950s, when it stood on the eve of its great leap forward, Quebec was, in every sense, a distinct society. Backwardness, after all, is a form of distinctiveness. Quebec had a predominantly small-town, agricultural population which lagged behind the Canadian one in education and literacy; its public culture was authoritarian; demographically, its family structure was unique in North America, with families of ten children the norm.

Quebec's Quiet Revolution was meant to overcome the distinctiveness of backwardness, and it has succeeded. From having the highest birthrate in North America, Quebec now has among the lowest. From having the worst educated population in North America, Quebec now has among the best. From being the most devoutly religious community in North America, it is now among the least observant. From having an authoritarian political culture, it now prides itself on the freedom and openness of public debate.

Quebec's distinctiveness used to be like that of the Appalachians or the American South, a regionalism anchored in relative rural poverty. Now, just like these other regions of North America, it has opened itself up to a continental way of life. To an outsider, the Quebeckers hitting the road for cottage country on a Friday night, in their Cherokees and Winnebagos, baseball hats on their heads, radios tuned to the local country and western station, could be in Minnesota or any other American state or Canadian province. Until they open their mouths, that is.

All of Quebec's anxiety about its modernization, its incorporation into the North American grain, has focussed on preservation of language. La survivance is, above everything else, the survival of a language. The core demand of Quebec nationalist politics has been that Quebec become a unilingual nation. Nationalists fetishize language, yet the obsession that all signs, including Stop, should be in French is comprehensible if one is aware that signage is often the only sign that one is in Quebec, and not Minnesota or Vermont.

Nationalism has often been a revolt against modernity, a defence of the backwardness of economically beleaguered or declining classes and regions from the flames of individualism, capitalism, Judaism and so on. Until the 1960s, Quebec nationalism often spoke in this tone. It does not do so now. This in itself is surprising. Given the speed with which modernization of the society has occurred since then, it might have been expected that Quebec nationalism would become a vocabulary of regret for what modernity has done to the distinctiveness of Quebec society. On the contrary. Nationalists invariably stress that theirs is the cause of modernity, of the reforming, secular state: attacking the power of the Church in education and moral life, advancing women's rights and sexual freedom, seeking to give Quebec a secure place at the very heart of the North American economy. In Quebec, being a nationalist means being a progressive, being modern, being a French North American.

The contrast between English Canadian and Quebecois attitudes to Americans is striking. In English Canada there has been an anguished debate for generations as to whether Canadian culture can preserve its distinctiveness amid the nightly electronic deluge of up to sixty cable TV stations in most Canadian homes. At Videotron, Quebec's largest cable TV company, they beam all the American soaps into Quebec homes, but they know that the most popular shows – the ones that get up to 80 per cent of the Quebec population staying home at night – are the ones written and acted in Quebec. As long as they can see what they want in their own language, Quebecois believe their culture will be secure.

Quebecois think of their language as a kind of invisible shield protecting their cultural integrity from the North American norm. The French language allows Quebecois a degree of cultural self-assurance towards the Americans which English Canadians can only envy. Yet the same Quebecois display none of the same self-assurance in relation to their own non-French-speaking minority. They incessantly fear that their declining birthrate and the rising tide of non-francophone immigration will dilute the French presence in North America. They seek controls of immigration policy to maximize the selection of French speaking immigrants. They legislate to restrict the rights of people to send their children to English-language schools. The language police are despatched to happily bilingual towns in the Eastern Townships to photograph tiny English cardboard signs in corner stores. Storekeepers are prosecuted, much to the irritation of bilingual anglophones and francophones alike. There is a pettiness in language politics which belies the cultural self-confidence the Quebecois project about their capacity to survive and flourish.

AT THE
TWO CLOWNS CAFÉ

At the Two Clowns Café in old Montreal, on an arctic night, I meet a group of half a dozen nationalist Quebecois to talk about language. On my part, this encounter is charged with the same expectation I felt, age 8, climbing that cemetery hill. Now, as then, I am going to meet the Other. This is ridiculous, I know. After all, don't we have the same passports? Drink the same beers – Molson, Labatt? Aren't our memories full of the same heroes – Maurice

Richard, Jean Béliveau, of the immortal Montreal Canadiens of the 1950s? Yet our political assumptions turn out to be so different that we might as well be living in different countries.

In the group at the Two Clowns is Nicole, exactly my age, an organizer for Quebec's teachers' union, the CEQ. Her union is independentist and so is she. Nicole and I discover that we share sports heroes, literary ones too (Parisian writers), and an affection for the hard bright winter mornings after a snowfall. We also share a memory: the October crisis of 1970. For me, it was the moment when the Canadian government broke the back of radical nationalism in Quebec. The Prime Minister, Pierre Trudeau, ordered the arrest of more than 500 Quebecois intellectuals and militants, following the kidnap and murder of a Quebec politician, Pierre Laporte. For Nicole, it was the moment she discovered she could no longer call herself a Canadian. For she was among those arrested, held without trial and then just as suddenly released. 'And why?' she says angrily stubbing out her cigarette. 'Not because I was making bombs in my basement. I wasn't. But because I had certain friends.' This was a moment of fissure between us, a moment which mutual good will and an affection for the same things could not overcome. For me, Trudeau remains the champion of that ideal of federalism I have wanted to believe in all my life. For Nicole, he is the betrayer, the native son who would stop at nothing to smash the nationalism of his own people.

Beside Nicole, who dominated proceedings with her outspoken convictions and raucous laughter, there were some young postgraduates finishing up their doctorates in law and anthropology, together with a young, soft-spoken blonde woman who was the chair of one of the oldest moderate nationalist societies in Quebec, the Société Jean Baptiste, which among other things organizes the great parade through Montreal on Quebec's national day, 28 June.

It was a typically Montreal conversation, switching between English and French with astonishing rapidity. Why, I asked, did Quebec have to be unilingual, if all of them were so fluently bilingual? Because, the president of the St Jean Baptiste society said, 'there are six million of us, and two hundred and fifty million of you in North America.'

Besides, said a young female anthropology student, 'the immigrants arrive here and they all want to learn English and if they do, we will lose Montreal.'

'Lose Montreal?'

'Yes! Lose Montreal. It will become an English-speaking island in a French nation, and that is intolerable.'

'Intolerable,' they all said.

'You all worry about survival. But you *have* survived, for God's sake. Why are you so worried?'

The woman from the St Jean Baptiste society replied, 'Yes, we have survived, but look at the cost. We would have been twelve million by now, but half of us left for the States.'

'You want to stop them?'

'Of course not. But the point is, we are surrounded by a foreign civilization and we must protect ourselves.'

I still couldn't understand it. The language is completely secure. The signage laws ban the public use of English. Quebec, alone among Canadian provinces, enjoys substantial jurisdiction over immigration and has secured the right to recruit French-speaking immigrants. The English public-school board is not allowed to accept pupils of French-speaking parentage (although the private English schools are full of children of Quebecois who want their children to grow up bilingual).

'There,' says one. 'What other society allows a publicly funded school system in a language other than the majority?'

'Fine,' I replied. 'I'm not saying Quebecois are intolerant. You're not. I'm asking why do you feel so insecure. Why do you believe your language needs a state of your own to protect it?'

'We are not insecure,' Nicole says, with exasperation. 'We just want to be at home, with ourselves.'

'Yes, frankly, we are tired of being a minority in Canada. We want to be a majority in our own place.'

'Whoah,' I cry. 'That sounds ominous. What about the tyranny of the majority?'

'That's not tyranny, that's just democracy,' says one bespectacled law student.

'Suppose you're right,' I say. 'Suppose you need a state to protect your language. Are you sure it's viable?'

'Of course. We are Quebec Inc!'

'But what if you're wrong? *You* won't pay the price – you all have qualifications. You know who will pay? The pulp workers in Trois Rivières. They're the ones who'll pay for a nationalist experiment that goes wrong.'

'What a vicious statement!' Nicole exclaims, in mock fury. 'Apologize. Apologize.' She is laughing, but also half serious.

'Answer the question.'

'I work for a union, dear. Don't tell me about the workers. Don't divide us either. They are as much for independence as we are.'

And so it goes, as the beer empties accumulate at our table, and the bar gets noisier and noisier. Some of the group say nothing, as if holding something back, letting the pressure inside them build. In a hush between songs from the bar band, a young woman anthropology student says to me, very quietly, 'Look, we just want a place where they treat us like adults. We just want to be treated like grown-ups, not like children.' She is close to tears, and it dawns on me, in the silence that follows, that in her imagining of this community that we are supposed to share, she sees it as a family, where I, and my English kind, are the parents who never listen, and her Quebec is the young woman desperate to take her place in the world as an adult.

What can you say to such a deep myth? It is a feeling, and notoriously, feelings cannot be argued with. But they may be as productive of mischief as my childhood belief that there were Frenchies at the top of the cemetery cliff who would steal our bicycles if they could.

It is late at the Two Clowns and time to go. As I draw my winter coat around me in the frigid arctic air outside, one of the young men who had said nothing all evening comes up and whispers quietly, 'It's strange how loud we talk, isn't it? As if we Quebecois were still trying to convince ourselves of something.'

TWO CONVERSATIONS

Lise Bissonnette is my age, pert and businesslike, a newspaper editor, a columnist, a complicated and subtle supporter of sovereignty for Quebec. I talk to her in the new offices of her paper, *Le Devoir*, founded by the great nationalist hero of Edwardian Quebec, Henri Bourassa.

No, she said, she didn't want to be called a nationalist. 'The narrow sense of a nation, you know, the ethnic meaning of the word nation' – she made a gesture of distaste – 'it's foreign to me.' It is curious how few people anywhere, when seen to be nationalists from the outside, think of themselves as nationalists from the inside. The word, she says, suggests closing in on yourself, and for her culture in Quebec should be open to the world.

I ask her whether being a nationalist, in the Quebec context, necessarily means a commitment to the sovereignty of an independent Quebec state. Through most of its history inside Canada, Quebec nationalism has been about getting more from Canada, not about getting out of Canada. So I tell her the old joke – 'What Quebec wants is a sovereign Quebec inside a united Canada' – and ask her whether it remains true. 'Of course,' she says. 'Why not? Everywhere in the world, people want it both ways. There are risks to independence, so Quebeckers may not love Canada, but they like it, and they want to keep the links, as a kind of reassurance.' Even when they voted for Trudeau, she says, Quebeckers were not necessarily voting for federalism and for Canada. They were voting for one of their own. 'They were playing tribal politics.' Trudeau himself would be surprised to hear this. His view of Quebec nationalism was that it is a language game played by the local elite to wrest maximum advantage from Ottawa and to ensure their domination of provincial politics. Ordinary voters, he insisted, see through the game, and when they vote for him, they vote for Canada.

But why, I persist, do you need a state if you already have exclusive jurisdiction in so many fields? Not true, she counters. Federalism in Canada 'is getting to be more centralized by the day. The federal government is entering the field of education and manpower training and we must resist that.' That is not how English Canada sees it. It has rejected proposals for the further decentralization of the federal system on the grounds that the country itself will not survive further provincial autonomy. Again, what is or is not true is not at issue. The crucial point is that our imagining of the same community barely intersects at all.

Why, I ask her, do Quebecois invest so little emotion in the idea of federalism, in the vision of two peoples living together within a single state? She leans forward on her desk and is briskly dismissive. 'First of all, English Canadians have been saying that for a very short time. You didn't hear much about that in the Sixties, when people were still fighting against the simple idea that French could be an official language in this country. In my view, the dream of the binational state is a Toronto cultural establishment way of seeing the country, and it is not shared by the majority of the people.'

But, I persist, in a world being torn apart by ethnic nationalism, isn't there something to be said for a federalism which keeps ethnic groups living together in peace? She won't budge. That's an English Canadian idea, she says, politely but firmly. Canada has failed. It says it is a bilingual, bicultural state. But go to Halifax or Vancouver and you'll see it's not true. The only place that approaches the ideal is Montreal. Quebec, she seems to be saying, has turned out to be better at practising the multi-ethnic, multicultural ideal than Canada itself.

She's not sure she'll ever see a Quebec with its own foreign embassies and its own seat at the United Nations. But she does believe that all the momentum of Quebec's history is leading it away from Canada.

Alain Dubuc is chief editorialist for *La Presse*, Montreal's largest French language daily. He describes himself as a 'non-separatist nationalist', someone who feels, in other words, that his nation is Quebec, but his state remains Canada. Mind you, he says, 'I don't really care about Canada. I don't have much energy to put into that country. All my energies go towards Quebec.'

But if you feel so little for Canada, I ask, why do you want to stay in confederation? 'Because,' he says, with an engaging laugh, 'we're stuck with it. We're two organisms that have grown together and created some bonds, and these are strong.' After all this time, separation would be cumbersome, expensive, risky.

If that is so – and it must be true that the separation would be costly and traumatic – why do some Quebecois nationalists continue to insist upon it? You must remember, he says, that our parents did really suffer. 'They were not black South Africans, but they were poor, and they didn't have as many chances in life as the anglophones in Quebec. They had to bow to the English, and they had to speak English when they didn't want to. We still have this image of being "*porteurs d'eau*", hewers of wood and drawers of water. It is part of our folklore, and our nationalism is also part of our folklore.'

But that would imply, I suggest, that the nationalist agenda is just about settling old scores. And if it's just about settling old scores, is it relevant to today's Quebec? Dubuc smiles and shrugs. 'Of course it's not. How do we adapt to globalization of the economy? How do we deal with thousands of people arriving from other cultures? In an independent Quebec these problems would be exactly the same.'

In that sense, therefore, the separatist agenda in Quebec is irrelevant? Dubuc nods. 'The separatist nationalists have a very nineteenth-century conception of the state, which has a government, an army, a flag, a place in the United Nations, this kind of thing. Having a state is a very costly tool, and it's not obvious that if you separate, you will solve your problems. So having your own borders, boundaries and flags . . .' He waves his hand dismissively. 'It's a kind of dream.'

If that's the case, however, why has the ideal of a bilingual, binational Canada never caught on in Quebec? Dubuc smiles. 'The irony is,' he says, 'that the only place in Canada which approaches this ideal, the only place where you find French- and English-speaking people working together, is in Montreal.'

So, I say, 'Quebec is the only place where the Canadian dream – my Canadian dream – actually worked out.'

'Exactly,' he says with an ironic smile.

If these two conversations were any kind of guide to what the writers, journalists and editorialists of Montreal argued about, it was clear that there was no impassioned and convinced defence of federalism left in Quebec. Trudeau and his generation of Quebecois labour leaders, writers and civil servants had fought for a Quebec at home in Canada, but the only people they seem to have convinced with their idea of the binational, bilingual state had been the English Canadians. And this conversion, which began in the late 1960s, came too late. For by this time, the tide of Quebecois opinion had moved irrevocably away. What my conversations with these two journalists seemed to show was that Trudeau's generation had had no children in Quebec.

This does not mean that there are no defenders of Canada in Quebec. The polls seem to indicate a three-way split: a steady third of the electorate opposed to any variant of the sovereignty option, a third in favour, and a third who can be convinced either way. But what seems evident is that, if Canada has defenders, they are like Dubuc – disabused, unemotional ironists who think that sovereignty is an outmoded nineteenth-century abstraction, irrelevant in a modern global economy. On the opposing side are figures like Lise Bissonnette, who argue that the struggle to keep Canada together is a wasteful diversion of the Quebec elite's attention. It should turn its eyes exclusively to the business of building a Quebec culture and economy. Thus the essential argument within the Quebec elite is within terms set by nationalist argument, i.e. between those who believe a nation must have its state, and those who believe the nation can achieve everything it wants without one.

English Canadians still ask, with anguish and perplexity, what is the grievance in French Canada that would justify separation. But that may be the wrong question. Nationalism in Quebec has long ceased to be the nationalism of resentment. The old scores have been settled. It is now a rhetoric of self-affirmation. The basic motive driving it is no longer the memory or myth of past injustice; the motive that counts is the sense of power and accomplishment. It is a nationalism less and less hostile to English Canada, simply because for most Quebecois, as Anglo-Canadian domination of the economy has receded as an issue, English Canada as a whole has become less and less relevant. As Alain Dubuc said, 'I like visiting there but it is still a foreign country.'

It could almost be said that Quebec was bound to Canada only so long as it could construct a rhetoric of resentment around the relationship. Federalism is like some marriages which cohere, paradoxically, because both parties are united in their grievances towards each other. Now that these grievances are ebbing, they have less and less reason to share the same bed.

Quebec has ceased to define itself in terms of Canada. Both sides in the political debate inside Quebec take it for granted that a place like LG-2 has given Quebec the economic independence, the confidence in itself, that a people needs to become a nation state. Both sides of the argument, in other words, feel the power of those Quebec turbines beneath their feet, as reality and as symbol. The only remaining question is whether they need to run a sovereign state's flag up over the powerhouse.

TRIBE AND NATION

One essential problem with the language of self-determination and nationhood is that it is contagious. Quebec has discovered a people within who also call themselves a nation.

About sixty-five kilometres away from the big red door which leads to LG-2 sits a trapper's cabin, in the middle of a vast, flat expanse of snowy pine forest. A fire is going in the stove, and I am readying my snow gear for a day with Billy.

Billy is a Cree hunter, and these frozen forests are his kingdom. We are in the middle of the Cree nation, a vast expanse of forest, river, marshland and lake roughly the size of Germany. Billy's people, now numbering about 11,000, have been hunting and fishing in this land for 5000 years. Like many aboriginal peoples they have taken up the European word 'nation' to describe themselves, and while the word may not be native to their language, they definitely seem to be one. They have their own language and oral tradition, a way of life, based around cabins and trap-lines, and a knowledge of their environment so detailed it could be called a science.

Billy slings his carbine over his back, starts up his skidoo, and gestures to me to get into the blood-smeared sled that he has hitched up behind. Then we are off, hurtling through the forest trails, with fir branches snapping against my goggles and plumes of snow flying up behind. From time to time, Billy stops to examine the caribou tracks in the snow, while I stamp my feet and rub my face to keep from freezing.

Suddenly the caribou break into the clearing in front of me, a pair of large males, the size of horses, with shaggy, cream-coloured coats and ears bent in fear. They are close enough for Billy to get off a clear shot, but he pulls up instead, and we watch them bucking and plunging in the waist-high snow, struggling to make the safety of the tree cover. Within a few seconds they have vanished and the silence of the forest returns.

Billy worries that the caribou are deserting his country. His traps are empty too, and the hooks don't bring in the fish they used to. His village was moved to higher ground, his trap-lines were bisected by power lines and fire breaks. The mercury levels in the new reservoirs are poisoning the fish. His land is changing before his eyes. His misfortune, and the misfortune of his tiny nation, is that they stand in the path of the LG project. Hydro-Québec has dammed Billy's river, creating huge reservoirs and flooding his hunting grounds. The river is no longer his. It belongs to the white man from the south.

The word 'belong' and the idea of property that goes with it are as alien to the Cree as the word 'nation'. Nationalism may be one form of Western romanticism about nature, but in the Western tradition, patriotism is related to property and implies unlimited dominion over nature. To Crees, this is an alien and offensive concept. Billy does not believe he owns the land; he believes he is part of it, one of the creatures who depends upon it, not only for his life but for his vision of the world. Western nationalism, when seen beneath Billy's frozen blue sky, sixteen hundred kilometres north of Montreal, is not a rhapsody to the land, but a song of domination and capture. Nationalism celebrates the land of a nation the better to subdue it to human purposes. Billy's claim is to be its steward and servant.

The Cree have had money rained on them in compensation – hundreds of millions of dollars – for the taking of the land. They have trailer homes now, four-wheel drives, skidoos, and a guaranteed annual income from the government. Their village has a new community centre, and there is a supermarket where you can buy fresh apples and tomatoes. There is a new hockey rink where the teenagers can play in the evenings. But nobody forgets what has been lost. Even the teenagers circle the ice wearing hockey shirts which say 'Ex-Hunters of Chisasibi'.

The James Bay project is the powerhouse of a potential independent Quebec. Quebec calls it modernization, development, progress. Billy calls it an invasion. The rights of two nations are in conflict. One is very large, has multibillion dollar resources to put into place. The other is very small. All it has on its side is an argument: if you claim self-determination for yourself, how can you deny it to us? For Billy and the Crees, the dams, the power stations, the hydro lines, the reservoirs, are a symbol too – of their expropriation. The Cree are fighting back, and like aboriginal peoples all over the world, they are resorting to the language of nationhood and self-determination themselves. They are doing so because they shrewdly perceive that it is a language which hoists the Quebecois on their own petard. In documents filed with the UN Commission on Human Rights in New York, Matthew Coon Come, grand chief of the Crees, spells out his people's claim.

> Self-determination is a right which belongs to peoples. It does not belong to
> states. It is a right of all peoples. It is universal and non-divisible, that is,
> either you have it or you do not. It is not a right that is given to peoples by
> someone else. Please understand, you may have to fight to exercise this
> right, but you do not negotiate for the right of self-determination because it
> is yours already.

This rhetoric alarms Quebec. Self-determination appears to mean something different than self-government. Quebec has been quick to concede the latter, while denying the former. 'The only limit to aboriginal autonomy will be the integrity of Quebec territory,' a Quebec minister of native affairs said recently. He went on, 'In this sense, there is no question of permitting the creation of ethnic ghettos where the laws of Quebec would no longer take precedence.'

The Crees believe that self-determination is compatible with the territorial integrity of the state they live in. Self-determination need not be absolute; it need not imply formal statehood, flags, seats on the United Nations. In any event, the Crees are quick to point out, these are white men's inventions. Self-determination means an end to permanent dependence on government handouts and an end to being the passive spectators of the destruction of their lands. It implies something more than exclusive fishing and hunting rights over territory in the hydro-electric development; it implies more than the right to put up a checkpoint on the road into the main villages to limit the inflow of alcohol; it means something more than municipal self-government. Above all, it means stopping further hydro-electric development. The Quebec government has its eye on the Great Whale River system, to the north of La Grande; as well as on the Nottaway, Broadback and Rupert river systems to the south. If both were completed, the entire Cree nation – its rivers, forests and encampments – would be bound, hand and foot, imprisoned within a tight network of power lines, roads, dams and powerhouses. The Crees would become survivors on their own homeland.

And for what? The costs of development in the region are astronomically high – $12–15 billion. Already something like 40 per cent of every consumer's electric bill is spent servicing Hydro-Québec's debt for existing projects. Cheap power, Quebec says, is the core of its competitive advantage in the North American economy, and its electricity rates are among the lowest in North America. But they are cheap only if the debt load of development in the north is kept out of the equation. If the new projects go ahead the debt load will become crippling, and if energy-efficiency measures cause demand to drop, that load could become catastrophic. In other words, national development is pressing up against the very limits, not merely of the Crees' environment, but against the carrying capacity of the Quebec nation too. The future demand for Quebec power is uncertain. The North-Eastern American states are not looking to sign new contracts for Quebec power; in several cases, the Crees have been able to persuade American regulatory authorities to cancel such deals.

If Quebec were to say, enough is enough, some compromise between the nationalisms in conflict in the north of Quebec might be possible. Self-determination for the Cree does not mean statehood: it means cultural and economic survival, which in turn means being able to preserve a hunting, trapping and fishing economy in the interstices of a major economic development. Aboriginal ways of life have demonstrated enormous flexibility: the gun, the skidoo, the CB radio are all effortlessly absorbed into the traditional Cree hunter's way of life. But they need time to adjust, they need guarantees that further encroachments will not occur. There is no overwhelming economic argument for further construction.

If Quebec does proceed with Great Whale, and with the destruction of the Cree nation, it will do so because the rhetoric of national pride will have prevailed over economic good sense. The trouble with nationalism, as applied to economics, is that it invests projects with a symbolic importance which makes governments blind to realities. If the James Bay project is what the Aswan Dam was for Egypt's Nasser, what Kwame Nkrumah's hydro-electric and aluminium smelting projects were to post-independence Ghana, the message is one of warning. In these two latter examples, declarations of national independence took their societies to the edge of bankruptcy. It remains to be seen whether nationalist hubris will lead Quebec to overplay its hand. Quebec is neither Ghana, nor Egypt. It is an advanced and developed society. But the risks are there. When economic development is vested in the imperatives of national pride, nemesis awaits.

RIGHTS AND SURVIVAL

Cree and Quebecois both argue their demand for national self-determination in terms of cultural survival. This link between survival and self-determination is central to nationalist claims everywhere, but it deserves sceptical examination.

The survival of Crees as individuals is not in doubt: their birthrate, per capita income and level of education are all increasing. Given these facts they can certainly survive as individuals who think of themselves as Crees. Whether they can survive as a nation, that is, as a distinct people with a way of life rooted in the land, is less certain. You could take the view that it should be up to the next generation – the teenagers cruising the ice in their Ex-Hunters jerseys – to determine whether to remain true to the hunting and fishing economy which sustains the culture. If so, then it is not survival itself, but the right to choose which way to survive that is at issue. The old ways of life must be preserved so that the freedom of choice of future generations can be preserved.

In order to preserve that choice, the Canadian federal government has begun turning local government, policing and justice over to native peoples. Already, in many native communities of the north, justice is jointly administered by native elders and magistrates from the south. Canadian law remains paramount, but these communities enjoy a degree of self-administration which the Italian or Chinese peoples of southern Canada, for example, do not enjoy.

Meeting the claim of cultural survival, therefore, implies that native Canadians may come to have more rights of self-government than those enjoyed by the rest of the population. Provided that these rights do not infringe on the rights of other Canadians or amount to secession from the Canadian state – and they do not – federalism can thus accommodate some asymmetry in the rights individuals enjoy within a state.

But can federalism accommodate a situation where group rights accorded to one national people appear to encroach upon the individual rights of those who do not belong to that national group? This, at least for English Canadians, is the moral challenge represented by Quebec language legislation, which restricts signage in English and restricts access to English-language education.

Nationalists in Quebec maintain that entrenching the French language is the precondition for the very survival of Quebecois identity. They live on a continent of 300 million English speakers; their native birthrate is declining and every day immigrants arrive whose first language is not French and whose first preference in learning a new language is English.

Here the stand-off between Quebecois and English visions of political community is complete. Quebecois nationalists simply deny that basic freedoms *are* being curtailed by signage legislation; while the anglophone community simply denies that Quebecois cultural survival is at stake.

The same stand-off can be observed in the Baltic republics. In the Latvian republic, for example, the fact that ethnic Russians are in a majority in Riga, the capital, is held to justify a new citizenship law which makes the capacity to speak Latvian a condition of Latvian citizenship. Ethnic Russians born and brought up in Latvia lose their citizenship in the new republic unless they learn the rudiments of Latvian. As a minority, they lose the right to speak their language whenever and wherever they please for the sake of the cultural survival of the ethnic majority.

These are not just disagreements about rights; they are also disagreements about the very purpose of the state. Liberals tend to argue that states should not have purposes: any state which wishes to further some collective end will necessarily trample on the rights of those individuals who oppose that end. The federal policy of bilingualism, on this view, is a classic piece of liberal neutralism – protecting the rights of both linguistic groups, while privileging neither. To a Quebec nationalist, however, the state cannot afford to be neutral when the cultural survival of the nation is at stake. In the real world of modern nations, English – being the language of global commerce – will sweep other languages aside.

Many Canadian liberals – led by Pierre Trudeau – have argued that when a state protects collective rights, whether they be Quebecois or aboriginal, the result is inevitably to infringe on individual rights. The cardinal sin of nationalism, on this account, is that it invariably results in some form of majoritarian tyranny. In this sense, therefore, Trudeau has warned, Quebec may be an example of an ethnic state in the making. As long as it remains within Canada, its language policies can be constrained and in some cases overruled by reference to the Supreme Court and the Canadian Charter of Rights. Should Quebec become sovereign, individuals would lose this right of appeal, and the way would be open to majoritarian ethnic tyranny.

There is little doubt that the gut appeal of Quebec nationalism lies for most Quebeckers in the vision of being a majority in their own society rather than a permanent, if powerful, minority within a federal Canada. But most Quebeckers insist that theirs is not an ethnic but a liberal nationalism, based on equal citizenship. What other society, I kept being told, funds a public-school system in a language other than that of the majority? What other society has such a full panoply of human rights protection as that enshrined in the Quebec charter of rights?

What other nation, they also add, does not take steps to protect and develop the language of its cultural majority? All nations decree which languages will have official status, all nations run school systems in the language of the majority. The liberal ideal of a purely procedural state, one which took no view as to what language or values should be taught in the state's public schools, is a fiction. On this view, in safeguarding its cultural heritage, Quebec is simply behaving like any other nation state. At which point, of course, English Canada cries in anguish: 'But you're not a nation state!'

WHO BELONGS TO
THE NATION?

It is a cold February morning in Ayer's Cliff, a farming community about half an hour's drive from the Vermont border in southern Quebec. The fields of the

McKinnon farm are white and bare, and the wind is drifting the snow up against the barn door. Inside, Angus and Peter McKinnon, two brothers in their 20s, are milking a hundred head of cattle, while their father Dennis, looks on and reminisces. There used to be lots of English families around these parts, he says, and he rolls off their names – the Barclays, the Todds, the Buchanans – but now most of his neighbours are French. The farmers' association used to run its meetings in English, and the Ayer's Cliff town council used to be in English. But that was in the old days, and now times have changed.

Dennis McKinnon was one of the farmers who figured which way the wind was blowing, and sent his two boys to primary school in French. Though they did their high school and agronomy courses at McGill in English, his sons remain bilingual. 'You have to be,' says Angus. 'All the business round here is done in French.'

And so it is: at the town council, at the Quebec farmers' association meetings, at the feed store, at the machinery distributors, Angus speaks French. It is much more than a halting gesture at bilingualism. Angus is the real thing. a fluently Quebecois anglophone. Two generations ago, such a person would not have existed among the farmers of this rolling countryside.

The two communities are cordial, and they work together, on the town council, in the farmers' organizations, but they keep to themselves socially. Angus McKinnon's mother plays violin in the orchestra in Sherbrooke. She is from Belfast originally, but her French is good and she fits in well in a French-speaking orchestra. But she's never been invited home by any of the other players. When Angus goes out in his truck to a dance on a Friday night, he'll be driving a lot of kilometres to get to a dance of English-speaking farmers.

A hundred thousand anglophones have left Quebec since the first independentist government was elected in 1976. But Angus is not going to take the road to Ontario. For one thing, Quebec agriculture is among the best subsidized and best administered of any province in Canada, and certainly superior to anything south of the border, where there is little price maintenance and the dairy producers have to survive on tiny margins and bulk production. And then there are the cultural reasons for staying. The McKinnons and families like them have been in these rolling valleys for 185 years. They came up from New England, because they didn't want to be part of the new republic, because they wanted to stay loyal to Britain and the Crown and British institutions, and because the land in these parts was good.

Not that the history in the Quebec school textbooks ever tells their story. In Quebec history, where anglophones figure at all, they appear as the colonial elite, the anglophones who lived in Westmount in Montreal and ran the railways and the department stores and the big businesses on Peel Street. There wasn't much room in the story for the small farmers of the Eastern Townships. They didn't quite fit the picture of the master class.

The McKinnons aren't resentful people. For one thing, they're doing too well. Besides, they can't recall any overt insults. The Quebecois slang for an Anglo is tête-carrée – blockhead – but in all their time in the bars and pool-halls, shooting some racks with the French farmers around, they can't recall hearing that word.

But there are other things that hurt, all the same. They feel that they are just as much part of Quebec as the French, but the history books, the politics, the language legislation all convey the message that they don't really belong.

'They had the language police down here last summer,' Angus tells me when we are having lunch at a Greek grill in Coaticook, near his farm. The Parti Québécois (PQ) – the independentist party – hired some college students to go around the town taking pictures of English-only signs. Then they went back to Quebec City and reported the tradespeople for violating the language laws.

The interesting thing is, says Angus, waving a greeting to a French farmer and his wife who have come in for lunch across the room, 'everyone was mad here. Not just the English. Everyone thought: we have a community here, what are outsiders coming in for and driving us apart?' He sips on his coffee. 'I tell you, had we caught those students, we would have run them out of town.'

It wasn't Angus McKinnon's rights that were being violated by the sneaky way the students snuck into town and took photos of the signs. Rights language doesn't really describe the problem. The problem is one of recognition. Are English-speaking Quebeckers recognized by the majority as belonging to Quebec society or not?

The minority populations of Quebec, not just the native anglophones, but the immigrant communities as well, are intensely irritated by the phrase 'Québécois pur laine' or 'Québécois de souche', used by some Quebecois to distinguish those who descend from the original French-speaking inhabitants and those, of English, Irish or other extraction, who arrived later. In any event, the distinction is fraudulent. There are fervent Quebecois nationalists called O'Brien or O'Neil, for example. Centuries of intermarriage between English, French and aboriginal Quebeckers make a nonsense of the idea that some Quebecois are more purely French than others. Some fervent nationalists admit the distinction is fraudulent. When I talked to the head of the St Jean Baptiste Society, she confessed that while she could call herself a 'Québécoise de souche' on her mother's side, her father was actually Spanish.

In every modern nation, the nationalist myth that nations have a self-contained, 'pure' ethnic identity comes up against the recalcitrant desire of ordinary people to breed across ethnic lines. Faced with the contradiction between the myth of ethnic purity and the reality of ethnic intermixing, nationalists have to choose how to define membership in the nation. Does the Quebecois nation comprise all those who live there, or only those who were born French-speaking?

All nationalisms face such a choice. Is Croatia the nation of the Croatian people, or of all those – they may include Serbs – who chose to make Croatia their home? Is Germany the nation of the German people, or of the Turks, Yugoslavs,

Portuguese, Spaniards, Romanians and Poles who have chosen Germany as their home?

Recent declarations by Quebecois nationalist leaders have raised suspicion that their definition of nationality is ethnic. Jacques Parizeau, the PQ leader, has said that Quebec independence can be achieved, with or without the co-operation of the minority populations. This may be a statement of fact, but it appears to imply more than a little indifference to the opinions and rights of the minority.

On balance, however, modern Quebec nationalists are at pains to differentiate their conception of the nation from the ethnic idea that they associate with the catastrophe of Yugoslavia. Thus, in its arguments for sovereignty, the CEQ – Centrale d'Education du Québec, a Quebec teachers' union – rejects the idea that Quebec is the 'national state of the French Canadians'. The Quebec state, they argue, should be the national state of everyone who chooses to live there, 'regardless of their ethnic origins'. A national state, they insist, need not be an ethnic state.

Even if it did become an ethnic state, Angus McKinnon muses, we will never go the way of Yugoslavia. Why? 'Because there's the highway to Ontario,' says Angus with a laugh. 'We can always get on the highway and leave. The poor people in Yugoslavia can't leave, but we can. But I don't want to. This is the best place in the world.'

HOCKEY NIGHT IN CANADA

Dennis Rousseau is in his late 20s and works for Wayagamack, a paper mill in Trois-Rivières, on the north shore of the St Lawrence. His wife works as a book keeper in town, and they live, with their baby girl, in a two-bedroom bungalow on a suburban street a few minutes walk from the paper mill. Outside, it is about 15 below zero and snow is falling through the street lamps. In Dennis's front yard, there is a gigantic snow fort, and half of the kids on the street are attacking it with snowballs and the other half are defending it. Snowballs are whizzing through the night air around me, splattering against the fort, against Dennis's front door. He pulls me inside and shuts the door with a laugh.

Dennis is wearing a hockey shirt and jeans, and his thin blond hair is down to his shoulders. His Quebecois is fast, heavily accented, and sometimes too much for my French-French to understand. He apologizes that he doesn't speak English, and then points down to his 3-year-old daughter who is pushing a large plastic tractor across the living room. 'She's going to be in English immersion.' English immersion courses are in their first year in Trois-Rivières. 'We don't want to be cut off,' he says.

I was looking for someone who could talk to me about the economics of independence, from a worker's point of view, and union organizers in Montreal gave me Dennis's name. Besides, Trois-Rivières is the heart of Quebec, a unilingual town that used to be the capital of its pulp and paper industry. There used to be twelve mills in the region, going twenty-four hours a day, making the paper for the phone books and newspapers of a whole continent. No more. Demand is down, due to the recession, and in Alabama and Georgia they have plants which can produce the paper for less. There are only six mills left, and at Dennis's factory they have lost a third of the workforce in the last year.

'A lot of lay-offs at my mill. Over two hundred. Same at the Belgo, Kruger, and worst of all is the PFCP which used to have a thousand workers. Now it's closed. We've got seventeen per cent unemployment in Trois-Rivières. It's bad. I could lose my job any time. When I go out to the rink to play hockey with the guys I never know who's going to be there.'

Hardly the moment, I would have thought, for nationalist experiments. But that's not how Dennis sees it. 'The government ought to do something. We need a jobs policy, but Quebec doesn't have the power. Employment is federal. We need to get our hands on the levers.'

Dennis isn't a Parti Québécois militant, but he is a phenomenon – he represents the spread of Quebec nationalist doctrine from the cafés of Montreal intellectuals to the industrial heartland. Three years of recession have, paradoxically, turned him into a nationalist. 'We've got the businessmen, we've got the skills, we could make this place work, I'm sure of it.' The Canadian government, he thinks, only takes care of English Canada.

Why, I suggest, don't you make common cause with the workers in Ontario? They're having just as hard a time as you. Dennis won't budge. 'Ontario won't give us the powers we need. They say we have too much already.'

Dennis is a cheerful, open-hearted man, diffident with strangers, but with convictions no amount of arguing on my part can shift. It doesn't make much impression when I tell him the Canadian government has been pouring money into the fight against unemployment in Quebec. It doesn't matter that an independent Quebec might have just as much trouble keeping a tired old paper mill in business. He knows what he knows, and that is that a sovereign Quebec couldn't make a bigger mess of his life than Ottawa has already.

I can't help feeling that for Dennis nationalism may just be a welcome flight from disagreeable economic realities. One reality is that his mill used to be owned by a Quebec company. They failed to put in the necessary investment and sold it off to the Americans. The Americans are now investing, but it may be too late for the plant to compete against their own lower-cost plants down south. What, in other words, can Quebec ownership or Quebec sovereignty do in the face of the economics of competition in a continental market?

But, then again, if he thought the way I do, he would give up. Nationalism gives him hope, and in Trois-Rivières, you need all the hope you can get. The curious thing, of course, is that it is such a Canadian style of hope. We Canadians believe in government. Social democratic interventionism is as much in my bones as it is in Dennis's. The sad thing is that this common faith is leading us into different countries.

Although Dennis feels strongly, there is little or no aggression in what he says towards English Canadians. He did visit Niagara Falls once, and while he had some trouble making himself understood, he liked it 'down there'. Had Dennis ever been in my home town, Toronto? He shakes his head and grins. As for holidays, he and his wife would rather head south to the east-coast beaches in New Jersey and Massachusetts, or further south in Florida, where there are so many Quebecois in the winter that they run a newspaper in French just for them. This is part of a pattern I observe throughout my visit in Quebec. When you ask people where they go when they have a little free time, they all say the States. They never say Canada.

After a couple of beers, it is time for Dennis to head down to the arena for his hockey game with the works team. It's one of those places from my Canadian childhood, a big, gloomy, vaulted place, bitterly cold, with a lozenge of white gleaming ice in the middle, and no glass to keep the pucks from flying into the rows of hard, grey-painted bleachers where I take my seat.

This isn't just any hockey arena. It's like the sand lots of Santo Domingo, where the world's best baseball shortstops grow up; or like the pitches in north London where Arsenal players learn how to curve a ball into the net. Trois-Rivières is one of those places where hockey is played best in all the world; it is from arenas like this one that the National Hockey League (NHL) draws its talent.

I have hockey in common with Dennis, as any Canadian does. I grew up listening to NHL games on the radio in the days before television. I have all the same names in my head that he does – Geoffrion, Béliveau, Richard – from the Canadiens' teams of the 1950s and 1960s. I used to play in arenas like this.

I sit in the stand and I watch the Wayagamack boys play. Dennis is good: low, fast, crafty, hard-working, darting in and out of the play, digging pucks out from under people's skates, hitting people when he has to, a big smile playing on his face. When he's on the bench, he pushes the helmet back off his face, sips on a Coke and roars: 'Allez les boys! Allez les boys! Look at that guy's acceleration! Tabarnak!'

I sit watching him, levering himself over the boards to join in a power play, wishing I still had my skating legs and wondering, finally, why I feel such fierce separation from a Canadian scene which is just as much mine as it is his. We share all these things, and yet we don't. Language falls between us, even though I am bilingual. His Quebecois is not my French. We play the same game, in the same arenas, and we cannot quite connect. Class, perhaps? But it is much more a question of language and old resentments and a history of bitterness, real and invented, which seems more robust and full of life than any of our understandings.

A scene like the hockey rink in Trois-Rivières sets you thinking about what exactly it is that people must share if they are to live together in a political community. Is it mere sentimentality to suppose that people ought to share the same rituals, the same cold nights under the bright lights of a hockey rink, in order to feel a common belonging? Nation states, after all, can cohere even when the peoples who compose them share much less than I share with Dennis. The core of my separation from Dennis comes down to this. We cannot share a nation – we cannot share it, since I am English and he is French, and he was born in Quebec and I was not. Because we do not share the same nation, we cannot love the same state. I tell myself this might be just as well. Shared love for a nation state might be a dangerous thing. Perhaps the gentleness, tolerance and good-naturedness of so much of Canadian life depends, in fact, on that absence of a fiercely shared love. Yet one can sit in a hockey arena in Trois-Rivières on a Tuesday night, watching a young man skating his heart out, with a wild grin on his face, and wish, suddenly, that we did actually love the same nation and not merely cohabit the same state.

13   The powerhouse of Quebec independence: the dam at LG-Two.

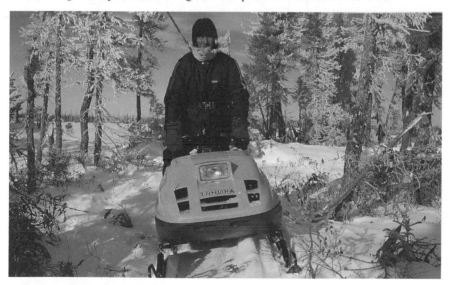

14   A Cree hunter checks his trap-lines by skidoo.

OVERLEAF 15   'Our real nation is Quebec': the St Jean Baptiste parade, Montreal, 24 June 1990.

LEFT 16   Mulla Mustafa Barzani, founder of modern Kurdish nationalism.

ABOVE 17   With the PKK guerillas, Iraqi Kurdistan.

LEFT 18   Milan, a PKK guerilla fighter from Melbourne, Australia.

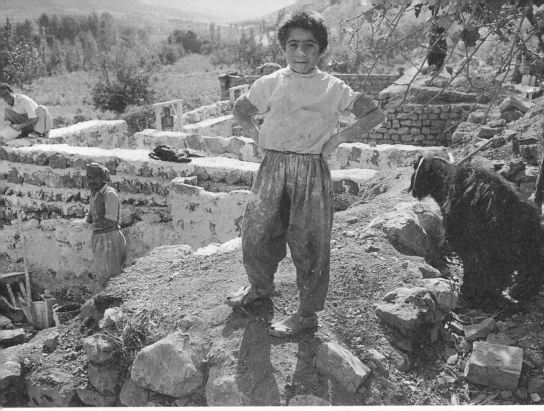

19 Rebuilding Kurdish homes destroyed by Iraqi chemical weapons in 1987.

20 Portraits of guerilla martyrs at a teashop between Amadiyah and Rawandiz.

21 The cargo cult: the Orangeman in his Lodge, King Billy crossing the Boyne behind.

BELOW 22 With Dick Sterritt (centre), maker of the Lambeg drum, and his father Ernie (right).

23 Belfast: Loyalist paramilitaries on the march.

24 The Loyalist community in insurrection:
burnt out cars and street murals, South Belfast 1993.

KURDISTAN

BORDERS

The mystique of nations is to appear eternal, to seem like elemental features of the landscape itself. Yet the borders of a nation lay the mystique bare. There, you realize how unnatural, arbitrary and even absurd the division of the world into nations actually is. The border walls bisect villages; the barbed wire may put two sides of the same street into different countries; the checkpoints may exile one half of a family from the other half; the lines on the maps may divide the same ethnic group into two different nations; that sinister straight line of border watch towers may violate the resolutely non-national contours of hill and valley.

The border I am now approaching is especially arbitrary. Behind me, the grasslands of south-eastern Turkey. Ahead of me, the steep green hills of Iraq. In between, a long, two-lane, concrete bridge over a tributary of the Tigris. I shoulder my pack and begin walking in the direction of the Iraqi hills in the dying light of a May afternoon.

What frock-coated gentleman in Sèvres or Lausanne decided that this side would be Turkey, and that side Iraq? The same people – the Kurds – live either side, 9 million on the Turkish side of the border, and 3 million on the Iraqi side. Yet until two years ago, nothing at the border post took any notice of these people's existence or even acknowledged that the border bisected their home-land. I am here because now, at last, things have changed. There is a handpainted sign up ahead at the end of the bridge, in Arabic and English script, which says 'Welcome to Kurdistan.'

But what Kurdistan is this? The land the Kurds claim as their own stretches across five nation states: Iraq, Turkey, Syria, Iran and Armenia. In the melan-choly offices of Kurdish exile groups in London, I've seen the map of this Kurdistan of dreams, stretching from the Syrian Mediterranean on the west, to Armenian Mount Ararat on the north-east, to the oil fields of Kirkuk in Iraq and the mountains around Kirmanshah in Iran. This is the land which a tribal mountain people, descended from the ancient Medes, have settled and claimed as their own for 4000 years, only to see their claims denied by the Turkish empire and the modern nations which rose upon its ruins. At the end of the First World War, when the Ottoman empire lay prostrate and Woodrow Wilson's principle of the self-determination of peoples was briefly in the ascendant at Versailles, the Kurds were promised a state. But between the Treaty of Sèvres of 1920, which promised them this homeland, and the Treaty of Lausanne of 1923, which ratified the new borders of Turkey, their claim was betrayed. Over this dream, the men in frockcoats dropped their border lines like a net.

It has been the Kurds' misfortune that their homeland is the meeting point of four of the most aggressive and expansionary nationalisms in the modern world: Turkish, Iranian, Iraqi and Syrian. The Kurds are thus a people whose struggle for a homeland has been deformed and deflected by nationalisms more virulent than their own.

The Kurds have always been regarded as a threat to the unity of the Turkish state founded in 1923 by Kemal Atatürk. Guided by Atatürk's centralizing, secular nationalism, the Turks set about forcibly assimilating the Kurds, denying them the right to speak their own language, educate their children in it or even call themselves Kurds. Until a decade ago, official Turkey described the Kurds as 'mountain Turks'. 'Kemalism' fused nationalism with the rhetoric of modernization: the goal of a modern Turkey was to end the Ottoman heritage of backwardness. The Kurds, therefore, were victimized, not just as an alien ethnic minority, fated to assimilate to the Turkish norm, but as a backward, barbarian people, fated to succumb to the modernizing energies of the Turkish state.

Likewise, to the modernizing nationalism of the Shah of Iran, the Iranian Kurds were a tribal throwback unaccountably standing in the way of a modern autocracy. Worse, they were Sunni Muslims, while most Iranians were Shias. After the Shah fell in 1979, the Iranian Kurds hoped their chances of autonomy would improve, only to discover that the fundamentalist revolution of the Ayatollahs was even more hostile to them than the Shah. Not merely did their stubborn mountain revolt stand in the way of the totalitarian control envisaged by fundamentalism; they were also religious renegades, Sunni obstacles in the path of Shi'ite universalism. Even now, Iran rockets Kurdish villages within Kurdistan and sends bomb-laden Mirages screaming over Iranian Kurdish villages inside the enclave.

The Ba'athist nationalism of Syria and Iraq was, at least in theory, less relentlessly centralizing than Turkey and less driven by ethnic intolerance. Iraqi Kurds were defined constitutionally as a national minority and retained the right to educate their children in Kurdish. Nominal autonomy was granted by recurrent Ba'athist regimes, but only as a result of stubborn revolt by Kurdish tribal and national leaders, the most famous being Mulla Mustafa Barzani.

When Saddam Hussein came to power in the 1970s, new oil wealth, coupled with Western and Russian military support, made possible a rapid transition to nationalist totalitarianism. Saddam used Arab nationalism to legitimize two imperatives: to modernize Iraq, and to make himself the most powerful and feared leader in the Middle East. The Kurdish revolt, begun in 1961 by Mulla Mustafa, and continued on and off ever since by his sons, presented the most substantial opposition to Saddamic totalitarianism and forced modernization. Saddam never succeeded in mobilizing long-standing popular ethnic hostility by Arabs towards Kurds. Instead, he fought them simply because they were the most consistent challenge to his particular form of despotism.

These four nationalisms have bedevilled the Kurd's own struggle to create a common national identity. Many Turkish Kurds speak only Turkish and recognize only the Roman alphabet. This divides them from Iraqi Kurds, who in most cases have kept their language and use the Arabic alphabet. Both the Iraqi and the Turkish governments have proven themselves adept at exploiting Kurdish differences. As in all nationalist struggles, there are those who resist and those who collaborate. In Kurdish, such collaborators are contemptuosly called *jash* ('little donkeys'). Saddam organized them into militias to fight the nationalist *peshmerga*. Kurds themselves admit that, for all the shared talk about a common homeland, they have actually fought each other more often than they have fought side by side. And besides the divisions sown among them by their neighbours, there are the divisions indigenous to the Kurds themselves: tribal and familial feuds, different linguistic dialects – Kurmanji in northern and western Iraq; Sorani in the south and east. Nationalist movements have chipped away at the tribal, regional and linguistic divisions which plague the Kurds, trying to create that unity which will at last make the nation possible. Yet that unity of purpose and vision remains elusive, and the question remains, with the Kurds as with other stateless peoples like the Palestinians: can nationalism create a nation?

How, in the absence of a state, in the face of such divisions, have the Kurds managed to survive as a people? Their secret, I suspect, may lie in their very traditionalism. This would reverse what is usually said about them, namely that their tribalism is a source of political division and weakness. Of course it is. But tribalism is also a subliminal source of cohesion, even for urban Kurds. As a people they have made the transition from a tribal to a national form of collective belonging within the last two generations, but their national consciousness is still shaped by the tribal bond. Their very backwardness, their stubborn enclosure within tribal loyalties, has protected them against assimilation and integration.

As I approach the little concrete hut, at the end of the bridge, where I hand in my passport, I can make out on the roof a bright new painting in acrylic of Massoud, Mulla Mustafa's son and heir as leader of the Kurdish Democratic Party. It has replaced the portrait of Saddam which used to hang there and was shot away in the first hours of the Kurdish intifada in March 1991.

At the sign, 'Welcome to Kurdistan', there is no real border post, just some brown-faced boys with automatic weapons who smile and say, 'Allo, Mistair.' A jet thunders overhead, so high up in the blue that you cannot see it, and the boys glance up and smile. 'America,' they tell me, returning my passport.

These jets, which patrol the no-fly zone over Iraq from their base in Incirlik, Turkey, are what stand between the Kurds and Saddam Hussein. How long they will fly, how long they will protect the Kurds, no one knows. The fate of stateless peoples is sealed in other people's capitals.

The sign at the border may say 'Welcome to Kurdistan', but the frontier itself actually bisects the dream homeland. Only 2.8 of the estimated 25 million Kurds are to be found there, most of them Iraqi Kurds by origin. Kurdistan is not a state, just an enclave. It has no flag of its own. It is not even allowed to call itself Kurdistan. Technically, it remains a part of Iraq and the Iraqi dinar remains the currency. It was set up in the spring of 1991, after Iraqi helicopter gunships chased the Kurds into the mountain passes. Allied forces drove the Iraqi army south, and Allied planes set up an air exclusion zone north of the 36th parallel, under which the Kurds were given the right to shelter, to return from camps in Iran and Turkey and rebuild their homes.

But if it is not a state, it is certainly acting like one. It has held elections, it has a parliament, a police force, the rudiments of a civil administration. Since Saddam has sealed it off from the rest of Iraq, Kurdistan is kept alive by the international aid convoys and Turkish trucks which rumble across the bridge. Yet there can be little doubt that the Kurds of Iraq believe that from this kernel, the enclave, one day a state will grow.

Kurdistan is something new under the sun in international law – the first attempt by the UN to protect a minority people against the genocidal intentions of its nominal ruler. Until Kurdistan, the international community stopped short of 'interventions' which challenged the territorial integrity and sovereignty of nation states. With the creation of the Kurdish enclave, it endorsed the idea that the duty of humanitarian intervention overrode the principle of the inviolability and integrity of sovereign states. If Kurdistan works, other nations which believe they can abuse indigenous minorities with impunity may see such enclaves hacked out of their territory. Kurdistan is all that remains of George Bush's 'new world order'. It remains the only place where a new balance between the right of people and the right of nations for the post-Cold War world was drawn.

Now that the world's most numerous stateless people have a small place that they can call their own, I wonder what it will do to them. Stateless peoples have a way of making visible the securities which people with states take for granted. The best way to find out what a nation state means to a people, what it does to their character, is to spend time among a people who have never had one of their own.

As my taxi grinds up the steep road past Zakho to Dahuk, I catch my first glimpses of Kurdistan. On the rocky, dusty verges of the highway, there are tents, some with US army markings, some with UNHCR markings, and inside them, lit by kerosene lamps, I see neat pyramids of Marlboro cigarettes, Mars bars, Turkish chocolate, bars of soap, packs of margarine, biscuits, packs of sugar and flour. Outside other tents I see neatly stacked rows of plastic jerry-cans, filled to the brim with pink petrol, guarded by boys whose hands and face are darkened with axle and engine grease. Saddam has blockaded Kurdistan's borders, and a desperately poor economy is only kept going by the ingenuity of the mule drivers who bring cooking oil and soap over the mountain passes from Iran, the Turkish trucks which thunder up this road, and these oil-smeared boys who sell smuggled petrol from jerry-cans by the roadside. The boys are barefoot and look cold in the darkness. Yet somehow the atmosphere is not of poverty and desperation, but of wonder and mystery – cheekbones and brown skin in the chiaroscuro of kerosene lamps, the bowed shapes of the tents, the flaps held back to reveal the smuggled treasures within. The boys stand by the flaps, their faces lit by the kerosene lamps, their eyes beckoning me to enter.

PESHMERGA

A white Toyota LandCruiser pulls up outside the front door of the dank hotel in Dahuk where I have spent my first night. I am pleased to see it. As I've discovered in Croatia and Serbia, the four-wheel drive is the vehicle of preference for the war-zones of the post-Cold War world. It has become the chariot of choice for the warlords who rule the checkpoints and the command posts of the factions, gangs, guerilla armies, tribes that are fighting over the bones of the nation in the 1990s.

In this case, the LandCruiser is provided courtesy of the Kurdish Democratic Party (KDP), the organization of Massoud Barzani. The KDP dominates in

Dahuk and in north-western Kurdistan, while the Patriotic Union of Kurdistan (PUK) run by Jalal Talabani has its strongholds in the Sorani-speaking eastern and southern portions. They share power between them in a coalition, but the gulf between them is wide and the history of mutual betrayal is long.

The KDP not only provides the LandCruiser – for a fee, of course – but also security protection.

Behjet and Taha are to be my *peshmerga*, my warriors, my security protection while I travel. They wear the *jemadane*, the black and white turbaned headdress of the male warrior, a short, tight-fitting brown military tunic, a magnificent waist-band of coloured cloth, called the *shuttik*, tightly wound into four ascending, intertwining strands which are tied at the side. Their trousers, called *shalvar*, balloon out dramatically and conclude in a pair of finely woven white cotton slippers, called *klash*. Both men have thick black moustaches and the watchful and dignified faces of mountain tribesmen. Behjet, the senior driver, wears a pistol in a worn leather case stuffed into his *shuttik*, while Taha shoulders a Kalashnikov on his back. Behjet's right knee joint is rigid – a war wound – and he walks with a pronounced limp. When he drives, he pinions his leg straight against the accelerator. When I tell him that he is to be my shepherd and I am to be his sheep, he smiles gravely. A shepherd is nearly as dignified a thing to be in Kurdistan as a *peshmerga*, and now he is to be both.

They are party men, and they have fought for the Barzanis all their adult life. I soon notice that when he takes me to the other parties, say to the PUK television station, or to the Commmunist Party HQ, Behjet becomes uneasy. These places are alien turf to him; the men with guns on the door eye him with equal suspicion. When I joke with Behjet about the long face he pulls whenever he is not among his own party, he laughs and says, 'No, no, all Kurds are brothers,' but his face tells me something different.

Behjet and Taha have guns. So, as far as I can see, does every other male I see on the streets. There are pistols worn in waistbands, pistol holsters gleaming from the inside pockets of suits, Kalashnikovs on shoulders, laid across tables in restaurants, hanging unattended on the backs of chairs, resting on the front seats of cars; ammunition clips inside the glove compartments; the barrels of guns sticking up among a tractor load of farm workers heading out to the fields in the morning light; guns lying beside men with bare feet bent in prayer. Once again, as in Serbia and Croatia, I am in a world where power comes from the barrel of a gun. And not just power, but prestige and male honour too.

Neither Behjet nor Taha flaunt their weaponry with the elaborately sexual display I had become used to at the Serbian and Croatian checkpoints. Perhaps this has something to do with being Muslims. At sunset, throughout our journey together, they retired to some quiet spot by the side of the road, removed their shoes, and quietly said their prayers. They did not touch alcohol and this must have contributed to the dignified, casual and desexualized way they handled weaponry. Among Europeans, by contrast, the gun culture at the checkpoints breaks a fundamental taboo. Most Europeans have lived since 1945 within states which enjoyed a monopoly of the means of violence. Such monopoly is the very core of what a nation state is. As the nations of the Balkans broke down, this monopoly collapsed. The arsenals of the armies were ransacked; hunting rifles came down from the attics; the arms traders moved in. For some young European males, the chaos that resulted from the collapse of the state's monopoly offered the chance of entering an erotic paradise of the all-is-permitted. Hence the semi-sexual, semi-pornographic gun culture of checkpoints. For young men, there was an irresistible erotic charge in holding lethal power in your hands and using it to hold up an aid convoy; terrorize a column of refugees, threaten a journalist; make some innocent civilians lie in a ditch with their hands over their heads, cowering beneath your gun sights.

In Kurdistan, by contrast, there has never been a state, so there has never been a monopoly of violence. The empires and nations which have ruled here never disarmed the *peshmerga*: they used them instead as militias and mercenaries. Guns are distributed to boys as soon as they reach adolescence. Carrying a gun is a sign that a boy has ceased to be a child and must behave like a man. The word *peshmerga* means not only 'warrior', but also 'the one who faces death'. The accent of meaning in the culture of the gun thus stresses responsibility, sobriety, tragic duty. For these reasons, therefore, I trust my *peshmerga* with their weapons. I can be sure there will be no crazy displays. Their weapons sit beside me on the front seat for two weeks, and after a day, I no longer give them any thought.

Yet, if there are guns everywhere, who is the man who gives the orders? In the absence of a nation state, there are no clear chains of command, no obvious lines of authority.

Behjet and Taha belong to the militias of the parties. But what about these police constables we pass, in blue and white uniforms, directing traffic with guns on their hips? What about these smart figures in military uniforms, with white puttees and red berets? These were the old Saddamic uniforms – based, I can see, on the old British regimental models from imperial days. Who gives them their orders? On a quick drive through the teeming market streets of Dahuk, full of shoeshine boys and barrows full of cucumbers and tomatoes and white onions, I see party guns, police guns and military guns.

No one is exactly sure who is in charge. Some of the police and the army belong to the old Saddamic days, and are the oldest geological strata of order. Some of them must have been *jash*, collaborators with the old regime. The worst of them, of course, the ones who tortured or took bribes, either fled or were done to death during the uprising of March 1991. The honest ones have stayed, to keep the traffic moving in the crowded squares.

Then comes the new Kurdish army: you see them drilling around the headquarters of the Dahuk governorate, awkward 16-year-olds, in ill-fitting military fatigues and dirty white Puma trainers, learning to march and shoot and fight for the first time. But they seem to be a new force; the backbone of the new state's fighting force remains the *peshmerga*, the traditionally dressed warriors of the party militias.

Behjet and Taha drive me to the party headquarters to drink the obligatory glass of sweet tea with the party bosses, receive their formal blessing and set off on our journey. Usually nothing can be begun or concluded in this part of the world without such tea ceremonies.

But there is no tea ceremony today, for the party headquarters is in a state of convulsion. It is election day for the seven posts in the party directorate for the Dahuk region. The big men come and go up and down the steps of the primary school. You can tell they are big men, because they do not wear the sober brown or grey-green khaki of the regular *peshmerga*; their *shalvar* are made of light, airy linen, with dramatic stripes down the seams and purple cuffs on their tunics; as they enter the building, an aura of deference expands around them; it is whispered that so-and-so was in charge of the military defence of Dahuk during the uprising of 1991; of another small, bustling, barrel-chested man with a superb red *jemadane* on his head, and an unruly sheaf of papers under his arm, it is said that he was commander of the mountain heights above the city.

The grandees saunter up and down in the front porch of the primary school, awaiting the result of the vote count inside, clicking their worry beads, discoursing in low whispers, in front of a life-sized portrait of Mulla Mustafa, with his dagger in his *shuttik*.

Inside, the count is going on in a large, blue classroom, the light through the windows gauzy with cigarette smoke, the tiles underfoot littered with butts, the room buzzing with the whispers and rumours of the hundred *peshmerga* who are standing at the back watching the count. Some of them are writing the results down on cigarette papers, shaking their heads, concentrating on what is happening at the front of the room. A man at a table picks up a ballot paper, calls out the name of the person voted for, and one of the tally-men standing at eight blackboards around the room makes a mark beside the name mentioned. Scrutineers cluster around the man reading out the names on the ballot papers to make sure he reads only what is there. This is an open count, a public ritual conducted so that everyone can see that the elections are free and fair. It all happens with indescribable speed and elegance, the names read out, the tally-man grunting that he has heard, the sound of his chalk scratching a point, the next name read out, in a steady, untroubled flow, while behind the huge crowd watches intently as chalk marks pile up beside the names. Some of the candidates are women, but there is not a single woman in the room. Kurdish democracy, like Kurdish warfare, is a man's affair.

Over the next two weeks, I visit the Kurdish parliament in Arbil and stare down from the visitors' gallery at the members, about a hundred of them, with eight women among them, some in traditional Kurdish costume, some in business suits, and a few religious leaders in magnificent robes and turbans. I can see that this is a real parliament, a place of genuine debate, in contrast to the cowed circus which Saddam used to convene once a year to show foreign visitors how well he treated 'his' Kurds. But the most impressive evidence of nascent Kurdish democracy is this electoral count in a small town schoolroom, with the men at the back, smoking, whispering and scribbling on cigarette papers. What I can't decipher is the relation between ancient and modern, between the tribe and the party, between the democratic equality of the election and the deferential, honorific relations between leaders and men.

I get an important clue about these questions one night, much later, when I am sitting on the darkened veranda of a house overlooking Sulaymaniyah, with the KDP party boss of the town, Muhyeddin Rahim. He is a thin, dark, wily man, tightly coiled and smart, who spent fifteen years representing the Kurdish cause in the USA, from a basement of his house in suburban Washington which was nicknamed the Pentagon of the Kurdish cause. We drink Scotch together, with the bottle under the table, so as not to give offence to the *peshmerga* who post guard from the shadows of the veranda. 'Off the record, Mulla Mustafa himself,' Muhyeddin confides to me, in his smoky voice, 'said to me, "Drink what you want. But be responsible. Do not lose your dignity. Do not throw yourself in the trash."' Muhyeddin speaks in an inimitable Kurdish-American slang. He loves going 'off the record'; he calls journalists 'you guys'. He could be a Washington lobbyist, but he is not. He wears his *jemadane* at a jaunty angle on the top of his head, like a matador's cap, and all night long armed men approach his table, in a deferential crouch, to whisper in his ear, to pass him an urgent phone-call, to clear away the dishes, to refresh his glass, to light his cigarettes, to bring him a new pack of Marlboros when he runs out.

I ask him what is most on his mind, and he says, right away, 'Outside support.' He is afraid of the fickleness of the Western conscience, our wandering moral attention span. If we do not keep our eyes on Kurdistan, Saddam will snatch it back. Muhyeddin eyes me through the cigarette smoke. 'No offence, but we cannot afford to trust anyone.'

How are your people doing? I ask him. 'Terrible. There are a million people in Sulaymaniyah,' he goes on. 'What do we have? A cigarette factory that doesn't work because we are short of raw materials. And a cement factory that doesn't work because we can't import fuel oil to run the machines. So everybody is unemployed. I don't know how long we can go on.' He takes a long drag on his cigarette.

'Come to my office. I'll show you what it's like.'

So I did. The minute he got out of his red Toyota, the petitioners began crowding around; old women in tears thrusting tightly wrapped knots of paper into his hand, detailing some injustice, some wrong they thought he could solve; a farmer whose legs were blown off when his tractor ran over one of Saddam's mines hobbled up on crutches, pulled up his trousers and showed us his stump; one old woman brought forward an old man driven crazy when their sons were taken away and shot; and, as Muhyeddin slowly edged his way through the crowd towards his office, beggars began pulling at his clothes, whispering, 'Give me a pound of sugar, give me a pound of flour . . .' It was a medieval scene, powered by a medieval belief: if you could only speak to the good king, all your troubles would vanish. But they do not vanish. Muhyeddin is a warlord, a party leader, not the good king who works miracles.

He himself is astonished that in the space of a year life has lifted him up from his Washington basement and dropped him back here to become boss of his home town. And he *is* a warlord, though he would find the word too 'Hollywood.'

I ask him who owned this house in the old days. 'A friend of a friend,' he says, looking at me slyly. 'He's in Baghdad now.'

Muhyeddin stares out at Sulaymaniyah by night. 'When I left here, fifteen years ago, there were no houses on this whole hillside. I came back, I hardly knew the place.' There must have been moments, in the Washington suburbs, when he wondered whether he still knew anything about the homeland whose cause he had made his own. I ask him whether it was hard to come home. No, he says happily, that would be your kind of problem, not mine.

Besides, he says, we are a modern party. We are not a tribe. He doesn't like this word tribal. It strikes him as condescending. When the modern Kurdish parties began, the power of the tribal chieftains, the *agha*, was immense. The people were in servitude towards them. But now the power in the land is in the hands of the parties.

He takes another secret call, confers with an aide, and then sneaks another clandestine sip of whisky. Then I ask him, 'Haven't you, hasn't the party leader, Massoud Barzani, simply become the new tribal chieftain?' No, no – he waves his hand. You misunderstand. Where are the landed estates of the Barzani family? Where is their great wealth? (Now the Talabanis – the Barzanis' great rivals – I could tell you about them, but that is another story.) Unlike Talabani, Barzani's power comes, not from tribal connections, but from his example. He has fought for his people all his life. That's why he has respect.

'Look,' Muhyeddin says, waving down at the curfewed streets of Sulaymaniyah. 'Out there is one of Barzani's brothers. He does nothing for his people. I am not obliged to give him respect. So enough of this tribal business.'

He makes me realize I am in the grip of a developmental fiction, according to which peoples must pass through stages, first the tribal, then the national, first the 'backward', 'primitive' and 'traditional', then the modern, and 'impersonal'. The

Kurds upset this fiction. There are no neat stages, no befores and afters, no neat lines between ancient and modern, between tribal and national. They are alternating identities, reconciled within single lives. In suburban Washington, on his day off, around the house, Muhyeddin would have worn trainers, a T-shirt, chinos, and would have had a can of beer in his hand. For meetings with the state department, there was the business suit. Back in Sulaymaniyah there is the *shalvar*, *shuttik* and his *jemadane*. He 'is' both of these uniforms: from the traditional comes devotion to his people; from the modern comes a cynical awareness of what is possible. He is both, and because there is a Kurdistan, he can *be* both.

It is time to go. He asks me where I am headed next. I say Halabja. He snaps his fingers behind him, whispers an order to a crouching figure, and then says, 'It is arranged.' What this means I only discover the next day, when I come into the lobby of my hotel. There, waiting for me in the driveway, is his own personal armoured jeep as escort, with a machine gun mounted on the roof of the cab and half a dozen tanned and smiling *peshmerga* in combat fatigues. It takes me a while to realize that they are only partly there to protect me. The road to Halabja is not especially dangerous. The real reason for the escort lies in the anthropology of warlord etiquette and display. The point of the escort is to show me respect, and to demonstrate the power, influence and authority of the man who had been smoking Marlboros and sipping scotch on the veranda beside me.

THE REPUBLIC OF FEAR

Behjet, Taha, our escort and I set off on our travels, up the dizzying mountain roads through the passes, down into the grass-green valleys, past the clusters of low, flat-roofed, double-roomed adobe houses which rise up the hillside and shelter with their backs to the crags. From Dahuk to Barzan, village after village, dynamited or bombed during Saddam's reign, is coming alive again. Piles of air-brick lie by the road; the sound of pickaxes, the slop of cement, the thud of shovels are to be heard everywhere. The turbaned shepherds are returning to the upland meadows with their flocks. The marshlands are being turned into rice-paddies; the huge plains are sown with wheat. And everywhere there are signs of Western charity. Dutch, Swiss, German agencies have paid to rebuild the villages which Saddam laid waste. New dispensaries are opening; fresh-water supplies and outdoor latrines are being laid on; water pumps are purifying the streams. The cycle of infectious disease is being brought under control. A homeland is coming to life, and everywhere people are glad to see you. The little barefoot boys selling almonds by the side of the road cry 'Allo Mistair' when they see my white face. The girls in purple *kiras*, bent under a weight of firewood, pause on the goat tracks and wave shyly at the LandCruiser. By the Bailey bridges over the brown rushing rivers, the guarding *peshmerga* salute in greeting.

Two years ago, such an opening of arms to outsiders would have been unthinkable. Saddam's agents would have shadowed any foreign visitor here and questioned anyone he spoke to. Two years ago, I would have met averted gazes, closed faces, turned backs. Perhaps too, in the most traditional mountain villages, I would have met with the suspicion visited upon all outsiders. All this has changed, with the coming of Kurdistan. Foreign aid workers tell me they have never worked in a more welcoming environment. The reason is obvious: without us, without the aid, the overflights, the fitful but ongoing international attention, there would be no homeland, no Kurdistan. We – the outside world – have helped a people become a nation. Every person knows this. And so they wave greetings at white faces.

When I stop to get a closer look at the rice-paddies, just being sown, the men in turbans slop out of the mud and come up and shake my hand. 'Allo, Mistair,' one says to me. 'When you cut Saddam's throat for us?'

A good question. Saddam still haunts Kurdish dreams. As if to remind Kurds that he is there, just across the mountains, he orders the electricity supply, which comes from Mosul, turned off so that Dahuk is plunged into darkness. As if to remind the Kurds that he still holds their economic fate in his hands, he withdraws the 25 dinar note from circulation. Since most Kurds hold their money in wads of 25 dinar notes, the effect is to wipe out the value of their savings at a stroke.

His grotesque chalets and palaces seem to be squatting on top of every mountain view; his prisons and barracks dominate every valley. These buildings are an exercise in the architecture of intimidation. The marble facings, the monumental terraces and gardens all say to the Kurds: you are nothing, I am everything. But the Kurds have taken their revenge. The palaces have been sacked and burned and ripped apart. Squatter families have run their washing lines up over the barracks and prisons. In Arbil, a family has even moved into Saddam's execution centre, near the parliament. A woman has set up her oven and bakes *nan* in the room where Kurds were once shot; goats ramble about in the cells; children pile stones and bricks up in the gutted window embrasures to provide protection against the wind and rain.

The fear Saddam still evokes charges the atmosphere with tension. The police chief in Sulaymaniyah showed me a cabinet case full of plastic bombs which Saddam's agents have attached to the lorries of international aid convoys or left in unmarked cars by the gates of primary schools. Recently, he sent troops across the border to three villages in the Arbil region to confiscate the harvest. In all these manoeuvres, Saddam's strategy is simple: nibble, nibble, while the West's back is turned, and when he is sure we're not looking: pounce.

At one of the new Kurdish television stations in Arbil, a local actor did a perfect imitation of the great dictator's television addresses, using a Spitting Image rubber mask. He thumped the table, shook his fingers at the screen, turning the old gestures of menace and intimidation into harmless grotesque. But when I asked him to take off the mask and let me take a photograph, he shyly refused, for fear that someone might mark him down for trouble if Saddam ever comes back. When I talked to the head of security for the Arbil region, he took me out of town into the middle of a field of ripening wheat. In town, a crowd might gather; in his own office, somebody might be listening.

The Iraqi army is twenty-five minutes from Arbil, massed behind defensive positions on a low, burnt hill which slopes down to the river at Kelek. Sometimes Saddam closes the border; sometimes he opens it. Today it is open, and through field glasses I can see the Iraqi border guards, strutting about in the heat haze, a kilometre away, processing a load of Kurdish workers standing on the back of a flat-bed truck. Then I watch the truck proceed cautiously across the concrete bridge and stop at the Kurdish checkpoint. There it is mounted on blocks and its undercarriage is inspected for explosive devices, often attached to the bumpers. The workers are off-loaded and their documents are checked. Iraqi agents are often smuggled into such convoys, and the Kurds do their best to weed them out. But the border procedures feel porous and unconvincing. They need metal detectors, search rooms – the whole paraphernalia of any normal state – but they can't even afford a proper metal barrier across the bridge, so people float through unnoticed, past the drink sellers and peanut hawkers and old women squatting by the road waiting for the bus.

The local *peshmerga* confer with Behjet, who reluctantly gives permission for his 'sheep' to be taken across the river to get a still closer look at the Iraqi positions from a vantage point on the other side. We leave the LandCruisers behind, since they may attract fire, and walk across the bridge to a village which lies just beneath the Iraqi guns. The local *peshmerga* spirit us through back alleys, telling us to keep our heads down and behind the walls. At the telephone exchange, they take me up a stairway, rocketed with artillery in 1991 and now a treacherous mass of rubble and twisted iron. Through binoculars, perched gingerly on top of a protecting wall, I watch the Iraqi soldiers watching us, sauntering to and fro between their dugouts, weapons over their shoulders, binoculars in their hands. They point at my binoculars and I duck out of sight. As I cross back across the river, feeling the Iraqis tracking me in their sights, I hear the distant thunder of unseen American jets high up out of sight in the stingingly bright blue sky.

GENOCIDE

Barzan must have been a beautiful village once, rising in terraces from the big river at the bottom of the valley, up through a sheltering cleft in the hillside through alluvial fields to the sheltering mountains behind. You can see how extensive it must once have been, from the piles of field stone, strewn about the lower terraces. These piles, through which poke the steel rods that once supported lintels and roofs, are all that remain of the traditional home of the Barzani tribe.

After the collapse of Mulla Mustafa's rebellion in 1975, Saddam took swift and terrible revenge. The entire village was dynamited, house by house, and the population was deported to camps near Kushtepe and Diyana, near Arbil. There Saddam's police kept them under close watch.

Then, in July 1983, at a time when the Barzani were in league with the Iranians, providing intelligence and reconnaissance support in the Kurdish hills against Saddam's troops, Saddam struck again at the Barzani tribe. His forces surrounded the camps at Kushtepe and Diyana, and rounded up every man wearing a red turban, a sign of membership in the Barzani clan. All males between the ages of 12 and 80 were loaded on to trucks and driven away towards Baghdad. They were never seen or heard from again. Their women were left behind to fend for themselves, never knowing what had happened. In March 1991, during the uprising, the Barzani widows fled to Iran. Since then, they have returned at last to their native village. Caritas, the Swiss charity, is building them new homes. They have running water, concrete floors, a corrugated iron roof over their heads for the first time. But none of it dulls the ache of not knowing what happened to their men.

The long grey hair of the Barzani widows flows unbraided and unadorned down their dark mourning garments. They sit barefoot and cross-legged at the entrances to their empty houses, with their surviving female children, waiting for the return of their menfolk. Their houses are empty, they explain bitterly; their storehouses of corn and jars of oil are empty too, for there are no men to provide for them. They survive on the charity of the foreigners. It is no way for a woman to live.

The Iraqi soldiers came in the night, they said, talking in the stunned monotone of people trapped in sorrow, and they took their men from their beds and their children from their cots. They took cripples and blind people too, all the men of Barzani. And no one knew where they had been taken. Some people had said there were mass graves, but nothing certain had ever been found. The hand of evil had swept their men off the face of the earth. Their faces streaked with tears, left to flow and not wiped away, the Barzani widows said they could not master this grief, because there was no end to it. The worst of it was that there was simply no defence against the pain of hoping, of believing that one day you would raise your eyes along the dusty, single-track road wending its way to the village through the mountains, and see a column of survivors returning at last.

Nationalism seeks to hallow death, to redeem individual loss and link it to destiny and fate. A lonely frightened boy with a gun who dies at a crossroads in a fire-fight ceases to be just a lonely frightened boy. In the redeeming language of nationalism, he joins the imagined community of the martyrs. All along the highways of Kurdistan, the portraits of *peshmerga* martyrs gaze down at you from the plinths where once hung portraits of Saddam. These portraits are the nationalist folk art of Kurdistan. In one, a warrior is shown standing amidst the high mountain snows; in another, by a lake, with a plover floating in mid-air, like the breath of hope. The pictures depict them in uniform, with their weapons on their shoulders, staring at the present, from the safety of death, looking back with a worried expression, as if wishing to be reassured that their sacrifices were not in vain.

The road from Barzan led eastwards, down from the mountains, past Sulaymaniyah into a vast valley floor sown with wheat. We passed turbanned men scything grass for their animals, and groups of villagers squatting by the roadsides with huge bundles of grass, waiting to be picked up by a passing truck; later, we would see them all, crowded impossibly but cheerfully on the back of some flat bed roaring past us, waving, while the old women sat glumly in veils on top of the grass bundles. We drove past rice-paddies, with men and women in bare feet, their clothing up about their knees, digging in the plants; and children, skin brown as their hair, selling sunflower seeds in little blue packets by the side of the road.

At its most elemental, nationalism is perhaps the desire to have political dominion over a piece of land that one loves. Before anything, there must be a fierce attachment to the land itself and a sense that there is nothing else like this, nothing so beautiful, anywhere else in the world. The mountains, the Kurds say, are their only friend, the only ones who never betray. But the mountains are also what bind them together as a people, sever them from others, give them a habitat and a home, create in them every day the desire that one day this will be truly theirs and no one else's. As Muhyeddin said, that night on his porch in Sulaymaniyah as I got up to go, 'Look, it all comes down to this.' He made a tight fist and held it up close to his face 'We want something, even if it is small, which no one will ever take from us.'

The road led south and east, through the lush plains of Shahrizor, towards the Iranian border. Just five kilometres from that border, sheltered on three sides by round treeless hills, now turning brown in the May heat, stands the town of Halabja.

On 16 March 1988 – at the time of the Kurdish New Year, and less than forty-eight hours after Kurdish *peshmerga* had seized the town from Iraqi forces – Iraqi planes swooped over the city dropping canisters of mustard gas, nerve gas and cyanide. Within a few hours, 5000 people lay dead.

There are films, taken by Iranian cameramen, hours after the attack. The colours of the children's clothes are bright; the blighted grass and leaves are still green; there is still colour in some of the faces; fathers lie in doorways, their arms over their children; mothers lie with their faces in the river, seeking to wash away the searing in their throats. It was the first chemical attack on a human population since the First World War. After it was over, the Iraqi army entered Halabja and dynamited the town.

At the outskirts I stop by an extraordinary pile of steel reinforcing rods and collapsed roof, beneath which there soon appear two cheerful children and a watchful mother, who is hanging out her washing on the angle between a cantilevered roof and a terrace. Then on the left as you go in, about seventy-five metres of pure rubble, not an undamaged concrete brick to be seen, then, on the right, proceeding up the main street, signs of attempts to dynamite the shops: pillars crushed under collapsing roofs; other pillars blown away, leaving only the exposed steel rods holding up the roof; huge artillery-shell-sized holes in the rear walls; on and on up the street, piles of rubble, roofs fallen in. But everywhere, despite everything, families are continuing to burrow out a life out in the ruins. Up the pitted street, past tea shops and feed stores, I come upon a man painting pictures inside a little library, including one picture of a woman in a red dress carrying a pitcher of water beside a stream near a tall flowering tree. The houses rise up a hillside; and from the contours of the hills, I can tell that this is a vision of the lost Halabja. Down another alley, I find sandal makers, impassively spinning the white yarn from which they stitch the immaculate white uppers of *klash*. Next door to the sandal makers, I find a neat-as-a-pin plumber's merchant with his cocks and stops and washers laid out in precise rows; next door to him, a carpenter, with a revolver lying on a seat amid some sawdust. Halabja market is full of pushcarts piled with beans and strawberries. I look at them and wonder whether their membranes and cells contain any memory or trace of chemical.

I come across a tall and distinguished teacher on her way back home for midday lunch from her primary school. We walk together through the ruins and she says, yes, here, he died, and there, in that pile, her body was found, and there in the basement of what was once a tea house – she is pointing to a dark hole in the middle of a pile of rubble – the *peshmerga* found fifty bodies. 'And one of them was my sister.'

When afternoon class resumes, she takes me to her primary school. How many children died in the attack? She does not reply, but instead goes to her blackboard and writes down a number: 198.

The children in her class watch her from their rough-planked desks: 7-year-olds in plaits tied with bows, black-eyed, giggling behind their hands, their faces lit by the hot, slanting light through the barred windows. What do you teach them about Halabja? I ask. They know. They know, she says.

She claps her hands, and they flood out of the room in a tumult, assembling in the school yard with all the other classes, shouting patriotic Kurdish songs at the top of their voice for the foreign visitor; little exuberant voices shouting into the sunlight. They surround me, pressing close, a school-yard full.

At the end, I drive up into the hills over the town, so that I can get the Halabja dust out of my lungs. I take a path up the hillside and find myself face to face with the mass graves of the victims. They are buried, in large, featureless caissons of concrete, overlooking the city now faint in the heat haze. I think of the Barzani widows, weeping in their doorways. Behjet and Taha take off their shoes, because it is the setting of the sun, and they kneel and say their prayers. The murmur of their prayers rises in the air behind me as I sit and look at the blighted town below.

Genocide is a worn and debased term, casually hurled at every outrage, every violence, even applied to events where no death, only shame or abuse, occurs. But it is a word which does mean something: the project to exterminate a people for no other reason than because they are that people. Before the experience of genocide, a people may not believe they belong to a nation. Before genocide, they may believe it is a matter of personal choice whether they belong or believe. After genocide, it becomes their fate.

Genocide and nationalism have an entwined history. It was genocide that convinced the Jews and even convinced the gentile world that they were a people who would never be safe until they had a nation state of their own. As with the Jews, so with the Kurds. To see Halabja, to sit by those faceless graves, is to know that the chemical attack marked them apart for ever, just as it revealed, beyond doubt or equivocation, what their neighbours were capable of feeling and doing.

The Kurdish leaders all tell you their goal is not a nation state. Such a goal is too large for us, Muhyeddin said that night on the veranda, too impractical, too unrealistic. It is a longing which will only render us mad, or fanatical. We must be content with autonomy within the existing states. We must swallow our longings and make our peace with the nation state order which was dropped over our land like a net after Versailles.

But after seeing Halabja, you realize one thing very clearly: autonomy will never do. It is a stopping point on a destination. But it cannot ever be the end of the road. For Halabja happened, and for a people who have known genocide, there is only one thing that will do: a nation state of their own.

GUERILLAS

It is raining in Raniya, and the rain is hammering on the tin roof of the hotel veranda where I am sitting. Black-veiled women, clutching their skirts about them, are running for cover through the downpour. Water is gushing down the gutters, carrying with it a tide of filth and offal and market leavings. The tea samovar is steaming, and the air is pungent with the smell of charcoal burning in the brazier. The hotel cook is slicing strips from a lamb's carcass hung up on a hook next to my table. Behjet and Taha sit beside me, with long faces. They are unhappy with their sheep. I am leaving their protection for a day and a night to visit a guerilla band in the mountains. I am about to be turned over to the protection of a young boy named Hassan, who has arrived with a LandCruiser and will drive me through the mountain passes to the guerilla camp. I am not just passing from one warlord's protection to another. From Behjet's point of view, I am going over to visit the enemy. For I am going to see the PKK, the guerilla organization of Turkish Kurds, who use the mountain hideouts of the Kurdish enclave to train for raids on the Turkish army across the frontier. Behjet's party, the KDP, opposes these raids for fear that the Turks will retaliate by closing the frontier and severing the main lifeline that keeps the enclave alive. In the autumn of 1992, the KDP *peshmerga* went to war against the PKK guerillas, to stop them using the enclave as a base. Now, however, there is an uneasy ceasefire between them. I am profiting from the ceasefire to pay a visit to what I know to be, by repute, one of the last national liberation movements of a classical Marxist kind.

I soon realize how foolhardy this trip may be. I have not paid the weather sufficient respect, and now it is taking its revenge. The bridges are out – washed away – and so we are soon weaving and bouncing our way through ploughed fields, seeking the flatter, stony shallows where the river will let us cross. We plunge into the river up to the tops of the tyres and struggle across.

Hassan is 18 with the wispy stubble of his first moustache on his upper lip. He speaks in a broad Sorani dialect, so mountain-bound that my translator can barely make out what he is saying. But he smiles gaily, no matter how vile or difficult the road, and I soon realize that he is a veritable maestro of the four-wheel drive. For four hours, he coaxes and cajoles the ancient car up a muddy, rutted, single-track road, more suited to the smugglers' pack-mules which keep passing us, than to a vehicle. Hassan gently nudges the big machine up the corkscrew bends, through the waterfalls which are carving up the surface, revving the wheels gingerly through the mudslides and rockslides which have carried the road away altogether. We pass villages which are being pounded by flash-floods, cascading off the mountains in an angry chocolate brown torrent. Villagers are vainly trying to canalize the water with corrugated iron ripped from their roofs. Children huddle with beasts inside dark doorways, waving to Hassan and me as we pass. After four hours, Hassan pulls up in an encampment of tents made of tree branches and white plastic sheeting. Smugglers, he says, and takes us inside to a large, snug, dry tent where, having removed our shoes and crawled to our places past a line of suspicious men eating rice with their hands, we are served delicious hot mint tea, which we drink to the sound of the rain hammering on the plastic sheeting. These smugglers run mule-teams over the steep passes into Iran, which lies only a kilometre or so over the mountains. In one corner of the tent I see stacks of Iranian margarine, cooking oil and sugar. If there is Iranian heroin, I do not see any. In a whisper, Hassan tells me the smugglers and the guerillas work together. Meaning? I can only assume the smugglers hand them a cut of their profits, in money or in kind, and the guerillas provide protection.

Within a kilometre of the smugglers, we reach the guerilla camp itself, set in a huge semicircular bowl which rises from a violent river raging at the bottom towards a flank of ridges which protect the camp from aerial attack. Dotted here and there on the hillside are dun-coloured, rain-soaked tents, a typical Kurdish adobe house with a radio antenna rising above its flat roof and at the centre a two-storey adobe house, in front of which a pair of ragged children are playing. The house, it turns out, is a barracks for guerilla officers upstairs, and it is there that I will sleep. Downstairs sleeps a Kurdish family of four and their goats, sheep and chickens.

As I stare at the hillside, I realize that there are women everywhere: single files of them, in combat gear, carrying rifles, running up the goat tracks towards the heights; others descending the goat tracks and disappearing, one by one, into what appears to be a large mess tent, dug into the hillside; while other female warriors, their hair pinned up beneath berets, mount guard on hill redoubts above me. The anxious-looking French-speaking 'liaison officer' who sticks by me explains. 'We are having a women's conference.'

He leads me up the goat tracks to the mess tent. Inside, fluorescent strip lights hang from the roof of the tent – there must be a generator in the camp, but how did they ever get it up the road? In the stark white glow, there are a hundred women, ranged neatly on rough hewn benches grouped around a central podium. Red, yellow and green banners – the Kurdish colours – hang from the roof of the tent. They say, 'Long Live Apo, Long Live the PKK'. In one corner, a woman is standing and is in the midst of a long, quiet, apparently reproachful speech, while the other women listen quietly, some taking notes. The astonishing thing is how young they all are: most in their teens, the oldest in their late 20s, unsmiling, earnest, youthful faces, some with rimless glasses, their hair pushed up beneath berets or tied in ponytails; all in the shapeless baggy uniforms worn by the men; Kalashnikovs leaning on their knees or resting on the corner of a bench, the whole atmosphere tense with earnest, adolescent attention.

It is a self-criticism session, my liaison officer whispers. He and I are the only males in the tent. Some recent guerilla raids, he says, went wrong, and lives were needlessly lost, because of errors in tactics and strategy. That is what the women are speaking about. One by one the girls rise to their feet and deliver little speeches, their heads down, their voices modest and sober, unrhetorical, controlled, but, to my ears, full of the plaintive, even anguished tone of true believers whose faith is being sorely tried.

The gathering recesses for fifteen minutes, and the girls pair off in twos, roll cigarettes and then stroll up and down, arm in arm, whispering and smoking. I follow them and get talking to a warrior girl named Milan. She is older than many of them – perhaps 25 – with brown hair buried beneath exactly the sort of grey deer-stalker style forage cap I remember from newsreels of Leon Trotsky in the Russian civil war. She wears the baggy trousers of the fighters, and a pair of Puma trainers, and she has 'Long Live Apo' neatly embroidered in red thread on the right breast of her military jacket. Apo is Apo Ocalan, leader of her party. Have you ever met him? I ask. But of course, she says, blushing with pleasure and embarrassment. She trained as a guerilla fighter in Ocalan's camp in the Bekaa valley in the Lebanon. 'That was where I learned Marxist dialectics, military tactics and Kurdish.'

Kurdish? I am astonished. Milan smiles and walks some distance in silence along the parade ground of rough stones that has been dug out of the hillside. 'You see,' she explains, 'I was born in Australia. In a suburb of Melbourne, actually. I didn't know I was Kurdish until I was seventeen.' Now that she has said this, I pick up the Australian lilt in her accent. She apologizes again. 'Forgive my English. I have not spoken it for four years.'

How does a suburban Australian girl end up as a Marxist nationalist guerilla in the hills of Kurdistan? Some longing for a certainty, powerful enough to pull up a life by the roots, must be at work here.

'It began when I asked my parents why I had this name. Milan. They told me it was Kurdish, but I didn't know what that meant, and they couldn't tell me. Fortunately the party had contacts in Melbourne.'

So I begin to see it – an Australian teenager, living inside a culture beyond roots, beyond the past, suddenly discovers that she has some. She discovers she has the most painful kind of national belonging there is, to a people who have no nation of their own.

Melbourne is not a place for causes. Going with the party is the most radical thing a Melbourne girl could possibly have done, and that is why she did it. She suddenly sees her life's vocation so clearly. She is young: the very extremism of the party, the radical nature of the call it makes upon her, is so imperative, that she succumbs immediately.

Within months of finding out about the PKK, she has left her family behind and is living in tent barracks in the Bekaa. When the party judges her ready, when she finally speaks the language of the nation she calls her own, they spirit her across the border to winter in the mountain passes and train for action. All she will say that casts light on this alchemy inside herself is that when she is here, in the mountains, she feels – here she pauses for words and looks out at the peaks – 'close to life'. More silence, then she says, 'I am alive here.'

But, I say, pointing at Iran, which lies just a kilometre away across the river below us. 'There's a lot of death here too.' The Iranian gun positions overlook the camp. 'But that is why,' she says, 'life is precious here. That is exactly why. I could lose it at any time.'

With a suburban clumsiness of my own, I persist. 'But how did you manage here? Life is hard.' She stops, kicks a piece of mountain shale with her shoe. 'Yes,' she says, 'we only had these on our feet this winter.' I am looking down at her white Puma trainers. My liaison officer has already pointed out to me the hobbling gait of a young man who lost all his toes to frostbite. 'Sometimes there was two feet of snow. I was often sick. My body is not ready for it,' she says, self-reproachfully, as if wishing she could jettison its Australian education in comfort, the inner softness that steals upon you when you live the life of the full refrigerator and the sunny beach. 'Soon, I will be ready for combat.' Already this gentle, soft-cheeked girl could kill me, would kill me, if her leaders ordered her to.

I want to hear the motors of indoctrination turn in her, and so I ask her what makes the PKK different from the other Kurdish parties in the struggle. 'They are tribal parties, who have made their peace with the traditional feudal and patriarchal nature of Kurdish society. We are the only party of the masses. We want to change the tribal, feudal and patriarchal nature of our society.'

Is that why so many young women join? 'Feminism is at the centre of our party. We want to change the condition of women in Kurdistan. First, we want to change it within the party itself. Then we want to change it outside, for all Kurdish women.' She does speak like this, in soft, fervent sentences that seem to come from outside herself, from the authoritative heart of the party, from all those hours in airless tents in the Bekaa, studiously writing on rough-hewn benches.

'Does he listen to you?' I suddenly ask, meaning Apo, the leader, the great one, whose name is lovingly embroidered in red thread on her breast. 'Oh yes, oh yes. He has encouraged the women to think for themselves, to speak up and make their voices heard.' This is not said in a forced or mechanical way, but with zealous credulity.

But Apo says a lot of things, and the path of his wisdom has a jagged and uneven shape. He began the armed struggle in 1984 with attacks, not only on Turkish civilian targets, but also on so-called Kurdish collaborators. Then, when these tactics proved too grisly even for his own supporters, he abandoned them and directed his guerillas against military, rather than civilian, targets. At first he was hostile to the creation of the Kurdish enclave; then he changed his mind and supported it. Sometimes he has practised peace with the Iraqi Kurdish groups, sometimes war. One wonders whether, in Milan's mind, the path of Apo's wisdom still runs smooth, or whether there is some tiny grit of doubt, deep down, in the machinery of incantation that whirs so smoothly as she talks. But casting for the doubt within her is perhaps a waste of time. What compels her about Apo, what makes her embroider his name, and, like all the men and women in the camp, place smiling pictures of him, like icons, in the corner of every tent, is that he has released them from doubt and from the burden of a questioning self. Milan's cause all but abolishes the division between individual and group. She has embraced a kind of belonging so intense that those who share it may look like mental slaves to an outsider like myself. To themselves, they seem at last to be free. For that is what is most striking about

Milan, as she smiles, shakes my hand and dashes back to the mess tent: she is truly happy here.

I soon discover that she is not the only one here who has returned from exile or expatriation. My own 'liaison officer', a rather gentle, soft-spoken and apologetic young man, who seems slightly ill-at-ease with the gun on his back, turns out to have been born among the Kurdish gastarbeiter in Germany. He served as the party's representative in Spain and France, without ever having lived in Kurdistan itself. His fellow liaison officer, a bluffer, more outgoing kind of man, turns out to be from Dortmund, and later, when we are sitting on the floor in their bare adobe-walled dormitory, drinking tea, they talk longingly of the expatriate world, and how isolated they feel high up in the mountains. Every evening, they take out their small Sony short waves and pull in the distant voices of Europe, especially the Turkish service of the BBC. With Milan, I had sensed how a cause could become a completely satisfying form of belonging. With those men, with their slightly shamefaced questions about whether I had ever been to Dortmund, had I ever been to such and such Kurdish restaurant in Frankfurt, I sensed nationalist belonging, high up on these Kurdish hillsides, as a kind of nobly chosen imprisonment.

When we have drunk many glasses of tea together, by the light of the spirit lamp hung over their horse-hair pallets, I ask the men whether it is possible to fall in love during the revolution. I see that I have touched a nerve. This is a guerilla camp, under military discipline – there is no place for relationships here. Marriage and children are out of the question. 'As long as Kurdistan is not free, we are not free to love and marry,' says my French-speaking liaison officer, with an unhappy look on his face. (When I report this remark to Behjet, on my return, he sighs and shakes his head. He is used to PKK political correctness and he has no time for it. 'A man who tells you he will not marry until Kurdistan is free is simply a man who does not want to marry.')

It is time, they suddenly tell me, rising to their feet, to take me to see the camp commander. He is, I now learn, none other than Apo Ocalan's younger brother, Osman. We make our way down along the goat tracks that snake this way and that in the darkness. The rain clouds have cleared and the sky framed by the mountains is lit with stars.

The leader is reclining on a horse-hair pallet, eating his dinner beneath a portrait of his brother. He is playing with his rice, sopping it up with a piece of *nan*, tossing extra rice back on to the plate with a bored flick of his hand. There is a large silver service revolver in his waistband, just visible beneath his black leather jacket. He is a brawny man, like his brother, and he doesn't like the foreign media. 'You all call us terrorists,' he barks, when I sit down. 'We are fighting for Kurdistan, and you call us terrorists,' he repeats, with a half-scowl, half-smile. It's a game, this bating, and it must go on until the matter of who will dominate the interview is settled to the leader's satisfaction.

'I didn't climb all the way up this mountain in the rain to interview terrorists,' I reply, and he grunts and looks away. His men hover in the doorway, waiting for a signal to take his plates away. He waves his finger, and they dart about clearing away the dishes, while the leader wipes the rice from his heavy black moustache.

I ask him why the Ocalan family joined 'the struggle'. We were poor, he replies, and the Turks treated us like dirt, that's why. My brother was smart in school, he always had the best grades, and he figured out that we had to fight. 'That's why we are here.' He looks down as he speaks, answers tonelessly and woodenly, suddenly the younger brother who doesn't write the lines, just speaks the ones that his smarter big brother thinks up. He says a lot more, but I switch off and wonder to myself, as I look at him, indolent bandit king at ease, how much nationalism there is in his motivation, how much pure banditry. What seems clear is that for him the ends matter much less than the means. The ends – a free, socialist, feminist Kurdistan – are better left to his brother, to true believers. He is obviously more interested in the means. It is the guns, the AK-47s, that speak for him, that speak *to* him.

Next morning, the guns begin speaking. I am led into the next valley, along a goat track, past sentries and look-outs, to a second training camp, to see a live ammunition practice. Ocalan is not there. The commander is an amusing grey-haired old fox, who sits cross-legged in the middle of his American army tent, with his officers around him, eating a dish of fried mint leaves, mixed with tomato. He orders a brigade to attack a redoubt below, and then sits back to watch the show, inviting me to join him, cross-legged beside him. Behind me, squatting on a slope, are several hundred guerillas, silently observing us both.

His soldiers are so terribly young, I think, as the attack begins. A rocket-propelled grenade, shoulder-launched from behind a rock below me, spatters harmlessly against the basalt face of the mountain opposite, sending up a plume of shale. I try to keep from starting as the machine guns open up on the white flag flying over the redoubt under fire. Under the cover of this hail of fire, members of the platoon begin sneaking forward, hiding behind rocks, edging forward on hands and knees, Kalashnikovs or pistols in their hands. The smack and thud of bullets into the dirt around them, the whine of ricochets, the after-blast of more grenades set the enclosed space of the mountain valley echoing. In a minute the leader of the platoon is at the base of the redoubt, and I see him lob a grenade up, see it pause in the air and then explode with a grey and unreal puff of smoke as in the movies. When the leader of the platoon grabs the white flag and then sets fire to the straw bales inside the redoubt to announce its capture, the massed guerillas on the hills behind me break into applause and chants of: 'Apo is our leader! Apo is our leader!'

Later, when their commander has dismissed them at the parade ground, and they are all dancing, in a semi-circle, arm over arm, chanting war songs, their Puma-clad feet pounding out a shared rhythm in the dirt, and the dust is rising around their shapeless brown trousers, I find myself struck by a sense of having seen this all before. Was it some footage of a Vietcong camp in the jungles of Vietnam? Was it with Che Guevara in the Bolivian mountains? Or was the echo in my mind much older, back to the grainy footage of the mountain guerillas of China, on Mao's long march?

I had managed, by climbing to the highest and remotest peaks of Kurdistan, to find a by now nearly forgotten relic of twentieth-century nationalism: the guerilla army waging a war of so-called national liberation, complete with Marxist texts, the wooden vocabulary I had heard from Milan, the red flags, the fervent communitarianism of this collective dance, and, above all, the abdication of the self before the all-powerful leader. I had supposed that the end of the Cold War had marked the end of all that. But it turned out to be alive and well in the mountains of Kurdistan. In its anti-feudal, anti-tribal rhetoric, in its feminism, it purports to be modern. Marxism, after all, is a form of modernism. But this is a game with shadows, for what, at the end of the twentieth century, seems more unmodern than a movement still in pursuit of a radiant tomorrow which half of the world is just awakening from as from a nightmare?

As I leave the camp, bound now for Turkey and then for home, two thoughts occur to me. The first is that, between these guerillas' visions of what a free Kurdistan should look like, and Muhyeddin's, there is little ground for compromise or reconciliation. When nationalist visions are in such a degree of contradiction, the usual result is war. Nationalism, as a rhetoric of modernity, has proved no more effective in uniting the Kurds than tribalism. Indeed, nationalism, when viewed from this Kurdish mountain top, seems like a form of tribalism, and one can only predict that tribal wars over the meaning and direction of the Kurdish struggle will continue for a long time to come.

The second thought – since the PKK is a Turkish movement, directed entirely at the Turkish occupation of the Kurdish homeland in southern Turkey – is that this particular guerilla movement is influenced by nothing so much as by the style and ferocity of its enemy, the Turkish army. I knew I had seen the weapon in Ocalan's brother's belt somewhere before. It was a Turkish military service revolver. Same arms, same ruthlessness. Nationalist movements and the state security forces which fight them often end up inside the same culture of violence. Enemies sometimes resemble each other as closely as brothers. That was the hypothesis I wanted to test, as I descended from the Kurdish mountain tops, said my farewells to Behjet and Taha, and recrossed the frontier into Turkey.

WITH THE FERRETS

Feret has an eager and forgettable young face. He wears interrogator's shades and a thirty-eight in his shoulder holster. He is 24 years old and he is with

Turkish special forces. I ask him what the special forces do. He smiles and says it is against regulations to tell me. But today he is taking me into the mountain villages where the Turkish army are fighting 'the terrorists' – his word for the PKK guerillas. He talks American. 'No way the terrorists are gonna win. No way.'

While he is out assembling the escort – an armoured car and two Landrovers full of Turkish soldiers – I tell my Kurdish driver that there is a small rodent, with sharp incisors, which London's East End gangsters are reputed to stick down the trousers of their enemies. My Kurdish driver smiles thinly, says nothing.

South-eastern Turkey is a land of opportunity for young ferrets. The whole area is like Northern Ireland, a vast military camp: the helicopters drone overhead; F-16s on strafing or reconnaissance runs scream over the tops of Kurdish villages; armoured personnel carriers and tanks squat astride every major rural road crossing; in the Kurdish market towns, there is a man with a walkie-talkie in every café. I have been shadowed for days. They lurk behind the pillars of the inner courtyard in the hotel. When I venture out in a car, they are just behind in small white Renaults, with video cameras, recording what I see, whom I speak to.

There are bright shining careers in counter-insurgency to be made here, and there are no obstacles in a clever boy's path: civil liberties are permanently suspended; you can arrest any Kurdish troublemaker you want; none of your superiors cares how you get your information from the bloodied suspects in the cells. True, there are some local journalists, from a Turkish paper called *Gundem*, who report so-called human rights abuses. But what's to stop you using your gun on them too? Eleven journalists have been shot already reporting the dirty war. Another one will hardly be noticed.

Foreign journalists, on the other hand, require special handling. Mind you, they're all hypocrites. Especially the British. They should know that fighting terrorists is a dirty business, but they come here and tell the Turks to be nice to the Kurds. They've got the IRA wanting to tear a large piece out of Great Britain, but they come to Turkey and tell us to grant 'autonomy' to the Kurds. Stop the repression? Stop the arrests? It's enough to make any good ferret sick.

But modern security culture is all about good public relations. So the ferret bites his tongue. 'You want a good show? That's what we're gonna give you,' he says. After all, Istanbul wants to host the Olympics; Turkey wants acceptance. Hadn't the director of security at the border between Iraq and Turkey said that he wanted to have 'human procedures, like you have in Europe'? As everyone knows, Europe's procedures are certainly human. It is good form in the counter-insurgency business to tell the foreigners how civilized and humane you would like to be. Even the ferret ventures a few remarks in this vein. As we rock and bump our way up the mountain tracks, past the army camps, barracks, airfields and surveillance posts, past Kurdish village women who mask their faces from the ferret, he admits that he wished the government spent a bit more on the roads and a little less on the security. The ferret is surely correct: never have I been in a country which spent more on ferrets.

The convoy finally reaches the Kurdish village they think it is safe for me to see. There are a hundred poor single-storey flat-roofed adobe houses, straggling up a hillside under the brow of a jagged cliff. On the clifftops, I spot the glint of Turkish binoculars. Down in the village, the women are laying ropes of sheep dung on the rooftops to dry as fuel for their fires. Children, sheep, chickens, are careening down the filthy winding tracks between the houses.

I have come to see the village guards, the Kurds who are armed and paid by the Turkish military to provide protection for the village. It is alleged that the guards terrorize their fellow villagers, commit atrocities in neighbouring villages and blame it on the 'terrorists'. The ferret knows I've heard these stories, so before I set out, I was shown a thick wad of photographs showing recent atrocities. There were so many pools of blood, so many glassy-eyed dead children beside their mothers, so many old men with small round puncture holes in their necks that I didn't bother to ask the obvious question. Did the 'terrorists' do this or the ferrets? Neither remembers any more, or cares. What matters is that terror works. Terror is the coinage of power. Make them fear you, say the terrorists, and the people will not collaborate with the police. Make them fear you, say the police, and they will not collaborate with the terrorists. And so it goes, the logic of escalating ferocity.

As the village children gather round the strange foreigner, a Kurdish man in a smooth silk suit with a machine gun on his back hits about with his fist, knocking the children away. Little boys yelp like beaten dogs and cower behind him. He comes up and shakes my hand: the local village guard commander.

It is never safe here, he says, gesturing at the hilltop behind me. Over that mountain, there is a village full of 'them'. Village guards are constantly ambushed on the roads at night. The school-teacher has been scared away by the attacks, so none of the children go to school. He lays about him again and strikes a boy close by with the flat of his hand. Kurdish men in poor country people's suits crowd around, their heads down, saying nothing. The ferret is close by, watching behind his interrogator's glasses. A Turkish army cameraman is filming every person I speak to.

I break away up one of the village tracks with the village grocer, a red-faced old man in traditional baggy Kurdish trousers, who whispers furtively as we walk. He is caught between the terrorists and the Turkish army. 'If we collaborate with the army, the terrorists try to kill us. If we collaborate with the terrorists,' he makes a gesture towards the ferret, who is gaining upon us, 'he will kill us.'

'What did he say?' the ferret asks, in a friendly, curious voice, as the convoy escorts me away. 'He says the army is doing a great job,' I say. The rest of the way home, through the prison camp that is southern Turkey, the ferret and I are silent.

The ferret is doing Atatürk's work, fighting to keep the unitary state of modern Turkey together. You can't compromise when the very unity of a nation is at stake. There is no price that is not worth paying. Pull the balaclava over your face; put some bullets in the chamber; go out and break some Kurdish doors down in the night. Pull them out of bed. Put a bullet through their brains. Dirty wars are a paradise for ferrets. But they are also a paradise for Apo Ocalan and his brother. Nationalism gives them both a cover for barbarism: one kills collaborators in the name of the liberation struggle; the other kills sympathizers in the name of the security of the nation state.

What will break this cycle? With enough terror, you can always stop terrorism. But can you stop a people from believing this place is their homeland? Can you stop people wanting their own state? The Kurds here know there is a tiny enclave next door, where a Kurd can be a Kurd, and they know what that feels like. You can smile, sing, make a joke in your own language. You can go up to a foreigner and talk to him. There are no consequences to fear in a place you call your own.

This border region between Turkey and Iraq is where I finally learn the human difference between a people who have their own place, and a people who do not. On one side, hearts and minds are open. On the other, hearts pound with fear. On the one side, they shout 'Allo Mistair' in greeting. On the other, they shrink from foreign contact for fear of trouble. Statelessness is a state of mind, and it is akin to homelessness. This is what a nationalist understands: a people can become completely human, completely themselves, only when they have a place of their own.

The longing for this is too strong to be stopped by terror. I leave the ferret at his barracks, double back into the mountain passes, elude my security tail and end up on a mountain road at dusk, my way blocked by a huge flock of sheep. A shepherd comes towards me through the rocky pastures. He is old, burned dark by the sun. He wears two rough, untreated hides sewn together like the armour of a warrior prophet. His eyes are blazing and he strides up to me, pushing his sheep aside with his crook. I ask him where I am, for I have lost my way on these high mountain roads. As if astonished that I should ever have believed anything else, he points to the bare burned hills around us, bathed in silver light, and he says, in a voice that is both soft and sure, 'This is Kurdistan.'

N O R T H E R N

I R E L A N D

MIRROR, MIRROR

The shutters are run down on the butchers and the betting shops, and crowds gather silently on the pavements. In the distance, from the tight warren of streets off the Shankill Road, comes the skirl of pipes and the tread of feet. A flat-bed truck appears first, bearing wreaths with the initials of the Ulster Volunteer Force picked out in red, white and blue flowers; then comes a hearse with a flower-decked coffin, followed by a silent army of men. There are perhaps two hundred of them, wearing big-shouldered, double-breasted suits, white shirts, black ties. Their dark glasses glint as they turn to scan the crowd. When they see a camera, a posse breaks ranks and comes over to pass the word. 'Now don't be filming. Wouldn't be wise.'

The Shankill is paying its last respects to Herbie McCallum. He had been providing protection for a Protestant parade, armed with a pistol and a grenade, when the police tried to re-route the march away from the Catholic Ardoyne. Scuffles broke out between Loyalists and the police. Some say the grenade was intended for the Catholics, others for the police, but the person who took the full force of the explosion was 29-year-old Brian 'Herbie' McCallum, father of two, paramilitary hero to his friends, Protestant terrorist to his enemies.

Before the rifles were fired into the air in the graveside salute, one of Herbie McCallum's commanders gave a speech in which he said:

To stand for capitulation. To stand silent, immobile in the face of treachery. To suffer ignominiously the malignment of our people, our culture, our history. To bow to the whims of mere pragmatists – is cowardice. Volunteer Brian Herbie McCallum and many many Ulster Volunteers who have made the ultimate sacrifice are testimony that this Nation will be defended.

Later the same afternoon, I am driving down Antrim Road, thinking how much it looks like my own street in north London. There are the same brick terraced houses lining both sides, with trimmed box hedges and rose bushes nestling beneath the bay windows. Everything is British and familiar, so what is this bus doing ablaze in the middle of the road? I am about thirty feet away, getting out of my car, and ahead of me a fireman is running towards the fire when an explosion throws him on to his back. When I look up again, the fireman is struggling to his feet and the bus is burning more fiercely than ever.

I've driven into a Belfast bus-hijacking. A minute before I arrived, a man with a gun had stepped out on to the road, ordered the driver and passengers off and then lobbed in a petrol bomb. Chances are the gunman may be watching, waiting to ambush the police. Armoured grey Land-Rovers have already blocked off the road. Officers in flak-jackets have taken up position behind walls. Judging from the fact that the street leads up from the Shankill, the gunman is a Loyalist.

Children quickly gather to splash around the hydrants while mothers stand out on the front steps in their aprons to watch the bus burn down to its frame. A woman comes over and says, 'You mustn't think this is how it is all the time. This is a great wee city. Don't get the wrong idea.'

I try not to get the wrong idea, but in the course of the next three hours, I come across two more hijackings, delivery vans left smouldering in the middle of residential streets, while police-marksmen cover them from suburban gardens. Over the normal sounds of a British city at night, I can hear the pop and crack of automatic weapons fire.

The two days after Herbie McCallum's funeral see the most extensive Loyalist rioting in Belfast in a decade. Forty buses and cars are hijacked and burned; there are twenty-eight gun attacks on the police and nine fire-bombings; when fire engines arrive in the Donegal Road area to put the burning cars out, the fire engine itself is hijacked, the crew thrown off it, and the tender set alight. Police called into Rathcoole, Woodvale, Shankill, Highfield and Tiger's Bay districts are fired upon. The police believe the rioting is a show of force, planned by those two hundred silent young men in dark glasses walking down the Shankill behind Herbie McCallum's coffin.

Ulster is a good place to end my journey, because it seems to reprise so much of what I've already seen on my travels: paramilitaries as in Serbian Krajina and Kurdistan; ethnic paranoia as in Croatia; the cult of male violence as in German skinhead gangs; a national security state as in Turkey. The helicopters constantly drone overhead, the Land-Rovers and armoured personnel carriers squat astride every major junction, and men in helmets stare at you down their gunsights.

Like most outsiders, I'd dismissed the Troubles as a throwback to the tribal past. Now, in 1993, Northern Ireland seems like a possible future writ large. No place in Europe has carried ethnic division as far as Belfast. The peace walls, put up in the seventies to keep people in the same street from fire-bombing and murdering each other, are now as permanent as the borders between nation states, twenty feet high in some places, sawing working-class Belfast in two.

Ethnic apartheid does reduce the death toll. In the mid-seventies, between 250 and 450 people were dying every year. Now the figure is under 100. At the same time, community segregation is growing. Sixty per cent of the population now live in areas which are more than 90 per cent Protestant or Catholic.

The segregation grows in molecular fashion: a tyre is slashed, a child is beaten up, petrol is poured through a letter box, by one side or the other, and another family decides to choose the safety of numbers. Belfast likes to talk about 'ethnic cleansing' – but molecular nastiness bears no comparison to genocide in Bosnia. If Sarajevo could look like Belfast one day, it would consider itself lucky.

In Northern Ireland, as in Croatia and Serbia, as in the Ukraine, ethnicity, religion and politics are soldered together into identities so total that it takes a defiant individual to escape their clutches. On one side people who have never been to a church in their lives have to live with the tag of Protestant. On the other, people who have no desire for a united Ireland but happen to be Catholic get labelled, once and for all, as 'nationalists'.

These labels imprison everyone in the fiction of an irreducible ethnic identity. Yet Northern Ireland's is not an ethnic war, any more than the Serbo-Croat or Ukrainian-Russian antagonisms are ethnic. In all three cases, essentially similar peoples, speaking the same or related languages, sharing the same form of life, differing in religions which few actually seem to practise, have been divided by the single fact that one has ruled over the other. It is the memory of domination in time past, or fear of domination in time future, not difference itself, which has turned conflict into an unbreakable downward spiral of political violence.

I am in Ulster to find out what Britishness looks and feels like when it has been put on the rack of a dirty war. In mainland Britain, Britishness is a casual puzzle, a subject for after-dinner conversation. In Ulster, it can be a matter of life and death. Loyalism, I thought, would serve as a mirror which would show me what the British might look like if their nation's life was on the line. I've chosen to visit in July because the great festival of Loyalism, the marching season, is about to begin. But after Herbie McCallum's funeral I'm already unsure as to what the mirror of Loyalism reveals. Protestant paramilitaries now kill more people in Northern Ireland than the IRA. Their victims range from innocent Catholics to British soldiers and members of the police. Here is a Britishness which is at war with Britain, a Britishness which swears allegiance to the Crown and the Armalite rifle.

The illusion that Britain is an island of stability in a world of troubles does not survive a day on the streets of Belfast. In reality, there is more death by political violence in Great Britain than in any other liberal democracy in the world. Since 1969 there have been 3,000 political killings and more than 50,000 people have been seriously injured. More people have died, per capita, of political violence in Great Britain than in India, Nigeria, Israel, Sri Lanka or Argentina, all nations which the British regard as more violent than their own.

There is nothing especially mysterious about this level and intensity of violence. Nationalism by its very nature defines struggles between peoples as struggles for their honour, identity and soul. When the stakes are raised this high, conflict is soon reduced to a zero-sum game. Victory for one side must mean total defeat for the other. When the stakes appear to involve survival itself, the result is violence. Such is the case in Northern Ireland. Two nation states lay claim to the province. Nine hundred thousand Protestants or descendants of Protestants wish to remain British. Six hundred thousand Catholics or descendants of Catholics mostly, but not invariably, wish to become Irish. Since one wish can only be satisfied at the expense of the other, it is scarcely surprising that the result is unending conflict.

What is more surprising than the level of violence is the willingness of the mainland to continue to pay the price. A relatively poor liberal democracy spends £3 billion a year and deploys 20,000 troops to back up a local police force in a struggle which can be contained but which cannot be won.

Such commitment would be unthinkable if the territorial integrity of the British state and the legitimacy of its authority were not both on the line. One might have expected that such a cause would rouse the deepest nationalist feeling. Yet all that seems to sustain the British presence is weary cross-party consensus that terror must not be seen to pay and that the troops cannot be withdrawn lest civil war ensue.

If the cause in question in Northern Ireland is defence of the Union, then already Ulster is not treated like a part of mainland Britain. There is an imperial

pro-consul, the Northern Ireland Secretary, who runs everything from negotiations with Dublin to the allocation of council housing. The currency is the
British pound, but the Northern Ireland banknotes are not tradeable as legal
tender on the mainland; British political parties do not compete for votes in the
province. Local democracy has been all but eliminated by twenty-five years of
direct rule from Westminster. Ulster knows it is already semi-detached.

Loyalists bitterly note the curious disparity between the outpouring of
nationalist feeling when Argentina invaded 'British sovereign territory' in the
Falklands and the indifference about Ulster. Mainland Britain would give Ulster
away if it could. Opinion polls give greatest support to options which entail
relinquishing British sovereignty over Northern Ireland or sharing it with
Ireland.

Even the British commitment to Ulster is hedged with conditions. Since the
Anglo-Irish Agreement of 1985, Britain is only committed to remain in Northern
Ireland so long as a majority of its people wish it. Thus the province is the only
part of the Union with an entrenched right of secession. For Loyalists, it is an
outrage that the British government should portray itself increasingly as a
'neutral' peace-keeper between one community which wishes to stay British and
another which wishes to become Irish.

If the cause in question in Ulster is the defence of the Union, then it is a cause
which moves few British hearts. Yet this is paradoxical. British nationalism has
always been of the civic variety: an attachment to the institutions of a state –
Crown, Parliament, rule of law, the Union itself – rather than to a nation. Yet like
Canada, India, Belgium and other multi-ethnic states, it is discovering that
attachment to the state may prove weaker than commitment to the nations which
comprise it. The Union, after all, is a constitutional contrivance, and who can feel
deep emotion about constitutional contrivances?

Ethnic nationalism attaches itself to the defence of a tradition and way of life,
and all of this could survive a re-drawing of the union. The British could cede
Northern Ireland and few in the mainland would feel the sting of shame or the
twist of remorse. Whether they should do so is another matter. But what exactly
does this tell us about Britain – that it has lost the nationalist impulses which
might once have rallied to Ulster's defence, or that it never had them in the first
place?

The English have always made the comparison between their own tolerant
moderation and the nationalist delusions of other peoples a touchstone of their
identity. Living on an island, having exercised imperial authority over more
excitable peoples, priding themselves in possessing the oldest continuous nation
state in existence, the English have a sense of a unique dispensation from
nationalist fervour. An ironic, self-deprecating national character which still

prizes the emotional reserve of its officer class approves of itself for declining the strong drink of nationalist passion.

Hugh Seton Watson, a great English historian of Eastern European nationalism, was convinced that there was no such beast on his own soil. A people who have never been conquered, invaded or ruled by others, he believed, could not be nationalistic. 'English nationalism never existed, since there was no need for either a doctrine or an independence struggle.' A Scottish nationalism perhaps, a Welsh nationalism too, but never an English nationalism.

After 1707, and the Union of the Scottish and English Crowns, a British national identity was forged which allowed the British to develop their unique double affiliation – to their nations of origin, and to the nation state and empire. As the original multi-ethnic, multi-national state, Britain was perhaps the first country where patriotism was directed to the imperial state, not to the nations which comprised it. In its imperial heyday, British civic nationalism focussed on the image of Britannia, ruler of the seas.

Imperialism was the form and expression of such British nationalism as there has been, and Britain's colonial peoples were never in much doubt about the incorrigible self-regard of their masters. Yet the masters themselves believed that their patriotism was by its nature different from the nationalism of other peoples. This view of nationalism as an illness which only infected foreigners provided a rationale for centuries of British imperial rule. Bringing the lesser breeds within the law meant freeing them from lesser tribal fanaticisms and teaching them the civil temper of the English race. Even when it proved that colonialism far from extinguishing ethnic loyalties actually helped to solidify them into nationalist consciousness, the British believed themselves confirmed as a people raised 'above' the tribal emotions of others. Hadn't they acquired the empire, according to a celebrated phrase, 'in a fit of absence of mind', and didn't they relinquish it with a degree of despatch which proved that they were free of grasping nationalist ambition? Imperialism may have been the face of Britishness for two centuries, but by its own reckoning, imperialism was a unique form of disinterestedness, a 'burden' diligently born and willingly renounced.

As the British adjusted to a new post-imperial era of genteel relative decline, they could find reasons to praise themselves for being immune to the lure of the kitsch of national self-regard. The stridently patriotic self-confidence of the Americans served as a perfect foil for the elaboration of a post-imperial national identity which regarded any form of British national self-regard as a comic turn.

The Cold War also acted to repress national self-definition not just in Britain, but across Europe. The normal national self-assertiveness and competitiveness of the Western European states were suspended for fifty years by the agreed necessity to present a united front against the Soviet threat.

At the same time, the relative prosperity of the fifties and sixties eroded British provincialism and began to weaken the British confidence in the charming and incorrigible distinctiveness of their way of life. A new black and Asian population arrived whose simple presence began to expose how very white and imperial were the symbols of collective belonging. The old national rituals began playing to a new audience; and in the process both the audience and the spectacle had to change. Even the monarchy ceased to be specifically British: it became the fairy-tale family romance for the entire planet.

Out of de-colonization, immigration, and genteel economic decline there emerged a new style of national identification which enjoyed and celebrated Britain precisely because it was essentially post-nationalist, because the demands it placed upon individuals were mild and fluid enough to enable each to be as British as he pleased.

I arrived in Britain from Canada in 1978. I rather liked Britain in supposed decline. It was relatively free of the provincialism of those nations which take themselves to be the centre of the world. It was less self-important than America; less complacent than Germany; less self-enclosed than France. It was in trouble and that made it an interesting place to live.

I both disliked and disbelieved the ambient rhetoric of national decline. It struck me mostly as a suppressed form of imperial nostalgia. Almost everything that was taken as a symptom of decline and decay – loss of empire, a new African, Asian and Caribbean population, traumatic economic restructuring – seemed signs of health rather than decay. Post-war Britain had been forced to change as radically as any society in Europe, and it had done so without falling apart, without ceasing to function as some kind of liberal democracy.

But as I have lived here longer, I have come to see that the space for a multi-cultural, multi-racial, post-national cosmopolitanism in Britain was much narrower than I had supposed. Those who speak on behalf of that kind of identity remain locked in a battle of ideas with those who still imagine a Britain on its own, safe from the incursions of Europe, defined by its monarchy and the sovereignty of its parliament. This is the cause at the heart of the thirty-year war over Britain's place in Europe, and only a fool would suppose that history is on the side of the cosmopolitans.

The depth of the resistance to Europe led me to suspect that I had been taken in by the British image of themselves as beyond the lower nationalist emotions of the Continentals. This is just another of Britain's stylish affectations. In reality, the British are among the most fiercely nationalistic of all peoples. Indeed modern nationalism is an English invention.

The very idea of the 'nation' acquired its modern meaning during the Protestant reformation in England. In the 1530s the Tudor state, under Henry VIII, led a nationalist revolt in the name of 'the English nation' against the Papacy and the Catholic Church. At the same time, the Tudor state initiated the conquest of Catholic Ireland. From the very outset of its nationhood, Englishness was defined antagonistically as the creed of an Anglo-Saxon Protestant nation locked in battle with continental Europe, the Papacy and the Catholic Irish. From the Marian persecutions of the 1550s, through the Spanish Armada of 1588, to the execution of Charles Stuart in the Civil War, the English nation defined itself against Catholic invaders from abroad and Catholic despots at home.

One of the turning points in the formation of English identity occurred when the Catholic King James II ascended the throne in 1685 and set about challenging the authority of Parliament and persecuting the Protestant faith. A national rising in 1688 appealed for deliverance to the Dutch ruler, William of Orange, who arrived in England, put James to flight and established both the sovereignty of Parliament and the supremacy of the Protestant religion.

James retreated to his Catholic domains in Ireland and began reconquering it as a prelude to an invasion of Britain. At the same time his ally and patron, Louis XIV of France, invaded Protestant Holland. The fate of Protestant Europe hung in the balance. All of Ireland was soon in James's hands, except the Protestant north. In 1689, the Jacobite armies laid siege to Londonderry, and for 105 days it held out, giving time for William of Orange to disembark and commence the re-conquest of Ireland. In June 1690, William of Orange himself came ashore at Carrickfergus. At the Battle of the Boyne, fought on 12 July 1690, he decisively defeated the Catholic pretender.

William of Orange's victory has entered British myth as the Glorious Revolution, inaugurating the imperial high noon of parliamentary sovereignty, religious toleration and constitutional monarchy. In Ulster, William's triumph became a founding myth of ethnic superiority. For Ulstermen, the Battle of the Boyne is exactly what the Battle of Kosovo is for the Serbs – the moment when a small people, in battle with mortal foes, defended Christendom for all of Europe. (While the Protestants won at the Boyne, and the Serbs lost at Kosovo, both cultures came to see themselves as heroic and misunderstood defenders of the faith.) Ulstermen's reward, as they saw it, was permanent ascendancy over the Catholic Irish, whom they now conceived, once and for ever, as potential rebels against the British Crown.

From 1688 until 1912 at least, the Ulster Protestants believed that their founding myth was also the founding myth of the British state – defeat of King James guaranteed a Protestant ascendancy in Ireland and constitutional monarchy in Britain. Yet this was not to be. Ireland proved to be the great failure of British state- and nation-building. The Protestantism at the very heart of the British identity made it impossible successfully to assimilate the Catholic Irish into the Union. When, in 1912, the British conceded Irish Home Rule, Ulstermen, led by Sir Edward Carson, rose in fury to resist, believing that the most loyal of all the Crown's subjects had been rewarded with a betrayal of the essential elements of Britishness itself, its Protestant core.

The inability of the British to think of Ulster as an essential part of itself has much to do with British awareness that their nation-building met its greatest failure in Ireland. The Troubles have reinforced in the British mind the conviction that Ulster is, after all, paradoxically and impenetrably Other, i.e. Irish.

Since Irish independence in 1920, Catholic Ireland has ceased to be one of the mirrors in which the British define who they are. Ireland and Britain are no longer brother enemies. Protestantism, once the very touchstone of what differentiated Britain both from Ireland and from Catholic Europe, is now a vestigial element of self-definition in a secularized country in which only 15 per cent of the population define themselves as regular church attenders. Not so in Protestant Ulster, where 65 per cent of the population attend services on Sunday. They, alone of the British people, remain face to face with the Other which has defined Britishness for centuries. No wonder theirs is the fiercest British nationalism on these islands; no wonder a visit to Ulster is to travel down through the layers of historical time that separate mainland Britain from a Britishness that once was its own.

TOMMY DOYLE

It is old but it is beautiful, and its colours they are fine
It was worn at Derry, Aughrim, Enniskillen and the Boyne
My father wore it when a youth in the bygone days of yore;
So on the Twelfth I always wear the Sash my father wore.

Tommy Doyle is wearing his Orangeman's sash and he is pacing to and fro in front of the Cenotaph, waiting for the Somme memorial service to begin. The Belfast Cenotaph, Tommy tells me, was the very first one erected in the empire after the Great War. It is in the shadow of Belfast City Hall, a great imperial building itself, erected when Belfast was the linen and ship-building capital of the British Empire. Next to the Cenotaph is a statue of the Marquess of Dufferin and Ava, Governor-General of Canada, Viceroy of India, complete with twin statues of a turbaned Sikh and a Canadian fur-trapper, their heads bowed in mourning for an Ulsterman proud, so the inscription reads, to be remembered as a 'great Irishman'.

Tommy, a trim 74-year-old with bright blue eyes, belongs to the post-partition, post-imperial era, when no Ulsterman would think of defining himself as an Irishman. Tommy is reputable Loyalism personified: deputy Grand Master of Ireland, Lodge Master of no 2 Belfast district; a devout churchman and teetotaller. He worked all his life behind the counter of a wholesale ironmonger, but it is Orangeism, not his work, which has been his life. There is not a fanatical bone in Tommy's body. He practises what his order preaches, which is to hate the sins of Romanism, but not the poor deluded Catholic sinner.

When a 'wee brown packet' arrived through his letter box, one morning in 1977, Tommy thought at first it might be a letter bomb. But after he had gingerly sliced open the seal and checked for suspicious-looking wires inside, a nice letter from Her Majesty the Queen came sliding out, together with a shiny silver Jubilee medal which he wears on ceremonial occasions, pinned to his Orange sash.

Tommy is also wearing his Sir Edward Carson tie, with 'No Surrender' inscribed upon it. Sir Edward Carson led the campaign against Irish Home Rule in 1912 and helped mobilize and arm the paramilitaries of his day, the Ulster Volunteer Force, raised to defend Ulster against Home Rule. When war was declared, this force volunteered to defend the empire, and they went off to die at the Somme as the 36th Ulster Division. In two days of battle, in July 1916, 5,500 men of the Ulster Division were killed or wounded. What Gallipoli was for the Australians, Vimy Ridge for the Canadians, the Somme was for Ulster. But while the blood sacrifice of Gallipoli and Vimy completed the national emancipation of two young colonial dominions, the Somme myth locked Ulster into the stasis of its basic myth of loyalism betrayed. Four years after the Somme, the returning Ulster Volunteer Force had their devotion rewarded with partition and the emergence of the Irish Free State.

All of the bitter ambivalence in Ulster Loyalism is encapsulated in the story of the Ulster Volunteers. A paramilitary unit raised to fight the British over Home Rule, fought and died to defend the empire in the Somme, only to lose Ireland with partition. In the 1960s, the Ulster paramilitary tradition revived, and took the old name to fight British betrayal once again.

Tommy's remaining cause in life is to build a memorial in France to the Ulster Orangemen who died in July 1916. He has the monument already designed and paid for by Orange Lodges around the world, and soon he will travel out to a field near Thiepval Wood in northern France and see his dream realized. He grew up in working-class Belfast streets where every third or fourth house held the memory of a son or a husband who had never come back. Tears come into his eyes when he tells about the 16-year-old lads found dead on the battlefield with birth certificates which faked their age to make them eligible for service. He seems truly haunted by this lost generation and if there is any bitterness in an otherwise sunny temperament it is in the suspicion that the British don't remember them half as tenaciously as he does.

But he brightens when he hears the pipe and drum bands coming up the avenue, and he sees his brethren from the lodges in the city marching towards the Cenotaph, with their bowler hats, their white ornamental cuffs on their serge suits, some carrying rolled umbrellas, others a sword, still others bearing the colours – the Union Jack and the Ulster Flag, with its bloody Red Hand in the midst of St Patrick's Cross. Wreaths are laid, 'Last Post' is sounded, the colours are lowered and a hundred ageing, worried-looking men sing in quavering voices Ulster's hymn, 'O God Our Help in Ages Past'.

When the Orange bands have marched away, Tommy takes me up to the central Orange Lodge, built in 1883, as it says on the pediment, directly below the twin Union Jacks and the statue of William of Orange on a rearing horse. The front façade is covered with steel mesh, spattered with white paint from a paint-bomb hurled from a passing car a few nights before. The lodge is a faded bunker of Britishness, dark as a tomb, because the windows have been sealed with steel anti-blast shutters. 'We need to spend some money on this place,' Tommy admits, surveying the faded brocade wallpaper, peeling at the top, the dusty portraits of lodge masters past and present, the discoloured mezzotints of Queen Elizabeth, circa 1953, the brass plaques in memory of Orangemen 'killed by enemies of Ulster'. Tommy takes me to the inner sanctum, the council chamber, where from the carved wooden throne at the head of the long baize table he presides over lodge meetings on Monday nights.

When we get talking about Loyalism itself, Tommy begins speaking like a somnambulist, drawing perfectly formed sentences from the depths of his unconscious. He is loyal, he says, 'to the religious and civil liberties established and confirmed by King William the Third of Orange, when he defeated the Catholic forces of King James at the Battle of the Boyne in July 1690'. When I remark that this is not what the British seem loyal to, he shrugs sadly and admits that it may well be so. 'They don't stand up for the Queen at the end of the pictures either.'

What it means to be British for Tommy is essentially what it means to be Protestant. The two cannot be distinguished, and between the two and the 'theocratic' state to the south there is an impassable gulf. Orangeism is his life because both of his loyalties, to the Crown and to his religion, are united in the Orange creed. It is what makes Tommy a happy man: he knows who he is and that he is doing God's work. But it also means he is a man who cannot change or learn. He is what he is. 'I'll tell you one thing,' he says as we get up to leave. 'If they took the cross of Saint Patrick out of the Union Jack, there wouldn't be much of a flag left. Now would there?'

I ask Tommy whether he is coming to the Orange Ball the same evening. Tommy blushes and says he is off home. Tommy is a total abstainer in the true Orange tradition, though he admits temperance is an idea whose time has run out. Still, you stick with what you believe. He has church tomorrow, and he has no time for capering about. 'Not my sort of thing,' he says, with a wink and a wave goodbye.

When I get to the dance-hall upstairs, I can see why Tommy took his leave. He wouldn't like the country and western music they are playing on the stage decked with Union Jacks. He wouldn't like the beer that is flowing from the pumps, or the way the men and women are dancing close. He wouldn't like the language one drunk is using on me as he tries to force me to leave. 'What the fuck are you doin' here? Get off, get off out of it.' The barman pulls him off me, and while some of the middle-aged ladies even lead me on to the dance floor, the place has a Serbian air of paranoia and resentment. Tommy might be embarrassed, as I am, by the drunken desperation that comes to hang over the scene as the hours go by, how these God-loving Orangemen and women start cursing and swaying from the drink, how at the end when everyone sings the Sash, they conga about the hall, waving the Union Jack, led by a man wearing nothing but a 'No Surrender' baseball cap, his Union Jack singlet and his Union Jack underpants.

Later that week I attend the annual Orange service commemorating William's victory at the Boyne. Several hundred middle-aged Orangemen and their wives, plus some marching bands, crowd into the Presbyterian Central Hall to hear a sermon on what the preacher calls that 'great charter of Protestant freedom', Saint Paul's epistle to the Galatians: 'Stand fast therefore in the liberty wherewith Christ hath made us free.'

There is much talk of liberty in Ulster Protestantism, but service to His vision sounds more like a long, grim imprisonment. The Ulster obsession with loyalty and betrayal is rooted within the Protestant struggle of the spirit against the flesh. Luther and Calvin, and two centuries of hellfire preaching, have left Ulstermen in a state of suppressed rage at the irrepressible disloyalty of their own impulses. All this is kept under uneasy control by the decorum of Protestant worship, yet it finds ways to burst out, even at the Orange service of consecration. At the end, when the collection is taken and counted, it is discovered that it is short of last year's total. In any other church I've been to, this would be a matter of silent regret. Not in Belfast. The disappointing result is publicly announced, the deficit enumerated down to the last pence to £126.35. 'This is a disgrace,' the officiating Orangeman thunders, 'a disgrace to Orangeism and its traditions.' Once again the flesh has triumphed. Once again the conscience has been found wanting before God, and on the most sacred day in the Orange calendar. The hall empties in chastened silence.

THE LAMBEG DRUM

There are two wars in Northern Ireland: a war between the Catholic and Protestant working classes of Belfast and Londonderry; and the war between the IRA and the Protestant farmers and townsfolk of the regions next to the border with the Republic. There is much loose talk about 'ethnic cleansing' in the border regions, as Protestant farmers and their families are driven off the land by the shootings and knee-cappings, the car and van bombs. The day before I drove through the lush green fields of County Armagh, the army had found a van loaded with 2,000 pounds of agricultural fertilizer and two timers ready to explode, aimed at Markethill, a pretty farming village already once destroyed by a bomb.

I went down to Markethill, an hour south of Belfast, to take a look at the border war and to meet a man I'd heard about, Dick Sterritt, who makes the Lambeg drum. Dick is a bear of a man in his late 20s, with a soft, lilting voice. The Lambeg drum is, he says, the 'heartbeat of Ulster', and the thunder that comes from its huge drum-head – 3 feet 1 inch wide – has been the sound of Protestantism on the march for three centuries. Dick will be marching with his Lambegs on the 12th of July at the Orange parade in Portadown, as he has done with his father, Ernie, ever since he was born.

Dick spends his year making and repairing drums and entering drumming competitions at the Orange Lodges around the county. Dick takes me to one sponsored by the Orange Lodge in nearby Scarva. The competitors and by-standers stand around in a circle in the parking lot of the Lodge and the drummers and their drums parade, one by one, like prize bulls in front of the judges. Three old men with score-sheets bend and listen to the sound, listening for that sweet reverberating quality in a drum which the makers call 'heart'. In any other drumming tradition – say the Caribbean – the accent would have been on the drumming and the prize would have gone to the most exuberant and inventive beat. Not with the Lambeg. The rhythm is as unvarying as Ulster tradition itself: a sudden high-pitched explosion of sound which continues for several minutes while the drummer goes purple in the face with effort. Try as I may, I can't tell which drum has more heart, and neither can the contestants. When the prizes are announced there is much good-natured bafflement at the decision. What seems to matter more than competition is the consumption of many glasses of Bush-mill's whiskey, and, needless to say, proceedings conclude with all present standing and singing 'The Queen'. When it is all over, Dick whispers to me, 'Our drumming wouldn't be safe in the Republic, now would it?'

The drums, like everything else in the Ulster tradition, came over with King William. They were kettle drums, played flat on either side of the saddle, and they have been the Ulsterman's defender ever since the Battle of the Boyne itself. Dick likes to tell the fable about the morning of the battle, when the Protestants were still asleep on one side of the Boyne water, and James's army was advancing to catch them by surprise. 'And there was a jenny wren, a wee bird, that began tapping on the drums, and it woke the drummer boy who sounded the alarm.' It's a strange thing, he says with a wink, how the Catholics nowadays like shooting those wee birds.

All of Dick's drums are elaborately painted and decorated: beside the Cock of the North, with a splendid crowing rooster on the shell, there is one, nearly eighty years old, called the Orange Conqueror, with King William's bewigged visage on it, and beside that a new one with a painstakingly painted picture of a young man with a pale pink face and red hair. He was a cousin of Dick's, a reserve constable with the RUC, who died in 1991 when a land-mine was detonated under his Land-Rover as he was leaving Armagh barracks.

'When I got the news, I went up to see my aunt, David's mother. The very first words she said to me was that David and you will not be walking up Markethill Street together on the Twelfth of July ever again. And I said to her, "Auntie Ivy, I'll always carry David on the Twelfth of July, because I'll put him on a drum."' Every year, Dick marches with David on his drum.

Dick's father, Ernie, a retired builder, listens gloomily. 'The thing is,' he says in his low, Armagh accent, 'they're selling us down the river. There shouldn't be foreign powers telling us how to run things here.' He means not just Dublin but Westminster too. 'The British man will never understand how to govern us,' Dick says. 'He doesn't believe that we belong.'

For Ernie Sterritt, mainland Britain is a disappointing place faraway. 'They used to sing "God Save the Queen" in the picture house,' he muses. 'Don't suppose they do that over on the mainland.' He sighs. 'It's all slipping away. Sure it is.' Dick listens and then he muses. 'They don't seem to have any story to tell, any song to sing,' Dick says. 'They don't seem to know who they are.'

Ernie shows me the Sterritt family tree, back to the seventeenth century, and Dick wants me to know that they are 'blackmouths'. In the days of Queen Anne, Dick explains, dissenting sects like the Presbyterians were under a ban and had to educate their children in the fields, behind the blackberry hedges, so in the blackberrying season, the children's lips and cheeks were stained black with the fruit. 'That was our name and it has stuck with us,' Dick says. He remains as suspicious of the established Anglican Church of Ireland as his blackmouth ancestors would have been. 'Only a thin piece of paper separates them from the Church of Rome,' he says darkly. Dick knows full well that there were times when blackmouths felt closer kinship with the Catholics, also labouring under religious ban, than with the local Protestant landlord, Lord Gosford. The dissenting tradition's abiding suspicion of the Anglican Establishments, in both its political and religious forms, adds another strain to Ulstermen's combustible Loyalism. There is a suppressed democratic impulse here in the Ulsterman's resentment of the mainland Establishment, suppressed because Loyalism never passes into a nationalism of its own, never detaches the Ulster people's cause from the Establishment's cause.

Dick takes me out for a drive in his red Renault 4 van, which he calls the goat wagon because he uses it to scour the countryside in search of goats big enough to give him a 37-inch drumskin. He gets some of his goats from the Catholic fellows around, but he always makes sure to call ahead, so that they can ring the spotter houses in the Catholic villages. That way his goat wagon won't be held up by the 'bandits'. That is how it is in bandit country. 'You wouldn't want to be out here at night,' he says, looking at the rolling fields with the Friesians chewing their cud by the gates. Some of the fence gates are booby-trapped by the Provies, and the copses will be full of British soldiers. Control over this county of Britain seems to sway back and forth between them. Every lane has a memory of that struggle. Dick passes one house and remembers a friend of his, a part-time soldier, who was kidnapped off his motorcycle while on his way home, tortured, shot and dumped in the road in front of his house. The army, fearing that the corpse was booby-trapped, had to drag it out of the village behind a Land-Rover, and his family had to watch it. 'It makes you wonder,' he says softly, 'what kind of a person would kill a man like that, knowing his family would have to see it.'

He himself has been set upon by some local Catholic boys in balaclavas, coming home from his pub on the Markethill High Street. 'Now, you can't have that kind of thing happening in your own home town.' A neighbour told him which Catholics were responsible, and over the next year, he sorted them out, one by one. 'Just taught them a lesson is all.'

But Catholics are only one of Dick's problems. He was on a bus with some Orangemen and a band heading for Londonderry, when some boys on board asked him to buy a raffle ticket for the benefit of the Loyalist paramilitary prisoners. Dick refused, saying that if they were in jail, they deserved it. When he got off the bus that night, the boys set on him and beat him up, in full view of some constables, who pulled him out of the fight and asked him if he would prosecute. In the heat of his anger, Dick said he would, but the matter never came to trial, because he got a phone call saying he shouldn't continue. 'Call it intimidation if you like,' Dick admits.

He has no time for the local paramilitaries and he points out the houses where the UVF flags are flying, the blue ones which signify that the house stands for an independent Ulster, one with no ties either to Britain or the Republic. This strikes Dick as crazy politics. 'They're short of cards for a full deck,' he says, shaking his head. Besides, he says, 'if the British weren't here, where would the farmers go for their subsidy?'

For all the trouble, he says, it's the greatest wee country in the world and he wouldn't live anywhere else. As we head down towards the border with 'the Free State', there are Friesians and Herefords in the steep, rolling pastures framed by holly and fuchsia hedges; white rose-bordered cottages; Union Jacks fluttering over the Church of Ireland steeples and the Red Hand Ulster flags flying over the bell-towers of the dissenting chapels and Orange Halls. Then with a bump and a twist in the road, and a quick dodge across a stream, we find ourselves face to face with a sign saying 'Welcome to County Monaghan, the Republic of Ireland'. No border checkpoints, no break in the lush green landscape, nothing to let you know that this is one of the most contentious borders on earth.

Dick is across it many times a year, for the race meetings. He loves a drink, a fine race-horse and a good story, and he never has any trouble south of the border. Sometimes he brings his Catholic friend, Kieran from Markethill, when Kieran is in the money, which isn't often. When he's put a couple of Power'ses under his belt, Dick will love to sing, and most of what he sings are rebel songs, the ones about breaking out of Omagh jail, about the girl with the blackband in her hair, and the one about the nightingale's lullaby. He'll mix the Fenian and the

Loyalist, the Southern and the Northern songs up one after another, till you can't tell which is which, or until the boys at his local pub start shouting, half serious, half in jest, that he should lay off the rebel songs and give them all a rendition of the Sash, which he does, to keep them happy.

I've come in search of what Britishness looks like in bandit country, and I find, of course, what I could never have expected: a man like Dick Sterritt, with his love of a drink and song and a story, quietly telling me that he will resist – he does not say fight – but resist till the end so as not to become what he so obviously seems to be already: an Irishman.

THE RATHCOOLE BOYS

Back in Belfast, Marty, Sheeran, Deeky, Paul and Mudd are painting the kerbstones of the Rathcoole Estate red, white and blue. In most of the Protestant estates, the kerbs are painted around this time of year, as a preparation for the 12th. Painting the kerbs is like putting up a wall mural of King Billy or of a Loyalist paramilitary, complete with Armalite and balaclava. It stakes out the territory. 'They do the same over there,' Deeky says, gesturing at the Catholic estate in the distance, only with the Catholics it is the Irish Tricolour and quotations from Bobby Sands, the hunger striker hero.

Until a few years ago, Rathcoole was the biggest public housing estate in Europe, and once upon a time it was mixed. Bobby Sands himself grew up there. Not any more. Rathcoole is rock-solid Protestant working class. Behind the white lace curtains in the tower blocks, in those immaculate front rooms of the semi-detached bungalows, with their three-piece suites and doilies on top of the television sets, there is the usual baffling Belfast mixture of decent, law-abiding people and paramilitary thugs who keep the local kids in order with an occasional knee-capping. Mudd, a 14-year-old glumly painting a kerb, is due one himself, for stealing cars and joy-riding around the Diamond, where the chippie and the dry-cleaner and the youth club are located.

The Diamond is not looking its best: during the rioting after Herbie McCallum's funeral, the chippie was trashed, and so was the youth club and there are fire-marks on the road where the cars were set alight. The boys won't say who was responsible, but they all cultivate a certain ambiguity about their involvement: they won't say they were there, and they won't say they weren't.

They couldn't exactly say what they like about being British, though they're applying the colours of the Union Jack to the kerbstones with the ardour of true patriots. 'It's the football,' Paul ventures. 'Yeah, Rangers, fantastic,' says Marty. Protestant Belfast worships the Glasgow Rangers, and Ranger scarves belong next to the Union Jack itself in Loyalist regalia. Few of the Rathcoole boys have ever been to mainland Britain, but they've heard that on the mainland estates no one would ever think of painting their kerbs red, white and blue. 'They don't have to, do they?' says Paul. 'They're not up against what we're up against, now are they?'

Marty's view is that the mainland estates don't paint their kerbs because 'they're all mixed up over there, all them different races and everything'. Here, he says, 'it's just us and the Taigs. So we have to show our colours, don't we?'

Marty, Paul, Sheeran, Deeky and Mudd don't have much to say about anything – at least not when I'm about – but when they don the purple uniforms of the Whiteabbey Protestant Boys Marching Band, a change comes over them. Each of them knows at least a hundred tunes on the small black ebony flutes they pull from their back pockets and a dozen rhythms on the short snare drums. All year long they practise in the gymnasium of the youth club, and in July during the marching season, there's hardly a night when they are not out marching and playing on the streets of Rathcoole and nearby estates. The band is more than their club; the music is their speech. They may not be able to tell you, in so many words, what Britishness or Protestantism means, but when the big, pimply boy starts hitting the big bass drum, and Sheeran starts them marching to the beat of his snare, and Marty, Paul, Deeky and Mudd take up the tune on the flute, they give a thundering account of who they are.

I follow them through the rain, to the Orange Lodge, as the traffic comes to a halt, as couples pushing their children in strollers stop and applaud them on their way, as the army sentries take up position to protect them from attack by the Catholic boys in the estate up the road. The drum brooks no argument; no wonder the Catholics call the marching bands the music of intimidation. But it has its own fierce beauty, and the boys will tell you there is nothing to equal the feeling you get when you're marching in the downtown and the sound is echoing off the high-walled canyons of the city.

THE DEE STREET
BONFIRE

On the stroke of midnight as 11 July turns into the 12th, Dee Street, like every Protestant street in the city, burns the Pope and the Irish Tricolour on top of its bonfire. For the past seventeen years, Mrs L. has sewn the Dee Street Pope herself, with a doll's head, spray-painted green, white and gold, crowned with a bishop's mitre. The Pope always wears red socks: indeed the Reverend Ian Paisley has been known to call His Holiness Old Red Socks.

In her immaculate front room, with its sideboard crowded with the trophies her family has won for pigeon-racing, Mrs L. also sews the Republican Tricolour from good silk she buys up at Crazy Prices. Her son, a spindly 14-year-old in a shell-suit, takes the lead in collecting for the bonfire. He's quite sure that this year Dee Street's is going to be the biggest one in the city.

Dee Street is a narrow double row of two-up-two-downs built in the last century for shipyard workers in the shadow of the yellow cranes of the Harland & Wolff shipyard. On the bare walls of the roads that lead into Dee Street, there are painted slogans: 'Ulster says NO!' 'Dee Street says NO!' 'Yukon Street says NO!' (When one of the local children paints me a picture of the street, the voice-bubble he puts on one of the children says 'NO!' too.)

All the front doors in Dee Street stay open, day and night, and kids wander in and out, from house to house. Unemployment is high and there are a lot of men in their 20s, heavily tattooed, hanging around the front doors, drinking and watching for strangers. On the wall facing the bonfire at the end of the street there is a mural of three Protestant paramilitaries wearing balaclavas and pointing automatic weapons.

Almost everyone I meet in Dee Street has lived there all their lives. One man who tells me he is 'a newcomer' finally admits that he has lived in the same house twenty-five years. He's only a newcomer compared to his wife, who was born in the street.

Dee Street has its wild men. There is Morris who has tattoos up and down his arms, and a heart tattooed on each ear-lobe, who wants to offer me his protection in return for a consideration. Then there is Lennox with his goatee, small narrow-set eyes and shaven head. People in Dee Street will tell you he is 'short of a slice for a sandwich'. He and Maddy, his girlfriend, had a child, and the mothers in the street offered to help them out, but the social services came and took the child away when Maddy was still in hospital. When Lennox found out, the neighbours came upon him storming up Dee Street, with murder in his eye and a can of petrol in his hand, shouting as to how he was going to burn 'the social' down to the ground.

Dee Street offers belonging with a vengeance – compassionate, warm and welcoming to its own; as unyielding as a stone to its enemies. It takes me days to convince them I mean no harm. I tell them I've just come to talk to the boys about the bonfire, but Mrs L. takes some persuading. Loyalists, like Serbs, brood on the way they are misunderstood.

Collecting for the bonfire begins in March. The Dee Street boys, ranging in age from 7 to 23, scour the streets, parking lots and factories and drag their trophies back in supermarket trolleys. By early July the collection is so large that they have to camp out all night to keep it from being stolen by the bonfire boys in adjacent streets. By 10 July, the Dee Street bonfire is an astonishing sixty-foot-high pile of cable drums, pallets and old sofas, boxes and barrels, railway sleepers and tyres.

Like the Rathcoole boys, the Dee Street boys have only the haziest idea of what goes on in the British mainland. Stewarty, who wears a Chicago Bears leather porkpie hat and a Rangers scarf, says he's heard of Guy Fawkes Night, but he couldn't tell you when it was. 'We have our bonfires and they have theirs, like.'

Stewarty's best memory of the mainland was going to a Rangers game in Glasgow, and how the Ulster chant 'We are, we are, we are the Billy boys!' rang round the stadium. But the rest of Britain, at least to judge from a couple of visits, seemed strange to him. Everywhere he went 'they called me a Paddy, as if I were Irish and responsible for all them bombings.'

Besides, he says, patting a neighbour's Rottweiler which has come up and is nosing about among the garbage at the edge of the bonfire, the English estates seemed cold and unfriendly. 'No kid's playing out in the street, like here in Dee Street. Nothing going on, like.' To tell you the truth, Stewarty admits, 'I get nostalgic three streets away in Belfast.' Dee Street is all he knows. He's got two children of his own, and he's never worked a day in his life. He couldn't anyway. If he did, the social might dock his 'brew' – Belfast for unemployment benefit.

I ask him where the Catholics live and he points behind him up the road, about four hundred yards. What would happen if you went up there? I ask, and one of the other boys says quickly, 'Kill you, sure.' And what happens if they come down here? 'They'd get a good hiding,' Stewarty says. It's just the way it is. They would do it to you if you were walking past. 'A couple of them might start doing the heavy. So you have to do the same. If they came down here they'd get a terrible hiding, not to kill them, mind, but just so as he remembers.' None of this is said with any venom. Indeed, Stewarty seems a bit embarrassed by it all, and wants it known that it might all be different if you lived in a mixed area. But not in Dee Street.

And what about those men? I say, gesturing to the paramilitary mural. A lot of the bonfire boys look away, uneasily, and one boy, the son of a British soldier, says quickly that they're illegal and you don't talk about them. But Stewarty says, digging at the ground with a stick, that they're there to punish 'rogues and thieves'. As far as Dee Street is concerned, punishment should be kept in the family: the police, or the 'peelers' as they are called, should stay out. Like if you steal a car, or if you 'do houses', then you get what's coming to you. And what's that? A knee-capping. Are you scared of them then? Stewarty looks at me shrewdly, 'You wouldn't expect me to say I wasn't, now would you?'

I come back on the night of the 11th to watch the Pope and the Tricolour being stuck on the top of the bonfire, and to watch the Dee Street boys marching up and down, with Lennox at the head, waving his Ulster flag like a madman and Mrs L.'s boy, Alex, beating out the rhythm on a cracked snare with only one skin. But word has got back to Mrs L. that I had been talking to the boys about Catholics and about paramilitaries, and she calls me into her sitting room. 'They're just kids,' she says. 'They'll say anything. But they don't necessarily mean it.' She'll have me know that she has to live here when I'm long gone, and it isn't easy. 'Look, I do my shopping up the road at Crazy Prices. With the Catholics.' If they get word of Stewarty's talk about giving them a good 'hiding', who knows what'll happen? And as for the paramilitaries, she says, 'I thought you were going to stay off politics.' We both know that if I don't get back in Mrs L.'s good books, I won't be long at the bonfire. I do my best to make her feel easier and she hears me out, smoking cigarette after cigarette in her front room, her face drawn and thin. She forgives me eventually and the word gets passed to leave me alone. At the stroke of midnight, the Dee Street boys' petrol bombs splatter against the pallets, and with a slowly gathering roar, the bonfire rises into flame. Lennox is waving the Red Hand flag, Morris is drinking from two cans of McEwan's at once, a huge crowd is eddying backwards from the rising heat of the flames; two men are cheerfully swearing at me for working for 'those faggot republicans in the fucking ITN [Independent Television News]'. When the Pope catches fire and the Republican Tricolour pitches down into the flames, the crowd lets out a low, visceral roar. Oblivious to everything, serenely drunk, Mrs L., surrounded by her kids, is last seen slowly circling the bonfire, twirling around with anyone who will dance with her, softly singing to herself:

> It is old but it is beautiful, and its colours they are fine
> It was worn at Derry, Aughrim, Enniskillen and the Boyne.

THE FIELD

'God is a Protestant,' the Ulstermen say, when explaining why weather on the annual Orange parade is usually clement. And so it is. The morning of the 12th of July dawns fair and bright. As the bands and lodge brethren gather in their thousands in front of the Central Lodge, Tommy Doyle is in fine fettle, greeting old friends and sipping a cup of tea. Eighty-five thousand Orangemen march across Northern Ireland on the 12th. Dick and Ernie Sterritt will be marching in Portadown. Actually, marching is the wrong word. 'Walking' is the preferred Orange term, suggesting as it does the right flavour of decorum and decency. But 'walking' is not how the Catholics see it. The thundering bands, the steady tramp of feet, and the verse from the Billy Boys song telling about how they're 'up to our necks in Fenian blood' are enough to keep most Catholics inside on parade day.

Orangemen will tell you nostalgically about the days when Catholics used to come and watch. As in Serbia and Croatia, both sides have an interest in conjuring up a lost paradise of inter-ethnic accommodation in which each side had amused respect for each other's rituals. It's easier for Loyalists to believe this than admit the truth, which is that Orangeism has always had a fiercely anti-Catholic edge and that the God-fearing, law-abiding side of Protestantism has always loved the intimidating and violent thunder of its own drums.

They march or walk to send a message to the other side, to say, here we are in our mighty throng, take heed and stay indoors. But they also march to send a message to themselves, to reassure and comfort the faithful. For Loyalism is much sapped with doubt about its long-term survival. The statistics from the 1991 census tell a gloomy tale. Twenty years ago, the Catholics stood at 34.7 per cent of the population. Today the figure is 41.4 per cent and rising rapidly. It is rumoured that among school-age children in Belfast the Catholics are up to 50 per cent of the total. The statistical picture of Protestantism is of an ageing population in decline, faced with a slow but steady haemorrhage of its best and brightest to the mainland. These numbers haunt the faithful, so much so that in the 12th of July booklet the Grand Master of all Ireland warns his fellow Orangemen not to put faith in 'deliberately falsified census figures', just as he warns them, darkly, that agents provocateurs may be lurking about the parade, wearing Orange Sashes.

So as they march up the Lisburn Road, heading towards Edenderry Field, with their banners held high, the Duke of Manchester's Invincibles and Cromwell's Ironsides, the Larne Protestant Boys and the Ballygally Flute and Pipe, the Rising Sons of the Somme, Carrickfergus, you count every Orangeman under 40 and you wonder how long the Order has to live.

But they do make a magnificent sight, the pipe and drum bands, the accordion bands and the bagpipe bands, as they stream beneath the great oaks flanking the downward-sloping cow pasture at the edge of Belfast that is known as the Field. Down at the bottom is a small raised platform to hold the dignitaries, and a few rows of chairs to hear the speeches, but of the thousands who march into the Field, only a hundred perhaps bother to listen. The rest all sprawl about on the grass, with a Union Jack or an Ulster Red Hand flag covering their faces from the sun, drums piled together, uniforms, leggings, socks, boots, in a tangle, among the chips and the crisp packets, the beer cans and the cigarette packs. Even the police take off their bullet-proof vests and lounge on the grass with their heads against the bumpers of their Land-Rovers. The speeches drone on, the age-old religious invective rises from the podium: 'Roman Catholicism is a perversion of true religion. Irish Catholicism is the most perverse of all religions,' I hear one reverend gentleman bellow. Another speaker thunders: 'The Protestants of Ulster are going to make Ulster great again and restore the greatness of Britain which has been sorely declining these past years.' Again, no one seems to be listening. While their elders thunder impotently on, young bandsmen fall fast asleep.

CARGO CULT

The great king from across the water disembarks from his white ships. In a great battle, he delivers the natives from their tribal enemies, and in victory guarantees their religion, and upon leaving confers on them mastery of their island for ever.

Having accomplished these magic designs, he departs, never to return. Ever after, the natives venerate his name, paint his picture, decorate their drums with his face, carry his portrait in their processions. They hold his memory sacred long after all trace of him has vanished from the traditions of the land whence he came.

According to the *Encyclopedia of Anthropology*, a cargo cult is a millenarian movement of native peoples who believe that the millennium will be ushered in by the arrival of great ships loaded with European trade goods or cargo. The goods will be brought by the ancestral spirits and will be distributed to natives who have acted in accordance with the dictates of one of the cults. Some cult leaders call for the expulsion of all alien, colonial elements as a precondition of salvation, while others insist on the abandonment of traditional ways of life and the adoption of European customs.

According to anthropologists who have studied such cults in the Pacific South Seas, the critical feature is that 'cargo cults are movements where whites lose control of their ability to police and direct the desires of their subjects. Having harnessed and in part created those desires for whiteness as part of a project of motivating villagers to take up development, the administration is horrified when those desires come to be turned against itself.' Anthropologists define the cargo cult as the result of an 'uncontrolled mimesis' in which native peoples take over the rituals and behaviours of whites only to subvert them and transform them into an object of worship which actually emancipates them from the European original.

British cargo cults are among the most tenacious and enduring in the world. In the Canada of my youth, in the salons of the Ritz in Montreal, the Royal York in Toronto and the Empress in Victoria, British Columbia; but also in the Raffles at Singapore, the Mandarin in Hong Kong; from the tea plantations of Sri Lanka to the hill stations of India, tea and cucumber sandwiches continue to be served and the rituals of a defunct empire float on in their ghostly afterlife. Here the loyalism implied by the ritual is merely nostalgic or elegiac. But there are insurgent cargo cults of Britishness, for example, as practised in the whites-only Rhodesia of Ian Smith after it declared unilateral independence from Britain in 1965. Here was a Britishness in revolt against Britain itself.

The sashes, the bonfires, the burning Popes and Tricolours, the Lambeg drums, the marching bands, the Red Hand flags, the songs: in all my journeys, I've never come across a form of nationalism so intensely ritualized. At one level, the reason for this is obvious. Here Britishness is ritualized because it is up against its antithesis and nemesis: Irish Republicanism.

Since the enemy are the 'nationalists', Loyalists are barred, not merely from using the term, but from thinking of themselves in this vein. Yet perhaps that is what Loyalism is – a nationalism that dares not speak its name. Loyalism, on this reading, is really loyal to itself, but since it cannot say so out loud, it says so tacitly, in rituals of belonging which elaborate an identity all its own.

The Red Hand sums up all of this ambivalence. You see it everywhere, on flags, on paramilitary murals, in candy replicas sold in every sweetshop. According to Celtic legend, two Scottish kings were swimming to Ulster. Whoever touched Ulster soil first would win the race and earn the right to rule the province. As the swimmers got closer, the one losing the race cut off his left hand and, with his right hand, threw it to the shore, thus claiming the prize.

It is a grimly appropriate symbol, especially in the way it consecrates the province as the bloody prize of a sacrificial struggle. It is both a respectable and an insurgent icon, figuring both on the official emblem of a province and on the paramilitary wall-paintings which lionize Loyalism's thugs. Celtic in origin and unknown to mainland Britain, the Red Hand shows just how tensely poised Loyalism is between identification and rejection, between fidelity and rebellion. Ulster worships at seventeenth-century Protestant shrines which mainland Britain no longer recognizes as its own. It elaborates a Britishness which it believes its mother has betrayed. It cannot pass into nationalist rebellion, since that would give comfort to its republican enemies, and it cannot subside into contented obedience, since that would trust the mother too far.

Yet it is also specifically British, above all, in its imperial memory of being masters once, and thus in its inability to conceive, let alone accept, becoming a minority in someone else's nation. It is also specifically British in its injured assertion of rights denied and betrayed, and in its inability to translate the sense of democratic injury into a genuinely democratic nationalism. This is true of mainland British nationalism as well. British national consciousness as a whole continues to see the nation embodied, not in the people, but in the Crown. The British think of themselves as subjects not as citizens, and popular commitment to the civic achievements of British history – the rule of law, the sovereignty of Parliament, the stability of the state – tends to express itself in an infantilized idealization of the monarchy. A nation of citizens, it could be argued, might prove more resolute and courageous defenders of these achievements than a nation of subjects.

Cargo cults are caricatures of their original. Yet caricatures reveal a truth, as fairground mirrors do. If Ulster is unable to decide what it is loyal to – its own people or the Crown – this may be because Britain as a whole no longer has an answer to the same question.

In the cargo cult of Ulster Loyalism, the ethnic and civic components of British nationalism are beginning to uncouple. Loyalism is an ethnic nationalism which, paradoxically, uses the civic symbols of Britishness – Crown and Union Jack – to mark out an ethnic identity. In the process, the civic content is emptied out: Loyalist paramilitarism, for example, makes it only too clear what a portion of the Loyalist community thinks of the rule of law, the very core of British civic identity. In the end, the Crown and the Union Jack are reduced to meaning what they signify when tattooed on the skin of poor, white teenagers. They are only badges of ethnic rage.

The same uncoupling could easily occur, indeed is already occurring, in Britain. Symbols of identity, like the Union Jack and the Crown, which once stood for the rule of law and the civic integument of a nation state, come to be debased, by disillusion, injustice and oppression, into pure symbols of whiteness. If a society no longer teaches its children that Britishness has a connection, not to ethnicity, but to justice, then its symbols are bound to figure on the placards of hatred.

As can be seen in Canada, India, Czechoslovakia, Belgium and elsewhere, Britain is not the only place where the civic and ethnic components of national identity are uncoupling. Most multi-national, multi-ethnic nation states are discovering that their populations are often more loyal to the ethnic units which compose them than to the federation and the laws which hold the state together.

What keeps ethnic and racial tension within bounds in the world's successful modern multi-ethnic societies is a state strong enough to make its authority respected. This remains true even in Northern Ireland. Despite the fact that British institutions do not command equal respect from both communities, the British state still manages, just, to hold the ring. What saves the province from becoming Bosnia is nothing more than the British Army, policemen who do their jobs and courts which convict upon evidence.

There is a larger moral to be drawn from this. The only reliable antidote to ethnic nationalism turns out to be civic nationalism, because the only guarantee that ethnic groups will live side by side in peace is shared loyalty to a state, strong enough, fair enough, equitable enough, to command their obedience.

THE HUNGRY AND THE
SATED

I end my journey where I started, thinking about the relation between arguments and consequences, between nationalist good intentions and nationalist violence. A rationalist tends to believe that what people do results from what they say they intend. Thus when nationalists say violence is warranted in self-defence and in seeking self-determination, a rationalist concludes that this is why violence occurs.

I am no longer so sure. So often, it seemed to me, the violence happened first, and the nationalist excuses came afterwards. The insensate destruction of Vukovar by both sides, for example, struck me as a perfect example of this. In that instance, nationalist rhetoric is best understood as an excuse for what happened, not as an explanation for what occurred.

Everywhere I've been, nationalism is most violent where the group you are defining yourself against most closely resembles you. A rational explanation of conflict would predict the reverse to be the case. To outsiders at least, Ulstermen look and sound like Irishmen, just as Serbs look and sound like Croats – yet the very similarity is what pushes them to define themselves as polar opposites. Since Cain and Abel, we have known that hatred between brothers is more ferocious than hatred between strangers. We say tritely that this is so because hatred is a form of love turned against itself. Or that we hate most deeply what we recognize as kin. Or that violence is the ultimate denial of an affiliation we cannot bear. None of this will do. There are puzzles which no theory of nationalism, no theory of the narcissism of minor difference, can resolve. After you have been to the wastelands of the new world order, particularly to those fields of graves, marked with numberless wooden crosses, you feel stunned into silence by a deficit of moral explanation.

In his essay 'What Does Coming to Terms with the Past Mean?' Theodor Adorno says, in passing, 'Nationalism no longer quite believes in itself.' There was a bewildering insincerity and inauthenticity to nationalist rhetoric everywhere I went, as if the people who mouthed nationalist slogans were aware, somewhere inside, of the implausibility of their own words. Serbs who, in one breath, would tell you that all Croats were Ustashe beasts would, in the next, recall the happy days when they lived with them in peace. In this divided consciousness, there was a plane of abstract fantasy and a plane of direct experience which were never allowed to confront each other. Nationalism's chief function as a system of moral rhetoric is to ensure this compartmentalization and in so doing to deaden the conscience. Yet it never entirely works. The very people who absorb such generalizations with such apparently unthinking zeal often still hear the inner voice which tells them that, actually, in their own experience, these generalizations are false. Yet if most people hear this inner voice, few seem able to act upon it. The authority of nationalist rhetoric is such that most people actively censor the testimony of their own experience.

Nationalism is a form of speech which shouts, not merely so that it will be heard, but so that it will believe itself. It was almost as if the quotient of crude historical fiction, violent moral exaggeration, ludicrous caricature of the enemy was in direct proportion to the degree to which the speaker was himself aware that it was all really a pack of lies. But such insincerity may be a functional requirement of a language which is burdened with the task of insisting upon such a high volume of untruths. The nationalist vision of an ethnically pure state, for example, has the task of convincing ordinary people to disregard stubbornly adverse sociological realities, like the fact that most societies are not and have never been ethnically pure. The nationalist leaders' call to ardent communitarian fellow-feeling has to triumph over the evidence, plain to every one of his listeners, that no modern society can beat to the rhythm of a single national will. That such fantasies do take hold of large numbers of people is a testament to the deep longing such people have to escape the stubborn realities of life.

Nationalism on this reading, therefore, is a language of fantasy and escape. In many cases – Serbia is a flagrant example – nationalist politics is a full-scale, collective escape from the realities of social backwardness. Instead of facing up to the reality of being a poor, primitive, third-rate economy on the periphery of Europe, it is infinitely more attractive to listen to speeches about the heroic and tragic Serbian destiny and to fantasize about the final defeat of her historic enemies.

The political systems of all societies – advanced and backward, developed and undeveloped – are prey to the lure to fantasy, and the only reliable antidote is the cold bath of economic, political or military disaster. Even then, societies cannot awaken from nationalist fantasy unless they have a political system which enables them to remove the fantasists. Societies with adequate democratic tradition have proven themselves vulnerable to the politics of fantasy. But a democratic system does provide at least for the punishment of fantasists whose lies catch up with them. At the same time, however, one cannot think of democracy as a reliable antidote to nationalism. The electoral survival of nationalist demagogues like Serbia's Milošević leads one to conclude that even in a nominal democracy like Serbia those who distract and divert people from reality usually enjoy greater political longevity than those who tell the truth.

These themes – fantasy, insincerity and inauthenticity – take us somewhat deeper in understanding the relation between nationalist argument and nationalist violence. We can begin to see how nationalist rhetoric re-writes and re-creates the real world, turning it into a delusional realm of noble causes, tragic sacrifice and cruel necessity. Yet there is a further element to add to the picture.

As everyone can see on their television screens, most nationalist violence is perpetrated by a small monitory of young males between the ages of 18 and 25. Some are psychopaths but most are perfectly sane. Until I had spent some time at the checkpoints of the new world order, until I had encountered my quotient of young males intoxicated by the power of the guns on their hips, I had not understood how deeply pleasurable it is to have the power of life and death in your hands. It is a characteristic liberal error to suppose that everyone hates and fears violence. I met lots of young men who loved the ruins, loved the destruction, loved the power that came from the barrels of their guns.

Perhaps liberals have not understood the force of male resentment which has been accumulated through centuries of gradual European pacification. The history of our civilization is the history of the confiscation of the means of violence by the state. But it is an achievement which an irreducible core of young males has always resented. Liberals have not reckoned with the male loathing of peace and domesticity or with the anger of young males at the modern state's confiscation of their weapons. One of the hidden rationales behind nationalist revolts is that they tap into this deeper sub-stratum of male resentment at the civility and order of the modern state itself. For it seems obvious that the state's order is the order of the father, and that nationalism is the rebellion of the sons. How else are we to account for the staggering gratuitousness and bestiality of nationalist violence, its constant overstepping of the bounds of either military logic or legitimate self-defence, unless we give some room in our account for the possibility that nationalism exists to warrant and legitimize the son's vengeance against the father.

My journeys have also made me re-think the nature of belonging. Any expatriate is bound to have moments of longing for a more complete national belonging. But I have been to places where belonging is so strong, so intense that I now recoil from it in fear. The rational core of such fear is that there is a deep connection between violence and belonging. The more strongly you feel the bonds of belonging to your own group, the more hostile, the more violent will your feelings be towards outsiders. You can't have this intensity of belonging without violence, because belonging of this intensity moulds the individual conscience: if a nation gives people a reason to sacrifice themselves, it also gives them a reason to kill.

Throughout my travels, I kept remembering the scene in *Romeo and Juliet* when Juliet is whispering to herself on the balcony in her nightgown, unaware that Romeo is in the shadows listening. She is struggling to understand what it means for her, a Capulet, to fall in love with a Montague. Suddenly she exclaims,

> 'Tis but thy name, that is my enemy;
> Thou art thyself though not a Montague.
> What's a Montague? it is not hand, nor foot
> Nor arm, nor face, nor any other part
> Belonging to a man. O! be some other name:
> What's in a name?

In the front lines of Bosnia, in the estates of Loyalist and Republican Belfast, in all the places where the tribal gangsters – the Montagues and Capulets of our day – are enforcing the laws of ethnic loyalty, there are Juliets and Romeos who still cry out 'Oh, let me not be a Croatian, Serbian, Bosnian, Catholic or Protestant. Let me only be myself.'

Being only yourself is what ethnic nationalism will not allow. When people come, by terror or exaltation, to think of themselves as patriots first, individuals second, they have embarked on a path of ethical abdication.

Yet everywhere, in Belfast, in Belgrade and Zagreb, in Lvov, in Quebec and Kurdistan, I encountered men and women, often proud patriots, who have stubbornly resisted embarking on that path. Their first loyalty has remained to themselves. Their first cause is not the nation, but the defence of their right to choose their own frontiers for their belonging.

But such people are an embattled minority. The world is not run by sceptics and ironists, but by gunmen and true believers and the new world they are bequeathing to the next century already seems a more violent and desperate place than I could ever have imagined. If I had supposed, as the Cold War came to an end, that the new world might be ruled by philosophers and poets, it was because I believed, foolishly, that the precarious civility and order of the states in which I live must be what all people rationally desire. Now I am not so sure. I began the journey as a liberal, and I end as one, but I cannot help thinking that liberal civilization – the rule of laws not men, of argument in place of force, of compromise in place of violence – runs deeply against the human grain and is only achieved and sustained by the most unremitting struggle against human nature. The liberal virtues – tolerance, compromise, reason – remain as valuable as ever, but they cannot be preached to those who are mad with fear or mad with vengeance. In any case, preaching always rings hollow. We must be prepared to defend them by force, and the failure of the sated, cosmopolitan nations to do so has left the hungry nations sick with contempt for us.

Between the hungry and the sated nations, there is an impassable barrier of incomprehension. I've lived all my life in sated nation states, in places which have no outstanding border disputes, are no longer ruled by foreigners or oppressors, are masters in their own house. Sated people can afford to be cosmopolitan; sated people can afford the luxury of condescending to the passions of the hungry. But among the Crimean Tartars, the Kurds and the Crees, I met the hungry ones, peoples whose very survival will remain at risk until they achieve self-determination, whether in their own nation state or in someone else's.

What's wrong with the world is not nationalism itself. Every people must have a home, every such hunger must be assuaged. What's wrong is the kind of nation, the kind of home that nationalists want to create and the means they use to seek their ends. A struggle is going on wherever I went between those who still believe that a nation should be a home to all, and that race, colour, religion and creed should be no bar to belonging, and those who want their nation to be home only to their own. It's the battle between the civic and the ethnic nation. I know which side I'm on. I also know which side, right now, happens to be winning.

FURTHER READING

Nations and nationalism

BENEDICT ANDERSON, *Imagined Communities*, Verso, 1983

ERNEST GELLNER, *Nations and Nationalism*, Blackwell, 1983

LIAH GREENFELD, *Nationalism: Five Roads to Modernity*, Harvard, 1992

ERIC HOBSBAWM, *Nations and Nationalism since 1870*, Cambridge: 1990

ELIE KEDOURIE, *Nationalism*, Hutchinson, 1960

ANTHONY D. SMITH, *National Identity*, Penguin, 1991

Germany

ROGERS BRUBAKER, *Citizenship and Nationhood in France and Germany*, Harvard, 1992

GORDON CRAIG, *The Germans*, Penguin, 1982

HANS MAGNUS ENZENSBERGER, 'The Great Migration', *Granta*, 42, 1992

MICHAEL HUGHES, *Nationalism and Society*, Edward Arnold, 1988

ANNE MCELVOY, *The Saddled Cow*, Faber, 1992

PETER PULZER, *The Rise of Political Anti-Semitism in Germany and Austria*, Halban, 1988

PETER SCHNEIDER, *The German Comedy*, Tauris, 1992

Ukraine

JOHN ARMSTRONG, *Ukrainian Nationalism*, Columbia, 1980

BOGDAN KRAVCHENKO, *Social Change and National Consciousness in Twentieth-Century Ukraine*, Oxford, 1985

IVAN L. RUDNYTSKY, *The Role of Ukraine in Modern History*, Harvard, 1987

OREST SUBTELNY, *Ukraine: A History*, Toronto, 1988

Yugoslavia

SLAVENKA DRAKULIĆ, *Balkan Express*, Hutchinson, 1993

PAUL GARDE, *Vie et Mort de la Yougoslavie*, Fayard, 1992

MISHA GLENNY, *The Fall of Yugoslavia*, Penguin, 1992

BRANKA MAGAS, *The Destruction of Yugoslavia*, Verso, 1993

JACQUES RUPNIK, ed., *De Sarajevo à Sarajevo*, Editions Complexe, 1993

MARK THOMPSON, *A Paper House: The Ending of Yugoslavia*, Hutchinson/Radius, 1992

Kurdistan

JOHN BULLOCH AND HARVEY MORRIS, *No Friends but the Mountains*, Viking, 1992

PHILIP G. KREYENBROEK AND STEFAN SPERL, *The Kurds*, Routledge, 1992

SHERI LAIZER *Into Kurdistan*, Zed, 1991

KANAN MAKIYA, *Cruelty and Silence*, Cape, 1993

Quebec

WILLIAM DODGE, *Boundaries of Identity*, Lester Publishing, 1992

RON GRAHAM, *The French Quarter*, Macfarlane, Walter and Ross, 1992

MORDECAI RICHLER, *O Canada O Quebec*, Viking, 1992

PETER RUSSELL, *Constitutional Odyssey*, Toronto, 1992

CHARLES TAYLOR, *Multiculturalism and the Politics of Recognition*, Princeton, 1992

PIERRE TRUDEAU, *Federalism and the French Canadians*, Macmillan, 1968

Northern Ireland

ARTHUR AUGHEY, *Under Siege*, Hurst, 1989

JONATHAN BARDON, *A History of Ulster*, Black Staff, 1992

GEOFFREY BEATTIE, *We are the People*, Heinemann, 1992

LINDA COLLEY, *Britons*, Yale, 1992

ROY FOSTER, *Modern Ireland*, Penguin, 1988

TONY PARKER, *May the Lord in His Mercy be Kind to Belfast*, Cape, 1993

PICTURE CREDITS

ACKNOWLEDGEMENTS

I must plead guilty to a deception. The book is written as if I was travelling alone. In fact, there were never fewer than five people accompanying me at all times, to make the BBC films that go with this book. Without their companionship, I am sure the book would never have been possible.

My thanks to Alan Yentob for commissioning the television series, and to his successor, Michael Jackson, for supporting it throughout. My gratitude to Pat Ferns of Primedia and to Geraint Telfan Davies of BBC Wales for conceiving the series in the first place, to Phil George of BBC Wales for leading the team throughout, and to Michael Chaplin of BBC Wales for lending the project his influence. In the Cardiff office, Tessa Hughes, Val Turner and Marian Williams made the travel arrangements and provided essential logistical support. On the road, three excellent cameramen, Brian McDairmant, Andrew Carchrae and Jacek Petrycki came up with the images. Jeff North, Bob Jones, Tony Meering and Patrick Boland recorded the sound. Ian Moss, Lawrence Gardner, Ralph MacDonald and Mike Carling served as camera assistants. Colin Thomas and Tim Lambert were the directors and producers of three films apiece, and the final shape of the films is as much their work as mine. Many of the ideas in this book began in their heads.

In all of these journeys, I depended heavily on my translators, researchers and fixers. In Ukraine, Lina Pomerantsev; in Germany, Elfi Pallis; in Quebec, Françoise Lemaitre Auger; in Kurdistan, Sheri Laizer; in Northern Ireland, Mary Carson; in Croatia, Alan Birimac and Mark Thompson, whose fine book on the collapse of Yugoslavia influenced my whole view of the area; in Serbia, Lazar Stojanović and Suzana Jovanović.

Portions of the text first appeared – in different form – in the *New Republic*, the *New York Review of Books* and *The Observer*.

Finally, my thanks to Martha Caute and Suzanne Webber of BBC Books and to Jonathan Burnham of Chatto for driving this book through a series of publication deadlines we all thought were impossible.

I cannot begin to convey my gratitude to everyone involved. There are few pleasures to match a happy division of labour.

INDEX

Numerals in **bold face** *indicate a chapter or section devoted to a subject entry.*

Dreaming
An Introduction to the Science of Sleep

Dreaming

An Introduction to the Science of Sleep

J. ALLAN HOBSON, MD

OXFORD
UNIVERSITY PRESS

OXFORD
UNIVERSITY PRESS

Great Clarendon Street, Oxford OX2 6DP

Oxford University Press is a department of the University of Oxford.
It furthers the University's objective of excellence in research, scholarship,
and education by publishing worldwide in

Oxford New York

Auckland Bangkok Buenos Aires Cape Town Chennai
Dar es Salaam Delhi Hong Kong Istanbul Karachi Kolkata
Kuala Lumpur Madrid Melbourne Mexico City Mumbai Nairobi
São Paulo Shanghai Singapore Taipei Tokyo Toronto

Oxford is a registered trade mark of Oxford University Press
in the UK and in certain other countries

Published in the United States
by Oxford University Press Inc., New York

© J. Allan Hobson 2002

British Library Cataloguing in Publication Data

Data available

Library of Congress Cataloging in Publication Data

Data available

ISBN 0–19–280304–2

1 3 5 7 9 10 8 6 4 2

Typeset by RefineCatch Ltd, Bungay, Suffolk
Printed in Great Britain by T.J. International Ltd., Padstow, Cornwall

Contents

List of boxes

List of figures

List of tables

Introduction

D reaming has fascinated humankind since the dawn of recorded history. As dreaming is so vivid, so complex, and so emotional, it has inspired religious movements, artistic representations, and introspective scientific theories. All of these pre-modern expressions have been based on the idea that dreams contain messages that cannot be delivered in any other way.

Thus, it was thought by the early Judaeo-Christians that God communicated his intentions via certain prophets to his human subjects. This concept was the centrepiece of medieval dream theory with its postulates of the 'Gates of Horn and Ivory'. Religious reformers such as Emmanuel Swedenburg were able to meet God's angels in dreams and he thereby received instructions about founding the Church of the New Jerusalem.

Early Western artists, such as Giotto, used dreaming as a vehicle for the pictorial representation of prophetic inspiration. Sleeping saints and churchmen are shown in the same pictorial frame as the visions that their dreams inspired. In modern art, the surrealists expressed through their wild paintings the conviction that dreaming was a more authentic state of consciousness than waking. Salvador Dali, Max Ernst, and René Magritte all painted in dream language. Dali was the most surreal, Ernst the most psychoanalytic, and Magritte the most neuropsychological of these artists.

At the turn of the twentieth century, the best known of all dream investigators would be Sigmund Freud, who set out to base his theory of the mind on brain science. His knowledge of the brain was so incomplete that he was forced to abandon his famous 'Project for a Scientific Psychology', and he turned to dreaming for insights about what he construed to be the dynamic unconscious. He decided, as had all his symbolist predecessors, that dreams concealed hidden meanings elaborated as one part of the mind, and that the unconscious tried to break through the protective barrier of consciousness. Freud thus threw dream theory back to the time of Biblical scholars, Artemidorus, and other early interpreters of dreams.

This book takes up where Freud left off when he abandoned his Project. It tries to build a new dream theory on the now solid and extensive base of sleep science. To accomplish this goal, I have given a concise summary of the findings of basic brain research, sleep lab studies, and recent clinical studies of sleep and dreams. Throughout the book, I use examples taken from my own dream journal to illustrate how our new theory of dreams, called activation–synthesis, can be used to explain in physiological terms universal dream features previously ascribed to psychodynamic factors. Once this is done, the mystery of dreaming is largely stripped away, leaving the content nakedly open to understanding without complex interpretation.

The main goal of this book is to show how a scientific theory of dreaming has been developed and strengthened over the past 50 years. In the process, the book offers the reader a unique opportunity to reconsider his or her own dream theory and, into the bargain, to learn about the fascinating discoveries of modern sleep science.

I

What is dreaming?

What causes dreaming? Why are dreams so strange? Why are they so hard to remember? A true science of dreaming requires a reliable definition that can lead to the reliable identification of this state and methods of measuring its properties. During the course of work on the brain, which led to the suspicion that it might be brain activation in sleep that causes dreaming, we realized that the most scientifically useful way to define and measure dreaming was to focus on the formal features rather than the content—by this is meant the perceptual (how we perceive), cognitive (how we think), and emotional (how we feel) qualities of dreaming, whatever the details of the individual stories and scenarios might be.

The radical change in emphasis, from the analysis of content to the analysis of form, exemplifies what scientists call a paradigm shift (a rapid change in pattern or theory). Through a formal approach, we found an entirely new and different way of looking at a familiar phenomenon. Whereas previously students

of dreaming had invariably asked 'What does the dream mean?', we asked what the mental characteristics of dreaming are that distinguish it from waking mental activity. We are *not* saying that dream content is unimportant, uninformative, or even uninterpretable. Indeed, we believe that dreaming *is* all three of these things, but it is already crystal clear that many aspects of dreaming previously thought to be meaningful, privileged, and interpretable psychologically are the simple reflection of the sleep-related changes in brain state that we start to detail in Chapter 3.

To provide a firmer grasp of the distinction between form and content, I offer an example, taken at random from my own dream journal, which is one of hundreds that I have recorded over the years. To give a complete sense of how my journal reads and to allow the reader to compare his or her own notes on dreaming with mine I quote the entry in full. I know that you will dream of subjects quite different from mine, but I suspect that the form of your dreams is similar.

10/5/1987 En route to New Orleans for a debate on dreams at the American Psychiatric Association's annual meeting: Two nights ago, a dream of Richard Newland

> *It is a house maintenance nightmare. I have too much property to maintain. Richard and a friend are 'helping' me but it is an uncertain alliance, with the twin threats of incompetence and inattentiveness.*
>
> *There are several scenes all with the same emotional theme: anxiety about maintenance details.*
>
> *In one scene we are walking along in hilly country, perhaps toward the house, but the destination is not clear.*
>
> *Then we are in a house, not at all like mine but assumed by my dreaming brain to be mine, and Richard's friend is spray painting the white wall (we have none in our house) with blue paint (neither do we*

have any blue rooms). The paint sprayer is a tank device of the type used to apply copper sulphate to grapevines or to exterminate cockroaches. Suddenly, the paint is being sprayed not only on the wall but upon a painting hanging on the wall.

My fears are confirmed. I yell at Richard to bid his friend stop.

For some reason, he has to go upstairs to turn off the machine (although it appears to be fully portable and self-contained) and this takes an inordinate length of time as the painting continues to suffer.

There follows a long dialogue with Richard who, while retaining continuous identity as Richard, changes physiognomy repeatedly. His face changed as follows: a gnome-like Napoleon Carter with a cherubic sun-burned face; a wry smile and a Chinese coolie-type hat; a calf face—as in A Midsummer Night's Dream *(the ad for which did not include the calf!); and as far as I can tell, never included Richard!*

I can't remember other faces or other action from this long episode.

Before discussing the distinctions of form against content that this dream so clearly illustrates, I should comment on the

circumstances of its recording and the timing of its occurrence. I was on an aeroplane, where I do a great deal of my journal writing. I was flying to New Orleans for a highly publicized and well-attended public debate on dreaming. I usually record dreams on the morning after their occurrence. The fact that I waited two days in this case probably resulted in loss of detail. But, as I will presently show, there is more than enough detail to make clear the distinction between dream form and dream content.

As far as the *content* is concerned, the dream is about my concerns for the upkeep of my farm in northern Vermont, which I have owned since 1965. Richard Newland is the son of my farmer neighbour, Marshall Newland, with whom I have had a long and complicated but successful and gratifying relationship. In spite of widely divergent priorities we have managed to get along and to help each other.

For me, the meaning of the dream is transparent: I am anxious about my property and about entrusting it to people who are careless about their own houses. This characteristic, known in psychological terms as emotional salience (or relevance), is all I need to understand the dream, which is a variant on the theme of incomplete arrangements that is so recurrent in my dreams and in those of most of my friends. For reasons that I discuss more fully in Chapter 2, I see no need and no justification for treating this dream as a disguised, symbolic expression of anxiety about other related themes (my wife's interest in another Vermont neighbour, for example). While admitting that it could be appropriate and more useful to notice such an association, it does not help in understanding what caused this dream, determined its comical bizarreness, and made it so hard to remember.

EAST BATON ROUGE PARISH LIBRARY
BLUEBONNET REGIONAL
Expiry date: 25 Mar 2018

Borrowed on 03/23/2018 17:53 Till

1) Dreaming : an introduction to the
   science of sleep
   Due date: 04/13/2018
   No.: 31659025885167
2) The happiness diet : a nutritional
   prescription for a sharp brain,
   balanced mood, and lean, energized
   body
   Due date: 04/13/2018
   No.: 31659041520996

Total on loan : 2

To renew items call 225-763-2240
or visit www.ebrpl.com.
03/23/2018 - 17:53

Form as opposed to content

To answer the questions about causes and characteristics of dreams, it is helpful to take a formal analytical approach.

As is typical of most dreams, I am so involved in the scenario that it never occurs to me that I am dreaming. As I see Richard Newland (and his unidentified friend), see my house (even though it is clearly not mine), see the blue paint as it is sprayed on the walls, and move through the sequence of scenes, I accept all of these unlikely features as real on the strength of my hallucinatory perceptions, my delusional beliefs about them, and my very strong feelings of anxiety and apprehension.

What this means is that our sense of psychological reality— whether normal dreaming or a psychotic symptom—is set by the strength of percepts and feelings as well as by our thoughts about them. Internally generated perceptions and emotions are two formal features of dreams and they are cardinal features. To explain their intensity (compared with waking), we might expect to find that parts of the brain that generate emotions and related percepts are selectively activated in sleep. We see in Chapter 5 that this is precisely what happens!

My Richard Newland dream is not simply perceptually vivid and emotionally salient, it is also cognitively bizarre, by which I mean that, despite the persistence of the main themes, there is a flagrant disregard for the constancies of time, place, and person. Notice that Richard's friend is not identified; notice also that the house that is supposed to be mine could not possibly be so; and notice that the scenes—however poorly recalled and described—meld into one another: first we are outside walking, then inside painting. Notice, most of all, that Richard's face assumes a series of non-Richard features without ever

challenging either the assumption that he is Richard, or that I am not awake but dreaming, as even a glimmer of self-reflective awareness would declare me to be.

These are the cardinal cognitive features of dreaming: loss of awareness of self (self-reflective awareness); loss of orientational stability; loss of directed thought; reduction in logical reasoning; and, last but not least, poor memory both within and after the dream. The fact that the incongruities and discontinuities of my Richard Newland dream are connected by association does not explain the looseness of those associations. Thus, it is true that the unusual spray-painting device resembles an agricultural tool; it is also true that Richard's transformed face is, first, that of another Vermont farmer neighbour, Napoleon Carter, and later a calf (Richard and his dairy farmer father, Marshall, had many calves); and it is remarkably true that Shakespeare himself celebrated the transformation of characters—turning them into each other and even into animals—in *A Midsummer Night's Dream*.

What causes the processing of such extreme associations (hyperassociative processing)? Freud, like his followers, religiously believed that dream bizarreness was a psychological defence against an unacceptable unconscious wish. This seemed unlikely to many people in 1900. At the beginning of the twenty-first century, it seems impossible to us.

Just as we expect (and find) selective activation of brain circuits underlying emotion and related percepts in rapid eye movement (REM) sleep, so we seek (and find) selective *inacti*-vation of brain circuits—and chemicals—underlying memory, directed thought, self-reflective awareness, and logical reasoning.

You may be more or less pleased by the story. You might prefer to believe that your dreams are secret messages of

personal portent. But whether you like the story or not, you must surely be as dismayed as we were to realize that we did not really need brain research to take this formal approach to dreaming. Common sense alone should have dictated at least that form and content were complementary. The distinction is made with ease in other fields: consider linguistics, where grammar and syntax are complementary; consider poetry, where meter and verse enhance one another; and consider the visual arts, where genre and subject matter interact for strong effect. So, why not the domain of mental life itself? Why not in dreams? Isn't the form of dreams an important contributor to content?

As shown in Chapter 2, some brave souls did make this distinction, but their feeble voices were drowned out by the clamour of the interpreters who pandered to the deep-seated human need to believe that dreaming, as for every apparent mystery, has a deeply veiled meaning inscribed by a benevolent hand whose ways are known only to a few chosen mediators.

Dreaming and how to measure it

Let's begin our analytical odyssey by accepting the most broad, general, and indisputable definition of dreaming: mental activity occurring in sleep. But what *kinds* of mental activity occur in sleep? Many different kinds, for example:

Report 1. As soon as I fell asleep, I could *feel* myself moving just the way the sea moved our boat when I was out fishing today.

Report 2. I kept thinking about my upcoming exam and about the subject matter that it will contain. I didn't sleep well because I kept waking up and was inevitably pulled back to the same ruminations about my exam.

Report 3. I am perched on a steep mountaintop, the void falls away to the left. As the climbing party rounds the trail to the right, I am suddenly on a bicycle, which I steer through the group of climbers. It becomes clear that I make a complete circuit of the peak (at this level) by staying on the grass. There is, in fact, a manicured lawn surface continuing between the rocks and crags.

All these reports qualify as descriptions of dreaming according to our broad definition, although they are very different from one another and each is typical of the kind of sleep in which it was experienced.

Report 1 contains an internal percept, the sense of rhythmic movement imparted by the sea to a boat and to those on board the boat. This report is typical of sleep-onset dreams, especially on nights following novel motor behaviour such as skiing, or boating, or even—as in Robert Frost's poem—*After Apple Picking*. The subject has been boating, and the sense of motion, which abated immediately upon putting his foot on shore, recommences at sleep onset and reproduces, exactly, the physical experience of boating. We will have more to say later about this stimulus-induced dream, especially when we look at the theme of motor learning later in the book. For now, let us emphasize how short and relatively simple this sleep-onset dream experience is. Even though it is hallucinatory, as is Report 3, it is impoverished in its brevity and its narrow scope, its lack of characters other than the dreamer, and its emotional flatness. Many sleep-onset dream reports are richer and more variegated than this one, although they are all brief and lack the elaborate plot development of Report 3.

Report 2 is limited to thinking, or what psychologists call

cognition. There is no perceptual structure, and hence no hallucinatory aspect. There *is* emotion, however. The dreamer is anxious about performance on a test and this anxiety appears to drive obsessive thinking very much in the way that it might be expected to do so in waking. The thinking described is non-progressive. The dreamer doesn't even rehearse the content of the exam material in a way that might be adaptive. Accounts of rumination such as this are often given when individuals are aroused from sleep early in the night. If they are collected in a sleep lab—as described in Chapter 3—they are associated with the low levels of brain activation that typify what we call slow wave sleep (seen on the electroencephalograph or EEG) or non-REM sleep (NREM; this refers to the lack of eye movement). Mental activity in NREM sleep later in the night, when brain activation approaches that seen in REM sleep, can assume many of the properties of Report 3.

Report 3 is a typical REM sleep report: it is animated; it is dramatic and complex; it is bizarre; it is hallucinatory; it is delusional; and it is long, about eight to ten times as long as Reports 1 and 2 (which were given in their entirety), whereas only a small excerpt of Report 3 is given here. In the rest of Report 3, there was a scene change from the mountain peak to Martha's Vineyard Island (though I was still on the same bicycle), and then to a shopping centre, a restaurant, a dance, and a meeting of faculty colleagues. The dream also exemplifies typical dream features, such as character instability, because one of my colleague's wives is seen as a blond when, in reality, she is a brunette. The sense of movement, which is continuous, becomes particularly delightful when I become practically weightless and glide along a golf fairway. At the dance there is 'a Baltic group wearing embroidered peasant garb and stamping the floor to a loud band (I can hear the drums especially).'

There is simply no comparison between the richness of Report 3 and the restrictions of Reports 1 and 2, even though Report 2 fulfils this more rigorous definition of dreaming.

Report 3 more fully illustrates a mental experience occurring in sleep, which is characterized by:

1. Rich and varied internal percepts, especially sensorimotor (movement), auditory (drums), and anti-gravitational (weightlessness) hallucinations.
2. Delusional acceptance of the wild events as real despite their extreme improbability (a bike on a mountain peak?) and physical impossibility (gliding weightless on a golf fairway?).
3. Bizarreness deriving from the discontinuity (at least six locations) and character incongruity (a blond brunette?).
4. Emotional intensity and variety (fear, elation, and exuberance).
5. Poor reasoning—I can make a complete circuit of the peak by staying on the grass!

When we think about how the very different experiences in the three dream reports were brought about, and even what they may mean, we can easily understand the first two simply in terms of brain activation that reflects, in sleep, the dreamer's previous experience (the boat trip) and concerns about the future (anxiety about an exam). In both cases, the residual brain activation of sleep onset and early night sleep is enough to reproduce faithfully a very small part of waking experience. Report 3, however, needs a much more elaborate explanation to account for its description of events, many of which never happened and never could have happened. Brain activation, which must be powerful, and highly selective, can account for some aspects—the hallucinatory imagery and the associated movements, for example. But activation cannot

Does everyone dream?

All human beings who have been studied in sleep labs have brain activation in sleep. Periods of brain activation during sleep are associated with rapid eye movements in the sleeper. These rapid eye movements give the brain-activated phase of sleep its name: REM or rapid eye movement sleep. When awakened at the time of intense clusters of rapid eye movements, 95 per cent of sleepers studied in labs report dreaming. From this evidence, it is generally assumed that everyone does, in fact, dream in sleep; any impression to the contrary is related to the difficulty recalling dreams.

If dreaming is not interrupted by awakening, it is rare to have recall. Poor or no dream recall by many people is a function of the abolition of memory during these brain-activated phases of sleep. As the chemical systems that are responsible for recent memory are completely turned off when the brain is activated during sleep, it is difficult to have recall unless an awakening occurs to restore the availability of these chemicals to the brain.

account for the bizarreness and the loss of logical reasoning. If brain activation were global in REM sleep, we would expect orientation and cognition to improve, not deteriorate. These changes must result from something else, something that changes the whole mode of operation of the brain and the mind. As we see in Chapters 4 and 5, this change in mode is affected both chemically and by selective brain deactivation. The net effect is that, in dreaming (compared with waking), some mental functions are enhanced while others are diminished. It's as simple as that! And every bit as complicated.

How were dream data collected?

The reports that have been presented so far are all mine. They were recorded at home or on the road in my personal journal, which now runs to 116 volumes covering the last 25 years of my life and includes over 300 dream reports. Dream reports such as these have the great advantage of being easy and inexpensive to obtain, numerous, and, to me at least, undeniably authentic. Even though I have no recall of these dreams until I read the reports, I have the reports and I see in them the striking formal features that I have emphasized in this chapter.

These reports do, however, have corresponding deficiencies, which need to be overcome if dream science is to be universally valid. To test the generality of the findings and to be sure that I wasn't just making up dreams to fit my theory, we need to have reports from many other sources and individuals, collected under very different conditions. The dream data that we have analysed before arriving at our conclusions have thus been taken from other dream journals, sleep lab reports, and home-based reports.

Other dream journals

The best dream journal that I have found is called *The Dream Journal of the Engine Man*. Its author was a railroad buff. I like it because it was recorded in the summer of 1939 (when I was only six years old) and could not therefore have been influenced by my theories. I also like it because the descriptions are so detailed and so free of interpretation. Some are even accompanied by simple but expressive drawings. To control for the fact that the Engine Man, like me, is male, we have collected journalistic reports from our female colleagues and students. All show the same robust formal differences from waking consciousness that I have emphasized here.

Sleep lab reports

Thanks to our colleagues Milton Kramer (University of Cincinnati) and John Antrobus (City College of New York), and our own sleep lab team, we have over 1,000 reports that were collected by experimentally awakening participants in studies.

We know that sleep lab awakenings change the character of the reports in at least two ways.

1. They introduce thoughts, feelings, and percepts related to the laboratory situation, but this has no effect on dream hallucinations, delusions, or bizarreness.
2. They increase recall and the naturalism of the dream recalled. For example, more positive emotion is found in post-awakening reports, indicating that we normally sleep right through our more pleasant dreams, whereas our unpleasant ones are more likely to awaken us and tilt the scales towards negative emotion.

A major disadvantage of sleep lab reports is that they are

very expensive to obtain and tend to come almost exclusively from younger individuals. Students at the universities where the labs are located are easily recruited. Finally, due to expense, they tend to be limited in number of reports per participant. No one who is a sleep lab participant can yet match the 256 reports of the Engine Man, or my 300+ reports.

Figure 1 Line drawing made from a photograph of a subject sleeping with the Nightcap, together with Nightcap output and analysis. Top trace: histogram plot of eyelid movements; second trace: hypnogram of computer-scored Nightcap data; third trace: histogram plotting head movements.

Home-based reports with physiological controls

With the hope of obtaining the best of both dream science worlds, we have developed the Nightcap, a home-based sleep monitor that allows us to know what state the participants were in before their reports, to compare spontaneous awakening with experimental awakening reports, to obtain abundant data from each person, and, best of all, to obtain reports in natural settings (Figure 1). Using this approach we have been able to accomplish two feats that have never before been attempted.

One is to obtain a very large number of reports from each of three sleep conditions: sleep onset, NREM, and REM sleep. The other is to obtain comparable reports from two states of waking by beeping the same participants with a home pager during the daytime. Thus, the same participants who give us dream reports also give us reports of their waking consciousness. This last advantage is crucial to our effort to extend our understanding of mental life back into the waking state, and to obtain comparable quantitative data from the minds of the same individuals when awake and asleep.

Summary

It is ironic to note that the first task of a science of the mind—to describe, define, and measure polar states of consciousness such as waking and dreaming—has only recently assumed a serious status. Although artists and poets have long championed this approach and have appropriately celebrated the differences between conscious states, scientists have shied away from their study because they had no objective measures of subjective experience and because subjective experience was considered to

be hard to trust or deal with. But there is no substitute for a direct approach to human consciousness, an approach that takes subjective experience as data. Part of the solution to this problem is technical: we now possess laboratory and field methods for establishing the parameters of brain correlation with mental experience. Another part of the solution is conceptual: by focusing on the formal aspects of mental states we remove the distractions and intractability of enormous individual differences in mental content. As we see in Chapter 2, most of the important differences between waking and dreaming can be captured by formal analysis, so that content analysis can thus be unburdened from the impossible task of explaining, in its own terms, formal differences.

2

Why did the analysis of dream content fail to become a science?

Although there were a few important predecessors of the formal approach to dreaming described in Chapter 1, most dream theorists preferred to focus on content. Impressed with the apparent unintelligibility of dreams, these theorists assumed that there was a rebus, or transformational set of rules (algorithm), which presented the deeper meanings of the dream in disguised symbolic, metaphorical, and sensory terms. Interpretation has always been the main goal of content analysis, whether for medical diagnosis (in the hands of the early Greeks), fortune telling (in the work of Artemidorus), religious prophecy (in the Bible), or psychological divinations (in the proto-scientific schema of Sigmund Freud).

As he was so close to us in time and spirit, and because our brain-based theory is so different from his, in this chapter we focus on Freud's psychoanalytic model as it was developed in his *Project for a Scientific Psychology* (1895) and *The Interpretation of Dreams* (1900). Freud wanted his psychology to have a solid

foundation in brain science, but he was 100 years too early to build it as we now can. For this reason, he was forced to resort to speculative philosophy, the medium of all pre-modern dream theories that analyse content. The differences between Freud's content analytical scheme and modern theory are shown in Table 1.

Table 1 Differences between Freud and activation–synthesis: two models that offer different explanations of the altered state of dreaming

Dream phenomena	Psychoanalysis	Activation–synthesis
Instigation	Repressed unconscious wish	Brain activation in sleep
Visual imagery	Regression to sensory level	Activation of higher visual centres
Delusional belief	Primary process thinking	Loss of working memory resulting from DLPFC inactivation
Bizarreness	Disguise of wishes	Hyperassociative synthesis
Emotion	Secondary defensive response of ego	Primary activation of limbic system
Forgetting	Repression	Organic (physical) amnesia
Meaning	Actively obscured	Transparent, salient
Interpretation	Needed	Not needed

DLPFC, dorsolateral prefrontal cortex.

For all pre-modern analysts of dream content, the dream as it is experienced by the dreamer is not what it appears to be; rather, it is the distorted read-out of a sick body (Greek *Oniro-diagnosis*), or an encoded message about the future from the gods (whether pagan as with Artemidorus or Judaeo-Christian as in the Bible). Sigmund Freud picked up the distorted message idea and acted as the high priest whose psychological skills could

tell the patient things that he would otherwise not know about himself. All of these systems, including psychoanalysis, are essentially religions in that they are based on faith in an agency that gives hidden directives, which can be understood only through the intervention of someone who can interpret the 'message'.

Nourishing these ideas was the general assumption that the world and its people were created by, maintained by, and beholden to a higher power, a god or gods that constituted the ultimate agencies of earthly phenomena. While Freud was an avowed atheist—his rejection of religion was practically phobic—he fell back into the hidden agency idea with his belief in a dynamic unconscious mind that was in constant competition with consciousness. In dreaming, this competition became war-like, so that the mind was forced to resort to extreme defences to avoid being overwhelmed.

At a deeper level, all schemes that analyse content are essentially two-pronged: there are always two agencies—us and them, the body and the spirit, the ego and the id, the brain and the mind. Part of the change in paradigm exemplified by the shift from dream content to dream form is the adoption of the philosophical conviction that the physical world is the only world that there is, that the brain and the mind are therefore inextricably united, and that dreaming is a distinctive form of conscious awareness caused by the state of the brain in sleep. To be fair to Freud, we must acknowledge that he really knew that these things were true (or believed them as fervently as we do), but that the interpretive tradition was too powerful and too tempting for him to resist, especially as he knew next to nothing about the brain.

Still, we can express our astonishment at the failure of so

Can dreams foretell the future?

Since time immemorial, the mysterious nature of dreaming, which we now know is determined mainly by its formal qualities, has led people to believe that dreams were messages from the other world. Dreams have been regarded as prophetic communications which, when properly decoded, would enable us to foretell the future.

There is absolutely no scientific evidence for this theory and considerable scientific evidence against it. It is certainly true that individuals who are concerned about a traumatic event, such as the threat of the loss of a loved one who is sick, will dream about that loved one more than would otherwise be the case. We know from our experiments on lucid dreaming that it is possible to influence dream content simply by having a subject in mind while going to sleep. Therefore, dreaming about a loved one at a time when that loved one's life is threatened is not in the least bit surprising. If the dreamer then calls and finds that the individual has died, it is understandable for him or her to assume that the dream was a premonition of that death. But this is a mistake. It is simply a coincidental correspondence between a situation about which one has legitimate and intense concern and the occurrence of the event that one fears.

We can turn the question around and ask what constitutes scientific proof of the occurrence of dreams that are

premonitions (premonitory dreams). The answer is that we would need to do what are called prospective studies, studies in which many individuals are sampled in terms of their dream life and judges who know nothing about the dreams or individuals (i.e. are blinded) are asked to make predictions or correspondences between these dream events and events that occurred in real life. A problem that arises here is that individuals who believe in premonitory dreams will usually give one or two striking examples of 'hits', but they never tell you how many premonitory dreams they had that were *not* associated with the event that in fact occurred. To do a scientific study of dream prophecy, we would need to establish some base of how commonly coincidental correspondences occur between dream and waking reality. Until we have that evidence, it is better to believe that the assumption is false.

many dream theorists to grasp the dream form theory. When Leonardo da Vinci asked:

'Why does the eye see a thing more clearly in dreams than when awake?'

We would expect such a great genius to offer the speculative but naturalistic answer:

'Because the visual image production system of the brain is selectively activated in sleep!'

And when Shakespeare ascribes to Bottom the recognition that 'I dreamed a dream so strange as to pass all understanding', why doesn't he go on and close the circle by hypothesizing that:

'Because the brain's memory mechanisms are so seriously disrupted during sleep we cannot escape bizarre mental experiences that would otherwise occur only during madness.'

Indeed, the analogy with madness offers clues about the creation of dreams by the brain precisely because the form of dreaming is very much like certain kinds of madness. The combination of frequent visual hallucinations (in the perceptual domain), instability of orientation, and recent memory loss (in the cognitive domain) should have made physicians, such as Sigmund Freud and Carl Jung, recognize that the mental illness that dreaming simulated best was delirium, the psychosis associated with the acute brain dysfunctions caused by toxicity (alcohol and drugs), anoxia (inadequate supply of oxygen to the brain caused by circulation deficiencies), and acute head trauma. Jung said, 'Let the dreamer awake and you will see psychosis.' Fair enough. But what kind of psychosis will you see? The fact that it is delirium should have suggested that a major shift in brain

function was necessary to account for such a major change in mental state. We return to this discussion in Chapter 7.

With regard to mental state, we need to note two important points: one phenomenological, the other methodological.

For phenomenology, the term 'mental state' implies global features: every aspect of mental activity changes when the mental state changes. The easiest way to effect a global change in mental state is to engineer a global change in brain state. For methodology, the clinical assessment of mental state has always been achieved by an examination known as the mental status exam. Uniting neurology and psychiatry, the mental status exam is a comprehensive checklist of mind functions that are known to be disrupted by organic brain disease, i.e. brain disease caused by a physical rather than a mental condition.

To introduce the far-reaching implications of dream science to a general science of consciousness, consider the following categories of the mental status exam:

- Consciousness: clear or clouded?
- Attention: focused or distractible?
- Intellectual: sharp functions or dull?
- Perceptions: externally driven or hallucinated?
- Cognition: logical or illogical?
- Emotion: stable or unstable/uncontrolled?
- Memory: good or poor?
- Abstraction: symbolic or concrete?

Even this very incomplete list makes us realize how careless we have been in not applying the mental state concept to dreaming and the mental status approach to its analysis.

Below is another report that will help us see the global nature of mental state changes in dreaming:

9/3/1981   Red Car, Dream no. 16

> I am trying to organize a group for a departure. I find one member at the foot of a hill, near some water. I urge him to go up the hill to a rendezvous point for departure.
>
> Suddenly, or perhaps always, he is in a red car, which runs along beside me up the hill. The peculiar thing is that the front of the car, including the driver, is underground. Yet its trajectory is smooth and the ground is unbroken!
>
> As we climb, the car moves ahead of me and I make a strong but vain effort to keep up with its progress. The car then crosses from left to right and runs—still half underground   into a wall. I wonder if the driver will have hurt his head in the crash.
>
> The scene changes.
>
> I am in a locker room and approach my son Ian who has been hurt. At first his legs appear to have been amputated at the knees and I feel dread. But as I approach, what I took to be stumps are his blood-smeared kneecaps (very bright red blood—like the car—and he is smiling, not crying). I am relieved and wake up.

My *consciousness* is clear as a bell. In fact, I see—and feel—everything in this dream with a *surreal intensity* that would have pleased André Breton as much as Leonardo da Vinci. The intense hallucinatory *percepts* grip my *attention* in a vice that won't let it do anything else but watch in fascination—and in *horror*—as the half-buried car hurtles uphill and crashes despite my effort to control it. The emotions of *horror* and *dread* (*fear*) survive the scene shift—to the locker room—where I am *relieved* to find that my son is OK. Although it is not explicitly noted, my cognition is defective and my logical reasoning poor. How could the car do what it appeared to do and without disrupting the ground? 'Seeing is believing' is one answer.

My Red Car dream reveals another kind of association—one marked by a high degree of emotional salience. My son, Ian, *was* badly injured in an automobile accident and one of his legs *was* threatened and saved. So it is natural for my memory of associations—associative memory—to link the red car crash to my son, Ian. *But* (and it is a large *but*) I do not see Ian in the hospital setting where I actually beheld him at the time of his accident. And he had only one leg damaged, not two. This departure of the dream scenario from long-term memory of personal experiences, called episodic memory in psychological terminology, is typical and needs to be explained. Episodic memory may feed dream content useful fragments for plot construction, but it does not supply the details that are, in waking, so easily remembered. Why? What is going on? We should not ignore cases like this because there is nothing less at stake than how memory works. This means that dream science is a set of rules for understanding unconscious aspects of memory formation, but not in the sense intended by theorists who analyse dream content.

Extending the suggestions of Chapter 1, dream science now

needs much more careful consideration of the numerous subcategories of mental state. A list of such subcategories and the ways that neurobiology explains them are given in Table 2. Having stumbled, almost by accident, on the now obvious fact that the bizarreness of dreams is a reflection of orientational instability, we want to know much more about other memory functions. Are declarative and/or episodic memories used in dream plot constructions? To what extent and with what constraints? The terms 'declarative' and 'episodic' refer to specific memories of personal or historical events, e.g. I went to Boston last weekend. This kind of memory is contrasted with 'semantic' memory, which consists of general facts, e.g. Boston is the capital of Massachusetts. Another class of memory is 'procedural', e.g. I know how to drive my car to Boston.

And what about thinking? We already know that thinking is suppressed in dreaming and that it is only slightly effective when it does appear.

Table 2 The psychological basis for the differences between waking and sleeping

Function	Nature of difference	Hypothesis of cause
Sensory input	Blocked	Presynaptic inhibition
Perception (external)	Diminished	Blockade of sensory input
Perception (internal)	Enhanced	Disinhibition of networks storing sensory representations
Attention	Lost	Decreased aminergic modulation
Memory (recent)	Diminished	Because of aminergic demodulation, activated representations are not restored in memory

Why did the analysis of dream content fail to become a science?

Memory (remote)	Enhanced	Disinhibition of networks storing mnemonic representations increases access to consciousness
Orientation	Unstable	Internally inconsistent orienting signals are generated by cholinergic system
Thought	Reasoning ad hoc Logical rigour weak Processing hyperassociative	Loss of attention, memory, and volition leads to failure of sequencing and rule inconstancy; analogy replaces analysis
Insight	Self-reflection lost	Failures of attention, logic, and memory weaken second- (and third-) order representations
Language (internal)	Confabulatory	Aminergic demodulation frees narrative synthesis from logical restraints
Emotion	Episodically strong	Cholinergic hyperstimulation of amygdala and related temporal lobe structures in the brain triggers emotional storms which are unmodulated by aminergic restraint
Instinct	Episodically strong	Cholinergic hyperstimulation of hypothalamus and limbic forebrain triggers fixed action motor programmes, which are experienced fictitiously but not enacted
Volition	Weak	Top-down motor control and frontal executive power cannot compete with disinhibited subcortical network activation
Output	Blocked	Postsynaptic inhibition

From J. Allan Hobson and Edward Pace-Schott, *Fundamental Neuroscience*, 2nd edn., Nov. 2002

Among the generally unsung heroes of the dream form theory, brain state = mental state, looms the Romantic Movement figure of David Hartley, famous as the father of British Associationism. Associationism asserts that memory is organized according to categorical similarities among objects, people, ideas, and so on, to every category of content. A good example, from my Richard Newland dream in Chapter 1, is the associative linking of spray painting with sulphating of grapevines. Although the purposes are very different, the processes are similar—to cover a large surface area with liquid, it is useful to turn the liquid into tiny particles and to spread these via a pressurized vapour system. Another example, in the Red Car dream, is the association of the hallucinated car crash with my son's accident.

What caused the failure of psychoanalytic dream theory?

Freud must have had in mind the fragmentary nature involved in incorporating episodic memory when he coined the term 'day residue' and dubbed it the dream stimulus. Subsequent scientific work on memory sources of dreams has shown, however, that even this notion is mistaken. In Tore Nielsen's data, the incorporation of confidently identified memory sources is actually low for the day immediately preceding a given night's dream; it becomes higher as one moves backwards in time to a peak at day 6 before dreaming. In the French neurophysiologist Michel Jouvet's dream data, the peak of incorporation is 7 days before the dream and never includes content from locales to which he has just travelled, a surprise even for theories that emphasize emotional salience, as well as those that emphasize recency.

Freud's work suffered from two fatal scientific defects, which his brilliant rhetoric could not overcome. One was the absence of relevant brain science, which he knew was indispensable and would some day force revision of his theories. For this he cannot be blamed. He was a creature of his time and his ambition pushed him a century ahead of that time. But because Freud *was* trained as a biological scientist, we can in all fairness ask why he was so careless as an observer. Why were his data so limited? Why was his focus so narrowly fixed?

As far as the data are concerned, Freud made no attempt to collect dream reports from people other than himself, and even those reports are few in number (about 40 are cited in the 700 pages of his *Interpretation of Dreams*) and fragmentary (his word counts, of less than 100, are many times less than most modern samples). In the 1890s, as today, it was an easy matter to collect an extensive, representative sample and to treat the data-set as a whole rather than using the piecemeal, axe-grinding, controversial technique that Freud used to discuss each one.

Freud's scholarship is evident in his detailed discussion of the scientific literature before 1900. However, he is controversial and exclusive rather than dispassionate and balanced in discussing the work of others. In many cases, his derisive dismissals seem justified, but, for one who was sure that the brain was important, he is cavalier in his treatment of such intellectual giants as Wilhelm Wundt (who correctly assumed that the dreaming brain would show a selective increase in some of its functions, e.g. vision, and a selective decrease in others, e.g. memory and reasoning). For Freud, the idea that any dream content was nonsensical, i.e. gratuitously associative, was anathema. He therefore thought that Wundt's suggestion that the

bizarre nature of dreams reflects a delirious series of links of loosely connected contents must be wrong.

Freud ignored two important predecessors. One was David Hartley, who ascribed the bizarre nature of dreams to too many associations; he had a functional theory to go with his hypothesis, a hypothesis that was probably correct. Dreaming, for Hartley, served to loosen associations that were otherwise inclined to become obsessively fixed. 'And that would be madness,' Hartley asserted. Certainly, dreaming is a hyperassociative state (i.e. a state in which many, many associations are made), as Freud could have quickly determined had he examined dream reports before rushing to interpret them.

The second great predecessor was Wundt's teacher, Herman Helmholtz, who also inspired Freud's own mentor, Herman Muller, and helped to create the anti-vitalist spirit of the age in which Freud's theory took root. In discussing dreaming in his classic *Physiological Optics*, Helmholtz was a formalist in his approach to hallucinated movement. As Helmholtz noticed, the sense of the self moving through the dream space is one of the most robust formal features of dreaming. When today we refer to 'sensorimotor hallucinations' we are only echoing Helmholtz's recognition that the dreaming brain is capable of simulating acts of movement (motor acts) extremely convincingly. Helmholtz recognized that this meant that motor control—in waking—must be highly predictive. More specifically he theorized that the nervous system created its own image of the expected consequence of movement.

This principle has become enshrined in movement physiology as the 'efferent copy hypothesis'. If, and only if, we are able to predict, and project, an image of movement outcomes are we able to move effectively. The almost magical ease of dream

movement (witness my weightless gliding and the flight patterns of lucid dreamers) is due to this self-contained, closed-loop activation, in sleep, of movement patterns that are felt by us to be complete and have an outcome. This, of course, implies activation of generators of motor patterns in the brain, for which there is now abundant evidence.

The best that poor old Freud could do with flying dreams was to argue that they represented displaced sexual desire. Freud's rebus, you will recall, was that unconscious wishes—and sexual wishes needed to be kept unconscious—escaped the censor's denunciation when the ego was weakened by sleep. If the now free-to-be-expressed sexual impulses were not disguised, by the pleasurable but not sexual hallucination of flying, the dreamer would be awakened by the consciousness of these forbidden desires. Freud never mentioned his own sexual dreams. Perhaps he never had any—or never remembered them. But this is unlikely. And any research participant—or any of his patients—could have told him that sexual dreams, complete with orgasm, occur in the very same people who enjoy flying dreams.

The kind of argument that I am now advancing is dismissed as Freud-bashing by the many, still passionate defenders of psychoanalysis. It is true that I want to discredit Freud emphatically, but only because we are all still in danger of accepting subsequent psychological explanations for dream phenomena that are likely to have physiological mechanisms with quite different psychological meanings from those that we can now imagine. For example, we might experience exotic movement, including sexual movement, in dreams in order to refresh movement programmes that are crucial to survival. We might also regard dreams as efforts to revise those programmes in terms of

emotionally salient or important memories. Thus, my son's accident is an important aspect of my bicycle dream. In fact, he had another terrible accident on a bicycle before we stopped him from riding with his own impaired motor control system. Ian's bike accident is fixed in my memory as a warning: this could happen again to him and to me.

Can associations ever really be free?

Associations are not associations unless they have meaningful connections. The meaning of their connection is determined as much by the context in which they are evoked as by their historical source. So, just as Freud, the atheist, was doomed by his authoritarian speculations to create a new religion of which he was the highest of priests, so he was destined to suggest certain associations for the dream content of his clients, even as he tried desperately to distance himself from hypnosis and the criticism of suggestibility. This was particularly true of his work with hysterical patients, whose highly hypnotizable nature he recognized. And he knew from his experience at the Salpêtrière Hospital in Paris in 1885, that the neurologists Pierre Janet and Jean-Martin Charcot were able to get whatever result they wanted from their hysterical patients, especially in the theatrical context of medical teaching amphitheatres.

Freud's idea that he could avoid suggesting content by laying a client down on a couch (encouraging a pre-sleep relaxation) and sitting behind him or her (to remove any personal impact) seems grossly naïve in retrospect. Sleep onset is a particularly fruitful state for the elaboration of fantasy and dream-like mental activity that incorporated local conditions shamelessly. And any patient, hysterical or not, would know—by 1910 at the very

latest—what Freud expected in the way of 'associations'. Now that the false memory phenomenon is so well known, it is easy for us to see what mischief Freud's 'scientific' precautions must have cost him. To avoid repeating these mistakes, we need to be much more critical, and much more versatile, than Freud was.

One way to free the formal approach to dreaming for immunity from the charge of self-fulfilling prophecy is to keep our mind genuinely open with respect to psychological meaning, to resist any formulaic approach to interpretation, and to refuse any interpretation that is not straightforward and tied to physiology. This means that we have to settle for less than Freud wanted. As made clear in Chapter 11, there remain many aspects of dreaming that we cannot explain today, although, as this book attempts to show, many aspects of dream content *can* be explained today using the formal approach. Those that cannot be explained will have to wait. But, with the field moving as fast as it is today, the wait will not be long, and it will be worthwhile because we will finally obtain what Freud could only dream of: a psychology that is perspicacious and free from doubt.

Brain–mind isomorphism and the science of dreaming

The word 'isomorphism' means similarity of form or shape, and brain–mind isomorphism that every form of mental activity has a similar form of brain activity. Therefore, if we detect a dream form, we can seek a corresponding brain form. In dreaming, the simplest example is activation. To explain the awakening of the mind in sleep we should expect to find a similar (but not of course identical) awakening of the brain during sleep. As we see

in Chapter 3, we do find this—the brain is electrically activated in sleep and, when this happens, the mind is turned on too. Naturally. It's that simple.

A more detailed example should clinch our point. If, in our exploration of the brain in sleep, we find physiological evidence that memory systems are disabled, we should expect to find that memory is altered during dreaming and that dreams would be difficult to recall. We already know that the second prediction is true, but just how true we cannot yet say precisely. The first prediction has, however, scarcely been entertained. Is it generally true that I cannot exercise my episodic memory when I am dreaming? Does this affect dream content?

These examples are chosen to highlight two important points about the doctrine of brain–mind isomorphism. One is that it is just as fruitful to map from the brain to the mind as it is to map from the mind to the brain. The second is that we must choose carefully the appropriate level of each domain at which to focus our isomorphic efforts. In the beginning, and we are still very much at the beginning, we will find that global and psychologically general levels will be more generous than detailed and psychologically personal ones. Individual differences have never been generous to psychology. And how many of them are real? Although it may disappoint you if you hanker after a fortune-telling interpretation of your dreams, our attention to the mirrored formal aspects is necessary to the scientific understanding of dreaming as a universal process. Later in this book we will see how it can be used to help individual dream interpretation by relieving it of an impossibly difficult task and helping us to discover the usually clear emotional salience of our dreams.

3

How is the brain activated in sleep?

Consciousness is so rapidly and dramatically reduced during sleep that it was natural to assume that the brain simply turned off at sleep onset and turned on again just before awakening. Indeed, some people do sleep all night in that deep, oblivious, and uninterrupted way. Some, but by no means all. And no one sleeps that way all the time. There are periods of life change and stress when mental activity seems to go on all night. Are these to be attributed to our not really being able to sleep at such times? Perhaps. But what about dreaming? How could such elaborate and exciting mental activity arise in an inactive brain?

This question was answered in a wide variety of erroneous ways. As dream recall was generally poor and needed awakening to be present at all, many scientists—Sigmund Freud among them—wrongly assumed that dreaming occurred only in the instant before awakening. Now it is certainly true that dreaming can occur just before awakening. And we have already noted that

dreaming can be so unpleasantly exciting as to provoke awakening, leading to another erroneous assumption: that all dreams are unpleasantly exciting, i.e. all dreams are characterized by negative emotions such as anger, anxiety, or fear.

Another erroneous theory was that dreaming arose in response to external sensory stimuli that were strong enough to activate the brain, but not strong enough to produce arousal. Again it is true that train whistles, indigestion, and spouses coming home late can influence dream content. But they often don't, and dreaming doesn't depend on such stimuli even when they do gain entry to the sleeping brain.

It turns out that most dreaming occurs under the calm cover of sleep and is the result of a built-in mechanism of brain activation that operates in all of us every night of our lives. It is the goal of this chapter to explain how the brain activation of sleep was discovered and how it gradually initiated the paradigm shift, or change in pattern, from dream content to dream form that has been the subject of my first two chapters. Before beginning our story, it is important to appreciate that, just as it took a full half-century (1900–53) to recognize the reality of brain activation in sleep, it has taken another half-century (1953–2001) for us to come to terms with this discovery. And there are still many diehards who refuse to relinquish the hopeless fantasy of the total power of interpretation offered by dream content analysis.

Why did it take so long to discover brain activation in sleep?

We are inclined to assume that it is the slow progress of technological development that impeded scientific advances in studying

dreaming. But this is a face-saving sop for those who were so conceptually blinded that they could not imagine the simple experiments that could have led to the brain activation conclusion. As Michel Jouvet shows in his novel *Château du Rêve*, most of our vaunted twentieth-century discoveries about sleep could have been made earlier by the most useful scientific instrument of all: direct observation. The direct observability of sleep is especially easy to achieve in our infants and children, the very individuals who most dramatically reveal the brain activation of rapid eye movement (REM) in their behaviour.

And it almost happened, although never quite. Instead of simply observing sleepers—and seeing with one's own eyes the periodic occurrence of small facial and eye movements, as well as muffled cries, penile erection, flaccid muscle tone, depressed spinal reflexes, and a host of other autonomic or self-regulating measures (take respiratory rate for a simple example)—those few scientists who were interested enough to perform anything faintly resembling a sleep or dream experiment interfered with the sleep of the participants in their studies. It was the induction of dreaming that these scholars, most of whom were French, were interested in. Could they induce a participant to dream of a certain odour by opening a perfume bottle under his or her nose? The answer was yes, as they found out, but it was very, very difficult. And, meanwhile, they missed the chance to observe natural sleep.

We must admit that staying up all night observing other people sleeping is not everyone's idea of fun. It requires unusual motivation and a modicum of self-discipline, even if one is tempted by the prospect of discovery. If Freud had only imagined that dream behaviour could be observed—he was certainly motivated enough to do it—he would quickly have realized that

all he needed to do to be a sharp observer was to sleep in the daytime. His phobic concern about suggestion could have been further quieted by the premium placed upon doing nothing but watching.

But, in reality, it's even easier than that. For anyone to observe REM sleep behaviour directly, it can be done with bed partners, especially in the wee hours of the morning, most conveniently on vacation, in the summer time when the hillock of the cornea can be seen in the early dawn light to glide to and fro under the closed—or perhaps half-open—eyelids. The eyelids themselves dance and twitch sporadically and, when they do, one has only to give a light tap on the shoulder and ask what is going on in the mind. Informed consent is as admirable in these informal conditions as it is in university sleep labs, but don't let that stop you.

If you don't have a willing bed partner, you can observe your big sister's baby or anyone's pet cat or dog, and have the same thrill of discovery. Of course you can't expect an answer if you ask *them* if they are dreaming. But you can answer that question for yourself now that you know that the REMs that give brain-activated sleep its most popular name are a direct readout of the internal activation. Not that dreaming occurs exclusively in REM sleep. It doesn't. REM sleep just happens to provide the most ideal condition for its occurrence.

In Chapter 4, we take up the question about the dreaming brain that, so far, only our animal collaborators can answer; in Chapter 5, we consider the implication for the development of the abundant, florid REM sleep of all mammalian newborns. My point here is simple and descriptive. The first step of any natural history endeavour is to observe (quietly and carefully) and to record one's observations (thoroughly and systematically). It is

as embarrassing as it is instructive that this was never done by anyone aspiring to either sleep or dream science before 1930. How many other breakthrough discoveries now elude us because we are conceptually boxed in by gratuitous assumptions that there is nothing to observe and/or that we can obviate direct observation via intuition or speculation?

The electroencephalogram and the sleep lab

Neurophysiologists were every bit as slow as psychologists to move dream science forwards. They knew about reflexes but they didn't know about spontaneous activation. Instead they assumed that the brain was as dependent on stimulation for all of its activated states as was the mind in sleep.

Two of the greatest minds in the history of science studied reflexes and believed that mental activity was stimulus-dependent. The Nobel Laureate Charles Sherrington argued, forcefully, that the reflex was the functional unit of the brain. He never really listened to his imaginative student, Thomas Graham Brown, who tried to convince Sherrington that it was the spontaneous activity of paired 'half-centres' that set the stage for reflex responsiveness. The basic difference between Sherrington's reflex and Graham Brown's half-centre concept is that the reflex brain was completely dependent upon external stimuli, unlike the half-centre brain which was capable of spontaneous activity. Sherrington made the mistake of assuming from his own conscious experience that his brain simply turned off when he went to sleep.

Ivan Pavlov, justifiably famous for showing that reflexes can be conditioned, shared Sherrington's assumption that the mind was blank in sleep (wrong!) because the brain was inactive

(wrong again!) and unstimulated (wrong once again!). As we see in Chapter 4, it was not until well after the discovery of REM sleep that the activation of the nerve elements known as neurons (neuronal activation) was shown to be continuous in sleep. This means that our brains never turn off completely, and hence they are always capable of *some* level of mental activity, even if waking and dream consciousness both depend on a robust level of brain activation.

Electrophysiology began to correct the picture in 1928 when the German psychiatrist Adolf Berger succeeded in recording brain waves from the surface of his patients' heads using an amplification and recording device that came to be known as the electroencephalograph (or EEG). The EEG revolutionized sleep and dream science as much as it altered clinical neurology because it provided an objective tool for assessing dynamic brain activity in normal individuals as well as in patients with epilepsy. Figure 2 illustrates an EEG, together with other variables used in modern sleep science. Against great scepticism that his so-called 'brain waves' were artefacts of movement or muscle activity, Berger won the day when he showed that the EEG underwent distinctive changes in sleep. To cut a long story short, behavioural sleep was invariably associated with a tendency for the brain waves to slow (in frequency) and to increase (in amplitude). This change marks the onset of what we now call slow wave or non-REM (NREM) sleep.

It wasn't long before the EEG was used to study sleep in the forerunners of today's sleep labs. The capacity to record physiological variables has grown so dramatically in the twentieth century that we tend to forget how simple the early devices were, and how startling the discoveries made with them. Today's 'polygraphs' are all direct descendants of Berger's baby, a

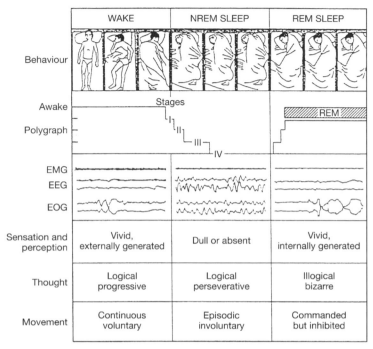

Figure 2 Behavioural states in humans. States of waking, NREM sleep, and REM sleep have behavioural, polygraphic, and psychological manifestations. The sequence of these stages is represented in the polygraph channel. Sample tracings of three variables used to distinguish state are also shown: electromyogram (EMG), which is highest in waking, intermediate in NREM sleep, and lowest in REM sleep; the electroencephalogram (EEG) and electro-oculogram (EOG), which are both activated in waking and REM sleep and inactivated in NREM sleep. Each sample is approximately 20 seconds.

glorified voltmeter that can raise the power of electrical signals three orders of magnitude from the microvolt (thousandth of a volt) range on the surface of the body to the volt range of the recorders. Variations on the theme of EEG are its better-known

predecessors, the electrocardiogram (ECG), which measures the heart's activity, and its two offspring, the electro-oculogram (EOG), which measures eye movement, and the electromyogram (EMG), which measures muscle tone.

How was brain activation in sleep discovered?

It was the combination of EEG and EOG that enabled Eugene Aserinsky and Nathaniel Kleitman to make their 1953 discovery of brain activation in sleep. They called the brain activation phase of sleep REM (for rapid eye movements) because of the association of the activation of the eye movements (oculomotor activation) with activation of the brain. They asserted that dreaming might be another associated event. It was the EMG (together with the EEG and EOG) that allowed Michel Jouvet and François Michel to show that muscle tone supporting posture—and hence postural movement—was actively abolished in REM sleep.

Before 1953, it was recognized that sleep was not uniform/intractable, any more than it was inert. In other words, electrical patterns of brain-wave activity changed continuously, denoting both global and local flows of brain activation. It was assumed, erroneously, that only the intense brain activation of REM was capable of sustaining dreaming. As the REM periods occurred periodically at 90 minute intervals and occupied 1.5 to 2 hours per night, this seemed like more than enough time to accommodate dreaming. It is certainly many times more than the instant before awakening.

It turns out, however, that dreaming can also occur at sleep onset (no surprise because the EEG is still relatively activated)

Do we dream in black and white or in colour?

Modern lab evidence suggests strongly that we dream in colour. To what, then, do we attribute the common misperception that dreaming occurs in black and white? The answer is very clear—it is the poor memory. Recall of dreaming is a function not only of brain activation in sleep but also of awakening conditions, which determine whether dreams will be recalled at all, whether they will be recalled clearly, and whether they will be recalled at length. In all clear, lengthy reports we see colour descriptors in abundance. We dream in colour. In our thousands of lab dream reports, there is not a single instance of a well-recalled dream being in black and white, as would be expected if this were indeed normally the case.

and in other phases of so-called NREM sleep, especially late night stage II sleep when the brain is almost as active as in REM sleep, often called stage I. That leaves stages III and IV, which occur early in the night and are considerably less likely to be associated with dreaming.

The point of this introduction to sleep lab science is to show that, although technology was not really necessary to describe dreaming scientifically or to describe sleep behaviourally (because both could have been done via careful direct observation), it was indispensable in showing that brain activity is continuous—and continuously variable—in sleep.

Who discovered REM and the EEG sleep cycle?

Eugene Aserinsky was interested in studying attention in children, so sleep was a nuisance to him because, no matter how hard he tried to keep them alert, sleep invariably took over the minds of his young participants. As many teachers of the young have seen, Aserinsky noticed that when his participants' attention flagged their eyes tended to close. He therefore decided to put electrodes near the childrens' eyes in order to record their eye movements while they were awake, and this helped. Aserinsky was, however, astonished to discover that, when his young participants finally succumbed to sleep, their eyes darted back and forth and up and down behind their closed lids. He had inadvertently discovered REM sleep—and the first participant was his seven-year-old son Armand. Aserinsky was a persistent scientist but he was also just plain lucky. Why? Because REM occurs at sleep onset *only* in children!

As Louis Pasteur opined, 'In the field of observation chance favours the prepared mind'. When Aserinsky reported his observations to Kleitman, his mentor recognized their significance for a science of dreaming. By extending this observation on the eyes into sleep, and by recording the EEG and the heart and respiratory rates in adults, Aserinsky and Kleitman were able to observe the regular ebb and flow of activation affecting the brain, the eyes, the heart, and even breathing throughout sleep. When this activation was maximal—with a wake-like EEG, clusters of REMs, rapid heart action, and fast, shallow breathing—awakenings yielded long, complex dream reports, similar to the one below.

11/7/1981 Country House in Winter, Dream no. 19

We are at a country house in winter, like the farm in East Burke but different. K.D.K. is there and we are skiing. I am looking, with a sexual motive, for A.T. whom I have not seen for at least 20 years and whom I never loved. She may be upstairs in this home, which may or may not be

> mine. The second floor is reached by climbing a twisted wooden shaft
> with inadequate branch-like steps. It is a struggle. When I pull myself
> up—noting that the heating is on and therefore that the house must be
> inhabited—I find myself in the arms of a sleeping J.C.
>
> J.C. suddenly wakes up—with a look of not-surprising terror on
> his face—and tries to orient himself. I see and feel his murderous, self-
> protective fear as he struggles to decide if I am I, and if I am real. This all
> happens in an intense instant, summarizing all of the emotional com-
> plexity of our relationship. I try to reassure him saying, 'J.C., it's me, I
> love you.' And. . . .

Dreams with frankly sexual themes such as this one are relatively rare in sleep lab settings, where being the content is more likely to reflect concern about sleeping while being observed and being subjected to awakening. (In fact, this dream occurred when I was on a trip to China and sleeping in a hotel in Guangzhou, of which there is not the faintest record in my dream.) The dream is, however, typical of those reported after awakenings from REM sleep, whether in the sleep lab using the Aserinsky–Kleitman theory, at home using our portable Night-cap monitoring system, or in hotels in Guangzhou, China.

11/7/1981 Country House in Winter, Dream no. 20

> I am again climbing toward an ambiguous bedroom. This time the thread
> of the spiral ascent is to the left upward. There are two routes: one is safe,
> but long, through grass at the base of a rock butte; I take the other, more
> vertical and direct ascent on the edge of the rocks. I am glad that I was
> forewarned (by C.?) that the rock was rotten because I quickly adapt
> to the succession of slides of large slabs of the cliff side. Each time I take a
> step, some of the granite falls away. These huge chunks of rock make not a
> sound as they fall, out of view, to my left. Finally, with relief, I am at the
> summit, which is a grill-like threshold on to which I level myself with two

hands. I thank my benefactress—hostess (C.?) for having prepared me
to cope with this hazardous ascent.

The universal characteristics that this REM sleep dream evinces are intense frequent hallucinations (called hallucinosis in psychology)—in this case the climbing movements are all perilously gripping—and a complete lack of self-reflective awareness. The setting is typically indefinite: it is my house but not really; the characters are vaguely defined—in this case particularly C.; emotions such as fear and elation are strong.

It is as if my brain were activated in a particular, selective way to form hallucinations and emotions that are sensorimotor (coordinating perception and action) in character, causing these elements to be combined in a completely novel but personally meaningful way. This is the 'synthesis' part of the dream process that Robert McCarley and I wanted to identify in our 1977 activation–synthesis thesis. In Chapter 5, we learn more about

evidence for this hypothesis, which can come through the application of imaging techniques to sleep and dream science.

During the early days of the sleep lab era (about 1953–75), the goal was to establish correlations between details of the dream plot, as described by participants, and details of physiology, as described by the EEG or polygraph. I call this the strong one-to-one isomorphic hypothesis, which attempts to link mental activity to peripheral physiology in real time. The goal was not achieved. Thus, early claims that the eye movements of REM sleep could be predicted from the sequence of directional changes in the dreamer's hallucinated gaze could not be substantiated. Although dream content did occasionally reflect the sudden increases and decreases of respiratory efforts, as would be expected in turning, talking, or painting, more often it did not.

In retrospect, the failure of this ambitious theory is not surprising: it never worked very well in waking either. It perpetuates the notion of the philosopher and psychologist William James, who held that emotion was the perception of peripheral physiology (e.g. anxiety occurs when I sense my rapid heart rate). This idea was discredited and eclipsed by Walter Cannon and Philip Bard's centralist theory of emotion, which says that the feelings that we have are a function of selective activation of that part of the margin of the brain known as the limbic brain (see Figure 11); they may then be associated with a wide variety of peripheral physiological changes.

An even more serious disconnection between dream psychology and brain physiology was threatened. When first David Foulkes, and later many other psychologists, reported that dreaming *could* be associated with almost any EEG stage of sleep, they reached the unlikely conclusion that the mental activity of dreams had nothing to do with sleep neurophysiology. Believe it

or not, this mind–brain dissociation hypothesis is still passionately defended. Needless to say, most of those who held these views were the disappointed champions of strong content analysis; some were even die-hard Freudians, and none was a practitioner of physiological sleep science.

Among the many compelling reasons to reject the assertion of brain–mind dissociation is the still overwhelming evidence that REM sleep is the most favourable base for fully realized and sustained dreaming; that NREM sleep is at best only half as favourable; that sleep onset is even less so; and that while awake, dreaming is essentially impossible. At this stage of our scientific knowledge all we can say is that dreaming is increasingly probable if the several brain conditions of REM sleep are present. The psychological counterpart of this correlation is given by the formal analysis and not content analysis of dreams. In dream reports we therefore seek to measure the degree to which they are hallucinatory (not what is seen) or thoughtful (not what is thought).

What is the biology of sleep and dream science?

Meanwhile, even as the dream debate grew fractious and became sterile, the sleep lab was unearthing a treasure trove of physiological findings of great interest to dream science, as well as to behavioural biology generally. The Aserinsky–Kleitman discovery was made in 1953, the same year that Watson and Crick published their epochal double-helix model for DNA. There are two important implications of this coincidence. One is that biology came of molecular age at the same moment that dream

science came of physiological age. In the subsequent half-century, biology has changed beyond recognition—in fact, it is now in danger of becoming nothing but the molecular biology of the gene.

Sleep and dream science, meanwhile, has only begun to approach molecular biology in terms of either conceptual ideas or methodology. This is both because the descriptive task of sleep and dream science was so enormous and because the concepts that were drawn into the field, especially from psychology, were not equal to the scientific opportunities presented. Not everyone, even today, wants to make mental activity physical. Too many cultural and private belief systems are threatened by the idea that consciousness in dreaming, as in waking, is a brain function. The immortality of the soul is a prime example. If the brain dies, doesn't the mind die with it?

One idea that the biological revolution in dream science forces us to take seriously is that, although it constitutes an undeniably interesting and informative state of altered consciousness, dreaming has no particular function in and of itself. As conscious experience, dreaming is nothing but our occasional awareness of brain activation in sleep. In this view, it is the brain activation underlying REM sleep itself that performs the vaunted functions of dreaming: establishing psychic equilibrium, integrating recent and past learning, casting our inventory of personal information in emotionally salient (or relevant) terms. All of these important functions can and certainly must be performed whether or not we are aware of them. If they depended on our conscious awareness of dreaming, we would be in big trouble—especially those who have no dream recall whatsoever.

The burden of proof now falls clearly, and heavily, on those who maintain that an awareness of dream content actually helps

us. For example, I am enlightened by finding through recall of Dream no. 19 that my psychosexual conflicts with a former friend and his wife are still alive in my mind. But, even if my interpretation of this dream is correct, how does it help me to know this fact? By making me aware that yes, after all, there is an unconscious, or that yes, after all, sexuality *is* polymorphous and ambiguous—that despite superficial appearances to the contrary, all is not entirely kosher in Hobson's unconscious mind.

Such sophistication might endear me to my psychoanalytic brethren, leading to a wider acceptance of my ideas, increased book royalties, and even referral of patients. Thus, my physical survival as well as my intellectual procreation could be enhanced. But it seems far more likely that I would do as well, or better, if I never had my spiral staircase dream or, rather, never recalled and therefore never interpreted it—the 'dream work', if any, is done unbeknownst to me, by REM sleep and its friends in my unconscious brain.

This is just the kind of 'reductionism' that psychologist opponents of physiologically based dream theory fear. Foulkes has argued passionately against what he perceives to be 'physiology's effort to take the problem of dreaming off of psychology's hands'. To some extent he is correct. If the main formal features of dreaming can be shown to be physiologically determined, then content analysis does not have to account for them. Instead of lamenting this situation, however, dream psychology could do well to breathe a heavy sigh of relief at seeing this onerous burden lifted. Freud himself was pushed to the psychoanalytic wall in trying to explain dream hallucinosis as a psychological defence. His effort to explain poor dream memory in terms of active repression (rather than simple amnesia) was equally forced. Worst of all, his effort to account for dream

emotion in terms of either wish fulfilment or disguise fell flat on its face because so many dreams contain unpleasant negative affect and because so many are undisguised.

Reductionism was Freud's strong suit. He tried to explain, as all would-be scientists do, the greatest number of variables in terms of the fewest assumptions. In hitting upon his wish fulfilment–disguise censorship model he was reductionist in the extreme. *Every* steeple is a phallus. *Every* dimple is a vagina. The problem is that Freud's reductionism was wrong, and it was wrong, in large part, because he did not observe behaviour, measure neurological function, or collect dreams systematically using the mind-set and tools of natural science.

Now, we have the facts of human sleep physiology. Now, we know—beyond the shadow of a doubt—that our consciousness in waking, sleeping, or dreaming is a brain function. It is high time to move on and to create the great, bold, and neurobiologically based theory to which Freud himself aspired. Reductionism cannot explain away phenomena. Dreaming will always be vivid, bizarre, emotional, unreasonable, and hard to remember. But how (the question of mechanism) and why (the question of function) may be explored scientifically using physiological tools. As content analytical dream theory reveals, it is the danger of circularity that has given subjectivity a bad name. Now we have a brave new world of scientific dream theory in which circularity can be transcended and dreaming can still be enjoyed, discussed, and interpreted.

In this chapter, we take seriously the idea that it is REM sleep that constitutes the ideal physiological conditions for dreaming, and attempt to use the data collected in cellular and molecular level studies of sleep in animals to answer the how and why questions of dreaming in greater detail.

4

Cells and molecules of the dreaming brain

By 1890, the scientific world was aware that the brain consisted of billions of individual cells called neurons (100 billion at the last count). In the first half of the twentieth century, while sleep and dream science were being prepared at the more global level of the electroencephalograph (EEG), neurobiologists were learning more about neurons than had even been imagined in anyone's speculative philosophy—and that anyone includes Sigmund Freud, Charles Sherrington, and Ivan Pavlov.

Among other things, by 1950 it had become clear that, as each neuron was bounded by a semipermeable membrane, it had the capacity to concentrate an electrical charge across that membrane by actively pumping ions such as sodium, potassium, and chloride in and out of the cells. This membrane potential, as it was called, could be raised (inhibition) or lowered (excitation) as a result of the influence of chemical molecules secreted by neighbouring neurons, which delivered their influences via

specialized junctions called synapses. The chemicals secreted from nerve endings were called neurotransmitters because they permitted cell-to-cell signalling in the brain.

When a neuron was sufficiently excited, its membrane potential could suddenly reverse its sign and the resultant differential in voltage, or action potential, could spread from the cell body over the entire surface of the neuron, including its endings, which were thereby induced to secrete their own brand of chemical neurotransmitter. The neurotransmitters that are directly responsible for neuronal excitability include glutamate (excitatory) and gamma-aminobutyric acid or GABA (inhibitory).

Most of the very successful work in cellular neurobiology was conducted under the protective umbrella of Sherrington's reflex doctrine, which provided sufficient information to help work out how neuronal circuits were organized. The reflex circuit model could explain the following: the spinal reflexes involved in posture and movement; the encoding of stimuli in sequences of action potentials in neurons, which could lead to sensation; and even the coordination of the sensory and motor systems needed to account for movement (motor) behaviour.

The reflex doctrine could not, however, help the pioneer sleep and dream scientists very much, because no link could be established between the activity of circuits of neurons (neuronal circuits) and the EEG. It had long been assumed that the EEG was the register of voltage changes in the brain (i.e. cerebral action potentials), although this could not explain the patterns of the EEG seen in sleep (e.g. spindles and slow waves), unless neuronal activity was continuous, i.e. spontaneous, as well as reflexive. Consequently, work at the cellular and EEG levels proceeded along entirely separate but parallel tracks, similar to those that Descartes thought God had used to set mind and body

the consolidation and advancement of procedural learning. As procedural learning is the acquired ability to do things when consciousness may not be involved, the subjective experience of dreams could never suggest even this high-level functional principle. And how could we know, from our dreaming, that our capacity to regulate our own temperature was being assured by REM sleep?

Using the techniques of electrical stimulation and surgical alterations of the brain that led to Moruzzi and Magoun's concept of activation of a reticular system in the brain, the French neurophysiologist Michel Jouvet, working in Lyons from the mid-1950s onward, established once and for all that brain activation did occur and that it occurred spontaneously in sleep. He also proved that REM sleep was organized by the brain stem, including this reticular formation. By discovering the active suppression of muscle tone that invariably accompanies REM sleep, Jouvet also helped us understand how the brain could be turned on without producing waking behaviour. As the motor system was actively blocked at the level of the spinal cord, real movement was impossible even if the upper brain elaborated and commanded the rich behaviours that we perceive in our dream scenarios.

12/3/1980 Parachute, Dream no. 29

> *A group of parachutists descends from behind forward—the sky is blue, the chutes white—suddenly and unexpectedly, one chutist passes the others rapidly—it is now clear that this is a contest—and the new man, from Navy, will win easily. But is his chute open? Yes. To guide his descent he climbs the cords—like a fetus shimmying up his own umbilical connection!*

Do animals dream?

All mammals have the same kind of brain activation during sleep as humans. Whether or not they dream is another question, which can be answered only by posing another one: Do animals have consciousness? The answer to that question has been hotly debated. Many scientists today feel that animals probably *do* have a limited form of consciousness, quite different from ours in that it lacks language and the capacity for propositional or symbolic thought.

Animals certainly can't report dreams even if they do have them. But which pet owner would doubt that his or her favourite animal friend has perception, memory, and emotion? These are three of the key aspects of consciousness, and they could be experienced whether or not an animal had verbal language as we do. When the animal's brain is activated during sleep, why not assume that the animal has some sort of perceptual, emotional, and memory experience?

In terms of the important scientific use to which we could put animal sleep in the study of human dreaming, it makes little difference what the answer to the question about animal dreams might be. All we need know, in order to learn from our animal colleagues, is that they have the same kind of brain activation in their sleep as we do. We then go on to make the fairly safe assumption that animals have the same mechanisms of brain activation in sleep as we do.

How does the study of REM sleep in cats help?

In 1957, William Dement, a co-worker of Aserinsky and Kleitman, vigorously investigated the REM sleep–dream connection in humans, and discovered that cats also had periods of brain activation and REM in their sleep. This provided the experimental model necessary for investigation of the cellular and molecular basis of brain activation in sleep, and the chance to integrate phenomena at the level of cells and molecules with the EEG and the distinctive forms of mental activity in human sleep. We didn't need to know whether cats dreamed to make this integration. All we had to do was assume that the REM sleep of cats was engineered in the same way as REM sleep in humans.

The hypothesis of REM sleep correspondence across species was greatly strengthened by the subsequent finding that all but the most primitive mammals had periodic brain activation during sleep. If they had eyes, they also had REMs in their activated sleep phases. Besides shoring up the homology hypothesis, this surprising fact suggested that REM was biologically important to all mammalian life, whatever its relationship to human dreaming. Conversely, it suggested that the correlation of REM and dreaming was a very limiting way of thinking about the functional significance of brain activation in sleep.

As it turned out, both of these new ways of looking at sleep were useful and important. For example, it has become clear that REM sleep subserves body temperature regulation (thermoregulation), perhaps the most basic of all mammalian housekeeping functions. Many experiments indicate that REM also facilitates

in perfect but independent motion. Cartesian duality dies slowly; it is still alive and well in most of us because we cannot yet see how a physical object, the brain, can have subjective experience. This is the so-called 'hard problem' of philosophy.

The basis of brain activation

Just before the middle of the last century, two classic sensori-motor physiologists, Giuseppe Moruzzi and Horace Magoun, working at Northwestern Medical School in Chicago, discovered that the experimental stimulation of the brain stem of cats could cause a shift in the EEG pattern from that of sleep to that of waking. In other words, they established an experimental basis for brain activation in sleep. Their results, published in 1949, antedated the discovery of rapid eye movement (REM) sleep by four years, but set the stage for investigating brain activation in sleep by challenging the deeply entrenched concept that all brain activation had to come from the outside world via sensory stimulation.

Indeed, Moruzzi and Magoun's hypothesis of a non-specific system that was activated by a reticular (net-like) component of the brain and that could operate independently of sensory input encountered stiff resistance. This resistance was only gradually overcome by their subsequent studies demonstrating independence of the activation from the sensory pathways. Prolonged sleep-like unresponsiveness occurred when this reticular system was damaged leaving the sensory pathways intact. These follow-up studies were being conducted just as the discovery of REM sleep was being made (again in Chicago).

In this dream, I myself am not moving as I was in earlier examples, but the perceived movement of three parachutists is nevertheless dynamic and emotionally gripping. The impending doom of such dream movement is typical and suggests not only the co-activation of anxiety in the limbic brain, but also the generation of unfamiliar or intrinsically impossible movement patterns at the level of the brain stem itself, where the neurons controlling body position in space are located.

Jouvet's most radical and definitive experiments supported this idea. When he isolated the brain stem below the level of the junction of the two areas of the brain known as the pons and the midbrain and, even when he removed all of the brain above this level, he could still observe the periodic suppression of muscle tone, and occasional eye and body movements, including the rhythmic stepping that would be used in real locomotion by a

normal cat during waking. In other words, one of the key formal features of human dreaming, the sense of continuous motion, may arise at the very low level of parts of the brain stem that generate motor patterns. In any case, such generators *are* present in the brain stem and *are* activated in REM.

Like Aserinsky and Kleitman, Michel Jouvet knew how to exploit the chance discoveries very well. He was trying to study something else (Pavlovian conditioning) when his cats, like Aserinsky's children, fell asleep. As he was also trying to monitor the cat's attention in waking, his neck muscle electrodes picked up the atonia (lack of tone) of REM sleep. In science, as elsewhere in life, it is an ill wind that blows no one some good! And later, luck found Jouvet ready again. As he was a neurosurgeon, studied cats, and wanted to integrate the EEG of structures such as the brain stem and the thalamus located under the cortex (subcortical structures), Jouvet was able to observe the paroxysmal (PGO) waves that arise in different areas of the brain—the pons of the brain stem reticular formation (P), the geniculate body of

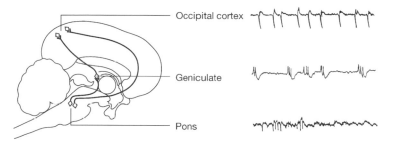

Figure 3 The visual brain stimulates itself in REM sleep via a mechanism reflected in EEG recordings as PGO waves. Originating in the pons (P) from the neurons that move the eyes, these signals are conducted both to the lateral geniculate (G) body in the thalamus and to the occipital cortex (O).

the thalamus (G), and the occipital cortex (O)—during REM sleep. These waves, which were markedly reduced in waking, indicated that the brain activation of REM sleep was physiologically as well as psychologically distinctive. Figure 3 shows recordings of PGO waves from the cortex, thalamus, and brain stem.

What chemical control is there of the brain–mind states?

Although counterintuitive, the discovery of brain activation in sleep was rapidly accepted by those dream scientists who had sudden and transformative ah-ha experiences when they read about it. In the ensuing excitement about the similarities between waking and dreaming consciousness, few stopped to wonder what bit of this sleep-dependent brain activation could account for the *difference*, which, after all, is every bit as important as the similarities:

- Why is dreaming so strongly sensorimotor, a feature unmatched in even the most vivid waking fantasies?
- Why is dreaming so rarely self-reflective, when waking consciousness is so often dominated by internal thought?
- Why is dreaming so limited by improvement in recall? In particular, why do we lose the capacity to recount actively declarative memories (memories that are learned quickly and consciously) and gain the capacity to activate remote ones?
- Why is almost all dreaming forgotten?
- Why are dreams so bizarre?

Could physiology help us answer these questions as well? Certainly not if all we paid attention to was brain activation and the common aspects of its occurrence in waking and sleep.

To answer all these questions about the distinctive features of dream consciousness, it was necessary to know not only that the brain was switched back on in sleep, but also that this switch process was effected by quite different mechanisms from those of waking. After all, we usually don't wake up during REM and we already knew, from Jouvet's early work, part of the reason why we don't move: our muscles are actively inhibited. This guarantees the continuation of immobility and it helps us understand why we often awaken feeling paralysed in our dreams.

Moreover, we knew from the PGO wave discovery that REM sleep activation had distinct pulses. Each PGO wave, and there are something like 14,000 PGO waves per day in the cat, delivered a pulse of activation to the brain, similar to what would happen if we were startled by an unexpected stimulus during waking. This fact meant that dreaming was a mental state made up of both sustained electrical brain activation and very strong, very discrete arousal stimuli. The PGO waves could thus mediate distinctive aspects of dream mental activity such as the intense absorption (the dominance of percepts over thoughts) the bizarreness (based on discontinuity and incongruity of times, places, and people), and the constant sensorimotor content (as if the brain were compelled by the self-activation process to elaborate one movement scenario after another).

Neuromodulation and the brain state

None of this explains why memory is pre-empted. Nor does it explain how PGO waves arise in REM sleep. To unlock those puzzles, we needed the key provided by the discovery of control by neurons, i.e. neuromodulation, a special kind of chemical neurotransmission by which the brain is able to change its state

globally. Brain state is set by the mode of information processing: when the brain switches mode from external to internal information sources; when it switches from a store-and-remember to a don't-store-and-forget mode; and when it switches from linear–logical to a parallel associative mode. All of these mode switches can go on in small but significant ways in waking, but they become obligatory, pronounced, and fixed when the brain enters REM sleep.

We now suppose that the reason for the change in brain state is the dramatic change in neuromodulation that distinguishes REM sleep from waking. In 1960, the presence of brain stem cells containing the neuromodulators noradrenaline (norepinephrine) and serotonin were reported by the Swedish neuroanatomist Kjell Fuxe. It has since become clear that these cells change their output when animals go to sleep and most dramatically when they enter REM sleep. To cut a long story short, the serotonin and noradrenaline cells that modulate the brain during waking reduce their output by half during non-REM sleep but are *shut off* completely during REM sleep. This means that the electrically reactivated brain is working without the participation of two of its chemical systems that mediate the awake state. These very systems have been strongly implicated in precisely those awake state functions (such as attention, memory, and reflective thought) that are lost in dreaming.

To understand this almost alarmingly simple hypothesis, it is important to recognize what is so special about these neuromodulatory neurons and their chemical messengers:

1. They are relatively few and relatively small.
2. They are highly localized to a few brain stem nuclei.
3. They are pacemaker cells in that they are rhythmical and spontaneous unless they are inhibited.

4. They fire at relatively low rates, in metronome-like fashion.
5. They project their fine, multiply branching processes all over the brain and spinal cord.

Vernon Mountcastle has called this unique collection of cells a 'brain-within-the-brain'. By this, he means that they constitute a mode-switching mechanism that can automatically and forcibly change the microclimate of the rest of the brain. An analogy to the temperature and climate control system situated in the cellar of a modern home, but influencing all its rooms, comes to mind.

Figure 4 shows how the neuromodulatory cells of the brain stem (area called the pons) project up to the thalamus and cortex and down to the spinal cord to mediate the EEG changes of REM sleep.

Now the emphasis on the power of the formal approach to the study of dreaming should become clear even to those who still long for the mystique of fortune-cookie dream interpretation. We can see that, when the brain self-activates in sleep, it changes its chemical self-instructions. The mind has no choice but to go along with the programme. It sees, it moves, and it feels things intensely but it does not think, remember, or focus attention very well. This, in turn, shows clearly that our so-called minds are functional states of our brains. The mind is not something else—it is not a spirit, it is not an independent entity. It *is* the self-activated brain whose capacity for subjectivity remains to be explained but whose form of subjectivity can now be understood.

This is the most radical assertion of modern dream science. Waking and dreaming are two states of consciousness, with differences that depend on chemistry. Can you digest the proposition? Or does it stick in your craw? Do you say, yes, but . . .

Figure 4 Schematic representation of the REM sleep generation process. A distributed network involves cells at many brain levels (left). The network is represented as comprising three neuronal systems (centre) that mediate REM sleep electrographic phenomena (right).

and fill in the dots with a host of questions that are designed to express your curiosity about as-yet unexplained details, and defend yourself against the humiliation of having your dreaming reduced to a brain state? You know that *you* are more than a brain state, don't you? But how do you know that? By your

subjectivity, you reply (which I haven't yet explained, have I?). So you still have a loophole, but please admit that the net is closing. And, please, bear with me as I attempt to show you how lucky you are to be such a fabulous, automatic, and reliable set of brain mechanisms that you can dream, imagine, create, and feel in your sleep. In due course, I will also try to assure you that, as being a brain does entail a subjective aspect, you are the free agent you always supposed yourself to be. You don't have much free choice but the little you do have can go a long, long way.

The biochemistry and pharmacology of REM sleep

This is a good time to review the correlation of dreaming with sleep and to drive home my point that this correlation is continuous, partial, and statistical rather than discontinuous, complete, and categorical. As the state of the brain changes continuously, it only gradually changes it mode. It does not suddenly switch from one state to another. Furthermore, the continuous and gradual modulatory changes do not affect every single neuron of the brain identically or even simultaneously. These generalizations, which all flow from neurobiological work on the state control systems of the brain stem, have far-reaching implications for a general theory of mind as well as for a specific theory of dreaming.

Mental states, such as waking and dreaming, are as many splendoured in their details as are the waking and sleeping brain. For example, perceptions may arise internally as well as exter-nally during waking: fantasies of near hallucinatory intensity can intrude on waking and train whistles or telephone rings can

invade dream plots. In the spirit of statistics, however, the probabilities of these two phenomena are reversed in waking and dreaming, and these probabilities are set by the neuromodulatory systems, Mountcastle's brain within the brain. In waking, external stimuli are far more likely to be accurately perceived than in dreaming. In dreaming, internal stimuli are far more likely to give rise to hallucinatory imagery than in waking. We need to understand the mechanisms of this contrast much better because nothing less than our sanity is at stake. Later, when we examine the impact of the neuromodulation theory on mental illness, we will see that *all* the drugs that are now used to treat psychoses have a role to play on the neuromodulators. We also see that they do so in ways that are often consonant with the role of these chemicals in shifting the balance of the brain to be awake or dreaming.

Chemical microstimulation

Once the behaviour of the serotonin- and noradrenaline-containing neurons of the brain stem had been recorded with microelectrodes and charted across the sleep cycle, it was natural to wonder what would happen if we conducted more active experiments by intentionally interfering with their natural propensities. The experimental technique called chemical microstimulation was devised, and it proved to be highly successful in studying yet another neuromodulatory system of the brain stem, the cholinergic system, so named because its effects on target neurons are mediated by acetylcholine, a molecule long known to effect movement by changing the charge of (i.e. depolarizing) muscle fibres and causing them to contract and move our limbs.

As it turned out, acetylcholine was a prime mover not only

of muscles, but also of the central brain state. Acetylcholine-containing neurons fire in both waking and REM sleep, so they may help to mediate EEG activation in both states. Their excitability is apparently enhanced in REM sleep because of the decrease in inhibition from the serotonin-containing neurons, which you will remember are turned off in REM. In their variety and complexity, these neurophysiological details can become confusing. The main point to keep in mind is that in REM sleep the brain, although electrically as activated as in waking, is activated in a chemically very different way.

This conclusion was dramatically supported by chemical microstimulation experiments, which showed, unequivocally, that REM sleep could be induced by injecting very small amounts of a cholinergic drug into the area of the brain stem known as the pons. Moreover, the pattern and timing of the REM sleep-enhancing effect depended on what part of the pontine brain stem was chemically altered. If the drug was placed in a particular area of the brain (the reticular formation on either side of the midline), cats fell asleep faster, entered REM sleep sooner, and stayed in it longer than when inert chemicals were used. Much, much longer! Cats normally have spontaneous REM sleep periods that run from 4 to 10 minutes in length, and they might show 60- to 70-minute REMs when stimulated by a cholinergic. These chemically enhanced REM sleep periods were not only longer, but stronger, with more REMs when the drug was present.

Were we producing chemical dreams? This question is moot in cats, although even in humans, where similar effects are obtained, we would say only that we can enhance dreaming by enhancing REM sleep. As scientists, we think that all dreams are chemically mediated. So, yes, we are producing dreams chemically by helping the brain to do so.

These results have been widely replicated and accepted, which means that the brain side of dream science is now firmly established. Scientific acceptance of cholinergic REM enhancement came slowly. We had to show that a variety of cholinergic drugs could work, that they could all be blocked with anticholinergic (atropine) treatment, and that even drugs such as neostigmine, which work by blocking the normal enzymatic breakdown of acetylcholine, can enhance REMs. We can safely conclude that REM sleep dreaming is mediated by acetylcholine when noradrenaline and serotonin are at very low levels.

What all this means about the function of REMs is another question. What is the effect on learning and memory of making the brain so strongly cholinergic in REM sleep? Acetylcholine has long been implicated in learning and memory, so the REM story contributes in a significant way to an emerging picture that is consistent with our partial, statistical model of the brain as mind. Here is a sample hypothesis: we can trigger memory fragments with acetylcholine but cannot make new ones without noradrenaline and serotonin.

I said that it made a difference where the cholinergic drug was placed. When the microinjection is made in an area of the brain that is at the furthest edge of the pons (the far lateral pons), at points near to where the acetylcholine-containing neurons are found, the effects are quite different and informative; we see delayed rather than immediate REM enhancement. This is particularly surprising because the drug *does* immediately enhance PGO waves that we had previously thought might be the cause of REMs. Their dissociation in long-term enhancements of REMs proves, however, that they cannot be the cause. Besides, by temporarily uncoupling the PGO waves from REM, the delayed enhancement is prolonged, lasting 6–10 days instead of

4–6 hours after more medial injections into the reticular formation.

We ourselves are only slowly digesting these findings, which seem to point us in the direction of molecular biology rather than dream theory. This may indicate, as do other signs in the field, that the gap between REM sleep and DNA, both discovered half a century ago, may be closing. Our reasoning is as follows: the reticular site, where cholinergic stimulation produces immediate and short-lived REM enhancement, is a trigger zone; by contrast, the lateral pontine site mentioned earlier, where low immediate PGO waves and long-term REM enhancement are produced, is a control region. The difference between the two sites is that one—the control region—actually contains cholinergic neurons whereas the other, the trigger zone, does not.

Under normal circumstances, the timing and amount of REMs (and hence dreaming) are controlled by the excitability level of (among others) the cholinergic neurons. And that level is subject to a wide variety of genetic and experimental factors that contribute to long- and short-term differences in sleep, which are correlated with normal development, learning, and memory, and even mood and temperament. The brain–mind functions well if, and only if, the cholinergic system is operating within certain limits. These limits are set by biological and behavioural mechanisms that the chemical microstimulation theory of REM sleep can help us to understand.

5

Why dream? The functions of brain activation in sleep

We have already given our answer to the question of why we dream based on physiological mechanisms: because the brain self-activates in sleep. We have already hinted that dreaming itself may be an epiphenomenon of brain self-activation, so dreaming may occur for reasons that are quite different from those that we would infer from the psychological study of REM sleep dreaming.

In the last chapter we noticed, moreover, that rapid eye movement (REM) sleep always involves intense brain self-activation, occurs in all mammalian species, and is carefully controlled by a genetically regulated chemical system. This means that, without a doubt, REM sleep is important to mammalian biology. It is highly conserved across species, quantitatively regulated within species, and varies with the stages of brain development. In this chapter, we examine the last two points by considering the changes that occur during development, and the effects of upsetting the system by making REM sleep impossible or, at least, very difficult.

Do babies dream?

The human newborn baby offers one of the best opportunities to observe REM behaviour directly. This is not only because REM occurs at sleep onset (as Eugene Aserinsky noticed in the young participants in his studies), but also because the movements associated with the pulse-like aspects of brain activation are more intense and less completely inhibited than they are in adults. Consequently, not just humans, but newborns of all species show dramatic muscle twitches of the limbs and trunk, together with highly expressive contractions of the facial muscles: as if dream emotions were being read out directly. Babies show pleasure, fear, surprise, and disgust in the facial expressions of REM sleep. Do they feel these emotions? Are these emotions the building blocks of dreams? In short, do babies dream? Our scientific answer to these rhetorical questions must be 'We don't (and can't) know'. But our personal inclination might well be 'why not?'.

The human fetus begins to show highly organized and spontaneous movement very early in its uterine life. By 30 weeks of gestation, these movement patterns within the organism include the eyes (REMs), the face (early or primordial emotion?), and the limbs (primordial locomotion?). All of these findings have profound implications for our concept of the brain–mind and how it develops. Clearly, nature has provided its most elaborate creation — the human brain–mind — with its own means of self-activation. In his recent book, *I of the Vortex*, the neurophysiologist Rodolfo Llinas has suggested that endogenous motility contributes to the fundamental sense of agency that is the essence of self-hood!

So we sleep, perchance to dream. And we dream, perforce

When does dreaming start?

One of the most striking findings of modern sleep research is that the immature individual, whether a human baby, a kitten, or a puppy, has a lot more brain activation in sleep than it will when it grows up. What this means is that a brain substrate for dreaming is present at birth. Whether babies have dreams is moot, just as it is with animals. The baby is developing consciousness, and has primordial perception, emotion, and memory, but he or she does not yet have language. Propositional or symbolic thought depends on language. If babies do dream, their subjective experience cannot possibly be of the same quality as that of adults.

Psychologists who have studied the development of dreaming in children find that the accounts of dreaming that are similar to those of adults start to appear at about age three, when the infant is acquiring language and propositional thought. Children's dreams then become more and more complex and interesting up until about age seven, when most of the formal adult dream characteristics are reported. Taken together with animal evidence, this suggests that brain activation is not enough to produce dreaming. The upper brain circuits that support language and propositional thought must be functional in order for dreaming to occur. The fact that human and other mammalian newborns have so much more brain activation in sleep than adults, together with the fact that the dreaming of children is

relatively impoverished, also suggests that REM sleep is important for development in some ways that dreaming does not predict.

to reactivate the brain basis of self-hood that is embedded in our built-in capacity to generate movement. Put another way, our dreams—so constantly and elaborately animated—remind us that we were born with an already huge talent for movement and for the sensorimotor perceptions of movement that become the centre of our sense of self as agents. Speculating further, we might imagine that every night, after 90 minutes and for at least two hours, we are 'born again', where that phrase, borrowed from fundamentalist religion, has an entirely somatic (bodily) and secular meaning. If I do not yet make myself entirely clear, let me add that the formalist approach to dreaming reveals that fictitious movement—the sense of moving in dream space—is a powerful point in favour of Llinas' theory. Another point is that the only dimension of orientation that is secure in dreaming is the sense of self—I am always at the centre of the vortex that is my dream.

The following dream report is rich in bizarreness, but it also illustrates the insistent movement of the dreamer through dream space. Whether I am in the hotel, the temple, or on a Vermont hillside, I am always moving, looking, noticing, or talking.

18/6/1984 Quest, Dream no. 33

> *The overall theme was a quest—I was looking for something, or perhaps just a way (in both the geographical and strategic senses of the word).*
>
> *One scene was in a restaurant/hotel with the usual confusion of rooms, levels, and people. It seemed like a reunion in the dining room because there were some people from Harvard there though none was identified. My job was to find the back door so as to exit directly to the street and not backtrack to the lobby. I opened several doors only to find that they were in fact windows which had been closed, by carpentered*

panels, from the outside. I noticed that wooden wedges had been inserted between the window frames and the panels, an elaborate contrivance for which the function was not apparent. It seemed odd that the panels would be so spaced rather than fitting flush.

I gave up on the shortcut exit plan and started back to the lobby.

Then the scene shifted to a classical temple, Greek or Egyptian There was a narrow stair passing below a stone arch with a prominent keystone. I remarked how one of the pleasures of working at Harvard was exposure to beauty. This seemed to explain the strange scene shift adequately.

But, abruptly, I was walking on a Vermont hillside, covered with snow, looking for an old woman. The snow was slightly off-white making me wonder if there were fresh manure just under the surface. Despite the risk, I decided to eat some snow to quench my thirst. It was tasteless.

I was then talking with someone like Marshall Newland about the old woman whom I had not yet reached. He offered an aphorism that seemed, in typical Vermont fashion, to sum up the situation:

'I may be hard to find, but when you get there, you can count on my presence.'

This seemed to mean that reliability was the reward of persistence.

The 'I' of this dream is amazingly secure given the whirling inconstancies of place and action. This report also illustrates the strange impoverishment of thinking that typifies dreams that are as animated as this one. This suggests that it is sensorimotor action, not cognition, that is important to the developmental processes that we are discussing. In other words, my sense of

agency is first linked to movement; only later is it elaborated in thought.

Do fetuses dream?

In the womb (or uterus), at 30 weeks' gestation, the human fetus is spending almost 24 hours of each day in a brain-activated state that constitutes a first level of REM sleep. At birth, an unequivocal REM sleep state occupies at least half of not less than 16 hours of sleep each day. This guarantees at least eight hours of automatic, off-line brain activation each and every day. Ask yourself why? And let your answer run its full course: to develop the human brain. To make up the mind—in a word to become an increasingly effective mover and an increasingly distinctive self.

So, it probably doesn't really matter whether babies dream except in so far as subjectivity must develop part and parcel with movement competence, if the hypothesis of movement—agency–self is to have any credibility at all. By now, we can certainly reject as gratuitous any assumption that infantile dream content is meaningful or fulfils wishes in a psychoanalytic sense. Far from indicating psychological defensiveness, the early occurrence of motion and emotion in REM sleep argue for the opposite: a redundant, reliable, and remarkable offence designed to self-organize behaviour and tie it to subjectivity. Figure 5 illustrates the dramatic changes that occur in sleep and waking during the human life cycle.

Why do babies have so much REM sleep? What shuts the system down as development proceeds? These important questions have not yet been answered definitively because the study of sleep development is still (please pardon the expression) in

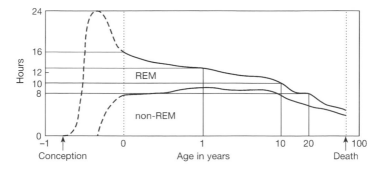

Figure 5 The relative proportions of each 24-hour day that are devoted to wake, REM sleep, and non-REM sleep change dramatically over our lifetime. Exactly how and when these states develop in early uterine existence is not known (dotted lines), but data from premature infants suggests that REM sleep is almost all of life at 26 weeks of gestation age. After 26 weeks, waking increases progressively and inexorably until death.

its infancy. But, it is very likely that the following biological facts hold true:

1. *The brain stem:* as the seat of the most primordial (first-line) regula tory systems (temperature, cardiovascular, and respiratory to name three), the brain stem must develop earlier than the upper brain, in particular earlier than the part of the brain housing the thalamus and cortex (thalamocortical brain) which will later support the emergence of consciousness.

2. *The cholinergic system* of the brain stem: as the mediator of internal bodily (endogenous) activation, this system must develop earlier than the serotoninergic and noradrenergic systems (i.e. systems involving the chemicals serotonin and noradrenaline), which will be needed as the individual shifts priority from sleeping to waking.

3. *Later development* of the other systems of chemicals known as amin- ergic systems (chemicals include histamine and dopamine) is what

shuts down infant sleep and especially REM sleep, reducing it by at least 400 per cent from infancy to early adult life.

How much sleep do we need?

What happens if we do not get the sleep we need and how much do we need it? You can answer these questions for yourself just as well as I can. But, before you try, you should realize two things: the first is that sleep has now been accorded the variability inherent in all biological phenomena, i.e. short sleepers (four to six hours a day) are no more 'abnormal' or unusual than longer sleepers (eight to ten hours a day). Even if most adults sleep six to eight hours, it doesn't mean that they always do so. Sleep, like body weight, fluctuates according to the complex interaction of internal set-points, social customs, climate, and personal experience. The second is that, even when we sleep very little, we are able to compensate extremely well, especially if the stakes are high. If we are motivated—either by reward or the need to avoid disaster—we can normally manage to squeeze a little more cognitive competence out of our weary brains.

Now give your answer. My answer is that I now need eight to ten hours (and still don't feel completely refreshed). When I was younger I survived on four to six hours. As a medical house officer and sleep researcher, I sometimes went for 36 consecutive hours without any sleep whatsoever. But, whatever my baseline, I have always noticed that sleep curtailment compromises my ability to be attentive and to organize my own mental activity efficiently and effectively. To read, to write, to listen, and to tell, I need a good night's sleep. And, recognizing that fact, I try my best to get it. When I was sleep deprived, and/or

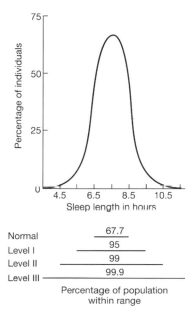

Figure 6 Like all biological functions, sleep length varies widely. If the number of people who sleep for various durations is plotted on a graph, the result is a bell-shaped curve. Estimations of the chance of falling within 1, 2, or 3 standard deviations from the mean are shown below. Only one in a thousand people falls outside these limits, but such short or long sleepers do exist.

stressed, I was far more likely to have intense, bizarre dreams such as the one I reported earlier in this chapter (Dream no. 33, page 75).

Why have lab studies of sleep deprivation had so much difficulty achieving consensus about the costs of sleep losses and the inferred benefits of sleep gains? To understand this issue, it is helpful to go back to the early days of the 1960s, when the discovery of REM sleep unleashed a storm of experimental enquiry.

The good news is that the storm was unleashed. The bad news is that the studies were often driven by the scientifically naïve and flawed ideas of psychoanalysis. The history of so-called 'dream deprivation' is a good case in point. As REM sleep was correlated with dreaming, it tended to be equated with it. Deprive the participants in a study of REM sleep and you will deprive them of dreams. True enough, but only partially true.

As dreaming normally occurs at sleep onset and in non-REM (NREM) sleep (and no one has yet investigated the possibility that this tendency increases when REM sleep is curtailed), William Dement and his psychoanalyst–neuroscientist colleague Charles Fisher were sure that dream deprivation (REM deprivation, really) would cause people to become psychotic because they would not have the psychic escape valve that dreaming—and only dreaming—made available to them. Needless to say, some of the participants did become psychotic when their sleep deprivation was prolonged. Everyone who lived through this period remembers the stories of students who became psychotic after 10 days of REM deprivation. As a publicity stunt, the disc jockey Peter Tripp was kept awake for 72 hours in his broadcasting booth. Tripp's normal hypnomanic radio chatter was gradually replaced by fixed paranoid delusions.

In retrospect, none of these studies was morally justified because the working hypothesis was that dream deprivation would, if pushed far enough, drive the individuals crazy. Although I am disappointed with the lack of clarity that still clouds this area of science, I would not myself either submit to such treatment or expose others to it.

Sceptics such as Anthony Kales did much more careful work on this problem, and invariably showed that normal humans are

surprisingly immune to sleep deprivation. When they assessed sleep deprivation's effects using quantitative psychological tests, they found no differences between selective REM sleep reduction and total sleep reduction, and only very small impairments with either. What these studies seemed to show was that there was nothing particularly special about REM sleep—or dreaming—for the maintenance of psychic equilibrium. Indirectly, these results also weakened the naïve 'hydraulic' hypothesis that it was pressure to dream that, when released, caused psychosis.

These studies did not, however, mean—as many incorrectly supposed—that sleep was without salutary effects on the mind. The idea that sleep is a waste of time is still deeply embedded in our culture, along with our commitment to achievement, doing, and material success. If you were asked to name the most accomplished American entrepreneur, you might well nominate Thomas Edison, our candidate (as inventor of the light bulb) who prided himself on his ability to be very productive on very little sleep. Thomas Edison might have been a true short sleeper, genetically endowed with a high-energy brain that allowed him to be more active, more wakeful, and more creative than most of us.

For every Edison, there is another person who will never invent anything, will never feel well rested, and should never attempt medical school. Such 'long' sleepers should take satisfaction in their sensitivity, their capacity to feel, to be, and to reflect. Poetry and literature are compatible with the stay-in-bed lifestyles of the Marcel Prousts, Samuel Taylor Coleridges, and Graham Greenes of the world. All three celebrated sleep and dreaming quite actively and began to set up a culture of internal reflection, skill in creating one's own values, and

narrative production that is every bit as needed by the world as light bulbs. What, after all, are we to read when we are awake at night?

In the rest of this chapter, we see that sleep is much more than a Band-Aid for the brain–mind's cognitive competence. We see that sleep is essential to life in ways that psychology could never imagine. In Chapter 6, we learn that cognitive competence *does* suffer—mightily—from sleep loss, although this effect can be demonstrated experimentally only when tasks that demand prolonged attention and complex sequences of thought processes are used to challenge sleep-deprived individuals. Later, when discussing depression in Chapter 7, we return to sleep–mental illness connections, and realize that the same brain-stem systems that control and trigger dreaming mediate mood and mode of thinking.

Is sleep essential to life?

If we do not survive, we do not reproduce. What do we, as mammals, need to do in order to survive? We need to eat, and to convert dietary calories into fuel for bodily functions; we also need to avoid predation, especially when we are vulnerable—at night, for example. So far, so good. We need to eat without being eaten.

But we must also stay warm (or cool) enough to function effectively. This involves maintaining our core body temperature within the very narrow range of daily fluctuation (no more than 0.83 degrees Celsius, or 1.5 degrees Fahrenheit). If we become overheated, our brains do not work well—in fact they go to sleep, which is why tropical cultures are more likely to create siestas than Thomas Edison's. If we become cold, our

brains are equally upset. The mountaineer's mnemonic for cold exposure says, first you fumble, then you mumble, and then you stumble, and finally, you tumble.

For us, technological kings of the beasts, 'predation' may seem like an idle threat. But think of life in the inner city and tell me how much you enjoy walking at night in ill-lit neighbourhoods. Think of the threat of infection against which we must constantly fight to avoid pneumonia (colds and sore throats are bad enough), to avoid invasion of our bloodstreams by the micro-organisms that inhabit our intestines (and normally aid digestion without asking for more than a part of our meals), and to maintain immunity to avoid invasion by a vast army of destructive viruses (such as influenza A, hepatitis B, and so on through the alphabet). These are our predators as much as lions are for zebras!

It turns out that all of these functions suffer when sleep deprivation becomes extreme. The recent experiments of Allan Rechtschaffen and his group, at the same University of Chicago where sleep and dream science began in the early 1950s, made it impossible—or at least very difficult—for one of a pair of rats to sleep. The other rat was free to sleep whenever the sleep-deprived rat was awake. In this way, it was possible to reduce sleep greatly in the one without significant reduction in the other.

It is important to emphasize the fact that these experimental conditions were so extreme that it is difficult to imagine them occurring naturally. It is also important to note that it takes two weeks, a surprisingly long time, for the most severely debilitating effects to set in. Finally, we can take some comfort from the fact that, at any stage in the proceedings, recovery is complete when sleep is allowed. We should *not* assume,

however, that the results of experimental sleep deprivation of a type that we will probably never experience are irrelevant to our own concepts of sleep hygiene. Anyone who has ever noticed that even minor sleep loss leads to increased risk of infection will get this point easily.

The first defect, in what inevitably became a fatal syndrome in sleep-deprived rats, was the tendency for the skin to break down, to lose its continuity and integrity. By the end of the second week, this was associated with highly motivated heat-seeking behaviour—rats always found the warmest corner of their cage. What then ensued challenges credibility: the rats lost weight and the weight loss was so unrelenting that it could not be countered by constant eating! In other words, the caloric value of food declined, presumably as more and more of the animal's own energy resources were devoted to keeping warm. The capacity to regulate the body temperature was also lost. The very essence of mammalian adaptation—and the reflex property on which brain function depends—is temperature regulation. Without sleep, temperature regulation and normal brain function cannot be maintained. The implication, which I find irresistible, is that all of us refresh our thermoregulatory capacities every night as we sleep.

By the end of the third and fourth weeks, the sleep-deprived rats began to die off. They were metabolically starved in the presence of enough food to keep the control rat sleek, plump, and as happy as a rat can be under such circumstances. Death occurred when the sleep-deprived rats could no longer fend off infection. They were invaded by bacteria from their own bowels—eaten up by normally symbiotic hitchhikers that were no longer satisfied just to go along for the ride.

Now, you might say that we have come a long way from

dreaming and even from brain activation in sleep, but I don't think so and I hope that a moment's reflection will show you why. To explain why sleep normally defends us from such fates, we must assume that it is the change in brain state, with all its chemical and electrical transformations, that keeps us healthy. A second reason, admittedly theoretical, is that our drive to sleep is so intense, so demanding, and so enduring that it *must* have important survival functions.

What about the brain activation part? What about dreams? How are dreaming and thermoregulation related to one another? My answer is that only mammals have thermoregulation and only mammals have REM sleep, so it is likely that these two functions—and dreaming—are tied together in some way. What could that 'way' be? Here we can only speculate, but before doing so let us take note of another surprising fact. It is only in REM sleep that mammals can *not* thermoregulate. We can put all of this together in a theoretical way for future experiments to investigate.

Food-finding and food ingestion all depend on waking behaviour which, in turn, depends on brain activation. In the case of waking brain activation, systems involving chemicals such as norepinephrine and seratonin (aminergic systems) operate and we know that thermoregulation depends on them. All waking functions consume energy and are risky for, although essential to, survival.

Brain activation in sleep is brought about in a very different way: the aminergic systems are turned off, so thermoregulation is impossible, although thermoregulation is not needed in REM sleep because the animal is thermally safe in its nest—safe from heat loss and predation. The brain activation of sleep is by nerve fibres that have the same effect as a chemical known as

acetylcholine (and their effect is called cholinergic); it is energy-conserving and safe, but every bit as essential to survival because it allows the animal to restore the effectiveness of its core regulatory systems. At the same time, the brain–mind is off-line and free to reorganize its cognitive repertoire as well as its more basic bodily functions. We say much more about this later.

What is the function of dreaming?

It has recently been suggested by the philosopher Owen Flanagan that dreaming is an epiphenomenon (a causal occurrence or functionally insignificant phenomenon), i.e. it has no function as such. Taking this position is rather extreme, but scientifically tenable, because there is no evidence that the content of dreams has a significant influence on waking behaviour. It may help us to notice, via our dreams, that we are complex emotional creatures, but we know this already. Recall of dreaming *cannot* be all that important because there are so many individuals with little or no dream recall whatsoever who function quite nicely.

Even if the conscious experience of dreaming and its recall are epiphenomena, the brain process that underlies dreams could perform a number of functions. The most popular current theory is that the activation of the brain in sleep is necessary for us to reorder the information inside our heads, to get rid of certain obsolete memories, to update memories, and to incorporate new experiences into our memory systems. We discuss this theory in more detail in Chapter 9. In addition to this cognitive function, the activation of the brain during sleep could have a lifelong developmental role. As we have just seen, REM sleep is far more prevalent in newborn infants than it is in adults. This suggests that it is the construction of the brain

itself that is one of the functions of brain activation in sleep. There is no reason for us to think that development stops once we have acquired language; we go on throughout our lives needing to reconstruct our brains and our minds.

Can the formal analysis of dreaming tell us something about how our cognitive repertoire is restored? Do we lose memory for the same reason that we lose thermoregulatory capacity— the disablement of the aminergic systems on which both depend? The net effect of resting and restoring the aminergic systems at night is to strengthen our next day's capacity for thermoregulation and acquisition of information. Along with memory and thermoregulation, we can therefore also ascribe alertness, attention, and even analytical intellect to aminergic effectiveness. In Chapter 6 we take these possibilities a step further by discussing regional brain activation.

Our dreams are emotional, and something that psychologists term 'hyperassociative', because our brains are activated by cholinergic rather than aminergic chemicals. Thus, we restore the most fundamental aspects of our cognitive capability—the capacity to order our memories in a way that serves survival. Emotional salience or relevance is a general mnemonic rule. Our level of emotional competence has a high survival value and underlies the more precise information needed to function socially. In other words, we need, first and foremost, to know when to approach, when to mate, when to be afraid, and when to run for cover. These are the skills that sleep refreshes every night of our lives by activating our brains, with no regard for the details of declarative memory (memory that is learned quickly and consciously). As with thermoregulation, and immunity to infection, our instincts to flee, fight, feed, and fornicate are crucial to survival and to procreation.

6

Disorders of dreaming

In this chapter, we look at the way in which the brain systems mediating dreaming can become exaggerated or distorted, with unwelcome consequences. Here, we are on the edge of the medicine of sleep disorders, a topic of great interest to modern sleep science.

Nightmares and night terrors

Throughout this book, we have emphasized the important role that brain activation in sleep plays in helping us to understand human dreaming. The same rule applies to the understanding of frightening dreams and nightmares. We've already emphasized the fact that dreaming includes intense emotion, which is often negative. In fact, dreams from which we spontaneously awaken are characteristically dominated by anxiety, fear, and anger. So, in a sense, the question of what causes nightmares is the same question as what causes negative emotion in dreams. The

answer is the same, too. It is brain activation and, in particular, activation of an important and ancient area called the limbic brain.

What kind of brain activation causes nightmares rather than pleasant dreams? The obvious answer is that it must be the emotion centres of the brain that mediate negative emotion that are activated in nightmares, and activation of the emotion centres that cause positive emotion determines the pleasant nature of other dreams. Having said this, it is important to distinguish, in traumatic dreams, the difference between night terrors and nightmares.

Night terrors are pure emotional experiences that occur on awakening from sleep. Typically, they are associated with non-rapid eye movement (NREM) sleep, as are the recurrent dreams of post-traumatic stress. Together with the arousal from NREM sleep, there is intense activation of the heart, the breathing rate increases, and the blood pressure may rise to extremely high levels; the person awakens drenched in sweat and terrified, and often has little dream recall whatsoever from these awakenings.

This is quite different from the more typical experience that most of us have had at one time or another—to awaken from a dream in which we were trying to escape from imaginary pursuers, absolutely terrified. In the second case, which is more likely to occur in REM sleep, we have formed the perceptual scenario of an attack situation from which we are attempting to flee, and our emotion is appropriate to the dreamed action. Figure 7 shows the activation that is not in our control (i.e. autonomic activation) which is normally associated with REM sleep. As can be seen, increases in heart rate, blood pressure, and respiratory rate can begin in NREM sleep.

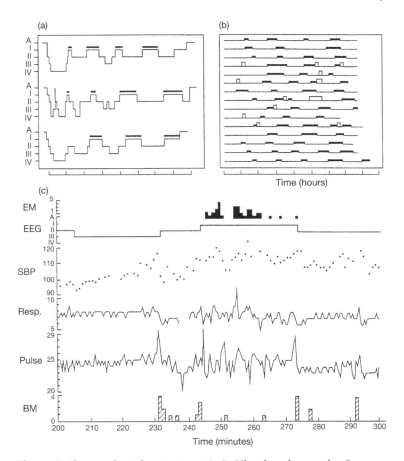

Figure 7 Sleep cycle with activation. (A, B) Ultradian sleep cycle of NREM and REM sleep shown in detailed sleep-stage graphs of 3 human subjects (A) and REM sleep periodiagrams of 15 human subjects (B). In (C) one such sleep cycle is shown to illustrate the changes in eye movements (EM), EEG, blood pressure (SBP), respiration (resp.), pulse, and body movements (BM) that are associated with REM.

In night terrors, especially post-traumatic night terrors, emotion may be the same as that experienced during waking, whether or not there is any associated dream content. The brain is activated in sleep and brain centres mediating emotion are preferentially activated in sleep as will be made clear when we discuss brain imaging data in Chapter 7. We can see, then, that nightmares, however unpleasant, are normal events in sleep, suggesting that the maintenance of these emotional systems of the brain, which ensure our survival, may be one of the functions of brain activation in sleep. Too bad we have to dream about it.

Sleep walking

Sleep walking, sleep talking, and tooth grinding are three of the so-called parasomnias, movement (or motor) behaviours that occur unexpectedly during sleep. When we recall that the answer to so many of our questions has been brain activation in sleep, it will not be surprising to notice that all three of these motor behaviours are a function of the activation of the movement systems in subcortical brain tissue—the motor pattern generators (or MPGs) that are referred to in Chapter 4. The motor systems that are activated are activated over and above the ability of the brain to quell motor output through inhibition.

During REM sleep, one of the most common dream experiences is of imagined motion. To ensure that we do not move, the system has to run an inhibitory, or blockade, process to stop the motor commands, which are hallucinated by us as dream movement, resulting in actual movement. One of the ways in which the brain guarantees no movement during sleep is

through inhibition; another is simply to dampen the use of the motor systems. This is well known because, to fall asleep, we have to assume postures that are immobile; we will not be able to go to sleep if we are unable to stop moving. So, the very onset of sleep is dependent on disabling the motor system. Later, when the brain is intensely activated during REM sleep, motor output has to be actively blocked.

Between these two extremes, in NREM sleep activation of motor command centres in the brain may occur that results in behaviours such as sleep walking, sleep talking, and tooth grinding. These motor behaviours are said to be 'dissociated' because normally they occur only during waking. Now they are occurring during sleep, and the assumption has been either that an awakening has occurred or that the person is dreaming. Both are wrong. There is partial brain activation—enough to support movement, but not enough to support waking. These states are hybrids, with features of *both* sleep and waking.

To understand this apparent paradox, we need to recognize that movement is programmed by the brain at many levels. The upper level of the brain, which gives us voluntary control over movement during waking, is pretty much out of the loop during sleep. The lower brain structures, many of which are necessary for movement, may, however, be activated while the upper brain is inactive. The result is automatic movement, such as may be seen in heavily sleep-fogged individuals who need to urinate getting up and going to the bathroom or to some inappropriate place, such as the flower garden, where they attempt to urinate.

In performing such sleep-walking acts, these individuals are partially aroused, but still deeply asleep in respect of the upper brain. We know this from lab studies in which brain waves have been recorded. The high-voltage slow waves of deep sleep

continue to be recorded while the individual sleep walks. One old wives' tale about sleep walking holds that it is a mistake to wake the person, usually a young person, up from such episodes. The answer to that one is to 'go ahead and try'. It is usually impossible, but don't worry about it because, if you can't do it or if you do succeed in waking them, there will be no adverse consequence whatsoever.

Post-traumatic dreams

What effect does trauma have on dreams? There are two para-doxically contradictory answers to this question: enormous impact and very little. We don't understand why, in some cases, the trauma is almost always dominant and, in others, it has such a small role to play in the shaping of dreams. One answer may be that victims of trauma, e.g. post-traumatic stress disorder patients who have had violent experiences in war, have a specific kind of awakening experience. Their sleep is interrupted by terrors akin to the night terrors of children, and, like in the night terrors of children, these do not occur in REM sleep when normal dreaming takes place. Instead, they occur in NREM sleep, the phase of sleep in which the brain is less completely activated, but in which powerful emotions can nevertheless make themselves felt.

Individuals who have had intrusive and disruptive trauma may have intrusive and disruptive emotional experiences during sleep, which create states of brain activation of their own. This encapsulation of trauma leaves intact the normal physiological process of brain activation in sleep that results in dreaming. This could help us account for the fact that many individuals who have had traumatic experiences (and I am one of them) never

dream about that experience at all—it just wasn't strong enough to take on a mental life of its own and it plays very little part in the construction of my dreams.

I was assaulted on the street by three men and nearly killed by them—my nose was blasted to smithereens and my nasal septum deeply separated from my skull; I needed painful plastic surgery (without anaesthesia). But this episode has never appeared in my dreams; what appears instead are frighteningly aggressive confrontations, although these appeared before the traumatic event as well as after. This is not the least bit surprising or unusual. One of the things that we fear most is being overpowered and assaulted by criminals or bullies. That has been a part of the fear of my life ever since I was a young child, so that in my dreams I may have what appear to be recurrent episodes of confrontation with powerful enemies whom I am helpless to repulse. I run away and they chase me, and sometimes they may even catch me, as they did in the real traumatic event that occurred. But then I wake up. They never go on and break my nose in the way they did in my real life experience. In fact, I rarely experience pain in my dreams.

Careful scientific studies of survivors of the Holocaust suggest that all sleep is invaded by the horrific replay of memories of experiences. This fact, coupled with the findings of post-traumatic stress disorder in veterans of military combat, suggests that, just as waking thought tends to be dominated by preoccupations with these unpleasant experiences, so does sleep mental activity tend to be dominated by them.

We now need to carry out studies to find out if awakenings performed in REM and NREM sleep yield different reports. This is important, not only to answer the question of how trauma shapes dreaming, but also to answer questions about the

function of dreaming. We still don't understand why the brain self-activates during sleep, yet evidence suggests that it is certainly not only to replay previous experience.

REM sleep behaviour disorder

The new kid on the dream disorder block is the REM sleep behaviour disorder (RBD), a very strange syndrome in which patients enact their dreams through movement. This is not sleep walking, although it *is* what sleep walking was erroneously thought to be. How does RBD come about?

The inhibition of movement or motor output, which normally quells the movement commands of dreams, is only quantitatively greater than the excitation of neurons that is the embodiment of these commands. If either inhibition declines or excitation increases, or both, movement will result.

In RBD, individuals (often middle-aged men who will go on to develop the movement disorder parkinsonism) begin to enact their dreams. One of my patients flails his arms, and hits his wife, as he dreams of driving a car and turning sharply on a curve. Another imagines that he is at a swimming pool and dives off the bed.

In every case, the dream report given by the patient on being awakened fits with the motor behaviour observed during the REM sleep dream. We know that these events occur in REM sleep from sleep lab evidence.

This sounds very much like evidence for the one-to-one theory of dream psychophysiology, proof of which eluded experimenters in the 1960s. It also suggests that REM sleep physiology can be pathologically distorted by inherent degeneration of the brain. In the case of RBD, the system controlling the

neurons (neuromodulatory system) that is suspect is dopamine, a chemical neurotransmitter which has an unclear role in normal sleep.

We know that dopamine deficiency is the cause of parkinsonism and that many RBD patients will develop this condition. Beyond that, it is not clear what is going on, although it *is* clear that prolonged use of a group of antidepressants known as the selective serotonin reuptake inhibitors (SSRIs) can lead to RBD. This suggests that serotonin, which is known to be a potent inhibitor of REM, may interact with brain dopamine systems and upset the balance between inhibition and excitation of the motor systems in sleep.

Dreaming, like any other mental state, is subject to pathological deformation. In Chapters 7 and 8 we explore this theme in more detail and show how normal dreaming helps us understand the organic (physical) basis of psychopathology, the organic basis of dreaming itself, and how disorders of dreaming help us to understand both normal dreaming and psychopathology.

7

Dreaming as delirium: sleep and mental illness

If dreaming and the psychosis of waking life are not dynamically interchangeable in the sense of Freud's model, how should we conceive of the compelling analogy that exists between them? After all, dreaming *is* a psychotic state, and it is as psychotic a state as we ever experience while awake. The internally generated perceptions have the hallucinatory power needed to make us hopelessly delusional. In the face of their detail and the powerful takeover of our minds, dream hallucinations make it impossible for us to realize that we are in the grasp of an altered state of consciousness. We are sure we are awake and believe our senses—and the associated emotions—despite the incongruities and discontinuities of dream bizarreness, which, were they to occur in waking, would immediately tip us off.

If these emotions occurred while we really were awake, our first reaction to improbable or impossible dream scenarios would be to say 'Pinch me, I must be dreaming!'. If that didn't work, we might try to wake ourselves up. Next, we might

wonder if someone had slipped a mickey in our cocktail, or whether one of the drugs we were taking for high blood pressure or migraine or spastic colon had side effects that our doctor had not warned us about. For sure, we would wonder whether or not we were getting enough sleep. We would probably do all these things before we concluded that we should see a psychiatrist, although we would know that we were going crazy for some physical reason or another.

This means that, formally speaking, dreaming and severe mental illness are not only analogous but identical. This, in turn, means not only that is it easy to imagine that physical changes in brain state can produce psychosis, but also that the perfectly normal changes of sleep have very dramatic effects on our mental capacities. What's going on here?

Do we go mad each night to prevent ourselves from doing so in the day time? Or do we go mad because the brain temporarily gives up certain of its controls in order to regain them, in better order, when sleep ends? We don't yet know the answers to these questions, although the evidence suggests that each has a grain of a more complex truth hidden in this still incomplete line of enquiry.

What kind of psychosis is dreaming?

Psychosis is, by definition, a mental state characterized by hallucinations and/or delusions. It is very difficult to hallucinate without being deluded; we go into this 'seeing is believing' principle in more detail later. But, as almost everyone knows, it is quite possible to be deluded without hallucinating. Normal suspicion—call it caution if you will—leads us to believe things about our lovers, colleagues, and governments that are either

completely untrue or highly exaggerated. In other words, we don't need to hear voices to be paranoid, although it certainly helps.

Which natural class of psychosis is dreaming most like: schizophrenia, major affective disorder (such as depression and mania), or an organic mental illness, e.g. delirium resulting from drugs or a high fever? If you are following my reasoning at all, you will quickly realize that the answer is organic mental illness. And, if you have any doubt, call the formal approach to your rescue.

Begin with the dream hallucinations. What sensory modalities do they use? Everyone will say 'vision' without hesitation. Although visual hallucinations are quite rare in schizophrenia and major affective disorder, they are the very hallmark of organic delirium.

Move on to the delusions: these are exclusively cognitive/intellectual and never paranoid as is typical of schizophrenia. They are rarely related to the body (i.e. somatic) as they can be in depression (a common feature of which is a mistaken conviction about lost, defective, or diseased body parts). The grandiosity and fearless elation of mania *are* shared with dream psychosis, although these features are also found in organic delirium, especially in its chronic, post-intoxication phase.

The clincher of the argument comes when we consider the cognitive deficits. When we are dreaming, times, places, and people change without warning. This orientational instability is a variation on the organic delirium theme of disorientation. Delirious patients, similar to dreamers, know only who they are, not where they are or what day it is, or even who is with them. In response to the disorientation, which is caused by the recent memory deficit, the patient with organic delirium makes up stories that are not lies but false beliefs, sincerely—and often

fatuously—advanced to cover the huge holes in memory. We call this trait 'confabulation'. Confabulation is *not* a word we usually apply to dreaming, but it fits. Fabulous is a related word, which *is* often used to describe dreams.

When we elaborate dream plots, we are telling ourselves stories, fibs, white lies, and myths about ourselves. In fact, we are so convinced that these myths are about the real us that we rarely, and then only reluctantly, reach the conclusion that we are delirious when we dream. In this view, it ought to be considered at least possible that dream content is as much dross as gold, as much cognitive trash as treasure, and as much informational noise as a signal of something. This kind of proposal, which Robert McCarley and I made in our original 1977 papers about the activation–synthesis hypothesis, has never been popular.

There are, however, many other reasons to take the dreaming-as-delirium argument seriously. Even if you believe that the peculiar utterances of your aunt with Alzheimer's disease contain deep or hidden meanings, you recognize that it is her loss of brain cells that causes her to make so many of them. In fact, Alzheimer's disease, and its many degenerative ailment cousins, all affect neurons, including the aminergic and cholinergic elements that we already know to be functionally eliminated (the aminergics) or enhanced (the cholinergics) in sleep. What I am saying is that not only are the mental phenomena analogous, but also the brain mechanisms underlying them.

Sounds bad, doesn't it? Going to sleep entails the enabling of a distinctive brain activation process akin to delirium: delirium is a state that we thought we could get only by being bad or by taking drugs such as alcohol, amphetamine, or atropine, or by outliving our brains—in the senile conditions of old

age. Suddenly we find out that it happens to all of us, every night of our lives, and probably more when we are being good than when we are being bad, and more when we are young than when we are old!

The good news is that all we need to do to cure ourselves of dream delirium is to wake up. This is a comforting thought in more ways than one. It means that we can stop the music if we don't like it (as therapists treating anxiety disorders and depression have discovered), but it also means that the concept of chemical balance, always so seductive and powerful, but, until now, so vague, can finally be specified. Mental state is a constantly negotiated compromise between the poles of waking sanity and dreaming madness. The following dream shows just how delirious my own mind can become when my brain is inhibited by the aminergic system and overstimulated by the cholinergic one.

28/8/1983 A House Burning, Dream no. 32

> I could see the smoke, just like when the sauna and, later, the farmhouse caught fire. This time it seemed again like the house but it was in the wrong place (across the road) and when I pulled the hose toward the source of the smoke, I was oblivious that it would not reach. There was snow on the ground. I dropped the hose and ran on to find that the smoke was issuing from a chimney (at the level of the ground) hence, no danger. This house—impossible in every way—somehow fit into the familiar complex of buildings that is the farm of my dreams. There is one large barn whose repairs I frequently contemplate—it does not resemble the real barn whose repairs I also—in reality—frequently contemplate.
>
> 'Who set this fire?' I inquired angrily.
>
> 'A boy' was the answer from a man faintly resembling a scout-master or teacher and—through his expression only—implying that

the 'boy' was Ian and that I should not be angry because of his handicap. He had that professional, holier-than-thou sort of patience that I myself some days evince when faced with irritated parents of troublesome children.

'He is around here somewhere.'

He was not but there was an abundance of well-meaning clinical types, a veritable workshop of do-gooders all of whom were discussing the wonders of kindness and love. This disarmed me only slightly. I was still concerned about the fire and eager to punish the fire setter.

Suddenly, there was a complete scene shift. Beside a stream, with rapid current and much white water, a ball (orange) is seen to shoot out into the maelstrom. It will certainly be lost if it reaches the waterfall. I call out to Julia, who is immobilized, at least to go to high ground so as to plot the course of the ball. (She has been playing with Karen Lavie who arrived that day with an orange ball.) Instead, she plunges into the stream and, with a manly swimmer's stroke, knifes through the current, seizes the ball, and carries it out the opposite bank. This seems, at once, miraculous and normal.

If this is not a delirious, psychotic experience, all of my psychiatric training is worthless. I have visual hallucinations, delusions, strong emotions (anger, anxiety, and elation), and, most definitely, disorientation, and its close cousin, confabulation. This story, which seems so crazy to my waking mind, seemed so normal to me in the dream.

What happens to sleep in mental illness?

What does this tell us about the chemical imbalance theory? Here again, most people can intuit the general answer. Anxiety

and other emotions (such as elation) that increase brain activation of the waking type, impede sleep. They do so by increasing the set-point for the aminergic systems, which mediate waking and inhibit sleep. Besides causing insomnia, which is unpleasant, these conditions also induce sleep deprivation or, at least, sleep curtailment. And we know, from our discussions in Chapter 5, that sleep deprivation may be positively unhealthy, not just dysfunctional.

When patients are becoming psychotic, for whatever reason, sleep is also likely to suffer, adding the risk of normal dream delirium to that of a schizophrenic or affective psychotic process, because individuals can be driven into states of delirium by extreme sleep deprivation. Think of brain-washing, trance states, and the confessions of treason extracted by political, psychological, and cultural rituals. All involve sleep deprivation. In the end, sleep-deprived individuals will do or say anything in exchange for sleep.

Sleep loss is therefore common in and contributes powerfully to the development of psychosis. In the case of schizophrenia (now thought to be a disorder of excessive dopamine release and/or heightened effectiveness of dopamine), we can hypothesize an indirect but positive interaction with the other modulators of the awake state, noradrenaline and serotonin, and a direct negative interaction with acetylcholine. Significantly for my dreaming-as-delirium thesis, no distinctive changes in sleep are seen in chronic schizophrenia.

When we come to consider major affective illness, our story becomes almost unbelievably enriched. In the first place, depression, which is now thought to be mediated by serotoninergic and/or noradrenergic insufficiency, is characterized by a marked tendency for REM to occur earlier, to be more intense,

and to last longer than it does in age-matched controls, or in the same patients when they get well. This means that major depression, which is also thought to be enhanced by cholinergic (acetylcholine) systems, is a functional disorder of the very same neuronal systems that control dreaming; by stretching the point a bit, it could mean further that to be prone to depression is to be prone to REM sleep and vice versa. The changes in the sleep of someone with depression, and the presumed neuromodulatory basis, are shown in Figure 8. This is a surprising conclusion because, as we have seen, dreaming is unlike depressive psychosis and depression is unlike delirium!

How can we square these apparent discrepancies? The first step is to admit that we don't know enough yet to do so. The second step is to point out the most promising avenues of investigation. One certainly arises from the fact that, although the most effective antidepressant medications suppress REM sleep (by beefing up the depressed aminergic system and toning down the hyperactive cholinergic system), they do so with quite a different time course. The disorder of REM sleep is fixed at once, whereas the mood disorder may take weeks to respond. This means that sleep and mood are linked by long-term, downstream brain processes, which we cannot yet describe but which almost certainly depend on changes in gene expression.

Another promising lead is the immediate relief of daytime depression by a single night of REM sleep deprivation. This finding suggests that, if there is something already wrong with mood control, REM sleep chemistry induces depression. Could this induction of depression be mediated by the cholinergic overdrive of REM? Perhaps, because we know that cholinergic drugs that increase REM acutely make depression worse.

We are left with the tantalizing approximation of two

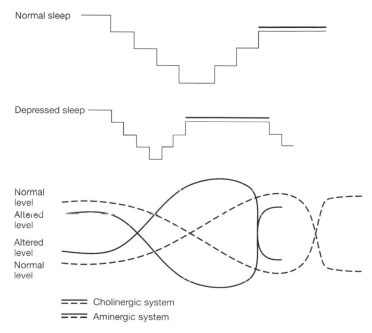

Normal sleep

Depressed sleep

Normal level
Altered level

Altered level
Normal level

=== Cholinergic system
=== Aminergic system

Figure 8 Many depressed patients experience an earlier onset of REM during the first sleep cycle. The first REM period may also last longer and be more intense than normal. The process is reversed by antidepressant medications that strengthen the aminergic and weaken the cholinergic systems.

models—one controlling sleep, the other controlling mood—which are about to collapse into each other, but not quite. Not yet. Those yearning for a unified theory of brain and mind must exercise patience and be satisfied that, in this case at least, the cup is well over half-full, whereas only 25 years ago it was completely empty.

8

The new neuropsychology
of dreaming

Sleep lab dream research very quickly reached a point of diminishing returns. This was because the one-to-one dream content theory was too ambitious and too unscientific to guide a physiological programme that was too superficial to provide detailed data about the brain. The result was a contentious and unproductive period of sleep and dream research lasting from about 1975 to 1995. Understandably disappointed, the grant committees of the American National Institutes of Health began to cut funding for sleep labs, especially those that were engaged in descriptive, correlative work on dreaming.

During this same period, neurophysiological work on sleep in animals was proceeding apace, providing details about the brain that could only be tentatively matched with human psychology using the dream form theory. This failed to satisfy many psychologists, who were understandably nervous about the applicability to humans of cellular and molecular evidence

obtained in cats, and who were unable or unwilling to give up the dream content theory. Believing that they had been unfairly deprived of support, some psychologists, led by David Foulkes, made a strong attack on physiologically oriented dream research.

Brain imaging to the rescue

In the second half of the last decade of the twentieth century, officially declared by US Congress to be the 'Decade of the Brain', brain imaging technology made it possible for the first time in human history to visualize the regional activation (and inactivation) patterns associated with changes in conscious state. Chief among these conscious state changes, and appropriately chosen as a first point of attack, were waking, sleeping, and dreaming. Although this scientific approach is still young, it is developing rapidly and has already revolutionized dream science by providing us with the opportunity to compare our formal dream versus wake measures with formal wake versus rapid eye movement (REM) sleep measures of regional brain activation.

Before describing how this method works, I show how two examples of dream formalism are explained by the brain imaging data. They are intensity of the hallucinations (which is often much exaggerated in dreaming) and directed thought (which is usually diminished or completely absent in dreaming). By going far beyond the spatial resolution of the electro-encephalograph (EEG), brain imaging allows us to record the regional brain correlates of hallucination and thought. Studies using a form of imaging called positron emission tomography (PET) show an *increase* in activation of just those multimodal regions of the brain that one would expect to be activated in

hallucinatory perception (the cortical areas of the parietal lobe, see Figure 9). They also show a corresponding *decrease* in the activation of an area of the brain known as the dorsolateral prefrontal cortex (see Figure 9); this brain area has been identified as the area of, or base for, working memory, self-reflection, and directed thought. In other words, in REM sleep—compared with waking—hallucination is enhanced and thinking is inspired because of the shift in regional brain activation.

How are such observations actually made? What relationship do they have to what we already know to be the global changes in brain chemistry and physiology underlying them?

If you have ever been referred for computed tomography (CT) or any of many magnetic resonance imaging (MRI) methods that have replaced X-rays in medicine and neurology, you have already enjoyed the fruits of the brain imaging revolution. Both of these techniques, and also PET, produce images of the brain itself—not just the skull—by computing density differences in the tissue (CT) or functional activation differences of the tissue (MRI and PET). This takes advantage of the fact that the density of the brain is altered by blood flow, together with activation and inactivation of neurons. Whenever neurons become more active, they require more oxygen, which is supplied by increasing blood flow to the activated region. Scans from PET and functional MRI make 'visible' such regional activations (and inactivations).

As computers are used to organize and manipulate the three-dimensional data, it is possible to look at the activity of many different brain regions, from many different angles, simultaneously. The computer, under instruction from the investigator, decides from what angle to take the image and at what

depth to focus its density analysis. It then produces a myriad of pixels, or points that measure density, plots them in two dimensions as a 'slice', and colour codes the density patterns to make them easy to read qualitatively.

For research purposes, PET is attractive because it has relatively high spatial resolution. It must be realized, however, that, even with PET, we are not at the level of cells and molecules that is provided by the microelectrodes and microinjection techniques used in basic sleep research. So a gap still remains. We tolerate this gap because PET tells us things that would take decades (or centuries) to realize if we could use these microinjection techniques in humans (which we can't), and because we know that it is just a matter of time before the gap is closed in animals.

Meanwhile we rejoice at the festival of findings obtained using PET to study sleep and dreaming in humans. Table 3 shows the brain regions that are activated (and inactivated) in

Table 3 Imaging of brain activation in REM sleep and the effects of brain damage on dreaming

Area of brain	PET studies on activation in REM	Brain damage studies of effects on dreaming
Pontine tegmentum	↑	—
Limbic structures	↑	↓
Visual cortex	—	—
Supramarginal gyrus	↑	↓
Dorsolateral prefrontal cortex	↓	—
Mediobasal frontal cortex	↑	↓

Key: ↑, increase; ↓, decrease; −, no change.

human REM sleep compared with waking, and compares the data with those emerging from the analysis of changes in dreaming after accidental destruction of the brain regions in question by disease, especially stroke. To aid comprehension, consult Figure 9, which shows the location of brain areas that are either hotter or cooler in REM sleep than in waking.

The following findings are of particular interest: activation of the area of the human brain known to be an important source of the chemically distinct brain activation pattern in animal REM; activation of a vast area of the marginal part of the forebrain which is known to mediate emotion and to motivate behaviour in humans; activation of the limbic areas controlling emotion, especially fear; and activation of multimodal 'association' areas of the brain.

These regional activation data are compatible with the formalist view that dreaming differs from waking in being more internally controlled, more hallucinatory, more emotional, and motivated more by instinct than in waking. In comparing the respective mind and brain forms of the two states, the dream scientist carries out a subtraction. In the first set of comparisons, we ask what parts of the brain are *more active* in REM sleep and whether they correspond to formal aspects of the mental state that are intensified in dreaming.

Dreaming is also characterized by a set of related, cognitive features that are *deficient* compared with waking, including diminished self-awareness, diminished reality testing, poor memory, defective logic, and, most strikingly, the inability to maintain directed thought. Imaging experiments now tell me that the area of the brain called the dorsolateral prefrontal cortex, which is normally activated in support of functions in waking, is deactivated in REM sleep. In other words, the subtraction

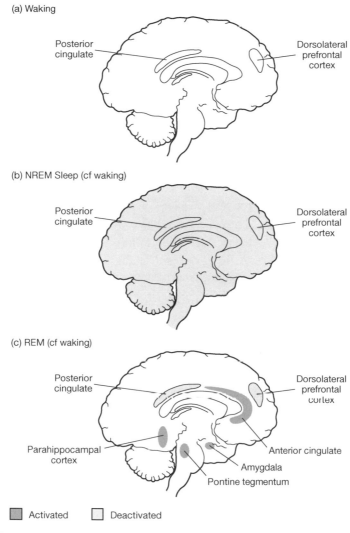

(a) Waking

Posterior cingulate

Dorsolateral prefrontal cortex

(b) NREM Sleep (cf waking)

Posterior cingulate

Dorsolateral prefrontal cortex

(c) REM (cf waking)

Posterior cingulate

Dorsolateral prefrontal cortex

Parahippocampal cortex

Anterior cingulate

Amygdala

Pontine tegmentum

■ Activated   □ Deactivated

Figure 9 Summary of PET study evidence of brain region activation in NREM and REM sleep. Compared to the blood flow distribution in waking (a), the global decreases observed in NREM sleep (b) suggest widespread deactivation consistent with the greatly diminished capacity of conscious experience early in the night. In REM sleep (c), many regions are activated about their levels in waking (solid black) while others are deactivated (shaded).

in this case shows waking to have more of both the psychological traits and the underlying regional brain activation.

To see such striking correlations is almost too good to be true and, in fact, they prompt us to consider a causal hypothesis in each case. The *reason* that dreams are so perceptually intense, so instinctive and emotional, and so hyperassociative is because the brain regions supporting these functions are more active. The *reason* that we can't decide properly what state we are in, can't keep track of time, place, or person, and can't think critically or actively is because the brain regions supporting these functions are less active. Could it be that simple? Why not? Much apparent complexity melts away when science comes up with a correct simplification. This is the true meaning of reductionism.

Now we must recall that regional brain analysis of diminished psychological function in dreaming shows an association with the lack of noradrenaline and serotonin in the REM sleep-activated brain—these two chemicals are known to be necessary for attention, learning, and memory (and by implication for orientation and active reasoning). Reciprocally, we must say that the uninhibited cholinergic system (active in this state) could contribute to the positive signs mediated by the regional activation of the areas of the brain involved with hallucinosis, hyperassociation, and hyperemotionality.

The story keeps getting better and better. We might even wonder what is left for a psychology of dream content to do. In Chapter 11 we return to this issue but, for now, let us simply say that all of the features of dreaming that Freud wanted to explain with his wish-fulfilment, disguise–censorship theory are explained in just the way he hoped might ultimately be possible—by the physiology and chemistry of the brain.

Can we take our programme of integration a step further?

Possibly. Suppose, for example, that the changes in regional brain activation during REM sleep in humans were somehow related to the shift in the modulation of the neurons, which could quite possibly be valid, because if blood flow is controlled by such modulators in the rest of the body, surely they should also do so in the brain. In other words, a simple way of effecting the complex pattern of regional brain activation and inactivation would be to change the balance of the modulation of neurons, so changing blood flow and then activation of the neurons. It is likely that modulators affect neuron function by both direct (synaptic) and indirect (vascular) actions. It won't be long before we get an answer from brain science.

The main point is that we can now see our own brain in action, something that I could only dream of 15 years ago.

6/7/1984 Headache, Dream no. 34

Having suffered from 'cluster' headache syndrome since January 19, 1984—I began to notice improvement in May and June with a decrease in frequency and intensity of the attacks.

Last night, I dreamt that I was examining my own head (as at a post mortem but this was not suggested in the dream). I pulled back the scalp and skull with intense curiosity, thinking 'at last, I will find out what had been causing this thing!' And, lo and behold, there was a cause—a large balloon-like mass (or was it air?) pressed the brain down into the lower third of the skull. It was concave on its surface.

When I looked closely at the left hemisphere, I noted that it was moth-eaten which explained my difficulty (almost certainly age-related) in remembering specific names. I was interested, but not frightened by what I saw; I was not the least bit aware of the paradox (tangled hierarchy?) that I was looking at my own I (= brain). For such a thing to occur there must, of course, be two brains—but then, the brain-within-the-brain will suffice.

I recall saying 'Now, wake up so that you can recall this remark-
able scene!'

The lucidity with which I was able to waken myself up makes this report suspect of conscious autosuggestion. But I did not, as far as I know, attempt to induce it. Instead, it simply read out my unconscious neurobiological self-analysis.

Does brain damage cause changes in dreaming?

As a result of the conceptual and political split between psychiatry and neurology caused first by the mind–body problem and deeply aggravated by Sigmund Freud's inadvertent dualism, it took dream science an inordinately long time to notice that

cerebrovascular accidents (better known as strokes) and epileptic seizures (better known as fits) could cause decreases and increases in the formal features of dreams, respectively.

Strokes occur when cerebral blood vessels close (as a result of arteriosclerotic plaques) or are blocked (by emboli—small blood clots usually coming from the heart). Strokes prevent the affected brain regions from receiving the oxygen that they need to do their job. A complete loss of dreaming can occur when there is damage to tissue in the brain known as the multimodal sensory cortex (part of the parietal cortex) or to the deep frontal white matter of the brain. Table 3 shows the reader that these are among the structures selectively activated in REM sleep, which is almost certainly not a coincidence. It indicates that these two regions are necessary for dreaming to occur.

You can activate the brain in sleep in whatever way you like, but you will *not* produce the psychological experience of dreaming without activating the parietal cortex or deep frontal white matter. Why not? Are these restricted and discrete brain regions the brain's seats of dreaming? Probably not. More likely they constitute connections allowing other brain regions to communicate with one another in such a way as to sustain dream consciousness.

When strokes are centred in the visual regions of the occipital cortex—again in associative rather than in primary processing zones—patients may report dreaming without visual imagery. To understand this finding we must realize that when visual stimuli, encoded by the retina, reach the primary visual cortex some simple properties of images (such as edges or bars) are represented but the complexity of whole images (houses or people's faces) are built up and represented elsewhere. There are more than 20 such secondary or associative visual areas in the cortex.

Do blind people see in their dreams?

The answer to this question depends on whether the blindness was present at birth or acquired later in life.

People who are blind from birth have no visual imagery at any time, neither in waking nor in dreaming, and this is because their visual systems have never had the necessary interaction with the perceptual world to develop perception or the encoding of visual images. Thus, when their brains are activated during sleep, they are unable to call up images because there are no encoded images present. Naturally, vision is not the only modality in visually impaired individuals; bodily sensations or the sense of position of the body in space is markedly enhanced, and enhanced in proportion to the loss of cues given by the visual system. So these individuals do have other hallucinatory dream experiences, just in a different mode from the visual.

People with acquired blindness have had previous vision. Their brains have developed perceptual capacities and the capacity to recall the images. They can create images awake with their eyes closed and they can create elaborate images when their brains are automatically activated during sleep. In fact, dreaming is the time when people with acquired blindness see most clearly. This recalls the question of Leonardo da Vinci: 'Why does the eye see a thing more clearly in dreams than when awake?'

One of our blind participants told us that he was particularly pleased to see in his dreams because he could revisit his family at will. This suggests that individuals with acquired blindness could and should be taught to recall their dreams and even to shape their content, because they can have convincing perceptual contact with family members long after they stopped being able to see them in the wake state. Our participant was able to describe in detail the gold braid on his postmaster father's hat, which he could see when he visited his father during his dreams.

Epilepsy is an abnormal condition in which the normal activity of affected brain regions may be enhanced as well as impaired, and so constitutes an experiment of nature that is the opposite of stroke. Ever since temporal lobe epilepsy came under experimental scrutiny—at the hands of the Montreal neurosurgeon Wilder Penfield and his neurophysiologist colleague Herbert Jasper—it was known that direct electrical stimulation of the human temporal lobe could produce 'dreamy states' not unlike those associated with spontaneous seizures.

These epileptic states were 'dreamy' precisely because they shared some formal features with normal dreams—they could be hallucinatory, hyperemotional, cognitively confused, and difficult to recall. Now that we know that the temporal lobe is selectively activated in REM sleep, we are bound to ask 'Is this just another coincidence?' The answer, again, is probably not. We need to take seriously the idea that REM sleep, which has pulse-like activity brought about by cholinergic systems, is provided with electrical stimulation to the temporal lobe; this spreads to nearby connected structures and causes us to have dreamy states similar to some aspects of epilepsy as well as to some aspects of psychosis. In both cases the mediating mechanisms are specifiably physical.

As with the imaging work, which complements almost perfectly what happens in dreaming, this aspect of neuropsychology is very new, very young, and very undeveloped. We can expect much more information as other aspects of the effects of brain damage on dreaming are investigated. What we can say unequivocally at this point is that, of course, since dreaming is a brain function, brain damage will affect it. How could it be otherwise?

9

Dreaming, learning, and memory

The idea that dreaming is involved in the reorganization of memory has been around for at least 30 years, but only within the last five has a strong, clear line of evidence been developed. One of the most important scientists working in this area is my colleague Robert Stickgold, and it is his work that forms the backbone of this chapter.

The basic hypothesis, for which evidence was previously consistent and positive but not impressively robust, is that rapid eye movement (REM) sleep subserves consolidation of memory. This hypothesis is appealing because the brain is activated and dreams are composed of memory fragments. This hypothesis has been borne out by recent experiments, although it now appears that non-REM (NREM) sleep is equally important. More interestingly, the dream–memory plot has thickened in two important ways:

1. Thanks to progress in cognitive neuroscience, the learning and memory processes that sleep may affect have been better characterized and differentiated.
2. Thanks to progress in basic sleep neuroscience, the brain dynamics that appear to support the differentiated aspects of learning and memory are now known in enough detail to allow modelling of the sleep learning processes.

As I have constantly repeated throughout this book, we need, always, to maintain a distinction between dreaming as a conscious experience and REM or late-night NREM sleep, the physiological states of the brain underlying the conscious experience. Just as REM sleep can run without our ever remembering dreams, so—we suppose—can learning and memory reorganization take place without our ever being aware of it. The best we can hope for is that our new, formalist approach to dreaming might help us to understand the rules of memory reorganization.

REM sleep and learning in animals

Two complementary theories were adopted in the early days of studying sleep and learning in experimental animals. Rats were used for this work because cats, despite much more being known about their brains, are such poor learners. Cat owners will object to this invidious comparison—surely their beloved pets are at least as clever as rats. But cats are domesticated and don't need to learn much to survive. Rats are still wild and need to adapt to much more difficult life conditions.

In the first theory, sleep was measured after exposure to new learning, and REM sleep was found to increase as learning

increased. In the second theory, REM sleep was prevented; this impaired learning. In both cases, the focus was on REM sleep. In the case of the post-exposure theory, the increase in REM sleep was often surprisingly delayed and time-limited, leading Carlisle Smith to propose the concept of a 'REM sleep window' for the consolidation of learning. This concept is akin to critical periods in development, which also involve learning, and which may also involve REM sleep because that state is so prevalent in immature animals.

As far as dreaming is concerned, the data that are most relevant to considerations of the timing of learning and of a REM sleep window in humans are the surprising delays in incorporating new location data reported by travelling dream recorders such as Michel Jouvet and the systematic lab work on the dream incorporation of experiential data by Tore Nielsen. As mentioned earlier, both sources indicate that it may take several days, even a week, for the brain to get around to using new information to change its mind. It is thus clear that, in considering behavioural repertoires, we are confronting long-term processes and we should not expect to find that all post-exposure learning takes place overnight.

How can recurrent dreams
be explained?

Dreaming has remarkably consistent features from individual to individual and from night to night. We call these features formal to indicate the difference from what we call content. By formal, we mean that dreams are visual and intensely emotional, have a peculiar logical quality, and times, places, and people are

infinitely plastic and changeable. In other words, dreaming is recurrently bizarre, and it is the recurrence of the bizarre features that we think determines the assumption by most people that the content is repetitive.

We know that content itself can be repetitive, especially in the case of traumatic dreams, which we discussed in Chapter 6. But when we ask normal inidviduals to produce records of the recurrent dreams they claim to have, we are impressed by the fact that what is recurrent is the formal features, e.g. anxiety may be a common element to dreams. Well, anxiety about what? Anxiety about exams, for example. That's not a bit surprising if we think that anxiety or emotion play a large part in dream construction. What things are people anxious about? They are anxious about performance and performance evaluation, and what performance evaluation is more stressful or important to people than exam performance? Consequently, we may have exam dreams as one of the recurrent themes.

Exam dreams are, however, often quite different from one another in orientational detail—they take place in different rooms and different places, and concern different subjects. What they all have in common is the dreamer's feeling that he or she is unprepared. This is not unusual in life, especially in the lives of busy, competitive people. In dreaming, it may be related to the fact that we have a great deal of difficulty vocalizing our thoughts. In other words, another formal feature of dreaming is the inability to remember. It is rare in dreams to remember something; it is strikingly peculiar that, although dreams are loaded with memory fragments, we don't stop in the middle of the dream and say, 'Hey, that reminds me of something' or remember, for example, that one of our dream characters has recently died. It is this defect in thought, added to the coupling

of anxiety to one of its most common associations, the fear of failure, that may determine what an individual calls his recurrent exam dream.

It may seem to the reader that we are attempting to explain away rather than explain recurrent dreams, but this is not the case. What is recurrent are certain emotionally salient themes that depend on certain formal properties of dreams, and these are deeply repetitive. Every dream is characterized by visual perception and strong emotion, most often elation, anger, or anxiety. With these emotions come our own historical experiences—the experiences that are associated with these emotions are likely to appear in our dreams.

Human learning and memory

The distinction between learning and memory is particularly clear in the case of procedural tasks that expose individuals to sensorimotor challenges—some of which are met entirely outside our awareness.

On a task of visual discrimination—the Karni–Sagi task, for example—individuals improve their performance without knowing how or why (as they learn the task); after sleep they then do better when re-tested (again without knowing how or why). On the visual discrimination task (or VDT) individuals must fix their gaze on a symbol, an 'L' or a 'T', at the centre of the screen and then indicate when an aberrant stimulus array (\ \ \ instead of / / /) is flashed in another part of the screen. As is usual in cognitive science, reaction time is the measure used and, within an hour of training, most individuals become very fast at this subliminal recognition.

Despite not knowing consciously how they do it, people get

quite good at this task and improve markedly during training sessions. Improvement is measured by the achievement of a high percentage of correct judgements as the time of stimulus exposure is reduced. We don't think of this as memory (and it may have little or nothing to do with dreaming), but it is probably typical of most of the things that we learn and so it is quite important. In other words, we learn a myriad of procedures without being able to describe them verbally. Most learning is unconscious. We call this kind of learning procedural memory to distinguish it from episodic and semantic memory.

The next day, when they are re-tested, Karni–Sagi subjects' performance correlates strongly with how they slept. If they have been deprived of REM sleep, they behave as novices showing no advantage of their previous exposure. If they sleep deeply early in the night and/or have long REM periods late in the night, they retain their learned skill and may even improve on it. The greatest improvements occur when both deep early night (NREM) and long late-night (REM) sleep are present. As can be seen in Fig. 10, the correlation between the product of the two sleep measures and improved performance is almost one. Suitable controls, for lapsed time and for sleepiness, show that it is sleep itself that confers the benefit of skills improvement.

This result is important for several reasons: one is that it is robust; another is that it is highly replicable; a third is that, because it is entirely unconscious, it cannot be faked; a fourth is that the learning probably takes place in a restricted area of the brain that can be specified—the primary visual cortex—which makes the experimental theory amenable to study using imaging techniques. Unfortunately, it is not a task that rats can learn so

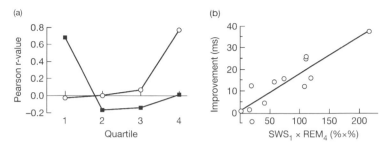

Figure 10 Visual discrimination task learning. (a) Correlation of learning with slow wave sleep (SWS) and rapid eye movement sleep (REM) across the night. For each quartile of the night, the Pearson correlation coefficient between SWS% and overnight improvement (filled squares) and between REM% and overnight improvement (open circles) was calculated. (b) Two-step model of memory consolidation. Improvement is plotted as a function of the product of the amount of SWS during the first quarter of the night and the amount of REM in the last quarter. Both amounts are quantified as percentages of the entire night. The strong correlation suggests a two-step consolidation process, including an early, SWS-dependent process and a late REM-dependent one.

we cannot easily expose the cellular neurobiology of the sleep benefits. As for cats, forget it!

Dreaming itself and learning

People who never master the Karni–Sagi task do not dream of taking the test in any way that relates to their competence. Are there waking–learning experiences that are so strong that they are in evidence within the mental state/thoughts of sleepers? We have previously alluded to the reports of skiers and sailors who notice a return of the illusion of movement of skiing or

Are dreams caused by indigestion?

Certainly not. The theory that dreaming is caused by indigestion was introduced in the nineteenth century by scientists who were otherwise unable to explain activation of the brain during sleep. They thought that such activation must come from external stimuli. Of course, if one has a stomach ache, or has eaten or drunk too much, the processing of the food and resulting chemical disturbances are likely to lead to awakenings, and these awakenings may be associated with dream recall. When one is lying asleep in such states of gastrointestinal brain activation, it is not unlikely that mental content will be related to the dietary indiscretion. This might mislead us into thinking that the dreams were, in general, caused by those external stimuli.

In fact, a day's external events have very little place in the genesis of dreams. Freud thought that dreams were triggered by recent memories, but we find that recent memory enters into dreaming very little. Fragments of episodic memory of biographical events are incorporated, but whole recollections are never reproduced as such. Instead, only partial fragments of recent memories enter into dream construction and, along with other materials from remote memory, become part of scenarios created entirely from scratch as brain activation proceeds.

sailing at sleep onset. We also know that mental experiences at sleep onset are dream-like. So, we may have to settle for sleep-onset dreaming if we want to see the effect of learning on mental content. If we are willing to accept this gift of nature, we may be able to learn from it, as our recent studies of novices learning the video games *Tetris* and *Alpine Racer* have taught us.

Individuals who are learning to play these popular games typically report intrusive game imagery at sleep onset—in other words, in sleep they still have declarative or episodic memory of their learning. This indicates, beyond the shadow of a doubt, that the brain has made a retrievable record of its experience, held it in 'memory', and replayed it later under the altered conditions of sleep. This gives us a very desirable handle and marker of waking experience that can be tracked in the brain as sleep proceeds.

Fortunately, there *is* an animal model for this phenomenon. Rats who are learning maze navigation will often show correlated firing of neuron pairs in the area of the brain known as the hippocampus, and this firing increases as they learn, as if neurons were making a physical link to represent the animal's orientational maps. The cross-correlation re-emerges at sleep onset, as if the rat's brain, like the brain of the *Tetris* or *Alpine Racer* player, was repeating in sleep the cerebral code from its daytime experience. The cellular and molecular basis of this phenomenon can now be studied.

Now brain activation in sleep can be seen in an entirely new light. It does—sometimes at least—reflect previous experience. 'Of course it does,' you say. 'I always thought that would be true.' But how could you be sure? And how could you find out exactly what was done with that day's experience by your brain

without a label or a marker? Now that we have one, we are in a much stronger position to ask such questions as the following:

1. As declarative memory (memory that results from conscious awareness and associations) depends so strongly on an intact hippocampus, are our daytime experiences temporarily stored there for further processing?
2. Are bits of declarative memory, but not entire scenarios, transferred out of the hippocampus when the brain is reactivated in REM sleep?

While waiting for a more systematic answer, consider this helicopter dream which illustrates many of the points about memory that I am trying to make.

14/7/1977 Helicopter, Dream no. 3

The day I took Chris to Pisa I saw two helicopters low over the outskirts of the city. That night, I dreamed of two helicopters going the other way. Then they appeared to be landing in our pasture in Vermont (Chris had

suggested, the previous day, that planes sometimes landed in high moun
tain Alps—which I doubted).

As one helicopter neared the uneven ground I noticed that the
pilot was Roger Horn (exhibit designer for Dreamstage)! I cried out—
in that silent way of dreams—to him to be careful and suddenly, very
suddenly, the helicopter became a tractor, a farm tractor with big wheels
which, on hitting the ground, flew apart, one large wheel rolling wildly

downhill while the rest of the tractor veered to the left with Roger now running behind.

Like a Chaplin film, it was all very choppy and comical—but frightening at the same time. Roger and the tractor now parted company and I watched as Roger ran headlong into the wall of a shed which he thumped with his noggin giving a resounding crack and then a reeling recoil of a dazed Roger.

With our experimental data and dream reports such as this, we are now in a position to create a new model of learning in sleep and dream memory that transcends all existing technical analysis. In the dream example given, the emotional salience (or importance) of peril, triggered by the helicopter observation, integrates two other perilous subjects: tractor operation in Vermont and my vulnerable friend, Roger. It is already clear that the brain does not store information like a tape recorder, a microfilm filing system, or even content-addressable memory— in other words, it doesn't simply take experience and lay it down somewhere in its depths for future reference.

What the brain does, instead, is to keep a rather impressive record of experience for a relatively short time, probably in the hippocampus and directly related cortical structures, which is accessible for about one week by day but inaccessible by night. This model can explain how and why I never dream of daytime experiences that are easy to recall the next day. The brain uses sleep to make bit-by-bit adjustments in its long-term repertoire of learning and memory, in a way that guarantees both efficacy and efficiency.

Take efficiency first. Suppose my brain, as Freud and many of his followers have assumed, kept a detailed record of everything. Nothing would be forgotten. There is simply not enough

storage capacity for this model to hold. All the evidence is against it. And it wouldn't work very well either. How would retrieval proceed? I would need a virtually infinite look-up system that would be extremely costly in time and space as well as physically impossible. Instead, my brain reworks my memories into a much more general fabric of inclinations to act and feel in certain ways in response to certain stimulus conditions.

As far as efficacy is concerned, this is a model of procedural memory with more than a sensorimotor aspect, because it includes considerations of instinctive priority and emotional salience. It is thus the Freudian unconscious broadened and made user-friendly. No longer a cauldron of dread desire, my unconscious procedural repertoire is both rich in sources and ready to respond. I don't have to think about most of what I do. It just happens: automatically, appropriately, and adaptively. My emotional brain 'knows' that helicopters, Vermont tractors, and nervous exhibit designers have something in common.

But I *do* need a conscious declarative memory system too, and it needs to be ample, accurate, and updatable, especially around issues of orientation.

- Who am I and who are the key people in my life?
- Where am I and how do I find my way to places of importance to me?
- When did this or that prominent event happen?
- What is my current programme, and what are my goals for the future?

This is the conscious aspect of my mind and, although I want it to work as well as the unconscious does, I am willing and able to tolerate constraints and to elaborate props and tricks to make it work. For example, I use my journal to keep a record of

my experience in time, my address book to keep in touch with the locations and phone numbers of key people, and my schedule book to plan the future. I simply can't remember all that stuff. I don't want to and I don't need to if I use these memory aids.

My dreams reveal how procedural and declarative memory systems intersect and interact in sleep. They always show respect for the universal aspects of my behavioural repertoire and they treat the orientational details in a relatively cavalier fashion in order to achieve efficiency—they trade precise historical accuracy for global emotional associativity. In other words, my dreams reveal how little detail of my daily experience—but how much of the emotional salience—gets mapped on to my procedural repertoire. After all, most of the details are redundant anyway. I already know who I am, who my key people are, where I live and work, and what I have done, am doing, and intend to do in the future.

10

Dream consciousness

In his approach to dream interpretation, Freud's emphasis was on the unconscious mind, where that mental agency was viewed as a constantly threatening, barely restrained collection of socially and psychologically unacceptable desires. In turning this idea on its head, and viewing the unconscious mainly as an ally, and a guide to survival and socially sensible reproduction, we are redefining the unconscious in a way that demands a new view of consciousness in general and of dream consciousness in particular. This chapter is designed to describe how modern sleep science has contributed to the dramatic progress of the last decade in understanding the brain basis of consciousness, and how that understanding has caused us to shift our model of dreaming in the direction of altered states of consciousness that have been recognized—and celebrated—since the psychedelic era of the 1960s.

Before taking up these two themes, we need to define consciousness in a way that is compatible with the formalist

approach to dreams and with the cognitive neuroscience approach to its brain basis.

Consciousness may be simply—and unarguably—defined as our awareness of the world, our bodies, and ourselves. The last quality, awareness of ourselves, includes awareness of awareness, the knowledge that we are conscious.

Consciousness is a brain function with both global and compartmental aspects. It succeeds in so far as it is a unitary state that integrates many different aspects of the brain–mind. Some of these are listed in Table 4. (See Figure 11 for physical orientation.)

There are two important models embedded in Table 4. One is the sequential processing model, beloved of the reflex theorists. The sequential model says that all neural information processing, including consciousness, proceeds from the outside in and from the bottom up; it passes through an integrator at the top and then proceeds down and out again. The other is the

Table 4 Areas of the brain dealing with the different components of consciousness

Component of consciousness	Locus in the brain
1. Sensation	Peripheral sense organs
2. Perception	Cortical and subcortical elaboration
3. Attention	Thalamocortical
4. Emotion	Limbic subcortical (amygdala)
5. Instinct	Limbic subcortical (hypothalamus)
6. Thought	Frontal cortex
7. Orientation	Parietal and frontal cortex
8. Narration	Left temporal cortex
9. Volition	Prefrontal cortex
10. Action	Spinal cord and muscles

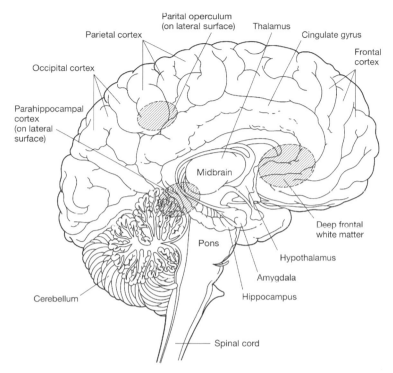

Figure 11 The structure of the human brain

modular approach, which is used by neurologists who wish to assess mental states, cognitive neuroscientists who wish to understand parts of the mind, and dream formalists who share both the clinical goals of the neurologist and the physical approach of the scientists.

A central problem for anyone faced with this set of modular and sequential processes is to understand how conscious unity can be so effortlessly achieved. At any moment, we are aware— or about to be aware—of many information sources, and yet our

conscious experience feels very seamless, smooth, and focused. This quandary has been called the binding problem, and theorists have approached it in a variety of ways—by 'binding' is meant the knitting together of disparate elements into a seamless whole. For starters, consider the five senses that may contribute to our construction of a perception. Most scientists assume that synchronicity of the many brain regions contributing information to consciousness is achieved via rhythmically harmonious activation of the many direct connections between them. This explains, up to a point, the unity of conscious experience, although it says nothing about how that experience is actually achieved or how that very unity can change—as it does regularly when we dream or take certain drugs.

These normal and artificial alterations in consciousness require another quite different binding mechanism, one that chemically unites the many brain parts underlying the components of consciousness. It is my contention that such chemical unification is achieved via the influence of the chemically coded neurons of the brain stem (neuromodulation). Sleep science has shown that neuromodulation changes dramatically when our conscious state changes from waking to dreaming. The model of aminergic–cholinergic interaction thus constitutes a basis for understanding the alterations of consciousness normally experienced every day, although it also helps us understand those that may be induced by drugs, or arise unbidden in mental illness.

Binding via synchronicity occurs in milliseconds to seconds. Binding via chemical modulation occurs in minutes to hours. We need both, and we must make the best of both until we understand the mother of all questions: how does the synchronous and chemically coherent activation of brain cells result in conscious experience in the first place? How, after all, is the

nervous system involved in subjective experience—what the philosophers call *qualia*—and what David Chalmers dubs 'the hard problem'? Chalmers asserts that neuroscience has not yet, and may never, solve the hard problem. If you love a mystery, and want to avoid the implications of what neuroscience is saying, you have a way out here. Neuroscientists are no more believable than anyone who waves his hands and says 'And then a miracle happens'. The brain is a colony of neurons: it *thinks* and therefore it *is*.

Qualia and the hard problem: mind and body as one

I myself believe that even the hard problem, the problem of *qualia*, and the mind–body problem itself, are effectively solved once we know that the world is represented in the brain by two reciprocal processes: the first is the a cause-and-effect mechanism of self-organization that brings us into the world, at birth, with a high degree of self-determination. This is genetically arranged. The second is our experience of the world through which we enter symbolic representations of experience into our circuits of neurons. This is achieved behaviourally.

Both of these processes, the innate and the acquired, have examples in the specific activation programmes of the brain. Viewed in this way, waking and dreaming are mirror images of one another which interact throughout our lives to create consciousness in the first place and to endow it with information for purposes of adaptation as we live out our lives.

You may feel that we are still short of explaining a mechanism for awareness or for the awareness of awareness. Think with

me for a minute about how we see and, then, how we see that we see. In the case of reflexive (automatic) vision, the eye encodes various aspects of light in the firing patterns of its retina (inner layer); these signals are sent on to the brain where they are integrated as wholly abstract, but highly specific and meaningful, representations of the world (as images). So far, I suppose, no one doubts the model. If you do accept this model, however, the mind–brain problem is effectively solved. The visual world is nothing but a sequence of activation patterns of neurons representing images. It is only one step to the representation of this representation (i.e. awareness) and one more step after that to representing the awareness (i.e. awareness of awareness) and we are fully conscious. Each step involves the activation patterns of neurons.

Dream consciousness

What does dream consciousness tell us about all of this? It tells us, beyond the shadow of a doubt, that our brains are capable of an impressively rich state of consciousness without the aid of any instantaneous input from the world or output to the world. Again we know, beyond the shadow of a doubt, that the state of dream consciousness depends on brain activation in sleep— activation, including its properties of high-frequency synchronization and chemical neuromodulation, which is best provided by REM sleep, a brain state that exists before waking and upon which waking always depends. Of course, the converse is also true—at least as far as dream content is concerned. We need conscious experience in waking to represent it as such in our dreams, and we need language to give dream consciousness its narrative character and to make dream reporting possible.

What about the formal aspects of dreaming? Are we not now entitled to claim that they are innate? Built in to our brains in the womb? Already functioning, at that early stage, to provide us with the organizational structure from which full consciousness will emerge? And doesn't that at least open the door to the possibility that some components of consciousness are in place well before others? In suggesting that the sensorimotor self-activations of the brain may be forefathers of the concept of *qualia*, I follow Rodolfo Llinas, who tracks *qualia* all the way down to single neurons. Consider the following report, noting especially its movement components.

Bridge, Dream no. 7–8/1977

> Last night, a terrifying bridge dream: Ian, Chris, and I are in the station wagon going up a ramp. We go off and land on a parapet—precarious but solid. I get out and go for help. This entails dropping off the parapet—some 40 feet down into water, into which I sink some 20 feet before touching bottom. Then I go up, like a shot, and try to get back in the car via a ramp. But it is one-way. Somewhere along the way, a man is lifting cars with ease.

Inspired by Llinas' bold theorizing, let us consider two related issues that are enlightened by dreaming of this sort. One is the perpetual sense of movement and the other is whether 'I' am the agent of that movement. It is I who jumps from the Dream Bridge. I drop 40 feet into the water; I go up 'like a shot'. But such dream movement is entirely virtual. It is fictitious. How can this be? We don't really move at all but are completely convinced that we are doing so. This means that Llinas is getting very warm indeed when he claims that the sense of self is embedded, at an early stage and an elemental

What is lucid dreaming?

In most dreams, we are convinced that we are awake. But, sometimes, dream events are so incredible as to make us wonder. This disbelief can be increased and converted into the recognition that we are, in fact, dreaming. By lucid dreaming, we thus mean the reacquisition during dreaming of an important aspect of waking consciousness that is usually lost, mainly the accurate recognition of the state that we are in. When we are awake, we know it and we can check on our knowledge very easily. We are able to make voluntary movements; we are able to control our thoughts; we are able, if we are sceptical, even to pinch ourselves and see that we feel things and are behaving in relation to external stimuli. In dreaming, we normally lose this self-reflective awareness; we are unaware of the state that we are in; we are unable to control our thoughts; and we are unable to make critical judgements.

During dreaming, some individuals become spontaneously aware that they are dreaming. This occurs naturally in children who are aged eight and above, and continues through adolescence. Later, it is difficult to rely on spontaneous occurrence of self-awareness during dreaming sleep. Lucidity can nevertheless be induced, and it is induced by techniques that anyone can follow. I put a notebook by my bedside along with a pen to record dream experience and then, before going to sleep, I tell myself that, being a normal human being, it is likely that I will

have two hours of absolutely fabulous dreaming tonight. To tune in on some of it I am going to notice when bizarreness occurs. I tell myself to notice things that could never occur in waking but typically occur in dreams, namely the changes of times, places, and people (especially the unusual occurrence of unidentified characters, characters with the qualities of one person who suddenly have those of another, and so on). This fluidity of the orientation functions—time, place, and person—is what is going to tell me that I am dreaming.

When I am successful, a part of my brain–mind wakes up and I am able to notice that I am dreaming and say so to myself. Having done so, I have created a kind of dissociation: part of my brain is in the waking state and part is in the dreaming state. And then I can have a lot of fun. I can watch the dreams, I can induce awakenings so as to increase my recall, and, best of all, I can influence the dream content. I can do whatever I please; well, almost whatever. I can certainly fly and can have whatever sorts of intimate relationships I choose with my other dream characters. This is usually enough to make people quite proud and pleased to have achieved lucid dreaming.

level, in the capacity of colonies of neurons to generate movement patterns. Although this does not entirely explain how the sense of self arises, it goes a long way to solving a problem that is otherwise difficult to manage: if 'I' am not the agent of movement, who, or what, is? The environment? Sensation? A reflex? It just doesn't make sense to think that way unless you are really lazy and want God to do it all!

The one orientational anchor that is never lost in dreams is the self, the 'I' who dreams, the I who thus swims, flies, flees, makes love, fears, and fights. True, some dreamers see themselves as dream actors (rather than being the centre of the action), but the self is always there. It is the construct of constructs, the organizational unit of consciousness. I dream, therefore I am.

How does dreaming alter consciousness?

Table 5 is designed to answer this question easily. In fact, Table 5 is a summing-up of facts that you already know, although it is important to be sure that you review them and that you have one last chance to refute or refuse the formalist approach before we turn to interpreting dreams. Ask yourself whether or not these claims apply to your dreams.

It is now possible to compare these brain functions with the brain regions specified in Table 4 to make our point about how these alterations are effected.

We begin by dispensing once and for all with the reflex model. The first (sensation) and last (action) are of entirely internal origin. The reason for this is twofold: first the input–

Table 5 Alterations of consciousness in dreaming

Component	Change compared with waking
1. Sensation	Almost entirely internally generated
2. Perception	Almost entirely internally generated
3. Attention	Seized by dream events, difficult to direct
4. Emotion	Elation, anger, and anxiety exaggerated
5. Instinct	Fighting and fleeing common
6. Thought	Illogical and undirected
7. Orientation	Severely deficient for time, place, and person (except self)
8. Narration	Highly confabulatory
9. Volition	Weak
10. Action	Constant fictitious animation

output gates are closed by active inhibition; second, the central representations of sensation and movement in the cortical and subcortical brain are self-activated.

As percepts depend on sensations and voluntary movement depends on muscle tone, perception (item 2 in Table 5) and volition (item 9) are altered secondarily. In the absence of external sensations, perception is derived from the self-activation of multimodal sensory areas of the cortex and related subcortical brain areas. Recall that formal vision, like images of houses and people's faces, is the responsibility of multiple and far-flung cortical areas. Some of these are linked to subcortical systems, such as the limbic lobe for example. So we can, at last, begin to imagine how our brain conjures up dream images through the self-activation of REM sleep. We suppose that the decision to act may also be impaired by the weakening of

working memory, which we discuss soon. This explains, in a summary way, four of the ten items.

Attention requires special comment. Dreams seize our attention and constantly co-opt it. We are so often surprised by the sudden turn of dream events that we cannot pay them the attention that they would command if we were awake. We assume that this attentional defect is partly a consequence of parasitic percepts arising spontaneously, but it may also spring from the lack of voluntary movement control that limits our ability to move and to think. We are awash in our own cognitive secretions, including elements of our own sensorimotor pro- gramme that are being run in rapid succession whether we like it or not. We thus suppose that attention in dreaming con- sciousness is weak for two reasons that are additive: one is a consequence of the disinhibition of sensorimotor programmes by aminergic systems; the other is the regional deactivation of the area of the brain called the frontal cortex.

Emotions (feelings) and instincts (primitive behaviours) are both enhanced by the activation of the limbic brain in REM sleep. In REM sleep, certain areas in the brain (namely the amygdala in the temporal lobe and the white matter of the base of the forebrain) are turned on. This is a finding on which all brain imaging studies conducted to date agree. This is Freud's 'id', and confirmation of its activation by modern neuroscience allows us affirmatively to include instinct and emotion as major instigators of dream plots. We can even agree that dream con- sciousness owes its often primitive character to 'release' of these brain programmes from the inhibition that holds them in check during waking. In this view, the ego/super-ego equiva- lents are the dorsolateral prefrontal cortex, which constitutes the 'I' that decides (in waking) whether or not to promote

real-life scenarios, culminating in instinctive behaviour. In dreaming consciousness, that I is asleep (as Freud suggested). Items 4 and 5 of Tables 4 and 5 can thus be understood in neurobiological terms.

Thought (item 6) and orientation (item 7) are both impaired by disablement of the aminergic systems and regional deactivation of the global and local memory systems of the brain. We want to know more about why declarative memories, which are presumably stored in the hippocampus and then moved out to the cortex, are so seldom available to dream consciousness. Clearly, all cognitive functions that depend on memory, except possibly emotional salience, are weakened in REM sleep. Dream consciousness is therefore both a poor analyser and a poor organizer of its content. Hyperassociativity and emotional salience are the rules that govern dream consciousness, not linear logic and specific, accurate, historical detail.

Putting it all together—integrating all of these disparate elements into a credible dream plot—is the job of what's left of the executive 'I'. Here we are on thin ice because we don't really know how the dream scenarios are composed, any more than we know how ideas are generated in waking. We emphasize narration because the reports we have of dreams read like stories. This is dangerous because the reports are necessarily given in waking and rely entirely on language, whereas the dreams themselves are experienced more like films. They are multimedia events, including fictitious movement of a type not yet stimulated easily, even in the most technically sophisticated film. Only virtual reality, where the subject's own movements affect perceptions, comes close to this dream experience. Thus, we use the term 'narration' advisedly to signal the coherence of dream experience, which is

all the more remarkable given the apparent chaos of REM sleep dreaming.

When we are dreaming, even without the help of the chemical unification conferred by noradrenaline and serotonin, and even without the focus and control of thought and action conferred by the part of the brain called the dorsolateral prefrontal cortex, our experience is nevertheless convincingly integral and convincingly real. Here again, it is hard to resist the idea that the ultimate reality of consciousness includes, and is strongly based upon, our brain's capacity to create a virtual reality, so close in all of its formal details to aspects of waking consciousness as to fool us, almost every time.

11

The interpretation of dreams

As this book has proceeded, I have first knocked Freud down, then picked him up again, dusted him off, and put him back on a pedestal. But it is not the same pedestal on which I would want to place our own dream theory. How can we now summarize the similarities and differences of the views of modern neuroscience with those of Freudian psychoanalysis? My colleague Bob Stickgold puts it well when he says, 'Freud was 50 per cent right and 100 per cent wrong'. In this final chapter we unpack this paradox, hoping to make clear what speculative philosophy can and cannot do, and to show that only experimental brain science can hope to correct any picture of ourselves based on intuition alone.

In what way was Freud 50 per cent right?

Cutting to the chase, what did Freud get right? His discussion of dreams correctly emphasized their primitive emotional character. Dreams are indeed instigated by the release in sleep of primitive drive mechanisms of the brain, and these primitive drive mechanisms do include the instinctive media of sex, aggression, and escape. The feelings that go with approach behaviour (elation, joy, happiness, love), avoidance behaviour (fear, anxiety, panic), and confrontational show-down behaviour (fighting, assaulting, shooting) are also all there. This is what Freud called the 'primary process', to distinguish it from the tamer, more civilized and rationalized secondary process of waking consciousness.

But there is a lot less sex than Freud assumed and a lot more of the negative emotions than he was prepared to deal with, because he placed so much influence on dreaming as wish fulfilment.

So much for aspects of his theory that concerned dream instigation. Was there anything right about his theory of dream plot construction? Emotional salience and hyperassociativity would seem to answer this question affirmatively. In other words, we see that Freud was correct in his basic assumption that dreams are (in part) driven by instinctive force (emotions) and that these emotions are loosely connected to mental content. Certainly the one great legacy of psychoanalysis is its emphasis on the importance of feelings, so often relegated to a secondary role by rational psychologies and philosophies. Dreaming does remind us emphatically that we have very powerful instincts,

emotions, and even inclinations to madness that must be held in check during waking hours.

Using this rebus (or set of rules), Freud was also correct in insisting that much more of waking consciousness than we were prepared to accept comes from our instinctive/emotional brains (or, as we would now say, our limbic systems). Moreover, we can expect to learn more about this part of ourselves by paying attention to our dreams and, perhaps, by using dreams as starting points in tracking associative trains of thought back to their imagined source in our instincts. I say 'perhaps' because this assumption has still not been proved. Even after 100 years of psychoanalytic practice, we have no empirical evidence for the power of dream content (over, say, waking fantasy or even neutral word list stimuli) to trigger associative trains of emotional salience. Indeed, as I soon insist, emotional salience is always the order of the day (or night) when it comes to associative thinking.

In what way was Freud 100 per cent wrong?

Freud's model of the unconscious was similar to Victorian sexual behaviour: the unconscious was seen as compelling, but sneaky and devious. In dreams, the unconscious wishes were always trying to disrupt consciousness, just as duplicitous sexual behaviour of waking was designed to dupe social convention. Thus, Freud's dream theory adopted the fatally flawed assumptions of disguise and censorship as the basis of dream bizarreness. The primary drive of the dream had to be expurgated or laundered and converted into the apparent nonsense of dream

bizarreness. This idea that only the remembered dream content was manifest and that it concealed a dormant instinct is the very heart of psychoanalytic dream theory. Without it, there is nothing left, except the emphasis on instinct and emotion. If, as we suppose, dreams reveal rather than conceal emotion and instinct, disguise–censorship is not only unnecessary but misleading. In fact, it is downright erroneous.

Without disguise–censorship, what is there left for an interpretation of dreams using a psychoanalytically constructed theory? If the dream-inducing instincts are not disguised and not censored, but entered into the dream plots directly, then the manifest dream is the dream, is the dream, is the dream! All we need to do in this case is to record our dreams and read the reports carefully! By carefully, I mean with an eye to associations, which may be remote and obscure, but meaningful to the construction of an historically honest view of ourselves. In this view, the so-called latent dream content is nothing more or less than the vast set of associations connected to each aspect of dream content. It could still be quite useful to investigate these as a way of learning more about parts of our mind that are important to us, whether or not we think of them as dream instigators or as elements that, precisely because they are of direct and undisguised emotional salience, get used in dream construction.

Although dream emotions are the same in men and women, they are associated with highly individual content. It is in this spirit that the interpretation of dreams—particular dreams of specific individuals—can still find a place in personal psychology and psychotherapy. In all likelihood, this is probably what has been going on in psychodynamic psychotherapy anyway.

Consider the following report of mine, which is as relevant

Are men's and women's dreams different?

We were very surprised when we conducted a study of emotion in dreams in a group of male and female college students. We had fully expected that the emotion profiles of these two groups would be as different as they are thought to be during the waking state. We expected men's dreams to be more aggressive and more violent and women's dreams to be more affiliative and tender, but we found that this was not the case, at least in our participants. The emotion profiles in dreams of men and women were strikingly similar.

There is very little difference in the tendency for men and women to have visual imagery in their dreams, very little difference in the tendency for them to have bizarreness in their dreams, and, most strikingly of all, there is very little difference in the incidence or intensity of the emotions. What this suggests to us is that the emotional intensity of dreams is something that is a given—it is a brain-based phenomenon that is experienced similarly by both men and women.

Through their biology and social interactions, men and women learn during waking to direct their emotional energies in different ways. Women are often more concerned with child rearing and child protection, and men are more often concerned with wage earning and competitive interactions with their peers. As a result of shifts in gender, these behaviours are changing as

we speak. But what apparently doesn't change very much is the representation of emotions in men's and women's dreams. Emotional salience is equally important to both sexes.

to the physiological discussion of Chapter 4 as it is to the question of individual meaning raised here. I suppose that I am the only person in the world who could have had a dream with this content.

12/3/1980 Homage to Jouvet, Dream no. 12

> *I arrive at a meeting (probably the New Mexico APSS meeting in 1969) and am greeting colleagues. Suddenly I notice that Jouvet is there. He recognizes me and smiles broadly (not his usual greeting). I am about to call out to him when I suddenly lose muscle tone in my legs and sink to the floor. I cannot communicate and feel lost.*

In my journal, following this report, I wrote the following comments:

- Limp legs: I first heard the French expression for this on the day that I went to a romantic rondezvous that needed to be discreet, to the Hotel de Beaux-Arts in Villefranche. When I returned to the lab, Jouvet said that I looked like I had *les jambes coupées*—an expression used to describe one who is sexually exhausted. My excuse to Jouvet for leaving the lab had been to meet my old friend D.B. at the main university library. I told Jouvet that D.B. had developed a foot fetish attachment to J.S. and that there were jokes about D.B.'s homosexuality. But there was nothing homosexual about my rendezvous at the Hotel de Beaux-Arts and Jouvet probably sensed that.
- Jouvet's smile: a beginning reconciliation after almost ten years of tension over personal and professional rivalry. Note that I had worked in Lyons in 1963–64 and that this dream occurred in 1980. Japan (1979) was the ice-breaker. Mexico (1980) will be the clincher. Jouvet's break with Hernandez-Peon—a Mexican friend and rival—began in Lyons when I was there in 1962. Today, I received a cordial letter from Jouvet—formal, but cordial.

- Atonia: Jouvet's great discovery, the abolition of muscle tone associated with REM sleep, is represented in my dream cataplexy. Like narcoleptics in real life, strong emotion—especially surprise—produces atonia. Perhaps I now recognize Jouvet's achievement in my behaviour.

Are these interpretations valid? How can I know? Certainly, I share the psychoanalytic patient's feeling that the interpretations 'ring true'. But this is the 'tally argument' so successfully demolished by Adolf Grunbaum. The fact that these associations are meaningful to me and that they possess compelling emotional salience confers no validity on them, either as dream instigators or accurate explanations of why I dreamed this dream, or that this is what this dream *really* means!

Science demands prediction

As Douglas Hofstadter has pointed out in his brilliant book *Gödel, Escher, and Bach*, the science of dream content interpretation founders on the rock of prediction. It is simply inadequate to conduct only retrospective analysis. Everything seems clear—and convincing—in the retrospectroscope. I dreamt of Jouvet because I had just seen him. OK. There is some evidence that antecedent events may form dream crystals around which the dream story forms. And, for sure, I am concerned about his feelings towards me and well aware of his important discoveries. So this 'interpretation' (I prefer to call it a discussion) cannot be a vindication of disguise–censorship because I am consciously aware of all of the anxiety-engendering conflicts that it depicts.

Could I predict this or any other dream that I have ever had? If there really were rules governing each and every dream plot, and I really knew those rules, I ought to be able to do so. My

guess is that I cannot and that you cannot. If after you have had the dream you can assign cause, your dream interpretation is subject to the post-hoc fallacy that demolished the logic of your interpretation. And mine!

Two caveats will help to make this point clear: one is the obvious failure of many, or even most, of our emotionally salient experiences to trigger dreams. As far as we know, and our knowledge is admittedly limited, there are many salient people, events, and impulses that we never dream about at all.

As an ambitious academic, I do have dreams about exam unpreparedness, credential inadequacy, and lost slides, misplaced lecture notes, being late, and the like. I call these 'incomplete arrangement' dreams and shortly offer an explanation of them.

But I never, and I mean *never*, dream of sitting at my desk, writing a paper, or reading a review critical of my grant application, even though I have those candidate dream stimuli all the time. Why don't they enter into my dreams? They are certainly emotionally salient. They concern survival, attack, defence, and all the rest. In other words, a scientific dream theory has to explain why a whole class of emotionally salient experiences cannot be a dream stimulus. Instead of these themes, I dream of related problems, which rarely, if ever, happen.

The other caveat is that the human mind is designed to see dream causality even when it could not possibly be present. How do we know this? By means of an experiment called dream splicing that was conceived by Robert Stickgold and carried out by our lab seminar group. We took 10 dream reports and cut them apart—with scissors—at the point of dramatic scene shifts in the plots. The resulting 20 dream fragments were then 'spliced'. We reassembled them so that one half were assembled

as reported and the other half as hybrids, their two halves coming from different dreams in different people. There was no way in which events in the initial segment of the hybrid dreams could be causally related to events in the second segment.

Before this experiment was conducted, I was one who firmly believed that I could see meaning in the sequence of dream subplots, even across scene changes. But as soon as I tried to decide whether a given report was spliced or not, I realized that I could not tell. Nor could anyone else. Even highly trained, practising psychoanalysts failed the dream-splice detection test if a scene change was involved. This simple experiment raises many disturbing questions:

- Why are we so sure that we can understand a person by knowing his or her history?
- Why are we so sure that any text can be read with the assumption of causal continuity?

In both cases—which are common, everyday occurrences—we have the same problem as the dream interpreter. We must project causal narrative structure on to events as a matter of course. It must be a category of mind to look for, and to find, causality in nature. Fortunately for us, it is often there. That's why we have survived and that's why science has progressed despite the errors into which our tendency to project narrative causality plunges us. But, we make at least as many mistakes in assigning causality as we make correct inferences. Sometimes we are able to see this, although usually not.

Dream science

The scientific method was designed to protect us from these errors of projection. A scientific experiment is an exercise in the elucidation of cause and the best experiments unmask false causation as much as they demonstrate true causation. In so far as our new dream theory is true, we can predict that brain activation of a given chemical and regional type will always produce hallucinosis, hyperassociativity, hyperemotionality, false beliefs, and other cognitive errors. This is as far as scientific prediction can now go with dreams, but it's far enough to put the formal psychological analysis of dreams out of the reach of content analysis.

We do not dream because our unconscious wishes or drives would, if undisguised, wake us up. We dream because our brains are activated during sleep, and we do so even if our primitive drives are turned on by that activation. In fact, such drives are not concealed. Rather, they are revealed in dreams. It is the specific neurophysiological details of that activation process, not psychological defence mechanisms, that determine the distinctive nature of dream consciousness.

Dream interpretation extends beyond its own narrow borders. We are all engaged in a kind of dream interpretation all the time. Why did so and so say such and such? Why do I feel anxious when I pick up the telephone? Why do I become angry at my daughter-in-law? Our experience with the interpretation of dreams shows us that it is dangerous to assume causality and that our answers to these questions had better not be just local and narrow, and analyse content.

What we need now is a set of truly general rules that help us to accept our dreams, our fears, and our rages for what they

are: expressions of brain activation in sleep and in waking that have their own deep and compelling reasons for being. In the twenty-first century we will learn much, much more about these deep reasons from brain research.

Conclusion

If the question is how do we understand the mystery of dreams, the simple answer is that there is no longer any mystery—at least no mystery worthy of the creation of mystical dream theories of the past. Surely, the work of sleep science is incomplete. We still do not know enough about how the brain–mind reorganizes itself during sleep and how dreams might be used for better understanding of this function. But, clearly, we know that these details are far more likely to reveal progressive, adaptive information processing during sleep than we have previously imagined possible.

In the place of dream mystique, we aim to install dream science. And the dream science we intend to install has a solid and broad base in neurobiology. The recent development of dynamic brain imaging technology, especially magnetic resonance imaging (MRI), makes this project particularly promising. For the first time in human history, we can see the regional activity of the brain as people wake, sleep, and dream. This is a true renaissance, a genuine revolution, and a major shift in the scientific theory of the brain and mind is to be anticipated.

As I have endeavoured to point out, nothing less is at stake than a scientific theory of human consciousness. As we already know that consciousness is a brain function, and that the state of the brain determines the kind of consciousness we experience, we can begin to build a model of conscious state determination on our solid and broad base in brain

science. Thus, the study of dreaming can be seen as a crucial part of a much larger project, one that will shake the foundations of philosophy, psychology, and psychiatry.

The study of dreaming is inextricably linked to the science of sleep. The science of sleep is inextricably linked to neurobiology. Thus, the science of dreaming is inextricably linked to neurobiology. So far, what have we learned about these linkages? We can summarize our progress by reviewing these important conclusions.

The first important conclusion is that dreaming, and other states of consciousness, are related to changes in the level of brain activation. Brain activation varies in a systematic manner during sleep and peaks of this function are highly correlated with dreaming. But, even the troughs of brain activation in sleep are far from the total inactivation intuited via introspection. In other words, the brain is always more active than not. Even when consciousness abates entirely, the brain is working in an impressively complex way. What is it doing? Important answers to this question are processing information, consolidating and revising memory, and learning newly acquired skills. This means that consciousness in both waking and sleep occurs only at the upper levels of brain activation, say 90–100 per cent.

The second important conclusion is that, independent of activation, the brain opens and closes its gates. But these are not the 'Gates of Horn and Ivory'. They are the gates of sensory input and motor output. Thus, as the brain self-activates in sleep, it shuts its gates so that outside information has difficulty accessing the brain. It is equally difficult for the sleep-activated brain to realize the motor acts that it generates. We experience them consciously as dream movement, but they are not,

fortunately, read out as movement. What this means is that the sleep-activated dreaming brain is off-line to normally effective inputs and outputs. It is doing its own thing, as it were. In this case, that thing is the very active processing of the sensorimotor and emotional data that we are consciously aware of as dreaming.

The third and perhaps most significant conclusion is that the brain not only self-activates and isolates itself from the world, but it changes its chemical climate very radically. In particular, two of the chemical systems necessary to waking consciousness are completely shut off when the brain self-activates in sleep. Without noradrenaline and serotonin, the dreaming brain cannot do certain things such as direct its thoughts, engage in analytical problem-solving, and remember its activities. It is this difference in brain chemistry that probably determines the differences between waking and dreaming consciousness.

None of these findings was predicted by dream theorists, before discoveries started being made in the second half of the twentieth century. But they all have enormous impact on the way that we think about our conscious experience. Without such knowledge, we were groping in the dark. With it, we can begin to shine light on our most interesting human attribute—consciousness.

Index